THE OXFORD BOOK OF
AUSTRALIAN
SHORT
STORIES

THE OXFORD BOOK OF
AUSTRALIAN
SHORT
STORIES

SELECTED BY
MICHAEL WILDING

Melbourne

OXFORD UNIVERSITY PRESS

Oxford   Auckland   New York

OXFORD UNIVERSITY PRESS AUSTRALIA

Oxford   New York
Athens   Auckland   Bangkok   Bombay
Calcutta   Cape Town   Dar es Salaam   Delhi
Florence   Hong Kong   Istanbul   Karachi
Kuala Lumpur   Madras   Madrid   Melbourne
Mexico City   Nairobi   Paris   Singapore
Taipei   Tokyo   Toronto

and associated companies in
Berlin   Ibadan

OXFORD is a trade mark of Oxford University Press

Introduction, selection and notes on contributors © Michael Wilding 1994
First published 1994

National Library of Australia
Cataloguing-in-Publication data:

The Oxford book of Australian short stories.

Includes index.
ISBN 0 19 553610X.

1. Short stories, Australian.   I. Wilding, Michael,
1942–   . II. Title: Book of Australian short stories.

A823.0108

This project has been assisted by the Commonwealth Government
through the Australia Council, its arts funding and advisory body.

Typeset by Best-set Typesetter Ltd., Hong Kong
Printed in Australia by Brown Prior Anderson Pty Ltd
Published by Oxford University Press,
253 Normanby Road, South Melbourne, Australia

CONTENTS

INTRODUCTION

'What is unique about the short story is that we all can tell one, live one, write one down,' Christina Stead wrote.[1] The story is that most accessible of literary forms. Everyone has a story. It has never been an exclusive or élitist form. The great short story writers have also been novelists, poets, dramatists. One of the appeals of the story is the way it attracts such a variety of practitioners. The story is in dialogue with novels, poems, plays, essays; it is not sealed off from other genres. It can contain the verbal concentration of a poem, the documentary transcription of the case-study, the sensuality of reverie, the awful authenticity of the confessional, the clarity of the exemplary, the exhilaration of the inspirational.

Australian writing has excelled in the short story. In part, of course, the difficulties of being a novelist in Australia helped to encourage the writing of stories. While publishers were cautious about committing themselves to Australian novels, the magazines would often print short stories. And when the magazines failed, as they often did, the short story writers could join the poets in giving readings. The succinctness of the form gave it a flexibility in terms of reaching a public. It was possible to fit stories into monthly reviews, weekly news magazines, daily newspapers, scandal sheets, trade union papers, men's magazines, women's magazines, academic quarterlies and little magazines.

Marcus Clarke's memoir, 'In a Bark Hut', captures the early days of European storytelling in Australia:

> When Thwaites had gone to bed in the corner—he was a most determined sleeper—M'Alister and I could pitch another log on the fire and prepare for enjoyment. Carefully filling our pipes, we placed the grease-pannikin on a mark made exactly in the centre of the table and 'yarned'. By 'yarning', dear reader, I don't mean mere trivial conversation, but hard, solid talk. M'Alister was a man of more than ordinary natural talents, and had he been placed in other circumstances, would have cut a figure. It was not

> easy to argue with him, and some of our discussions lasted until
> cock-crow. The arguments not unfrequently merged into story-
> telling, and in that department my memory served me in good
> stead. I had been a sickly brat in my infancy, and having unfet-
> tered access to the library of a man who owned few prejudices
> for moral fig-leaves, had, with the avidity for recondite knowl-
> edge which sickly brats always evince, read many strange books.
> I boiled down my recollections for M'Alister, and constituted
> myself a sort of Scheherazade for his peculiar benefit. He would
> smoke, and I would fix my recollections on a long strip of bark
> which hung serpentine from the ridge pole, and relate.[2]

Here we have an archetype of one set of origins for the Australian short
story. The long nights, the tobacco, the isolation of the bush, and the
recycling of the European heritage. We are back to the oral tradition, but
they are literary texts that are retold. The yarns were not self-generated,
but came from a complex past, to be recreated in a new context. At the
same time, it was not only a matter of texts, of free-floating fictions. The
stories emerged from arguments. There were issues at stake, values,
commitments. Storytelling was in continuum with argument and belief.

Clarke's early stories appeared in monthly reviews like the *Australian
Monthly Magazine* and the *Colonial Monthly*. He is remembered now as the
author of that classic novel of the convict system, *His Natural Life*; but he
wrote more than forty stories during his brief life-time (he was dead at
thirty-five) which range from romantic melodrama to realist sketches.
'Human Repetends' is a haunting treatment of the theme of reincarnation across the continents and centuries, a theme that was to be re-enacted
in Argentina in the following century by Jorge Luis Borges.

Clarke also pioneered the story of the Australian bush and outback.
But it is the later, native-born Henry Lawson who is generally privileged
as the great original of the Australian story. It was certainly Lawson who
established the enduring model of a laconic minimalism of language taut
with irony and repressed emotion. His portrayal of the life of the Australian bush has made him a nationalist icon; and though he spent most of his
life in poverty his portrait once adorned the ten-dollar note. His writing
not only expresses the feel of Australia, it also contains an argument. It
emerged from that brief flowering of radical optimism in the late 1880s
and early 1890s, a period of intense trade-union activity, of revolutionary
fervour and utopian optimism. It was a brief moment and much of
Lawson's bitter-sweet plangency of tone comes from his sense of hopes
defeated and ideals betrayed.

'The Union Buries Its Dead' is one of his enduring stories whose force
is timeless. There is a sophisticated art in its apparent artlessness, a
precision of pace and timing. But it also has its political specificities. Its
theme is union solidarity. What Lawson represents are the class divisions

within the labour movement; solidarity is expressed in the way the labourers attend the funeral of the unknown man; but the shearers still sit on the fence, and the drover goes off for a drink. The name the dead man 'went by', James Tyson, has a deeply sardonic implication. Tyson was one of the largest landowners in Australia, controlling around five million acres and notorious for his meanness. The dead man of Lawson's story is the antithesis of the real Tyson, one of the many who in the repressive period following the defeat of the unions in the 1890s found it convenient to adopt a new name. It is not a limitation of Lawson's stories that they benefit from some historical contextualising. His work was firmly embedded in social reality; this is his strength, and a significant part of his appeal to his contemporaries.

Lawson portrayed the world of the selector, the struggling small farmer, and of the itinerant labourer, with a deep compassion and sympathy. His vision had a specificity and an iconographic memorability that justly led to his reputation as the foremost chronicler of the characteristically Australian; but it was always a politically informed, socially critical account of Australia that he presented. Barbara Baynton's stories continue in the Lawson tradition, the same world of struggle and hardship and impoverishment; but whereas Lawson's naturalism partook of a programmatic political analysis, Baynton's world opens out into a gothic drama of emotional horror that is profoundly sceptical of the 1890s vision of social cooperation. Both these tendencies have persisted throughout the twentieth century.

The weekly journal the *Bulletin* published much of the short fiction of the 1890s. Its preference was for concise, even terse, fiction, firmly based on lived experience. Its editor, J. F. Archibald, and its literary editor, A. G. Stephens, were unembarrassedly interventionist, ever ready to suggest cuts and condensation to achieve that economic style. They encouraged contributions from their readers, a democratic and egalitarian editorial policy that made the *Bulletin* 'the bushman's Bible', uniting the literary aspirations of contributors from across the continent.

The subject matter of the material was less narrowly based than later accounts have suggested. One of the most popular contributors was Louis Becke, who specialised in stories of the Pacific islands, where he had lived for many years. Australia's recognition of itself as an Asian-Pacific nation at the end of the twentieth century is a reconstitution of its nineteenth-century role as a foothold for imperialist economic expansion. Louis Becke chronicled the realities of that expansion, focusing on the commercial and the sexual. Becke's stories were immensely popular at the time of their publication but have been ignored in more recent years. They are often adventure yarns and adventure began to be displaced in literary contexts by a greater inward focus and a reduction of narrative interest. Not that Becke's stories lack themes for reflection and pondering.

Indeed the themes themselves, of racial and sexual encounters, became too uncomfortable for decolonising times.

Another uncomfortable theme is social class and its attendant discriminations. While not following the American claim that theirs is a classless society, Australians nonetheless do not relish the topic like the English. With Ethel Turner's 'The Child of the Children' we have a powerful exploration of class and its taboos and prejudices. This story first appeared in the *Windsor Review* in 1897 and its theme fore-shadows George Bernard Shaw's *Pygmalion* of 1913. Did the slum girl 'Flip' Huggins who takes the name Eliza Brown suggest the names of Eliza Doolittle and Professor Higgins? Did Shaw draw from the story, consciously or unconsciously?

The vigour of the 1890s has tended to cast a shadow on the next half century in the literary histories. This is unjust in terms of literary achieve-ment, although times were hard for Australian writers. Henry Lawson wrote an account of 'Pursuing Literature in Australia' and concluded:

> My advice to any young Australian writers whose talents have been recognised would be to go steerage, stow away, swim, and seek London, Yankeeland, or Timbuctoo—rather than stay in Australia till his genius turned to gall or beer. Or, failing this—and still in the interests of human nature and literature—to study elementary anatomy, especially as applies to the cranium, and then shoot himself carefully with the aid of a looking-glass.[3]

The great period of expatriation began. Miles Franklin, Henry Handel Richardson, Jack Lindsay, Christina Stead, Patrick White, James Aldridge, Randolph Stow, Charmian Clift, George Johnston, Peter Porter, and many others, spent extended periods away. Some never returned. This was not a uniquely Australian phenomenon, it was also a century of travel and expatriation for many English and American writers. Australia, however, was less relaxed about it than the USA. Expatriates form an acknowledged, respected and well-liked component of American writ-ing. Australia, like Britain, offers no such recognition. There was for many years, perhaps there still is, a sense of unease about expatriation, a sense of desertion. When anthologies did include expatriate writers the work represented was generally set in Australia. There was a strange, silent unwillingness to include writing about other places, as if Australian writing should be concerned only with Australia. I have resisted that convention in this selection. Australians are determined travellers and some of their finest writing reflects this interest in the wider world.

While expatriation gave a cosmopolitan experience to many writers, it also sharpened their perception of Australia, whether in memory, as with Henry Handel Richardson, or on return, as with Patrick White. And for all those writers who travelled, there were many more who stayed at home. The concern to chronicle the nature of Australia remained a strong feature of the story. There was a firm, realist commitment to social observation and a deep affection for the Australian environment, a concern to evoke the look of the landscape, the feeling of the bush.

A deep, human sympathy informs the realist writing of the 1930s, '40s and '50s. It is concerned with the hardships of the poor and under-privileged, and unselfconsciously sees the working people as its proper subject and attempts to give them a voice. In this it follows the tradition established by Lawson. Judah Waten's 'Mother' is a touchstone of pro-grammatic socialist realism. Critical orthodoxy has tended to present an opposition of the realist and the modernist. But the realist story was protean. It could, and did, evolve in a variety of directions. In practice many of the writers drew on both realist and modernist traditions. Alan Marshall's 'Trees Can Speak' is a fine example. From the intensity of the realist imagination a mythic representation emerged. The scrupulously realist observation delivers a haunting story that has all the spare, focused clarity of a fable. Charmian Clift's 'Three Old Men of Lerici' begins with realist evocation of place, but what emerges is surely an eternal mythic moment, an incarnation of Pan pipes. Dal Stivens has written some powerful naturalist stories, but with 'The Man who Bowled Victor Trumper' the realist, post-industrial wasteland is a setting for a visionary explosion of language and image. It is also a fine example of the tall story, the exploitation of excess, of which Stivens has been a marvellous exponent. The bushman's tall story with its improbable, indeed im-possible, exaggeration, is a characteristically Australian expression. From this vernacular tradition Stivens has developed clear, spare fables of haunting plangency, wit and beauty.

Excess of a different kind, but equally splendid, was the characteristic of Hal Porter. Porter set himself firmly against the functional, utilitarian language of the naturalist and realist tradition and struck a pose of mannered, ornate dandyism. It worked brilliantly, the foregrounding of language offering jewelled evocations of innocence lost; never could innocence have been lost so often.

The convenient critical polarity of realism and modernism regularly dissolves when we look at the creative practice of the writers. Marjorie Barnard begins 'Dry Spell' with the archetypal Australian reality of drought, and from this develops an apocalyptic scene of extraordinary resonance. Here, as in her often anthologised story 'The Persimmon Tree', she is demonstrably one of the pioneers of modernist development in the Australian short story, while maintaining at the same time that realist connection.

Henry Handel Richardson is best known for her trilogy *The Fortunes of Richard Mahony*. Conceived on an epic scale, it is in marked contrast to the delicate, oblique, powerfully suggestive stories she collected in *The*

End of Childhood. These are extraordinarily evocative accounts of the discoveries of sexuality and the associated fears, expectations and ambiguities. This was also one of the themes of Christina Stead's novel *For Love Alone*. While Stead, like Richardson, is best known as a novelist, a 400 page volume of uncollected stories appeared posthumously. 'A Harmless Affair' is a moving, complex story set in a milieu Stead knew well, that of the politically engaged intelligentsia. Katharine Susannah Prichard's work sprang similarly from a committed world view. 'N'Goola', taken from her last collection, is one of the stories in which she deals with the treatment of the Aboriginal people in Australia. Prichard dealt more sustainedly with these issues than any other Australian writer, using her popularity and prestige as one of the best known and most accessible Australian novelists to draw attention to an appalling aspect of Australian life.

Christina Stead believed that everyone has a story. In this it is a profoundly egalitarian genre, profoundly appropriate to that Australian egalitarian self-image. This was the tradition that continued through to the 1960s. Sometimes the committed realism of the Lawson line became less radical than nationalist; but even here the essential Australian image was of the democratic, the vernacular. It was just this vision of Australia that Patrick White confronted in his reaction against the 'exaltation of the average' and the writing that he characterised as 'the dreary dun-coloured offspring of journalistic realism'.[4]

White's late modernism, with its surreal and quasi-metaphysical tendencies, offered a new pole of possibility in Australian fiction. In its turn it was soon to be displaced by the post-modern as social reality was rejected in favour of abstraction and play. White's 'Clay' retains, for all its creative mannerism, a strong connection with the social reality it rejects. There was always an ongoing critique of the suburban, the bourgeois, the mundane in White's writing. The focus, however, was soon to move from the social and representative to a preoccupation with writing, with technique. In Murray Bail's 'Zoellner's Definition' and Kris Hemensley's 'Self Portrait' the list and catechism have displaced narrative; play and game have pre-empted representation. In a different yet related way Peter Carey's stories made their impact with the foregrounding of technique, of estranging manner. Here the refusal of realism took the form of a degree of abstraction, of allusory representation, of the quasi-fabular. These were post-modern fictions whose moral was not always apparent, depoliticised fables with an aura of signification that remained elusive. They had a striking and assured impact of concept, all the more striking in that it was a concept, rather than an image or symbol, that unified the fiction and delivered a meaning. Like a number of his contemporaries, including Murray Bail, Morris Lurie and Barry Oakley, Carey came from the world of advertising copywriting, a world in which the writer as prophet, the writer as visionary, the writer as moralist, the writer as historian, had been superseded by the writer as manipulator, the writer as technician of special effects. The skill lay in producing a powerful reader response. This was the post-modern aesthetic of the game, the enigma, the construct, the product.

The late 1960s and the 1970s were an exciting time for Australian short fiction. There was a lively sense of change and renewal. There was a sense of breaking through into new possibilities, both in formal aspects and in subject. There was a new emphasis on sexuality, there were confrontations over permissible vocabulary, and there was a focus on contemporary urban experience replacing the preoccupation with the outback that the earlier nationalists had tended to privilege.

At the same time there were losses. The new liberating focus on sexuality, on drugs, on what earlier had been taboo as deviant, decadent, criminal, unacceptable, was at one level a challenge to repressive social conventions; but it was also a distraction from and displacement of the traditional concerns of the social and political, of class and work, which now tended to be ignored. Censorship challenges over language absorbed a lot of energy, while the underlying socio-political structure went unexamined.

New social developments required new forms and approaches. There was a vigorous and stimulating outpouring of experiment, a new openness to international models, a conscious exploration of the potentialities of fictional form. There was a stylistic revolution and a reaction against the realist norms that had held sway for so long. Experiments in abstraction, spontaneity and de-narrativisation flourished. Again, this was two-edged. The Lawson tradition, which had become narrowly insular and nationalist and aggressively anti-experimental, was necessarily challenged, as was the conservative gentility that still oriented itself towards the less dynamic aspects of English writing. The turning towards American models, however, marked a subservience to a new cultural and political imperialism, even as it offered innovation and change. The writing that emerged in the 1970s was as its best refreshing, defamiliarising, stimulating and challenging, but it could also be emptily formalist, a new dandyism; with the surrender of social purpose it was often hard to tell which.

Social purpose reappeared, however, in programmatic new ways: women's writing, gay and lesbian writing, multicultural writing, Aboriginal writing. These new separatist agendas developed, often funded by governmental agencies, and the unifying, cohering concept of an Australian literature began to dissolve.

A look at the great practitioners of Australian fiction shows that women writers have always been central. Certainly Miles Franklin and Henry Handel Richardson adopted masculine forenames, which testifies to a perceived social discrimination, but their work together with that of

Barbara Baynton, Katharine Susannah Prichard, Eleanor Dark, Marjorie Barnard and Christina Stead is at the very forefront of fictional achievement. That is unquestionable. Significantly, they all established themselves before the Second World War. But there are many other excellent writers whose work is less well known, such as Ethel Anderson, Elizabeth Harrower, Thelma Forshaw, Charmian Clift and Mena Abdullah who were writing in the 1950s and the 1960s. The 1950s, however, introduced a reaction in gender equality as in so many other areas, and it was not until the 1980s that these imbalances began to be redressed.

The 1980s also saw a belated recognition of Australia as a multicultural society. Conscious attempts were made to encourage writers from different ethnic backgrounds. There had, of course, always been a multicultural component to Australian writing. Henry Lawson's father was a Norwegian immigrant who had followed the characteristic practice of Anglicising his name (from Larsen); his maternal grandfather was an English Gypsy. Lawson was always conscious of his origins: occasionally he signed work Henry Hertzberg Larsen. Judah Waten's writing deals powerfully with the experience of immigrant families in *Alien Son* and *Distant Land*. In the 1980s the categories of multi-culturalism and ethnic writing were officially promoted. This was not without its ambiguities. Most of the writers I knew at that time were profoundly sceptical of this categorisation and unhappy about its marginalising implications; they wanted recognition as writers, not as 'ethnic writers'. In selecting this anthology the work of writers from a wealth of backgrounds, some first, some second, some third generation, has naturally and readily presented itself.

An even more belated recognition is the acknowledgment of the indigenous peoples of Australia. The earliest Australian stories were oral, in myth, in song cycle, in traditional narratives. These have continued to endure and to be told after European settlement. Paddy Roe's 'Lardi' is from a selection recently recorded by Stephen Muecke. There are also Aboriginal writers who have used European forms, notably Kevin Gilbert, Sally Morgan and Ruby Langford in non-fiction and memoir, Jack Davis in drama, and Mudrooroo (formerly Colin Johnson) in the novel. The first Aboriginal writer to publish a book was Oodgeroo Noonuccal. Best known as a poet, she also wrote a memorable volume of stories, *Stradbroke Dreamtime*, from which 'Carpet Snake' is taken.

But to categorise by gender and race is not the whole story. Writers are not limited to writing solely about their own ethnicity or their own gender. Issues of gender, race and ethnicity appear in a much more complex way throughout these stories. What I hope this selection shows is the expansiveness of the imagination, the prolific creativity and the richness of sympathy and perception of Australian writing. These are stories that lodge in the memory, stories to which the reader can return again and again, and which unfold new dimensions at each return. Their strengths and interest are such that outmanœuvre any preface. Having stressed the seriousness of the issues, then to forget the elements of comedy, of play, of pleasure in the short story would be a terrible mistake. There are pleasures in the story that the narratives of criticism, politics, philosophy and history can never give. That is why stories are read.

Michael Wilding

NOTES

1 Christina Stead, *Ocean of Story*, Penguin, Ringwood, 1986, p. 3.
2 Marcus Clarke, 'In A Bark Hut' (also known as 'Learning "Colonial Experience"'), in *Stories*, Hale & Iremonger, Sydney, 1983, p. 9.
3 Henry Lawson, 'Pursuing Literature in Australia' in *Henry Lawson: Autobiographical and Other Writings*, ed. Colin Roderick, Angus & Robertson, Sydney, 1972, p. 115.
4 Patrick White, 'The Prodigal Son' in *Patrick White Speaks*, Primavera, Sydney, 1989, pp. 15, 16.

NOTE TO READERS

Original spellings and punctuation have been retained in these stories.

MARCUS CLARKE

Human Repetends

'Come!' cried Marston, 'the story of your embodied ghost! Speak, thou gloomy Pythagorean!'

'Most men,' began Pontifex, 'however roughly the world has used them, can recall a period in their lives when they were absolutely happy, when each night closed with the recollection of new pleasures tasted, when the progress of each day was cheered by the experience of unlooked-for novelties, and when the awakening to another dawn was a pure physical delight unmarried by those cankering anxieties for the fortune of the hour which are the burden of the poor, the ambitious, and the intriguing. To most men, also, this golden time comes, when the cares of a mother, or the coquettish attention of sisters, aid to shield the young and eager soul from the blighting influences of worldly debaucheries. Thrice fortunate is he among us who can look back on a youth spent in the innocent enjoyments of the country, or who possesses a mind moulded in its adolescence by the cool fingers of well-mannered and pious women.

'My first initiation into the business of living took place under different auspices. The only son of a rich widower, who lived but for the gratification of a literary and political ambition, I was thrown when still a boy into the society of men thrice my age, and was tolerated as a clever impertinent in all those witty and wicked circles in which virtuous women are conspicuous by their absence. My father lived indifferently in Paris or London, and, patronized by the dandies, artists, and scribblers who form, in both cities, the male world of fashionable idleness, I was suffered at 16 to ape the vices of 60. Indeed, so long as I was reported to be moving only in that set to which my father chose to ally himself, he never cared to inquire how I spent the extravagant allowance which his indifference rather than his generosity permitted me to waste. You can guess the result of such a training. The admirer of men whose success in love and play were the theme of common talk—for six months: the worshipper of artists whose genius was to revolutionize Europe—only they died of late hours and tobacco; the pet of women whose daring beauty made their names famous—for three years; I discovered at twenty years of age that the pleasurable path I had trodden so gaily led to a hospital or a debtors' prison, that love meant money, friendship an endorsement on a bill, and that the rigid exercise of a profound and calculating selfishness alone rendered tolerable a life at once so deceitful and so barren. In this view of the world I was supported by those middle-aged Mephistopheles (survivors of the storms which had wrecked so many argosies), those cynical well-bred worshippers of Self who realize in the nineteenth century that notion of the devil which was invented by the early Christians. With these good gentlemen I lived, emulating their cynicism, rivalling their sarcasms, and neutralizing the superiority which their experience gave them, by the exercise of that potentiality for present enjoyment which is the privilege of youth.

'In this society I was progressing rapidly to destruction, when an event occurred which rudely saved me. My father died suddenly, in London, and, to the astonishment of the world, left—nothing. His expenditure had been large, but as he left no debts, his income must have been proportioned to his expenses. The source of this income, however, was impossible to discover. An examination of his banker's book showed only that large sums (always in notes or gold) had been lodged and drawn upon, but no record of speculations or of investments could be found among his papers. My relatives stared, shook their heads, and insulted me with their pity. The sale of furniture, books, plate, and horses, brought enough money to pay the necessary expenses of the funeral, and leave me heir to some £800. My friends of the smoking-room and the supper-table philosophized on Monday, cashed my IOUs on Tuesday, were satirical on Wednesday, and "cut" me on Thursday. My relatives said that "something must be done", and invited me to stay at their houses until that vague substantiality should be realized. One suggested a clerkship in the War-office, another a stool in a banking-house, while a third gener-ously offered to use his interest at head-quarters to procure for me a commission in a marching regiment. Their offers were generously made, but *then*, stunned by the rude shock of sudden poverty, and with a mind debauched by a life of extravagance and selfishness, I was incapable of manly action. To all proposals I replied with sullen disdain, and desirous only of avoiding those who had known me in my prosperity, I avowed my resolution of claiming my inheritance and vanishing to Australia.

'A young man with money and a taste for *bric-à-brac* soon gathers about him a strange collection of curiosities, and at the sale of my possessions I was astonished to find how largely I had been preyed upon by Jews, print-sellers, picture-dealers, and vendors of spurious antiques. The "valuable paintings", the curious "relics", the inlaid and bejewelled "arms", and the rare "impressions" of old prints were purchased by the "trade" for a third of the price which I had paid for them, doubtless to be resold to another man of taste as artless and as extravagant as myself. Of the numberless articles which had littered my bachelor-house, I retained but some three or four of the most portable, which might serve as remembrances of a luxury I never hoped to again enjoy. Among these was a copperplate engraving, said to be one of the first specimens of that art. The print bore the noted name of Tommaso Finiguerra, and was dated 1469. It was apparently a copy of a "half-length" portrait of a woman dressed in the fashion of that age, and holding in her hand a spray of rue. The name of this *grande dame* was not given—indeed, as I need hardly say, the absence of aught but the engraver's signature constituted the chief value of the print.

'I felt constrained to preserve this purchase for many reasons. Not only had I, one idle day, "discovered" it, as I imagined, on the back shelves of a print-shop, and regarded it as the prize of my artistic taste; not only had it occupied the place of honour over my mantel-shelf, and been a silent witness of many scenes which yet lingered fondly in my memory; not only had I seemed to hold communion with it when, on some lonely evening, I was left to reflect upon the barrenness of my existence, but the face possessed a charm of expression which, acknowledged by all, had become for me a positive fascination. The original must have been a woman of strange thoughts and (I fancied) of a strange history. The *pose* of the head was defiant, the compressed lips wore a shadowy smile of disdain, and the eyes—large, full, and shaded by heavy lashes—seemed to look through you and away from you with a glance that was at once proud and timid, as though they contemplated and dared some vague terror, of whose superior power they were conscious. We have all, I presume, seen portraits which by accident or design, bear upon them a startling expression, rarely seen upon the face of the original, but which is felt to be a more truthful interpreter of character than is the enforced composure which self-control has rendered habitual. So with the portrait of which I speak. The unknown woman—or girl, for she did not seem to be more than three-and-twenty—revealed in the wonderful glance with which she had so long looked down upon me, a story of pride, of love, of shame, perhaps of sin. One could imagine that in another instant the horror would fade from those lovely eyes, the smile return to that disdainful lip, and the delicate bosom, which now swelled with that terror which catches the breath and quickens the pulse, would sink into its wonted peacefulness, to rise and fall with accustomed equanimity beneath its concealing laces. But that instant never came. The work of the artist was unchangeable, and the soul which looked out of the windows of that lovely body still shuddered with a foreknowledge of the horror which it had expected four hundred years ago.

'I tried in vain to discover the name and history of this strange portrait. The artists or men of taste to whom I applied had neither seen another copy of the print, nor heard of the original painting. It seemed that the fascinating face had belonged to some nameless one, who had carried with her to the grave the knowledge of whatever mystery had burdened her life on earth. At last, hopeless of discovering the truth, I amused myself by speculating on what might, perchance, have been the history of this unknown beauty. I compared her features with the descriptions left to us of women famous for their sorrows. I invented a thousand wild tales which might account for the look of doom upon her fair face, and at last my excited imagination half induced me to believe that the mysterious print was a forged antique, and represented, in truth, some living woman to whom I had often spoken, and with whom my fortunes were indissolubly connected.

'A wickeder lie was never uttered than that favourite statement of colonial politicians—more ignorant or more impudent than others of their class—that in Australia no man need starve who is willing to work. I have been willing to work, and I have absolutely starved for days together. The humiliation through which I was passed must, I fancy, be familiar to many. During the first six months of my arrival I was an honorary member of the Melbourne Club, the guest of those officials to whom I brought letters of introduction, the temporary lion of South Yarra tea parties, and the butt of the local *Punch* on account of the modish cut of my pantaloons. I met men who "knew my people", and was surprised to find that the mention of a titled friend secured for me considerable attention among the leaders of such secondhand fashion as is boasted by the colony. In this genial atmosphere I recovered my independence. Indeed, had my social derelictions been worse than those incurred by poverty, I was assured that society could find it in its colonial heart to forgive them all. I was Hugh Pontifex, who had supped with the Marquis of Carabas, and brought letters of introduction from Lord Crabs. Had Judas Iscariot arrived armed with such credentials South Yarra would have auburnized his red hair, and had him to dinner. To my surprise, instead of being cast among new faces, and compelled to win for myself an independent reputation, I found that I was among old friends whom I had long thought dead or in jail. To walk down Collins-street was like pulling up the Styx. On either side I saw men who had vanished from the Upper World sooner than I. Tomkins was there to explain that queer story of the concealed ace. Jenkins talked to me for an hour concerning the Derby which ruined him. Hopkins had another wife in addition to the one whom he left at Florence, while Wilkins assured me on his honour that he had married the lady with whom he had eloped, and introduced me to her during a dinner-party at a trading magnate's. The game was made in the same old fashion, only the stakes were not so high. The porcelain was of the same pattern, only a little cracked.

'For six months life was vastly pleasant. Then my term of honorary membership finally expired, and I left the Club to live at Scott's. By and bye my money ran short. I drew a bill on England, and the letter which informed me of its payment contained a stern command to draw no more. I went on a visit to the "station" of an acquaintance, and on returning to town found that my hotel bill was presented weekly. I retired into cheaper lodgings, and became affiliated to a less aristocratic club. Forced to associate with men of another "set", I felt that my first friends remembered to forget me. My lampooned trowsers began to wear out, and I wondered how I could have been once so reckless in the purchase of boots. I applied to Wilkins for a loan, then to Tomkins and to Hopkins. I found that I could not repay them, and so avoided those streets where they were to be met. I discarded gloves, and smoked a short pipe publicly at noonday. I removed to a public-house, and talking with my creditor-land-lord at night, not unfrequently drank much brandy. I discovered that it is possible to be drunk before dinner. I applied for a clerkship, a messengership, a "billet" in the Civil Service; I went on the stage as a "super", I went up the country as a schoolmaster, I scribbled for the newspapers, I wrote verses for the Full and Plenty eating-house. I starved in "genteel" poverty until fortune luckily put me in the way of prosperity by suggesting Coachdriving and Billiard-marking. Thanks to an education at a public school, a licensed youth, a taste for pleasure, and the society of the "best men about London", I found myself at three-and-twenty master of two professions, driving and billiard-playing. You will understand now that my digression concerning pictures was necessary to convince you that all this time I never sold the mysterious print.

'One Sunday evening, towards the end of August, when the windy winter had not yet begun to melt into sudden and dusty spring, I was walking up Bourke-street. You, Falx, who have made a study of Melbourne city, know what a curious appearance the town presents on Sunday evening. The deserted road, barren of all vehicles save a passing cab, serves as a promenade for hundreds of servant-maids, shop-boys, and idlers, while the pavement is crowded with young men and women of the lower middle class, who under pretence of "going to church", or of "smoking a cigar", contrive to indulge their mutual propensities for social enjoyment. Those sewing-girls, who, at 6 o'clock in the evening, are to be nightly seen debouching from Flinders-lane or Little Collins-street, frequent these Sunday evening promenades, and, in all the pride of clean petticoats and kid gloves, form fitting companions for the holiday-making barbers, or soft-goods clerks, who—daring rakes! seek a weekly intrigue at the Peacock, on the unsavoury strength of a "Sunday" cigar. Examining these groups as I walked, I found myself abreast of Nissen's Café, impeding the egress of a lady. I turned with an apology, but the words melted on my lips, when, beneath the black bonnet of the stranger, *I found the counterpart of the unknown print.*

'For an instant surprise rendered me incapable of action, and then, with beating heart and bewildered brain, I followed the fleeting figure. She went down Bourke-street, and turned to the left into Swanston-street. When she reached the corner where the Town-hall now stands, a man suddenly crossed the moon-lit street, and joined her. This man was wrapped in one of those Inverness cloaks which the slowly-travelling fashion of the day had then made imperative to the well-being of

Melbourne dandies. A slouch hat of the operatic brigand type shaded
his face, but in the brief glance that I caught of him I fancied that I
recognized those heavy brows, that blunt nose, and that thin and treacher-
ous mouth. The two met, evidently by appointment, and went onwards
together. It was useless to follow. I turned and went home.

'I passed the next day in a condition of mind which it is impossible to
describe. So strange a coincidence as this had surely never happened to
man before. A woman has her portrait engraved the year 1469; I purchase
the engraving, try in vain to discover the name of the original, and meet
her face to face in the prosaic Melbourne of 1863. I longed for night to
come that I might wander through the streets in search of her. I felt a
terrible yearning tug at my heart strings. I burned to meet her wild sad
eyes again. I shuddered when I thought that in my wildest dreams I had
never sunk that pictured face so deep beneath the social waters as
this incarnation of it seemed to have been plunged. For two nights I
roamed the streets in vain. On the morning of the third day a paragraph
in the *Herald* explained why my search had been fruitless. The body of
a woman had been "found in the Yarra". Society—and especially unmarried society—has, as a matter of course, its average of female suicides,
and as a rule respectable folks don't hear much about them. The case of
this unfortunate girl, however, was different. She was presumed to have
been murdered, and the police made investigations. The case is sufficiently
celebrated in the annals of Melbourne crime to excuse a repetition of
details. Suffice it to say, that against the many persons who were presumed
to have been inculpated in the destruction of the poor girl no proof was
forthcoming. The journals aired Edgar Poe and the Mystery of Marie
Roget for a day or so, but no one was sent for trial, and an open verdict
left the detectives at liberty to exercise their ingenuity without prejudice.
There was some rumour of a foreigner who was implicated in the deed,
but as the friends of the poor outcast knew of no such person, and as my
evidence as to seeing a man of such appearance join the deceased was in
reality of little value (for I was compelled to admit that I had never seen
the woman before in my life, and that my glimpse of her companion was
but momentary), the supposition was treated with contempt and the
"case" dismissed from the memory of the public.

'It did not fade so easily from my mind. To speak truth, indeed, I was
haunted by the hideous thing which I had been sent to "view" upon the
coarse table of that wretched deadhouse which then disgraced our city.
The obscene and cruel fate of the unhappy woman whose portrait had so
long looked down upon me filled me not only with horror, but with
apprehension. It seemed to me as if I myself was implicated in her fate,
and bound to avenge her murder. The fact of my having speculated so
long upon her fortunes, and then having found her but to lose her before
a word could pass between us, appeared to give me the right to seek to

know more of her. The proud queen of many a fantastic dream-revel; the sad Chatelaine of many an air-built castle; had this portrait leapt to life beneath my glances as bounded to earth the nymph from beneath the chisel of Pygmalion? Had the lost one who passed me like a ghost in the gloaming come out of the grave in which they had placed her four hundred years ago? What meant this resurrection of buried beauty? What was the mysterious portent of this living presentiment of a dead and forgotten sin? I saw the poor creature buried. I wept—no unmanly tears, I trust—over her nameless grave. And then I learned her history. 'Twas no romance, unless the old story of a broken home and the cold comfort of the stony-hearted streets may be called romantic. She was presumed to have been well-born—she had been a wife, her husband had left her, she was beautiful and poor—for the rest ask Mother Carey, who deals in chickens. She can tell you entertaining histories of fifty such.

'At the inquest I met Warrend—you know old Tom, Marston?—and he sought me out, and took me home with him. We had been school-fellows; but though my taste for prints and pictures had now and then brought me into his company, I had seen but little of him. He was—as we know him—kindly, tender, and generous. He offered me his help. He was in good practice, and could afford to give me shelter beneath his bachelor roof. He wrote for *The Argus*, knew the editor, would try to procure work for me. That meeting, Noah, laid the foundation of such independence as I now claim. Shaken in health by my recent privations, and troubled in mind by the horrible and inexplicable mystery upon which I seemed to have stumbled, I was for some weeks seriously ill. Warrend saw that something preyed upon my spirits, and pressed me to unbosom myself. I told him the story, and produced the print.

'I must beg your grace for what I am about to tell you. You may regard the story as unworthy of credit, or sneer at it as the result of a "coincidence". It is simply true, for all that.

'Warrend became grave.

'"I have a copy of that print," said he, in a tone altogether without the pride usual in a collector. "I think a unique copy. It is the portrait of a woman round whose life a mystery spun itself. See here."

'He opened the portfolio, and took out the engraving. It was an exact copy of mine, but was a proof after letters, and bore in the quaint characters of the time the name, JEHANNE LA GAILLARDE.

'I fell back upon the sofa as if I had been struck in the face. The name of the poor girl whom I had buried was Jenny Gay! "Warrend," said I, "there is something unholy about this. I met a week ago the living original of that portrait, and now you a man whose name re-echoes that

of the Italian artist who engraved it, tell me that you know the mystery
of her life. What is it, then?—for before you speak I know I figure in the
scene!"

'Warrend, or Finiguerra, took from the book-shelf a little volume
published by Vander Berghen, of Brussels, in 1775, and handed it to me.
It was called *Le Coeur de Jehanne la Gaillarde*, and appeared to be a
collection of letters. In the advertisement was a brief memoir of the
woman whose face had so long puzzled me. I glanced at it, and turned
sick with nameless terror. Jehanne la Gaillarde was a woman whose
romantic amours had electrified the Paris of Louis XI. She was murdered
by being thrown into the Seine. "All attempts to discover the murderer
were vain, but at length a young man named Hugue Grandprête, who,
though he had never seen the celebrated beauty, had fallen in love with
her picture, persuaded himself that the murderer was none other than the
Sieur de la Forêt (the husband of the beautiful Jehanne), who, a man of
an ill-life, had been compelled to fly from Paris. Grandprête communicated his suspicions to none but his intimate friends, followed De la Forêt
to Padua, and killed him." As I read this romance of a man who bore a
name which reflected my own, I shuddered, for a sudden thrill of
recollection lighted up the darkness of the drama as a flash of lightning
illumes the darkness of a thunder cloud. The face of the man in
the cloak was recalled to me as that of a certain gambling lieutenant who
was cashiered by a court-martial so notorious that the sun of India and the
snows of the Crimea have scarce burned out or covered the memory of
his regiment's nickname.

'As Jehanne la Gaillarde was the double of Jenny Gay; as Hugue
Grandprête lived again in Hugh Pontifex; as the Italian artist was recalled
to life in the person of the man at my side, so Bernhard de la Forêt worked
once more his wicked will on earth in the person of the cashiered
gambler, Bernard Forrester. If this was a "coincidence", it was terribly
complete.'

—————⇒»•«⇐—————

'But 'twas a mere coincidence, after all,' said Marston, gently. 'You do not
think that men's souls return to earth and enact again the crimes which
stained them?'

'I know not. But there are in decimal arithmetic repeated "coinci-
dences" called *repetends*. Continue the generation of numbers through all
time, you have these repetends for ever recurring. Can you explain this
mystery of numbers? No. Neither can I explain the mystery of my life.
Good night. I have wearied you.'

'Stay,' cried I, rashly, 'the parallel is not yet complete. You have not met
Forrester!'

'No,' cried Pontifex, his large eyes blazing with no healthy fire, 'I have prayed that I might not meet him. I live here in Melbourne at the scene of his crime, because it seems the least likely place to again behold him. If, by accident, in the streets I catch sight of one who resembles him I hurry away. But I *shall* meet him one day, and then my doom will be upon me, and I shall kill him as I killed him in Padua 400 years ago!'

LOUIS BECKE

Challis the Doubter

THE WHITE LADY AND THE BROWN WOMAN

Four years had come and gone since the day that Challis, with a dull and savage misery in his heart, had, cursing the love-madness which once possessed him, walked out from his house in an Australian city with an undefined and vague purpose of going 'somewhere' to drown his sense of wrong and erase from his memory the face of the woman who, his wife of not yet a year, had played with her honour and his. So he thought, anyhow.

You see, Challis was 'a fool'—at least so his pretty, violet-eyed wife had told him that afternoon with a bitter and contemptuous ring in her voice when he had brought another man's letter—written to her—and with an impulsive and jealous haste had asked her to explain. He was a fool, she had said, with an angry gleam in the violet eyes, to think she could not 'take care' of herself. Admit receiving that letter? Of course! Did he think she could help other men writing silly letters to her? Did he not think she could keep out of a mess? And she smiled the self-satisfied smile of a woman conscious of many admirers and of her own powers of intrigue.

Then Challis, with a big effort, gulping down the rage that stirred him, made his great mistake. He spoke of his love for her. Fatuity! She laughed at him, said that as she detested women, his love was too exacting for her if it meant that she should never be commonly friendly with any other man.

Challis looked at her steadily for a few moments, trying to smother the wild flood of black suspicion aroused in him by the discovery of the letter and confirmed by her sneering words, and then said quietly but with a dangerous inflexion in his voice—

'Remember—you are my wife. If you have no regard for your own reputation, you shall have some for mine. I don't want to entertain my friends by thrashing R——, but I'm not such a fool as you think. And if you go further in this direction you'll find me a bit of a brute.'

Again the sneering laugh—'Indeed! Something very tragic will occur, I suppose?'

'No,' said Challis, grimly, 'something very prosaic—common enough among men with pretty wives—I'll clear out.'

'I wish you would do that now,' said his wife, 'I hate you quite enough.'

Of course she didn't quite mean it. She really liked Challis in her own small-souled way—principally because his money had given her the social pleasures denied her during her girlhood. With an unmoved face and without farewell he left her and went to his lawyer's.

A quarter of an hour later he arose to go, and the lawyer asked him when he intended returning.

'That all depends upon her. If she wants me back again, she can write, through you, and I'll come—if she has conducted herself with a reasonable amount of propriety for such a pretty woman.'

Then, with an ugly look on his face, Challis went out; next day he embarked in the *Lady Alicia* for a six months' cruise among the Islands of the North-west Pacific.

That was four years ago, and today Challis, who stands working at a little table set in against an open window, hammering out a ring from a silver coin on a marlinspike and vyce, whistles softly and contentedly to himself as he raises his head and glances through the vista of cocoanuts that surround his dwelling on this lonely and almost forgotten island.

'The devil!' he thinks to himself, 'I must be turning into a native. Four years! What an ass I was! And I've never written yet—that is, never sent a letter away. Well, neither has she. Perhaps, after all, there was little in that affair of R——s. . . . By God! though, if there was, I've been very good to them in leaving them a clear field. Anyhow, she's all right as regards money. I'm glad I've done that. It's a big prop to a man's conscience to feel he hasn't done anything mean; and she likes money—most women do. Of course I'll go back—if she writes. If not—well, then, these sinful islands can claim me for their own; that is, Nalia can.'

A native boy with shaven head, save for a long tuft on the left side, came down from the village, and, seating himself on the gravelled space inside the fence, gazed at the white man with full, lustrous eyes.

'Halloa, *tama!*' said Challis, 'whither goest now?'

'Pardon, Tialli. I came to look at thee making the ring. Is it of soft silver—and for Nalia, thy wife?'

'Ay, O Shaven Head, it is. Here, take this *masi* and go pluck me a young nut to drink,' and Challis threw him a ship-biscuit. Then he went on tapping the little band of silver. He had already forgotten the violet eyes, and was thinking with almost childish eagerness of the soft glow in the black orbs of Nalia when she should see his finished handiwork.

The boy returned with a young cocoanut, un-husked. 'Behold, Tialli. This nut is a *uto ga'au*, sweet husk. When thou hast drunk the juice give it me back, that I may chew the husk which is sweet as the sugar-cane of Samoa,' and he squatted down again on the gravel.

Challis drank, then threw him the husk and resumed his work. Presently the boy, tearing off a strip of the husk with his white teeth, said, 'Tialli, how is it that there be no drinking-nuts in thy house?'

'Because, O turtle-head, my wife is away; and there are no men in the village to-day; and because the women of this *motu* (island) have no thought that the *papalagi* (foreigner) may be parched with thirst, and so come not near me with a cocoanut.' This latter in jest.

'Nay, Tialli. Not so. True it is that today all the men are in the bush binding *fala* leaves around the cocoanut trees, else do the rats steal up and eat the buds and clusters of little nuts. And because Nalia, thy wife, is away at the other White Man's house no woman cometh inside the door.'

Challis laughed. 'O evil-minded people of Nukunono! And must I, thy *papalagi*, be parched with thirst because of this?'

'*Faiaga oe*, Tialli, thou but playest with me. Raise thy hand and call out "I thirst!" and every woman in the village will run to thee, each with a drinking-nut, and those that desire thee, but are afraid, will give two. But to come inside when Nalia is away would be to put shame on her.'

The white man mused. The boy's solemn chatter entertained him. He knew well the native customs; but, to torment the boy, he commenced again.

'O, foolish custom! See how I trust my wife. Nalia. Is she not even now in the house of another white man?'

'True. But, then, he is old and feeble, and thou young and strong. None but a fool desires to eat a dried flying-fish when a fresh one may be had.'

'O, wise man with the shaven crown,' said Challis, with mocking good nature, 'thou art full of wisdom of the ways of women. And if I were old and withered, would Nalia then be false to me in the house of another and younger white man?'

'How could she? Would not he, too, have a wife who would watch her? And if he had not, and were *nofo noa* (single), would he be such a fool to steal that which he can buy—for there are many girls without husbands as good to look on as that Nalia of thine. And all women are alike,' and then, hearing a woman's voice calling his name, he stood up.

'Farewell, O *ulu tula poto*' (Wise Baldhead), said Challis, as the boy, still chewing his sweet husk, walked back to the native houses clustered under the grove of *pua* trees.

Ere dusk, Nalia came home, a slenderly-built girl with big dreamy eyes, and a heavy mantle of wavy hair. A white muslin gown, fastened at the throat with a small silver brooch, was her only garment, save the folds of the navy-blue-and-white *lava lava* round her waist, which the European-fashioned garment covered.

Challis was lying down when she came in. Two girls who came with her carried baskets of cooked food, presents from old Jack Kelly, Challis's fellow-trader. At a sign from Nalia the girls took one of the baskets of food and went away. Then, taking off her wide-brimmed hat of *fala* leaf, she sat down beside Challis and pinched his cheek.

'O lazy one! To let me walk from the house of Tiaki all alone!'

'Alone! There were three of thee.'

'Tāpā! Could I talk to *them*! I, a white man's wife, must not be too familiar with every girl; else they would seek to get presents from me with sweet words. Besides, could I carry home the fish and cooked fowl sent thee by old Tiaki? That would be unbecoming to me, even as it would be if thou climbed a tree for a cocoanut'—and the Daughter of the Tropics laughed merrily as she patted Challis on his sunburnt cheek.

Challis rose, and going to the little table took from it the ring.

'See, Nalia, I am not lazy as thou sayest. This is thine.'

The girl, with an eager *Aue!* took the bauble and placed it on her finger. She made a pretty picture, standing there in the last glow of the sun as it sank into the ocean, her languorous eyes filled with a tender light.

Challis, sitting on the end of the table regarding her with half-amused interest as does a man watching a child with a toy, suddenly flushed hotly: 'By God, I can't be such a fool as to begin to *love* her in reality, but yet . . . come here, Nalia,' and he drew her to him, and, turning her face up so that he might look into her eyes, he asked:

'Nalia, hast thou ever told me any lies?'

The steady depths of those dark eyes looked back into his, and she answered:

'Nay, I fear thee too much to lie. Thou mightst kill me.'

'I do but ask thee some little things. It matters not to me what the answer is. Yet see that thou keepest nothing hidden from me.'

The girl, with parted lips and one hand on his, waited.

'Before thou became my wife, Nalia, hadst thou any lovers?'

'Yes, two—Kapua and Tafu-le-Afi.'

'And since?'

'May I choke and perish here before thee if I lie! None.'

Challis, still holding her soft brown chin in his hand, asked her one more question—a question that only one of his temperament would have dared to ask a girl of the Tokelaus.

'Nalia, dost thou love me?'

'Aye, *alofa tumau* (everlasting love). Am I a fool? Are there not Letia, and Miriami, and Elině, the daughter of old Tiaki, ready to come to this house if I love any but thee? Therefore my love is like the suckers of the *fa'e* (octopus) in its strength. My mother has taught me much wisdom.'

A curious feeling of satisfaction possessed the man, and next day Letia, the 'show' girl of the village, visiting Challis's store to buy a tin of salmon, saw Nalia the Lucky One seated on a mat beneath the seaward side of the trader's house, surrounded by a billowy pile of yellow silk, diligently sewing.

'Ho, dear friend of my heart! Is that silken dress for thee? For the love of God, let me but touch it. Four dollars a fathom it be priced at. Thy husband is indeed the king of generosity. Art thou to become a mother?'

'Away, silly fool, and do thy buying and pester me not.'

Challis, coming to the corner of the house, leant against a post, and something white showed in his hand. It was a letter. His letter to the woman of violet eyes, written a week ago, in the half-formed idea of sending it some day. He read it through, and then paused and looked at Nalia. She raised her head and smiled. Slowly, piece by piece, he tore it into tiny little squares, and, with a dreamy hand-wave, threw them away. The wind held them in mid-air for a moment, and then carried the little white flecks to the beach.

'What is it?' said the bubbling voice of Letia the Disappointed.

'Only a piece of paper that weighed as a piece of iron on my bosom. But it is gone now.'

'Even so,' said Letia, smelling the gaudy label on the tin of salmon in the anticipative ecstasy of a true Polynesian, '*pe se mea fa'agotoimoana* (like a thing buried deep in ocean). May God send me a white man as generous as thee—a whole tin of *samani* for nothing! Now do I know that Nalia will bear thee a son.'

And that is why Challis the Doubter has never turned up again.

BARBARA BAYNTON

Squeaker's Mate

The woman carried the bag with the axe and maul and wedges; the man had the billy and clean tucker-bags; the cross-cut saw linked them. She was taller than the man, and the equability of her body, contrasting with his indolent slouch, accentuated the difference. 'Squeaker's mate', the men called her, and these agreed that she was the best long-haired mate that ever stepped in petticoats. The selectors' wives pretended to challenge her right to womanly garments, but if she knew what they said, it neither turned nor troubled Squeaker's mate.

Nine prospective posts and maybe sixteen rails—she calculated this yellow gum would yield. 'Come on,' she encouraged the man; 'let's tackle it.'

From the bag she took the axe, and ring-barked a preparatory circle, while he looked for a shady spot for the billy and tucker-bags.

'Come on.' She was waiting with the greased saw. He came. The saw rasped through a few inches, then he stopped and looked at the sun.

'It's nigh tucker-time,' he said, and when she dissented, he exclaimed, with sudden energy, 'There's another bee! Wait, you go on with the axe, an' I'll track 'im.'

As they came, they had already followed one and located the nest. She could not see the bee he spoke of, though her grey eyes were as keen as a black's. However, she knew the man, and her tolerance was of the mysteries.

She drew out the saw, spat on her hands, and with the axe began weakening the inclining side of the tree.

Long and steadily and in secret the worm had been busy in the heart. Suddenly the axe blade sank softly, the tree's wounded edges closed on it like a vice. There was a 'settling' quiver on its top branches, which the woman heard and understood. The man, encouraged by the sounds of the axe, had returned with an armful of sticks for the billy. He shouted gleefully, 'It's fallin', look out.'

But she waited to free the axe.

With a shivering groan the tree fell, and as she sprang aside, a thick worm-eaten branch snapped at a joint and silently she went down under it.

'I tole yer t' look out,' he reminded her, as with a crow-bar, and grunting earnestly, he forced it up. 'Now get out quick.'

She tried moving her arms and the upper part of her body. Do this; do that, he directed, but she made no movement after the first.

He was impatient, because for once he had actually to use his strength. His share of a heavy lift usually consisted of a make-believe grunt, delivered at a critical moment. Yet he hardly cared to let it again fall on her, though he told her he would, if she 'didn't shift'.

Near him lay a piece broken short; with his foot he drew it nearer, then gradually worked it into a position, till it acted as a stay to the lever.

He laid her on her back when he drew her out, and waited expecting some acknowledgment of his exertions, but she was silent, and as she did not notice that the axe, she had tried to save, lay with the fallen trunk across it, he told her. She cared almost tenderly for all their possessions and treated them as friends. But the half-buried broken axe did not affect her. He wondered a little, for only last week she had patiently chipped out the old broken head, and put in a new handle.

'Feel bad?' he inquired at length.

'Pipe,' she replied with slack lips.

Both pipes lay in the fork of a near tree. He took his, shook out the ashes, filled it, picked up a coal and puffed till it was alight—then he filled hers. Taking a small fire-stick he handed her the pipe. The hand she raised shook and closed in an uncertain hold, but she managed by a great effort to get it to her mouth. He lost patience with the swaying hand that tried to take the light.

'Quick,' he said 'quick, that damn dog's at the tucker.'

He thrust it into her hand that dropped helplessly across her chest. The lighted stick, falling between her bare arm and the dress, slowly roasted the flesh and smouldered the clothes.

He rescued their dinner, pelted his dog out of sight—hers was lying near her head—put on the billy, then came back to her.

The pipe had fallen from her lips; there was blood on the stem.

'Did yer jam yer tongue?' he asked.

She always ignored trifles, he knew, therefore he passed her silence.

He told her that her dress was on fire. She took no heed. He put it out, and looked at the burnt arm, then with intentness at her.

Her eyes were turned unblinkingly to the heavens, her lips were grimly apart, and a strange greyness was upon her face, and the sweat-beads were mixing.

'Like a drink er tea? Asleep?'

He broke a green branch from the fallen tree and swished from his face the multitudes of flies that had descended with it.

In a heavy way he wondered why did she sweat, when she was not working? Why did she not keep the flies out of her mouth and eyes? She'd have bungy eyes, if she didn't. If she was asleep, why did she not close them?

But asleep or awake, as the billy began to boil, he left her, made the tea, and ate his dinner. His dog had disappeared, and as it did not come to his whistle, he threw the pieces to hers, that would not leave her head to reach them.

He whistled tunelessly his one air, beating his own time with a stick on the toe of his blucher, then looked overhead at the sun and calculated that she must have been lying like that for 'close up an hour'. He noticed that the axe handle was broken in two places, and speculated a little as to whether she would again pick out the back-broken handle or burn it out in his method, which was less trouble, if it did spoil the temper of the blade. He examined the worm-dust in the stump and limbs of the newly-fallen tree; mounted it and looked round the plain. The sheep were straggling in a manner that meant walking work to round them, and he supposed he would have to yard them tonight, if she didn't liven up. He looked down at unenlivened her. This changed his 'chune' to a call for his hiding dog.

'Come on, ole feller,' he commanded her dog 'Fetch 'em back.' He whistled further instructions, slapping his thigh and pointing to the sheep.

But a brace of wrinkles either side the brute's closed mouth demonstrated determined disobedience. The dog would go if she told him, and by and by she would.

He lighted his pipe and killed half an hour smoking. With the frugality that hard graft begets, his mate limited both his and her own tobacco, so he must not smoke all afternoon. There was no work to shirk, so time began to drag. Then a 'goanner' crawling up a tree attracted him. He gathered various missiles and tried vainly to hit the seemingly grinning reptile. He came back and sneaked a fill of her tobacco, and while he was smoking, the white tilt of a cart caught his eye. He jumped up. 'There's Red Bob goin' t'our place fur th' 'oney,' he said. 'I'll go an' weigh it an' get the gonz' (money).

He ran for the cart, and kept looking back as if fearing she would follow and thwart him.

Red Bob the dealer was, in a business way, greatly concerned, when he found that Squeaker's mate was ' 'avin' a sleep out there 'cos a tree fell on her'. She was the best honey-strainer and boiler that he dealt with. She was straight and square too. There was no water in her honey whether boiled or merely strained, and in every kerosene-tin the weight of honey was to an ounce as she said. Besides he was suspicious and diffident of paying the indecently eager Squeaker before he saw the woman. So reluctantly Squeaker led to where she lay. With many fierce oaths Red Bob sent her lawful protector for help, and compassionately poured a little from his flask down her throat, then swished away the flies from her till help came.

Together these men stripped a sheet of bark, and laying her with pathetic tenderness upon it, carried her to her hut. Squeaker followed in the rear with the billy and tucker.

Red Bob took his horse from the cart, and went to town for the doctor. Late that night at the back of the old hut (there were two) he and others who had heard that she was hurt, squatted with unlighted pipes in their mouths, waiting to hear the doctor's verdict. After he had given it and gone, they discussed in whispers, and with a look seen only on bush faces, the hard luck of that woman who alone had hard-grafted with the best of them for every acre and hoof on that selection. Squeaker would go through it in no time. Why she had allowed it to be taken up in his name, when the money had been her own, was also for them among the mysteries.

Him they called 'a nole woman', not because he was hanging round the honey-tins, but after man's fashion to eliminate all virtue. They beckoned him, and explaining his mate's injury, cautioned him to keep from her the knowledge that she would be for ever a cripple.

'Jus' th' same, now, then fur 'im,' pointing to Red Bob, 't' pay me, I'll 'ev t' go t' town.'

They told him in whispers what they thought of him, and with a cowardly look towards where she lay, but without a word of parting, like shadows these men made for their homes.

Next day the women came. Squeaker's mate was not a favourite with them—a woman with no leisure for yarning was not likely to be. After the first day they left her severely alone, their plea to their husbands, her uncompromising independence. It is in the ordering of things that by degrees most husbands accept their wives' views of other women.

The flour bespattering Squeaker's now neglected clothes spoke eloquently of his clumsy efforts at damper making. The women gave him many a feed, agreeing that it must be miserable for him.

If it were miserable and lonely for his mate, she did not complain; for her the long, long days would give place to longer nights—those nights with the pregnant bush silence suddenly cleft by a bush voice. However, she was not fanciful, and being a bush scholar knew 'twas a dingo, when a long whine came from the scrub on the skirts of which lay the axe under the worm-eaten tree. That quivering wail from the billabong lying murkily mystic towards the East was only the cry of the fearing curlew.

Always her dog—wakeful and watchful as she—patiently waiting for her to be up and about again. That would be soon, she told her complaining mate.

'Yer won't. Yer back's broke,' said Squeaker laconically. 'That's wot's wrong er yer; injoory t' th' spine. Doctor says that means back's broke, and yer won't never walk no more. No good not t' tell yer, cos I can't be doin' everythin'.'

A wild look grew on her face, and she tried to sit up.

'Erh,' said he, 'see! yer carnt, yer jes' ther same as a snake w'en ees back's broke, on'y yer don't bite yerself like a snake does w'en 'e carnt crawl. Yer did bite yer tongue w'en yer fell.'

She gasped, and he could hear her heart beating when she let her head fall back a few moments; though she wiped her wet forehead with the back of her hand, and still said that was the doctor's mistake. But day after day she tested her strength, and whatever the result, was silent, though white witnesses, halo-wise, gradually circled her brow and temples.

''Tisn't as if yer was agoin' t' get better t'morrer, the doctor says yer won't never work no more, an' I can't be cookin' an' workin' an' doin' everythin'!'

He muttered something about 'sellin' out', but she firmly refused to think of such a monstrous proposal.

He went into town one Saturday afternoon soon after, and did not return till Monday.

Her supplies, a billy of tea and scraps of salt beef and damper (her dog got the beef), gave out the first day, though that was as nothing to her compared with the bleat of the penned sheep, for it was summer and droughty, and her dog could not unpen them.

Of them and her dog only she spoke when he returned. He d—d him, and d—d her, and told her to 'double up yer ole broke back an' bite yerself'. He threw things about, made a long-range feint of kicking her threatening dog, then sat outside in the shade of the old hut, nursing his head till he slept.

She, for many reasons, had when necessary made these trips into town, walking both ways, leading a pack-horse for supplies. She never failed to indulge him in a half pint—a pipe was her luxury.

The sheep waited till next day, so did she.

For a few days he worked a little in her sight; not much—he never did. It was she who always lifted the heavy end of the log, and carried the tools; he—the billy and tucker.

She wearily watched him idling his time; reminded him that the wire lying near the fence would rust, one could run the wire through easily, and when she got up in a day or so, she would help strain and fasten it. At first he pretended he had done it, later said he wasn't goin' t' go wirin' or nothin' else by 'imself if every other man on the place did.

She spoke of many other things that could be done by one, reserving the great till she was well. Sometimes he whistled while she spoke, often swore, generally went out, and when this was inconvenient, dull as he was, he found the 'Go and bite yerself like a snake', would instantly silence her.

At last the work worry ceased to exercise her, and for night to bring him home was a rare thing.

Her dog rounded and yarded the sheep when the sun went down and there was no sign of him, and together they kept watch on their movements till dawn. She was mindful not to speak of this care to him, knowing he would have left it for them to do constantly, and she noticed that what little interest he seemed to share went to the sheep. Why, was soon demonstrated.

Through the cracks her ever watchful eyes one day saw the dust rise out of the plain. Nearer it came till she saw him and a man on horseback rounding and driving the sheep into the yard, and later both left in charge of a little mob. Their 'Baa-baas' to her were cries for help; many had been pets. So he was selling her sheep to the town butchers.

In the middle of the next week he came from town with a fresh horse, new saddle and bridle. He wore a flash red shirt, and round his neck a silk handkerchief. On the next occasion she smelt scent, and though he did not try to display the dandy meerschaum, she saw it, and heard the squeak of the new boots, not bluchers. However he was kinder to her this time, offering a fill of his cut tobacco; he had long ceased to keep her supplied. Several of the men who sometimes in passing took a look in, would have made up her loss had they known, but no word of complaint passed her lips.

She looked at Squeaker as he filled his pipe from his pouch, but he would not meet her eyes, and, seemingly dreading something, slipped out.

She heard him hammering in the old hut at the back, which served for tools and other things which sunlight and rain did not hurt. Quite briskly he went in and out. She could see him through the cracks carrying a narrow strip of bark, and understood, he was making a bunk. When it was finished he had a smoke, then came to her and fidgetted about; he said this hut was too cold, and that she would never get well in it. She did not feel cold, but, submitting to his mood, allowed him to make a fire that would roast a sheep. He took off his hat, and, fanning himself, said he was roastin', wasn't she? She was.

He offered to carry her into the other; he would put a new roof on it in a day or two, and it would be better than this one, and she would be up in no time. He stood to say this where she could not see him.

His eagerness had tripped him.

There were months to run before all the Government conditions of residence, etc., in connection with the selection, would be fulfilled, still she thought, perhaps he was trying to sell out, and she would not go.

He was away four days that time, and when he returned slept in the new bunk.

She compromised. Would he put a bunk there for himself, keep out of town, and not sell the place? He promised instantly with additions.

'Try could yer crawl yerself?' he coaxed, looking at her bulk.

Her nostrils quivered with her suppressed breathing, and her lips tightened, but she did not attempt to move.

It was evident some great purpose actuated him. After attempts to carry and drag her, he rolled her on the sheet of bark that had brought her home, and laboriously drew her round.

She asked for a drink, he placed her billy and tin pint besides the bunk, and left her, gasping and dazed, to her sympathetic dog.

She saw him run up and yard his horse, and though she called him, he would not answer nor come.

When he rode swiftly towards the town, her dog leaped on the bunk, and joined a refrain to her lamentation, but the cat took to the bush.

He came back at dusk next day in a spring cart—not alone—he had another mate. She saw her though he came a roundabout way, trying to keep in front of the new hut.

There were noises of moving many things from the cart to the hut. Finally he came to a crack near where she lay, and whispered the promise of many good things to her if she kept quiet, and that he would set her hut afire if she didn't. She was quiet, he need not have feared, for that time she was past it, she was stunned.

The released horse came stumbling round to the old hut, and thrust its head in the door in a domesticated fashion. Her dog promptly resented this straggler mistaking their hut for a stable. And the dog's angry dissent, together with the shod clatter of the rapidly disappearing intruder, seemed to have a disturbing effect on the pair in the new hut. The settling sounds suddenly ceased, and the cripple heard the stranger close the door, despite Squeaker's assurances that the woman in the old hut could not move from her bunk to save her life, and that her dog would not leave her.

Food, more and better, was placed near her—but, dumb and motionless, she lay with her face turned to the wall, and her dog growled menacingly at the stranger. The new woman was uneasy, and told Squeaker what people might say and do if she died.

He scared at the 'do', went into the bush and waited.

She went to the door, not the crack, the face was turned that way, and said she had come to cook and take care of her.

The disabled woman, turning her head slowly, looked steadily at her. She was not much to look at. Her red hair hung in an uncurled bang over her forehead, the lower part of her face had robbed the upper, and her figure evinced imminent motherhood, though it is doubtful if the barren woman, noting this, knew by calculation the paternity was not Squeaker's. She was not learned in these matters, though she understood all about an ewe and lamb.

One circumstance was apparent—ah! bitterest of all bitterness to women—she was younger.

The thick hair that fell from the brow of the woman on the bunk was white now.

Bread and butter the woman brought. The cripple looked at it, at her dog, at the woman. Bread and butter for a dog! but the stranger did not understand till she saw it offered to the dog. The bread and butter was not for the dog. She brought meat.

All next day the man kept hidden. The cripple saw his dog, and knew he was about.

But there was an end of this pretence when at dusk he came back with a show of haste, and a finger of his right hand bound and ostentatiously prominent. His entrance caused great excitement to his new mate. The old mate, who knew this snake-bite trick from its inception, maybe, realized how useless were the terrified stranger's efforts to rouse the snoring man after an empty pint bottle had been flung on the outside heap.

However, what the sick woman thought was not definite, for she kept silent always. Neither was it clear how much she ate, and how much she gave to her dog, though the new mate said to Squeaker one day that she believed that the dog would not take a bite more than its share.

The cripple's silence told on the stranger, especially when alone. She would rather have abuse. Eagerly she counted the days past and to pass. Then back to the town. She told no word of that hope to Squeaker, he had no place in her plans for the future. So if he spoke of what they would do by and by when his time would be up, and he able to sell out, she listened in uninterested silence.

She did tell him she was afraid of 'her', and after the first day would not go within reach, but every morning made a billy of tea, which with bread and beef Squeaker carried to her.

The rubbish heap was adorned, for the first time, with jam and fish tins from the table in the new hut. It seemed to be understood that neither woman nor dog in the old hut required them.

Squeaker's dog sniffed and barked joyfully around them till his licking efforts to bottom a salmon tin sent him careering in a muzzled frenzy, that caused the younger woman's thick lips to part grinningly till he came too close.

The remaining sheep were regularly yarded. His old mate heard him whistle as he did it. Squeaker began to work about a little burning-off. So that now, added to the other bush voices, was the call from some untimely falling giant. There is no sound so human as that from the riven souls of these tree people, or the trembling sighs of their upright neighbours whose hands in time will meet over the victim's fallen body.

There was no bunk on the side of the hut to which her eyes turned, but her dog filled that space, and the flash that passed between this back-broken woman and her dog might have been the spirit of these slain tree folk, it was so wondrous ghostly. Still, at times, the practical in her would be dominant, for in a mind so free of fancies, backed by bodily strength, hope died slowly, and forgetful of self she would almost call to Squeaker her fears that certain bees' nests were in danger.

He went into town one day and returned, as he had promised, long before sundown, and next day a clothes-line bridged the space between two trees near the back of the old hut; and—an equally rare occurrence— Squeaker placed across his shoulders the yoke that his old mate had fashioned for herself, with two kerosene-tins attached, and brought them filled with water from the distant creek; but both only partly filled the tub, a new purchase. With utter disregard of the heat and Squeaker's sweating brow, his new mate said, even after another trip, two more now for the blue water. Under her commands he brought them, though sullenly, perhaps contrasting the old mate's methods with the new.

His old mate had periodically carried their washing to the creek, and his mole-skins had been as white as snow without aid of blue.

Towards noon, on the clothes-line many strange garments fluttered, suggestive of a taunt to the barren woman. When the sun went down she could have seen the assiduous Squeaker lower the new prop-sticks and considerably stoop to gather the pegs his inconsiderate new mate had dropped. However, after one load of water next morning, on hearing her estimate that three more would put her own things through, Squeaker struck. Nothing he could urge would induce the stranger to trudge to the creek, where thirst-slaked snakes lay waiting for someone to bite. She sulked and pretended to pack up, till a bright idea struck Squeaker. He fastened a cask on a sledge and, harnessing the new horse, hitched him to it, and, under the approving eyes of his new mate, led off to the creek, though, when she went inside, he bestrode the spiritless brute.

He had various mishaps, any one of which would have served as an excuse to his old mate, but even babes soon know on whom to impose. With an energy new to him he persevered and filled the cask, but the old horse repudiated such a burden even under Squeaker's unmerciful welts. Almost half was sorrowfully baled out, and under a rain of whacks the horse shifted it a few paces, but the cask tilted and the thirsty earth got its contents. All Squeaker's adjectives over his wasted labour were as unavailing as the cure for spilt milk.

It took skill and patience to rig the cask again. He partly filled it, and, just as success seemed probable, the rusty wire fastening the cask to the sledge snapped with the strain, and, springing free, coiled affectionately round the terrified horse's hocks. Despite the sledge (the cask had been soon disposed of) that old town horse's pace then was his record. Hours after, on the plain that met the horizon, loomed two specks: the distance between them might be gauged, for the larger was Squeaker.

Anticipating a plentiful supply and lacking in bush caution, the new mate used the half-bucket of water to boil the salt mutton. Towards noon she laid this joint and bread on the rough table, then watched anxiously in the wrong direction for Squeaker.

She had drained the new tea-pot earlier, but she placed the spout to her thirsty mouth again.

She continued looking for him for hours.

Had he sneaked off to town, thinking she had not used that water, or not caring whether or no? She did not trust him; another had left her. Besides she judged Squeaker by his treatment of the woman who was lying in there with wide-open eyes. Anyhow no use to cry with only that silent woman to hear her.

Had she drunk all hers?

She tried to see at long range through the cracks, but the hanging bed-clothes hid the billy. She went to the door, and, avoiding the bunk looked at the billy.

It was half full.

Instinctively she knew that the eyes of the woman were upon her. She turned away, and hoped and waited for thirsty minutes that seemed hours.

Desperation drove her back to the door. Dared she? No, she couldn't.

Getting a long forked propstick, she tried to reach it from the door, but the dog sprang at the stick. She dropped it and ran.

A scraggy growth fringed the edge of the plain. There was the creek. How far? she wondered. Oh, very far, she knew, and besides there were only a few holes where water was, and the snakes; for Squeaker, with a desire to shine in her eyes, was continually telling her of snakes—vicious and many—that daily he did battle with.

She recalled the evening he came from hiding in the scrub with a string round one finger, and said a snake had bitten him. He had drunk the pint of brandy she had brought for her sickness, and then slept till morning. True, although next day he had to dig for the string round the blue swollen finger, he was not worse than the many she had seen at the Shearer's Rest suffering a recovery. There was no brandy to cure her if she were bitten.

She cried a little in self-pity, then withdrew her eyes, that were getting red, from the outlying creek, and went again to the door. She of the bunk lay with closed eyes.

Was she asleep? The stranger's heart leapt, yet she was hardly in earnest as she tip-toed billy-wards. The dog, crouching with head between two paws, eyed her steadily, but showed no opposition. She made dumb show. 'I want to be friends with you, and won't hurt her.' Abruptly she looked at her, then at the dog. He was motionless and emotionless. Besides if that dog—certainly watching her—wanted to bite her (her dry mouth opened) it could get her any time.

She rated this dog's intelligence almost human, from many of its actions in omission and commission in connection with this woman.

She regretted the pole, no dog would stand that.

Two more steps.

Now just one more; then, by bending and stretching her arm, she would reach it. Could she now? She tried to encourage herself by remembering how close on the first day she had been to the woman, and how delicious a few mouthfuls would be—swallowing dry mouthfuls.

She measured the space between where she had first stood and the billy. Could she get anything to draw it to her? No, the dog would not stand that, and besides the handle would rattle, and she might hear and open her eyes.

The thought of those sunken eyes suddenly opening made her heart bound. Oh! she must breathe—deep, loud breaths. Her throat clicked noisily. Looking back fearfully, she went swiftly out.

She did not look for Squeaker this time, she had given him up.

While she waited for her breath to steady, to her relief and surprise the dog came out. She made a rush to the new hut, but he passed seemingly oblivious of her, and, bounding across the plain, began rounding the sheep. Then he must know Squeaker had gone to town.

Stay! Her heart beat violently; was it because she on the bunk slept and did not want him?

She waited till her heart quieted, and again crept to the door.

The head of the woman on the bunk had fallen towards the wall as in deep sleep; it was turned from the billy, to which she must creep so softly.

Slower, from caution and deadly earnestness, she entered.

She was not so advanced as before, and felt fairly secure, for the woman's eyes were still turned to the wall, and so tightly closed she could not possibly see where she was.

She would bend right down, and try and reach it from where she was. She bent.

It was so swift and sudden, that she had not time to scream when those bony fingers had gripped the hand that she prematurely reached for the billy. She was frozen with horror for a moment, then her screams were piercing. Panting with victory, the prostrate one held her with a hold that the other did not attempt to free herself from.

Down, down she drew her.

Her lips had drawn back from her teeth, and her breath almost scorched the face that she held so close for the staring eyes to gloat over. Her exultation was so great that she could only gloat and gasp, and hold with a tension that had stopped the victim's circulation.

As a wounded, robbed tigress might hold and look, she held and looked.

Neither heard the swift steps of the man, and if the tigress saw him enter, she was not daunted. 'Take me from her,' shrieked the terrified one.

'Quick, take me from her,' she repeated it again, nothing else. 'Take me from her.'

He hastily fastened the door and said something that the shrieks drowned, then picked up the pole. It fell with a thud across the arms which the tightening sinews had turned into steel. Once, twice, thrice. Then the one that got the fullest force bent; that side of the victim was free.

The pole had snapped. Another blow with a broken end freed the other side.

Still shrieking 'Take me from her, take me from her,' she beat on the closed door till Squeaker opened it.

Then he had to face and reckon with his old mate's maddened dog, that the closed door had baffled.

The dog suffered the shrieking woman to pass, but though Squeaker, in bitten agony, broke the stick across the dog, he was forced to give the savage brute best.

'Call 'im orf, Mary, 'e's eatin' me,' he implored. 'Oh corl 'im orf.'

But with stony face the woman lay motionless.

'Sool 'im on t' 'er.' He indicated his new mate who, as though all the plain led to the desired town, still ran in unreasoning terror.

'It's orl er doin',' he pleaded, springing on the bunk beside his old mate. But when, to rouse her sympathy, he would have laid his hand on her, the dog's teeth fastened in it and pulled him back.

HENRY LAWSON

The Union Buries Its Dead

While out boating one Sunday afternoon on a billabong across the river, we saw a young man on horseback driving some horses along the bank. He said it was a fine day, and asked if the water was deep there. The joker of our party said it was deep enough to drown him, and he laughed and rode farther up. We didn't take much notice of him.

Next day a funeral gathered at a corner pub and asked each other in to have a drink while waiting for the hearse. They passed away some of the time dancing jigs to a piano in the bar parlour. They passed away the rest of the time skylarking and fighting.

The defunct was a young union labourer, about twenty-five, who had been drowned the previous day while trying to swim some horses across a billabong of the Darling.

He was almost a stranger in town, and the fact of his having been a union man accounted for the funeral. The police found some union papers in his swag, and called at the General Labourers' Union Office for information about him. That's how we knew. The secretary had very little information to give. The departed was a 'Roman', and the majority of the town were otherwise—but unionism is stronger than creed. Drink, however, is stronger than unionism; and, when the hearse presently arrived, more than two-thirds of the funeral were unable to follow. They were too drunk.

The procession numbered fifteen, fourteen souls following the broken shell of a soul. Perhaps not one of the fourteen possessed a soul any more than the corpse did—but that doesn't matter.

Four or five of the funeral, who were boarders at the pub, borrowed a trap which the landlord used to carry passengers to and from the railway station. They were strangers to us who were on foot, and we to them. We were all strangers to the corpse.

A horseman, who looked like a drover just returned from a big trip, dropped into our dusty wake and followed us a few hundred yards, dragging his pack-horse behind him, but a friend made wild and demonstrative signals from a hotel verandah—hooking at the air in front with his right hand and jobbing his left thumb over his shoulder in the direction of the bar—so the drover hauled off and didn't catch up to us any more. He was a stranger to the entire show.

We walked in twos. There were three twos. It was very hot and dusty; the heat rushed in fierce dazzling rays across every iron roof and light-coloured wall that was turned to the sun. One or two pubs closed respectfully until we got past. They closed their bar doors and the patrons went in and out through some side or back entrance for a few minutes. Bushmen seldom grumble at an inconvenience of this sort, when it is caused by a funeral. They have too much respect for the dead.

On the way to the cemetery we passed three shearers sitting on the shady side of a fence. One was drunk—very drunk. The other two covered their right ears with their hats, out of respect for the departed— whoever he might have been—and one of them kicked the drunk and muttered something to him.

He straightened himself up, stared, and reached helplessly for his hat, which he shoved half off and then on again. Then he made a great effort to pull himself together—and succeeded. He stood up, braced his back against the fence, knocked off his hat, and remorsefully placed his foot on it—to keep it off his head till the funeral passed.

A tall, sentimental drover, who walked by my side, cynically quoted Byronic verses suitable to the occasion—to death—and asked with pathetic humour whether we thought the dead man's ticket would be recognised 'over yonder'. It was a GLU ticket, and the general opinion was that it would be recognised.

Presently my friend said:

'You remember when we were in the boat yesterday, we saw a man driving some horses along the bank?'

'Yes.'

He nodded at the hearse and said:

'Well, that's him.'

I thought awhile.

'I didn't take any particular notice of him,' I said. 'He said something, didn't he?'

'Yes; said it was a fine day. You'd have taken more notice if you'd known that he was doomed to die in the hour, and that those were the last words he would say to any man in this world.'

'To be sure,' said a full voice from the rear. 'If ye'd known that, ye'd have prolonged the conversation.'

We plodded on across the railway line and along the hot, dusty road which ran to the cemetery, some of us talking about the accident, and lying about the narrow escapes we had had ourselves. Presently someone said:

'There's the Devil.'

I looked up and saw a priest standing in the shade of the tree by the cemetery gate.

The hearse was drawn up and the tail-boards were opened. The funeral extinguished its right ear with its hat as four men lifted the coffin out and laid it over the grave. The priest—a pale, quiet young fellow—stood under the shade of a sapling which grew at the head of the grave. He took off his hat, dropped it carelessly on the ground, and proceeded to business.

I noticed that one or two heathens winced slightly when the holy water was sprinkled on the coffin. The drops quickly evaporated, and the little round black spots they left were soon dusted over; but the spots showed, by contrast, the cheapness and shabbiness of the cloth with which the coffin was covered. It seemed black before; now it looked a dusky grey.

Just here man's ignorance and vanity made a farce of the funeral. A big, bull-necked publican, with heavy, blotchy features and a supremely ignorant expression, picked up the priest's straw hat and held it about two inches over the head of his reverence during the whole of the service. The father, be it remembered, was standing in the shade. A few shoved their hats on and off uneasily, struggling between their disgust for the living and their respect for the dead. The hat had a conical crown and a brim sloping down all round like a sunshade, and the publican held it with his great red claw spread over the crown. To do the priest justice, perhaps he didn't notice the incident. A stage priest or parson in the same position might have said: 'Put the hat down, my friend; is not the memory of our departed brother worth more than my complexion?' A wattlebark layman might have expressed himself in stronger language, none the less to the point. But my priest seemed unconscious of what was going on. Besides, the publican was a great and important pillar of the Church. He couldn't, as an ignorant and conceited ass, lose such a good opportunity of asserting his faithfulness and importance to his Church.

The grave looked very narrow under the coffin, and I drew a breath of relief when the box slid easily down. I saw a coffin get stuck once, at Rookwood, and it had to be yanked out with difficulty, and laid on the sods at the feet of the heart-broken relations, who howled dismally while the grave-diggers widened the hole. But they don't cut contracts so fine in the West. Our grave-digger was not altogether bowelless, and, out of respect for that human quality described as 'feelin's', he scraped up some light and dusty soil and threw it down to deaden the fall of the clay lumps on the coffin. He also tried to steer the first few shovelfuls gently down against the end of the grave with the back of the shovel turned outwards, but the hard, dry Darling River clods rebounded and knocked all the same. It didn't matter much—nothing does. The fall of lumps of clay on a stranger's coffin doesn't sound any different from the fall of the same things on an ordinary wooden box—at least I didn't notice anything awesome or unusual in the sound; but, perhaps, one of us—the most sensitive—might have been impressed by being reminded of a burial of long ago, when the thump of every sod jolted his heart.

I have left out the wattle—because it wasn't there. I have also neglected to mention the heart-broken old mate, with his grizzled head bowed and great pearly drops streaming down his rugged cheeks. He was absent—he was probably 'Out Back'. For similar reasons I have omitted reference to the suspicious moisture in the eyes of a bearded bush ruffian named Bill.

Bill failed to turn up, and the only moisture was that which was induced by the heat. I have left out the 'sad Australian sunset' because the sun was not going down at the time. The burial took place exactly at mid-day.

The dead bushman's name was Jim, apparently; but they found no portraits, nor locks of hair, nor any love letters, nor anything of that kind in his swag—not even a reference to his mother; only some papers relating to union matters. Most of us didn't know the name till we saw it on the coffin; we knew him as 'that poor chap that got drowned yesterday'.

'So his name's James Tyson,' said my drover acquaintance, looking at the plate.

'Why! Didn't you know that before?' I asked.

'No; but I knew he was a union man.'

It turned out, afterwards, that J. T. wasn't his real name—only 'the name he went by'.

Anyhow he was buried by it, and most of the 'Great Australian Dailies' have mentioned in their brevity columns that a young man named James John Tyson was drowned in a billabong of the Darling last Sunday.

We did hear, later on, what his real name was; but if we ever chance to read it in the 'Missing Friends Column', we shall not be able to give any information to heart-broken Mother or Sister or Wife, nor to anyone who could let him hear something to his advantage—for we have already forgotten the name.

HENRY HANDEL RICHARDSON

Conversation in a Pantry

It was no use, she simply could not sleep. She had tried lying all sorts of ways: with the blanket pulled over her or the blanket off; with her knees doubled up to her chin or stretched so straight that her feet nearly touched the bottom of the bed; on her back with her hands under her neck, or with her face burrowed in the pillow. Nothing helped. Going on in her she could still feel the bumps and lurches of the coach in which she had ridden most of that day. Then the log that had been smouldering in the brick fireplace burnt away in the middle, and collapsed with a crash; and the two ends, rolling together, broke into flames again. These threw shadows which ran about the ceiling, and up and down the white walls, like strange animals.

She was spending the night with Alice, and they had had a fire 'just for luxury,' and had sat by it for nearly an hour before going to bed. It would be her last chance of anything like that, Alice said: in schools, you never had fires, and all lights went out to the minute. And their talk had been fearfully interesting. For Alice was in love—she was over seventeen—and had told her about it just as if she was grown up, too; looking into the fire with ever such a funny little smile, and her blue eyes quite small behind their thick, curly lashes.

'Oh, don't you wish we could see into the future, Trix? And what it's going to bring us?'

But though she said yes, she wasn't sure if she did, really; she liked surprises better. Besides, all the last part of the time Alice talked, she had been screwing up her courage to put a question. But she hadn't managed to get it out. And that was one reason why now she couldn't sleep.

With a fresh toss, she sighed gustily. And, where her tumblings and fidgetings had failed, this sound called her companion back from the downy meadows.

'What's the matter, child? Aren't you asleep yet?'

'No, I simply can't.'

Alice sat up in bed, and shook her hair back from her face. 'You're over-excited. Try a drink of water.'

'I have. I've drunk it all up.'

'Then you must be hungry.'

'Well, yes, I am perhaps . . . a little.'

'Come on then, let's forage.' And throwing back the sheet, the elder girl slid her feet to the floor.

One tall white figure, one short, they opened the door and stepped out on the verandah.

31

Here it was almost as bright as day; for the moon hung like a round cheese in the sky, and drenched everything with its light. Barefoot they pattered, the joins in the verandah floor-boards, which had risen, cutting into their soles. Had they to pass open windows, dark holes in which people lay sleeping, Alice laid a finger on her lips. From one of these came the sound of snores—harsh snores of the chromatic kind, which went up the scale and down, over and over again, without a pause.

Turning a corner, they stepped off the verandah and took a few steps on hard pebbly ground. Inside the pantry, which was a large outhouse, there were sharp contrasts of bluish-white moonlight and black shadows.

Swiftly Alice skimmed the familiar shelves. 'Here's lemon cheese-cakes . . . and jam tarts . . . and gingersnaps . . . and pound cake. But I can't start you on these, or you'd be sick.' And cutting a round off a home-made loaf, she spread it thickly with dairy butter, topped by a layer of quince jelly. 'There, that's more wholesome.'

Oh, had anything ever tasted so delicious? . . . as this slice eaten at dead of night. Perched on an empty, upturned kerosene-tin, the young girl munched and munched, holding her empty hand outspread below, lest the quivering jelly glide over the crust's edge.

Alice took a cheese-cake and sat down on a lidded basket. 'I say, *did* you hear Father? Oh, Trix, wouldn't it be positively too awful if one discovered *afterwards*, one had married a man who snored?'

The muncher made no answer: the indelicacy of the question stunned her: all in the dark as she was, she felt her face flame. And yet . . . was this not perhaps the very chance she had been waiting for? If Alice could say such a thing, out loud, without embarrassment . . . Hastily squeezing down her last titbit—she felt it travel, overlarge, the full length of her gullet—she licked her jellied fingers clean and took the plunge.

'Dallie, there's something I . . . I want to ask you something . . . something I want to know.'

'Fire away!' said Alice, and went on nibbling at the pastry-edging that trimmed her tartlet.

'Yes. But . . . well, I don't quite . . . I mean I . . .'

'Like that, is it? Wait a tick,' and rather more rapidly than she had intended, Alice bolted her luscious circle of lemon-cheese, picked up her basket and planted it beside the tin. 'Now then.'

Shut away in this outhouse, the young girl might have cried her words aloud. But leaning over till she found the shell of her friend's ear, she deposited them safely inside. Alice, who was ticklish, gave an involuntary shudder. But as the sense of the question dawned on her, she sat up very stiff and straight, and echoed perturbed: '*How?* Oh, but Kid, I'm not sure—not at all sure—whether you ought to know. At your age!' said seventeen to thirteen.

'But I must, Dallie.'

'But why, my dear?'

'Because of something Ruth said.'

'Oh, Ruth!' said Alice scornfully. 'Trust Ruth for saying the wrong thing. What was it?'

'Why, that . . . now I was growing up . . . was as good as grown up . . . I must take care, for . . . for fear. . . . But, Dallie, how can I? . . . if I don't know?' This last question came out with a rush, and with a kind of click in the throat.

'Well, well! I always have felt sorry for you children, with no mother but only Ruth to bring you up—and she for ever prinking before her glass. But you know you'll be perfectly safe at school, Trix. They'll look after you, never fear!'

But there was more to come.

It was Ella, it seemed, Ella Morrison, who was two years older than her, who'd begun it. She'd said her mother said now she mustn't let the boys kiss her any more.

'And you have, eh?'

Trixie's nod was so small that it had to be guessed at. Haltingly, word by word, the story came out. It had been at Christmas, at a big party, and they were playing games. And she and some others, all boys, had gone off to hide from the rest, and they'd climbed into the hayloft, Harry MacGillivray among them; and she rather liked Harry, and he liked her, and the other boys knew it and had teased them. And then they said he wasn't game to kiss her and dared him to. And she didn't want him to, not a bit . . . or only a teeny weeny bit . . . and anyhow she wasn't going to let him, there before them all. But the other boys grabbed her, and one held her arms and another her legs and another her neck, so that he could. And he did—three times—hard. She'd been as angry as anything; she'd hit them all round. But only angry. Afterwards, though . . . when Ellie told her what her mother had said . . . and now Ruth . . .

But she got no further; for Alice had thrown back her head and was shaking with ill-repressed laughter. 'Oh, you babe . . . you blessed infant, you! Why, child, there was no more harm in that than . . . well, than in this!' And pulling the girl to her she kissed her soundly, some half-dozen times, with scant pause between. An embarrassing embrace, from which Trixie made uneasy haste to free herself; for Alice was plump, and her nightgown thin.

'No, you can make your little mind easy,' continued the elder girl on recovering her breath. 'Larking's all that was and couldn't hurt a fly. *It's what larking leads to,*' said Alice, and her voice sank, till it was hollow with mystery.

'What does it?'

'Ah!' said Alice in the same sepulchral tone. 'You asked me just now how babies came. Well, *that's how,* my dear.'

'Yes, but . . .'

'Come, you've read your Bible, haven't you? The Garden of Eden, and so on? And male and female created He them?'

'But . . .'

'Well, Trix, in *my* opinion, you ought to be content with that . . . in the meanwhile. Time enough for more when . . . well, when you're married, my dear.' Not for the world would Alice have admitted her own lack of preciser knowledge, or have uncovered to the day her private imaginings of the great unknown.

'But suppose I . . . Not *every* lady gets married, Dallie! And then I'd never know.'

'And wouldn't need to. But I don't think there's much fear of that, Trix! You're not the stuff old maids are made of,' said Alice sturdily, welcoming the side issue.

Affectionately Trixie snuggled up to her friend. This tribute was most consoling. (How awful should nobody want you, you remain unchosen!) All the same she did not yield; a real worm for knowledge gnawed in her. 'Still, I don't quite see . . . truly I don't, Dallie . . . how you *can* "take care," if you don't know how.'

At this outlandish persistence Alice drew a heavy sigh. 'But, child, there's surely something in you . . . at least if there isn't there ought to be . . . that tells you what's skylarking and what isn't? Just you think of undressing. Suppose you began to take your clothes off in front of somebody, somebody who was a stranger to you, wouldn't something in you stop you by saying: it isn't done, it's not *nice?*'

'Gracious, yes!' cried Trixie hotly. 'I should think so indeed!' (Though she could not imagine herself *beginning.*) But here, for some reason, what Alice had said about a husband who snored came back to her, and got tangled up with the later question. 'But, Dallie, you have to . . . do that, take your clothes off . . . haven't you? . . . if you . . . sleep in the same bed with somebody,' was what she wanted to say, but the words simply would not come out.

Alice understood. 'But *only* if you're married, Trixie! And then, it's different. Then everything's allowed, my dear. If once you're married, it doesn't matter what you do.'

'Oh, doesn't it?' echoed Trixie feebly, and her cheeks turned so hot that they scorched. For at Alice's words horrid things, things she was ashamed even to think, came rushing into her mind, upsetting everything she had been taught or told since she was a little child. But *she* wouldn't be like that, no, never, no matter how much she was married; there would always be something in *her* that would say 'don't, it's not nice.'

A silence followed, in which she could hear her own heart beating. Then, out of a kind of despair, she asked: 'Oh, *why* are men and women, Dallie? Why have they got to be?'

'Well now, really!' said Alice, startled and sincerely shocked. 'I hope to goodness you're not going to turn irreligious, and begin criticising what God has done and how He's made us?'

'Of course not! I know everything He does is right,' vowed Trixie, the more hotly because she couldn't down the naughty thought: if He's got all that power, then I don't see why He couldn't have arranged things differently, let them happen without . . . well, without all this bother . . . and so many things you weren't supposed to know . . . and what you were allowed to, so . . . so unpleasant. Yes, it *was* unpleasant, when you thought of undressing . . . and the snores . . . and—and everything.

And then quite suddenly and disconcertingly came a memory of Alice sitting looking into the fire, telling about her sweetheart. She had never known before that Alice was so pretty, with dimples round her mouth, and her eyes all shady. Oh, could it mean that . . . yes, it must: Alice simply didn't *mind*.

Almost as if this thought had passed to her, Alice said: 'Just you wait till you fall in love, Trix, and then it'll be different—as different as chalk from cheese. Then you'll be only too glad, my dear, that we're not all the same—all men or all women. Love's something that goes right through you, child, I couldn't even begin to describe it—and you wouldn't understand it if I did—but once you're in love, you can't think of anything else, and it gives you such a strange feeling here that it almost chokes you!'—and laying one hand over the other on the place where she believed her heart to be, Alice pressed hard. 'Why, only to be in the same room with him makes you happy, and if you know he's feeling the same, and that he likes to look at you and to hold your hand—oh, Trix, it's just Heaven!'

I do believe she'd even like him snoring, thought Trixie in dismay. (But perhaps it was only *old* men who snored.) Confused and depressed, she could not think of anything to reply. Alice did not speak again either, and there was a long silence, in which, though it was too dark to see her, Trixie guessed she would have the same funny little smile round her mouth and the same funny half-shut eyes, from thinking about George. Oh dear! what a muddle everything was.

'But come!' cried Alice, starting up from her dreams. 'To bed and to sleep with you, young woman, or we shall never get you up in time for the morning coach. Help yourself to a couple of cheesecakes . . . we can eat them as we go.'

Tartlets in hand, back they stole along the moon-blanched verandah; back past the row of dark windows, past the chromatic snores—to Trixie's ears these had now a strange and sinister significance—guided by a moon which, riding at the top of the sky, had shrunk to the size of a pippin.

ETHEL TURNER

The Child of the Children

She was an odd little mite, with eyes that were solemn when any of her committee were about, and humorously twinkling when she was quite alone. The droop of her mouth was meek, but the swift, laughing, upward curve betrayed a wicked and disturbing comicality. She was twelve.

The suburb was a large and wealthy one, and the women thereof, being led by an altar-cloth, gift-slipper and organ-fund parson, had tended for long into missionary ways.

They had made Turkey twill frocks for the little Indian wives, tea-cosies and pincushions to be sold for the benefit of the unspeakable, and therefore romantic, Celestial. Even the children constructed scrap-books, woollen balls, and dolls, in their thankfulness that they were not as other infants were, and dropped chocolate-destined pennies into a money-box that gaped hungrily to establish mission schools within the mysterious Great Wall.

But the cabling of distant horrors and the simultaneous induction of a man into the pulpit who called attention to the heathen in their midst produced a reaction. They held Dorcas societies, and presented their own poor with thick flannel petticoats—to the benefit of the pawnshops, for summer hung breathless over the land. They established a *crèche*, and tried to inculcate morals into the babies left there. They formed themselves into committees and went poking into all the little homes, forgetting that privacy was a thing to be revered. They took away the gaudily-painted scrap-books and the strings of beads which the children were making for eyes that had the charm of elongation. They told them rebukingly that there were beggars at their gates and poor nearer than the land of rice and idols.

So the rich little girls formed themselves into a committee, and when they had held half a dozen meetings to decide on the president, vice-president, secretary and treasurer, and had spent their first collection in badges and pink cards and red money-boxes, they set to business and adopted a child. An orphan not being available at the time, they sought till they found a little scrap of humanity who possessed the necessary quali-fication of having suffered sad parental neglect. She was one of a family of seven, the solemn-eyed mite, and had spent her little span of years with great happiness in the midst of misery. The very ups and downs of her life constituted happiness. Those who have beef to-day for dinner, and mutton tomorrow, veal the next day, and so on, cannot appreciate the subtle enjoyment of tinned salmon, bananas and ice-cream on Monday, and on Tuesday a twopenny loaf quite without accompaniment. Such was the seven's young fund of wit, laughter, wisdom and philosophy, that they were happy even when their parents were in gaol, or in the hospital, or away hiding, or drunk.

But once it happened that the bruised mother of them all lay ill, even to the point of conscience waking. Sometimes her dull eyes caught through a break in the dirt-dark window a glimpse of wide clean sunshine or the sky-purity of early dawn, and a feeble longing grew up in her breast for her seven little wicked ones to taste of such delight.

So when there came into the house one day an intrusive fine lady with a bunch of violets, a temperance tract and two little girls of the Children's Charitable Association, she listened to them in quite a subdued way, and even laid the tract aside on her pillow quite mildly.

And when she heard the object of the rich little girls was to adopt a child, take it entirely away from its evil surroundings, educate, clothe and keep it with their pocket-money, and fit it for an honourable position in life, she raised herself on her elbow, and with a break in her voice and heart offered the seven.

They would only have one, however, to the grief of her conscience and joy of her heart, which was a curiously soft one. She left the selection to them, and their choice fell on the twelve-year-old one because she looked the most picturesquely neglected of them all, and had flexible lips that drooped with proper gratitude.

They took her away with them and washed her, cut and combed her hair, and dressed her in garments very neat and plain, but bewildering to her by reason of their number. They were not even shocked to hear her name was Flip—Flip Huggins—for they had a new one ready-made for her—the result of a committee meeting that had agitated itself for two hours over the respective merits of Rebecca Jones, Susan Smith, and Eliza Brown. A ballot was taken, however, and the last one given to her to don with her new lilac print frock.

They boarded her out at a neat, tiny house. There were seven of them on the committee, and one went to see her every day. Every Saturday afternoon they met and sewed for her, holding a committee meeting the while. Towards the end of it she was always sent for.

'Well, Eliza,' little Laura, the daughter of a bank manager, used to say; 'and how have you been getting on this week?'

Eliza used to drop a curtsy that had as much humility in it as has a pretty soubrette on the stage. 'Fust rate, my lady, you bet your boots!' she would answer.

Of course this kind of reply necessitated rebuke and correction.

Laura, an unaffected, sweet-natured child, was obliged to object to the title.

'You know, Eliza,' she would say, 'I told you that you weren't to say "my lady".'

Eliza would smack her hand hastily over her mouth. 'It fairly burst out of me,' she would say. 'What an 'ed I've got on me!'

'And you mustn't say "fust",' another would say; ' "first" is the word, Eliza.'

'First,' Eliza would amend, curtsying again—'F-i-r-s-t' (spelling it slowly), 'first, first, first.'

'And "bet your boots" is very wrong,' another would correct.

Eliza used to lift up the corner of her useful galatea apron to her eyes. 'I'm an 'opeless 'ussy!' she would say. 'I ain't worth the cotting you sew my pinnies with!'

They would reassure her kindly, almost tenderly, for her self-abasement used to touch their little hearts. They would hasten back to the first question. 'How have you been getting on this week?' the President would begin again. And Eliza would answer carefully, painstakingly, as if really anxious to improve her speech, 'First chop—stiffen me if I ain't!'

They never kept up the attempt at speech purification longer than a quarter of an hour. Her versatility was too much for them.

For a month the attitudes befitting benefactors and benefited were kept up. For a month Eliza was seemingly humble and grateful, and the President, the Vice-President, the Secretary, the Treasurer and the Committee were graciously condescending and kind. And then one night the banker's old socialist brother came to dine with him, and from that time a new order of things began with the waif.

The brother was rich, and a bachelor, and Laura was his godchild; naturally she had always been taught to pay the greatest respect to his opinions.

He heard of the adoption of the child and sniffed.

'Better have left the youngster alone,' he said. 'I know these little fine ladies of the committee. They'll order the poor girl about and condescend to her till she's imbued with a hatred of the upper classes that will last all her life. By the time she's twenty she'll thirst to hide bombs in ball-rooms.'

'But, my dear Anthony,' said the banker's wife, 'you surely would not have Laura and the other children treat her as an absolute equal. There is no knowing where it would end.'

'My dear Madeline,' said the socialist, 'you know my opinion on these "betters." I consider she *is* an absolute equal, only she's not had all her privileges yet. Some day I'll adopt a little street baggage myself, and you'll see what you'll see!'

'Perhaps you are right,' said his sister-in-law amiably. 'You generally are, Anthony. But life is too short and one's social obligations too heavy to find time to experiment. All we propose to do is to give this unfortunate child board and lodging and a certain amount of education. If she repays us by making somebody a thoroughly good servant we shall be more than satisfied, for the race will be extinct soon. And we think it may be good training for our own children to let them have the responsibility of her.'

'Good fiddlesticks!' growled the socialistic uncle.

No one noticed how attentively Laura was listening: no one marked her exceeding quiet and thoughtfulness during the rest of the evening.

But the next committee meeting was like none of the preceding ones, for Laura had a 'plan,' and she was listened to with all the eagerness and attention which child-nature ever gives to anything adventurous.

She proposed to abandon the present method of Eliza's education and proceed for the future on entirely new lines—but secretly, of necessity. If the mothers heard of the innovation everything would be spoiled. 'Mothers don't understand things like this,' said Laura pathetically.

'Just let her be as if she's you or me? What fun!' said the jolly little daughter of a judge.

'But I don't quite see how we can manage it,' said the Vice-President. 'Lena's mother and my aunt go sometimes, you know, to see if she's getting on all right; wouldn't they find out?'

Laura owned that a great deal of caution would be necessary. 'What I thought,' she said, 'is this. We'll start from now and treat her just like one of ourselves. We'll have her in soon and tell her all about it. We'll teach her things she doesn't learn at that public school ourselves—dancing and French, and fancy work and things. And then in a year or so, when she is quite a lady, we'll take her to our mothers and surprise them. We'll show them the experiment *can* be done.'

'*How* lovely!' said the enthusiastic little girls. It seemed the most beautiful plan in the world to them.

They ran to fetch the little grass orphan and unfold their plans to her.

'You're *chiaccing*,' she said, with a disbelieving glance around.

They assured her eagerly of the genuineness of their intentions; all they required of her was to fall in with their ideas and leave herself entirely in their hands.

'I'm going to teach you dancing,' said the President. 'After school twice a week I'll come down to Mrs Brookes' and teach you in your bedroom.'

The Treasurer grumbled a little at this. 'I dance better than you, Laura,' she said. 'Professor Armande said I was the best in the class. I could teach her the Spanish waltz and the minuet, and you know you always forget them.'

Laura contended that she was President and had the right to choose. 'You can teach her German,' she said, 'or how to make those daisy mats.'

'I get most marks for French,' said the Hon. Secretary. 'I'll teach her French.'

'Well,' said an unimportant member of the committee, 'I'll teach her painting, and lend her my old box of paints.'

The adopted one, convinced of their good faith, fell into their plans with the utmost alacrity.

'But a year!' she said scornfully. 'I won't take 'arf that long. Why, I'll be a *perfect* lyedy in a month or two.' She even helped with suggestions herself.

'Eliza Brown,' she said 'ain't no kind o' name for a lyedy. You'll hev to fix another one up for me.'

They all saw the good sense of this, and an animated discussion as to the new nomenclature followed. Finally 'Dorothy Marjorie Gladys Fitz-Stephen' was decided upon and agreed to cheerfully by the one-time 'Flip.'

'An',' said the freshly christened one, 'red flannel petticoats an' striped pinnies ain't no kind o' clothes for a lyedy with three names an' a 'arf.'

'There's my pink party dress,' said the Treasurer eagerly. 'It's grown too short for me, and just hangs in the wardrobe. Mother will never miss it.'

'Pink 'ud suit me great,' said Dorothy Marjorie Gladys. ''As it got lace an' spangles on? 'As it got a sash? I 'ope it's cut down so me neck an' arms'll show.'

The President looked troubled.

'I don't see how you would get the chance to wear it yet, Dorothy,' she said. 'What would Mrs Brookes say to it?'

'My eye!' quoth Dorothy. 'Of course I'd wear this print thing over it when she was round. I could walk about me bedroom in it when she'd gone to bed. Get me used to bein' a lyedy, you know. I don't want to disgrace you when I comes out, you know.'

This seemed sensible too, and the Treasurer undertook to pack up the little frock and convey it surreptitiously to the cottage.

'Ain't none of you got pink stockin's with lace let in ter 'em?' said the embryo lady. 'I'd look frippy with grey 'uns under the dress.'

A member of the committee promised a pair. Her party dress was blue now, and she never wore her pink ones.

'An' a pair o' shoes, of course,' said the adopted one. 'You can't expect me to larn dancin' in copper toes.'

The Vice-President, the Secretary, and four members of the committee all measured feet with her, and it fell to the Secretary to provide a pair of these necessary articles of a lady's dress.

'Here are my gloves,' said the little President. 'I can run home without them easily. I want you to get in the way of going to school in them, Dorothy.'

Dorothy put her rough little fingers into them, after a hard struggle, and was delighted with the effect.

'Here's a bangle,' said the Treasurer, pulling a silver one off her wrist; 'but keep it well up your arm when Mrs Brookes is about.'

'I'll bring you a bottle of scent next time I come,' said the Secretary. 'Do you like heliotrope or wood-violet best?'

'You'd best fetch 'em both,' said Dorothy, 'an' I'll 'ave a smell at 'em afore I tell you.'

'Here's a handkerchief,' said a committee member, producing a tiny dainty one. 'My monogram's M. G., but it will stand for your middle names, Marjorie Gladys.'

'How lucky!' said the President.

The adopted sighed. 'Wot goes agen me orful,' she said, 'is me red flannul petticoats; just like workhus kids 'ave, they are—show's yours.'

The President turned back the hem of her little short frock and displayed underneath the torchon-trimmed white skirt, white flannel embroidered with silk. The Vice-President was requested to do the same; the Secretary, the Treasurer, the members of the committee, all wore white and daintily stitched petticoats.

'I'll bring you one of mine,' said the warm-hearted little President when she saw how the difference affected the one who wore scarlet flannel. 'And can't you spare one each, Nellie and Francey? she must have three at least; your nurse wouldn't miss them as she's a new one.'

Nellie and Francey promised, and the Secretary, eager to outshine them, slipped off her white muslin under-skirt, with all its tucks and embroidery, and presented it to 'Dorothy' on the spot.

'But what about Mrs Brookes,' said the anxious President.

'Dorothy' assured them it was quite safe. Mrs Brookes never looked into her clothes box, and even if she did she would only think the things were the cast-off clothes of the young ladies. Indeed, one of them could say a word to her that they were gifts, and there could be no objection.

And so the plan progressed.

In a couple of months Dorothy was able to speak to her public-school companions of '*mon père*' and '*ma mère*', and say '*s'il vous plaît*' when she wanted a bite of someone's banana, and '*merci*' when she got it. She was looked upon by them all as one of the most superior of girls. Did she not carry a scented cambric pocket-handkerchief? had she not a real silver bangle, with a threepenny piece attached, jangling on her wrist? True, her school frocks were strong prints and winceys like their own, but who else of them could turn up their bottom hems and display lace and fine stitching beneath? She learned to make daisy mats, she dabbed some red and green paint on paper, and was able to say she had painted a rose. She learned to dance. Every Monday and Thursday the President went down to the little house.

'Good afternoon, Mrs Brookes,' she would say.

'Good afternoon, Miss Laura,' the woman would answer. 'Do you want Liza? I think she's playing in her bedroom. Will I call her?'

But Laura always refused to cause her that trouble, and said she would go herself. Over the threshold into the clean little hall, up the oil-clothed stairs to the little room.

'Are you there, Dorothy?'

''Course I am! You *are* late! Look 'ere, if you can't get down sooner, Laura, I'm goin' out to play; I ain't goin' to larn dancin' if you keep me waitin' like this.'

'I couldn't help it, Dorothy dear, it was my music lesson, and I didn't know my piece. I was so busy making you a handkerchief satchel I hadn't time to practise it.'

'Is it lined with silk?' Dorothy would demand.

Perhaps Laura would have to confess that only mere muslin or sateen formed the inner part, and Dorothy would be quite displeased.

'You and Fan, and Min, and Floss, 'ave silk in yours, I'll bet,' she would say. 'Ain't you got a bit you could do it with? If I'm to be a lyedy you may as well do it proper.'

Then the lesson would commence, Dorothy being already tricked out in the pink party frock with the pink stockings and soiled white kid shoes.

She had learned to polka, and had taken to the highland schottische with the utmost avidity, but the intricacies of the waltz and mazurka Laura could not teach her, though she tried till she was breathless with having to hum the music and dance at one and the same time.

The lithe, active street child took to this pastime with the greatest *abandon*. Two or three times, when Laura had been able to smuggle her into her own house in her mother's absence, and give the lesson with one of the other girls at the piano, the music had made her like a little wild thing. She leaped, and hopped, and twirled, pirouetted and swayed about for all the world like a dancing dervish. It was quite useless for Laura to say the steps she took were none of them in the highland schottische; the moment the piano began the music of that stirring dance that moment she gave her legs and arms and body free play.

At the end of three months the committee decided that a year was far too long a time to wait to try the effect of the experiment on their mothers. And as Netta Burns' (the Vice-President) birthday was drawing near, with a lovely party promised to mark it, it was decided that the occasion should be taken to introduce Dorothy into the polite society for which it was now considered she was fit.

Netta had been granted permission to ask all her school-fellows to the party—the school being exceedingly select. And fortunately Mrs Burns had never seen the much-talked-of child of the children, having but recently returned to town.

Five of them went down to dress her on the all-important day; the ceremony had to be performed at five in the afternoon, although the party did not commence till seven, for there were their own five toilets still to be made. The waif was tricked out in a pale-blue frock belonging to the Vice-President; she wore white gloves that the Secretary had saved up to buy, and a beautiful blue sash of the Treasurer's. They frizzed her hair with hot curling-tongs, they lent her bracelets and brooches, then wrapped her up in a little red cloak.

'Don't *move*,' said the President. 'Sit still all the time on the bed, Dorothy; if you get the least bit out of order everything will be spoiled.'

'Will I start at 'arf-past six?' said Dorothy. 'I'd best be early, so you can fix me up if anythink's coming off.'

'No, seven will do,' they said. 'No one will come till seven, and it's not five minutes' walk; there will be such a lot coming just then, so you won't be noticed.'

'And don't talk much, Dorothy, dear,' said the little Vice-President; 'you know we haven't taught you quite everything yet, and if you say any of your funny things they'll find out.'

'Mum's the word,' said the child. 'I'll do nothink but nod or shake me 'ed, 'ceptin' at supper, then you'll 'ave ter let me gas a bit so I'll get the thinks I like.'

'Well, be *very* careful,' they said, 'and do sit still till the time; one bit of your hair is beginning to come uncurled already.'

'Will I sit 'ere on the pillow?' said Dorothy, seating herself with a great show of carefulness.

'Yes, that will do,' they said.

But when they had gone, and the utmost craning out of the windows showed no flutter of their pretty frocks, Dorothy stole downstairs, through the backyard and over the fence, seeing the gate was locked.

Who but trustful children could have imagined she could have missed so glorious an opportunity for displaying herself to her family?

Over the ground, up and down streets, went the little blue satin slippers. When at last she reached her own miserable lane she took off her red cloak and carried it daintily on her arm. How the boys cheered her and the girls envied! But there was no time for anything but a condescending little bow or two as she tripped through their ranks. In her own wretched little home tea was progressing; the times were evil and tea—milkless tea—formed the repast. Into the midst of them all rushed the gay, dazzling little figure. She devoured the dingy mother with kisses, she sprang into the arms of the grimy father, the sisters and brothers almost pulled her to pieces. Their astonishment was enormous; before, on the visits that none of her adopters knew she paid, she had been plainly and serviceably dressed, and she had kept the change secret that their surprise might be all the greater.

'I'm a lyedy now,' she said. And in her own mind there was not the faintest doubt but that she was. 'I've bin a lyedy for gone two months. I'm goin' to a swell party tonight; the 'ole lot o' you can come and stand at the front door and watch us goin' in.'

Of course they all went—the father, mother, and the six children who had not had the good fortune to be adopted. They grouped themselves on the pavement near the steps and watched in open-mouthed admiration the streams of glad little people arriving. Dorothy slipped in among a whole carriage load of little ones just come and was carried on with the rush away out of the people's sight. But when the stream of vehicles ceased and the strains of music began inside and the watchers found it dull and began to think of returning since they could see nothing at all, then into the midst of them again slipped Dorothy. 'I've been nicking all over the house,' she said breathlessly, 'an' I've fixed it all up grand. Tim and Ned can climb up the spouting there, an' that winder looks in the room the supper's set in; I've left two lats of the blind up. I've ripped a hole in the curtain at the dancin'-room winder; dad and mother can stand up close to it and look in and keep liftin' Tiny and baby up. And look here.' They looked, and were shown two handsome little opera cloaks. 'I nicked these out o' the dressin'-room,' she said; 'the woman thought I was gettin' 'em because it was cold downstairs. Jinny and Polly can put 'em on, and I'll smuggle 'em up into the room. It's 'Punch and Judy' show an' actin' goin' to be, an' every one sittin' down, so their boots won't show.'

She managed the difficult task with complete success. There were over a hundred children in the room, and all eyes were turned eagerly on the curtain that hid the stage. Just a few glanced round at the new entry, but they only saw three more little girls and looked away again.

The committee had seen and spoken to the waif, and intended to look after her presently and see she had an enjoyable evening, but just now they were engrossed with the acting.

Oh, how those three little girls enjoyed that acting! Jenny laughed hysterically the whole time, Polly shrieked with delight at each fresh witticism, Flip applauded frantically. The three or four 'grown-ups' in the room turned to look at them amusedly from time to time; their whole-hearted abandonment of happiness was good to watch.

It was not till the acting was over, and the chairs being cleared away for games and dancing, that the little ragged skirts and the burst old boots were discovered beneath the splendid capes.

One mite, resplendent in irreproachable foot-gear and dainty frock, nudged another one excitedly.

'Just *look* at those girls!' she said.

Flip caught the whisper and gave her sisters the word.

'Skip,' she said, 'and leave the cloaks.' Then she herself plunged in among the other well-dressed ones so as not to be compromised.

'Why,' cried another girl, 'that's my opera cloak!'

'And that's Florence Manning's!' cried another.

The poor little intruders saw there was no chance of watching the dancing, so they took their sister's advice. Before the grown-up people could be told they darted towards the door and forced their way without much difficulty through the groups of children there, who were too busy chattering to notice anything unusual. Once in the hall they were safe; the only servant there merely saw a lot of children running after two other children—it all seemed part of the party.

At the door the ragged ones paused for one second, pulled off their beautiful cloaks and flung them at their pursuers; the next minute the darkness had swallowed them up.

'Any'ow,' said Flip to herself, 'they've seen somethink.' When the dancing began she forgot her family who were flattening their noses on the glass, forgot the mothers who were to be impressed by her behaviour, forgot every injunction of her committee.

'Suppose you dance with this little boy,' said a lady to her who was endeavouring to find partners for everyone. But the waif shook her head vigorously.

'It's whips better dancin' on yer own nuts,' she said.

She fairly rushed into the middle of the floor and there began the wild antics the committee had so dreaded.

'Dorothy!' cried the President, catching at her arm and fairly forcing her to stop. Then in a whisper she besought her to be careful. 'You're spoiling everything,' she said.

'Oh, dry up! Let me 'ave a bit of fun for once!' was Dorothy's loudly spoken retort, and she went back to her hoppings and leapings amongst the dancers.

An exhibition of conjuring followed, given by Laura's socialistic uncle, who fancied he had a real gift for sleight of hand. He borrowed a hat and a handkerchief, and everyone distinctly saw him put the handkerchief in. But then he turned the hat so that they could all see, and shook it, and lo, it was perfectly empty!

They gazed at each other in awed surprise.

'Yah!' cried Dorothy's shrill voice; 'saw yer push it up yer sleeve.'

Of course everyone laughed, and the old gentleman went red with annoyance. But presently he essayed another trick. He borrowed another hat and displayed its perfect emptiness; he held up his empty hands.

'This is one of the most marvellous bits of prestidigitation known,' he said. 'You have all seen this hat holds nothing in the world. I will now see if I can extract anything from its emptiness. You can all observe my hands go nowhere but into the hat, and they are both open and turned to you. Yet what is this?' He began to pull out yards and yards and yards of different coloured ribbons; a fan followed, a baby's rattle—no end of mysterious things, 'Where can they have come from?' he cried, as if mystified.

The children breathed deeply and gazed at him entranced. But again Flip's contemptuous voice was heard. ' 'E 'ad 'em up his sleeves,' she cried, 'an' kep' jerkin' of 'em down. I seed a little packet with the ribbing in fall out.'

This time the touchy old gentleman flung down the hat and stalked straight off the stage, mortally offended, and nothing would induce him to conjure again that night.

Quite a blankness fell on the merry party; it was early for supper yet, but the hostess felt nothing else would break up the gloom. She had made a very decided mental note that never again would she allow Netta to ask a child she herself did not know personally.

'What is her name?' she asked Netta in great annoyance.

'Dorothy Marjorie Fitz-Stephen,' mumbled Netta.

'How did you come to know her? How did you ask her? Surely she does not go to anyone else's house?'

'She's been to Laura's house often, and to Flora's and Marion's. She doesn't make more noise than Nora Chilchester or Wilfred Boyle. Don't be horrid to her, mother.'

Mrs Burns still looked dissatisfied, but led the way to the supper-room.

When everyone was attended to she had time to observe the strange child. A gentleman came up laughing at the same moment. 'See that little youngster in blue,' he said; ' 'pon my word, I never dreamed any child—especially any girl—could eat as she has done. I've kept getting her jelly, cake, trifle—trifle, jelly, cake, and never once has she said, "No, thank you," to anything. Every fresh thing I ask her to have she says, "Rather," or "You bet," or "Trot it out," and empties her plate in an incredibly short time. There'll be a funeral tomorrow.'

'Look at her now,' he added, excitement in his tone. 'Well, this is past everything. When I was sixteen, and had a schoolboy's gluttony, I never equalled this small person. Do look at her.'

Mrs Burns peered across at the little girl in blue. She was standing, hidden as she thought by the stout socialist, and down the low-cut neck of her loose dress she was cramming cakes, sweets, fruits, everything she could lay her hands on. Then she slipped through the crowd and out of the room. 'Gone to eat in solitude on the stairs,' said the laughing gentleman. How was he to know of the family outside in the darkness waiting to be satisfied?

In a few minutes she was back again, and the performance was repeated. When she came back the third time and started to fill up the dress front still again, he followed her.

'The custard thing was scrummy!' he heard a boy's voice say. 'Couldn't you find another?'

'Didn't you nick a spoon or fork this time?' said another.

'No,' said the blue-clad mite; 'an' I ain't goin' to neither, so just dry up about it!'

'Zimmie want lol-lol,' said a tiny urchin.

'I'll slip back and get some more; there are some spiffin' choc'lats,' said the girl, and darted in again.

But there were several new arrivals in the supper room—mothers and fathers come to take the small ones home. Laura's mother recognised the child of the children instantly. 'What nonsense is this?' she said, laying her hand on the blue shoulder.

The committee gathered up with hanging heads and drooped lips; the failure of their experiment was very bitter to them.

'What is the meaning of this? Why are you here, Eliza?' repeated the mother of Laura.

The waif fell back instantly into the language of humility she always used to her grown-up patrons. 'I'm a 'opeless 'ussy!' she said, 'pack me off 'ome agen.' She took off her sash and offered it to the lady. 'Take it away,' she said; 'I ain't fit to look at it—I ain't fit to live.'

'How could you be so foolish, Laura?' said her mother, strong annoyance in her tone. 'What made you do such a thing?'

'We—we—we were making a lady of her,' was Laura's forlorn reply. Tears were in her eyes, her mouth trembled.

'What are they doing to my girl?' said her godfather, coming up. The child sprang to him. 'Oh, uncle,' she said, 'dear, dear, dear uncle! don't let her be made a servant of, will you? Oh, we had *nearly* got her to be a lady. *Darling* uncle! do take her yourself, will you? You said you'd adopt one some day.'

But the socialist looked resentfully at the spoiler of his tricks. 'No, thank you, Laura,' he said; 'I'll make my own choice when I do.'

The waif was returned to Mrs Brookes under the care of a servant. All the 'lady-like' clothes were taken from her; she was bidden learn to sweep and dust, as it befitted one whose profession would naturally be represented by a broom and a dust-pan.

At the end of a month, so melancholy to her was the transition from Dorothy Marjorie Gladys Fitz-Stephen to Eliza Brown, that she incontinently took to her heels one fine day, and, prevailing on her parents' indulgence, became Flip Huggins again.

ETHEL ANDERSON

Juliet McCree is Accused of Gluttony

Dr Phantom did not really care for children. It is doubtful whether any child had ever been invited to ride beside him in the dashing Hyde Park in which he made his daily rounds. This was a canopied and curtained vehicle, its four wheels rimmed with iron, and it was drawn by a piebald Waler, and driven by a white-gloved, personable murderer.

It was usual in those days for citizens of Sydney who applied for convict servants to ask for a murderer if any should happen to be available. They were in great demand, for, though apt to be impulsive on occasions of emotion, killers had generally been found to have warmer-hearted and more likeable dispositions than criminals of other persuasions. Dr Phantom, caring little for thieves, sheepstealers, pickpockets, lags, or the abductors of heiresses, employed, when he could do so, only murderers. Though he drew the line at poisoners (his dispensary being, he felt, a temptation) he was at this period particularly lucky; he was rich in the possession of 'First and Second Murderers'—as he designated them—and his servants' hall, in the neat red-brick Georgian house, some twenty miles from the capital, had never been more cheery.

On this energetic afternoon in early autumn, when a mellowing sun shone obliquely down on a humming and triumphing world, 'First Murderer' was on the box, a check-string with its wide band attached to his right arm, that had, on some earlier occasion, presumably wielded a lethal weapon (an axe was at that time the most popular tool), and Dr Phantom, sitting directly behind him, would jerk the cord to ensure attention before issuing directions as to which track should be followed, or at which house, shack, shanty, hovel or mansion he should stop.

In this beneficent district the fruit had never been finer.

The grapes growing in the direction of Dural had recalled to Dr Phantom a Tuscan summer.

The peach harvest, he noted, had never been more luscious. Lying at his feet two large baskets testified to an almost Olympian abundance; one was an Ossa of Jargonells, orange Bergamots, and 'Williams'; from a second willow-ark rose a perfect Pelion of grapes, apricots and plums (blue perdrigons), the first fruits of several orchards.

As Dr Phantom bowled along in his nicely shaded carriage his eyes lingered on the signs of an earlier optimism, on many a phalanx of raspberries, on plantations of gooseberries, and ordered battalions of strawberries. A particularly fine crop of these delectable berries punctuated the Undertaker's neatly kept plot with bright red nodules nestling on straw. It was an age when straw laid down on a roadway paid its sympathetic tribute to the difficulty of producing the coming gener-ation, and discreetly muffled the departure of age; and straw was plentiful.

On this garlanded highway, where even the hedges were bright with rose-haws, the good doctor experienced the pleasure afforded to a reason-ing man by the contemplation of a Universe based on reason.

He passed the chain-gang knocking sparks out of flint.

'They are dressing stone for the repair of the bridge,' he (rightly) concluded.

He skirted the milkman's trotting cart which pleasantly recalled to him the hip-waddles of a Zulu belle. The cart was painted yellow and a scarlet scroll was ciphered with the words 'Families supplied twice daily'.

'He is delivering the late afternoon milk,' Dr Phantom instinctively realised.

That, too, was a reasonable conjecture, though the statement on the cart was, perhaps, cryptic to the uninitiated.

Just outside Parramatta he observed the Rector entering Mrs Furbe-low's lean-to. 'The latest addition to that poor widow's family of twenty is about to pass, non-stop, through this vale of tears,' was his natural inference; he was right.

But a sight that baffled his intelligence as his Hyde Park clattered to a standstill by the kerb outside his partner's brass-plated, two-storied yellowstone house beside the bridge in Parramatta, was the apparition of seven little boys and girls, of ages ranging from four to, perhaps, ten or eleven years, each holding in their trembling hands a black papier-maché basin; each standing on a separate step of the stone stairway that led down to the slowly-meandering waters of the Lane Cove River.

His first thought had been 'Whooping-cough', but 'No', he reminded himself. 'I should have been the first to be informed of any such epidemic'.

He found his partner Dr Boisragon (pronounced Borrygan) standing on the top step of the flight.

He looked grave.

He looked even more stern than usual, and his handsome face wore an expression that might almost have been called 'pained'. Though he was dressed with his customary ceremony in a full-skirted marine blue frogged coat, with yellow Nankin breeches, nicely moulded over Welling-ton boots and his own (almost famous) legs, with a thick, gold bemedalled watchchain caressing a buff waistcoat, a black satin stock meticulously folded under white linen points, and with a stovepipe hat, cocked sideways, as he always wore it, he might have been going to a funeral; to the obsequies of the victim of someone else's rapacity and incompetence.

'The grapes,' Dr Phantom explained, handing him the larger of the two baskets which he had carried from the Hyde Park, 'are from Widow

Plunkett. The pears are selected from a basket given to me by Mr Jarvey, in recognition of the pretty compliments I paid him on his wall-fruit. The greenish apples are from Granny Smith, whose cottage near Castle Hill I passed in pursuit of a ruined stomach and a case of mumps out at Hornsby Junction.'

Accepting the basket Dr Boisragon touched the grapes reverently with his sensitive hands—he had a surgeon's hands—'The bloom!' he marvelled, 'How does Nature do it? Is it an efflorescence? Is it a quintessential patina?'

He set the heavy basket down on the parapet beside him and broke off a sizeable bunch of Muscatels.

'I must confess my ignorance.' Meditatively Dr Phantom peeled with his equally sensitive fingers a Yellow Monday peach of august proportions. 'No-one, to my knowledge, has conducted research into the mysteries of the bloom on fruit. It may be a sort of attar of perfection, like the fragrant scum one skims off a tank of rose-water. It may be a fructuous halo, or nimbus, like that bright manifestation of Holiness which (we are informed) accumulates round the heads of saints.'

He savoured his golden-fleshed peach.

'These,' Dr Boisragon murmured, converting another grape to a corporate Christianity, 'are gifts from the Gods of Plenty! What a country is ours! Begging the question of the scientific nature of bloom, I can rejoice in the luxuriance that showers on us such a prodigality of gifts.'

He took a bunch of white muscadines from the diminishing heap.

'But I am a sad man! I have a heavy heart! I am too conscious of the serpent that lurks in our Eden, of the wickedness of the almost irreclaimable YOUNG!'

He sighed heavily and with an absent mind voiced the opinion that 'The muscadine is, perhaps, the best white grape. Its juice is so pleasantly insinuating in texture, its flavour is so ethereal—a mixture of sharp and sweet—its bouquet (if one might call it so) is of so subtle an aroma.'

Dr Phantom chose an apricot. (It was an *abricot persique*.)

'Yes. In this glorious Eden of ours, I am confronted by sin in its most loathsome aspect, by error in its most leprous form.'

'Dear me,' Dr Phantom agreed, easily, and without much due attention. 'You are having, I gather, a party, a jollification, a romp-a-way for these children? Who are all these visitors?'

Dr Boisragon was eating a plum—a White Nutmeg.

Dr Phantom took a bunch of Black Frontignacs, and put them back.

'The three immature females in tartans and plaits are the indigent McMurthies, my poor sister Téméraire's brood. Her husband, as you know, is Captain of the brig *Rose*. The boy and girl standing on the step below them, whom I have heard referred to as 'the Coppertops', are my unfortunate eldest sister Jessica's grandchildren, Juliet and Donalblain

McCree. With my own hopefuls, James and Grizel, you have been acquainted from their birth—surely you recognised them all?'

The glances Dr Boisragon cast on the children were dour in the extreme. Dr Phantom excused himself, saying, 'Their colour is unusual. Are they not unnaturally pale?'

A douce sea-breeze, a zephyr faintly tinged and tinctured with ozone, and spiced with salt, which daily about this hour found its way up the estuary from Sydney harbour and the Heads and the Pacific beyond, stirred the hitherto placid waters of the river into infinitesimal wavelets, and blew the little girls' skirts about, flapping them like wings against their ankle-length *culottes*.

A number of seagulls, their presence so far inland perhaps presaging storm, were dipping and wheeling about the surface of a patch of ruffled water which, in the deeper reaches, hinted at a shoal of fish.

A group of saplings that dotted the sloping lawn right down to the water's edge also swayed and rustled, and their lively branches reminded Dr Phantom to enquire after—'The nectarine? Is it ripe? Did your poor wife enjoy it as much as you hoped? I see it has gone.'

An expression of deeper suffering clouded Dr Boisragon's already gloomy face.

'My wife did not have the pleasure of putting one toothmark on it. It was stolen.' He looked desolate. 'It was a Red Roman.'

It occurred to Dr Phantom that the group of children hugging their black basins looked, if possible, even greener about the gills, and, though he did not care for children, he averted his gaze from the rows of suffering upturned faces.

'Stolen? A bat? A parrot? Mr Jarvey told me of the depredations of many flocks of rosellas, or parakeets—or was it lorikeets?'

Half-sated Dr Phantom ventured on a jargonelle.

'It was stolen,' Dr Boisragon reiterated simply, dropping a handful of pips into a garden urn. 'I inspected it at three o'clock, when we first assembled on the lawn for our festivity. I decided to allow it one more hour of sunshine before giving it to my wife. Noticing how warm the sun had become, I went, an hour later, to pluck it—it had gone. It had vanished. Under the tree—not a sign of it. Down the slope? Not a vestige of it!'

He sternly regarded the flinching rows of upturned faces.

'I questioned the children closely. They all denied having stolen it.'

Dr Phantom ran a physician's discerning eye over the greening faces.

'Are the children sickening for something, do you think?'

'They are.' Dr Boisragon's tone was succinct. 'I gave them all an emetic. Nature never lies. I shall soon find out who stole and ate my nectarine.'

'Surely, by observation, you might have detected the culprit? Children are transparent enough. I once met a fraudulent financier. What struck me at the time was the complete absence of all experience in his blue eyes. Knowing nothing about his defalcations, I said at the time, "That young gentleman has got something to hide. He has obliterated his past from his expression." And he had, too! Look at those faces! The girls in plaits and tartans have eyes as black as sloes, without even a highlight in the pupils. I know that type. To learn how they feel—look at their mouths.'

The two doctors looked at the three tremulous mouths.

'I should say those girls were innocent.'

'Deduction is well enough in its way. I prefer the certainty of the scientific method.'

'Your boy James is like you. Is he six?'

'Yes.'

'Rule him out. By this time he should have learnt not to risk displeasing you.'

Though glad of this opinion on his son's probable innocence, Dr Boisragon was not certain he liked the inference.

'As for the coppertops, they are both suffering so acutely that their queasiness must soon take an active turn.'

It did.

Their breakdown was the signal, it seemed, for which everyone had been waiting. Seven black basins bore witness to the efficacy of Dr Boisragon's emetic.

Dr Phantom was just remarking, 'It strikes me that there is a guilty knowledge, a hint of a hidden appeal to one's sympathy, in the squirrel-like eyes of the girl coppertop,' when her basin demonstrated her guilt.

The regurgitation of the skin of a Red Roman was proof of it.

'Juliet McCree! You are both a thief and a liar.'

Dr Boisragon had never been more impressive.

'You wicked child! What have you to say to explain away your downright lie?'

He was forced to wait till she was capable of answering.

'What excuse do you offer for your felony?'

'Felony, Uncle Peter?'

'How do you excuse your theft of my nectarine?'

'I didn't steal it.'

Even Dr Phantom was shocked by such depravity.

'What—do you deny it? In the face of such evidence as that basin holds?'

'I just took it. I didn't steal it.'

'To take what is not your own is stealing.'

'But I didn't think it was not—' she retched—'was not—' she was violently ill—'was not—' she had scarcely got her breath when another paroxysm overtook her—'was not—' Dr Phantom turned away his eyes—'was not mine.'

That innocence was no shield from suffering was being aptly demonstrated by the six other children who were noisily and liberally con-
tributing to their basins.

'Wicked sinner! Look about you! Through your obstinate denial of
your guilt you have caused great suffering to your young relatives—poor
innocent children! Does that not shame you? Does that not soften you?'

Dr Boisragon grew more angry.

'Do you persist in saying that you did *not* lie to me?'

He took his pocket-book out of his buff waistcoat pocket.

'I will run through the notes I made when questioning you. Here
they are.' He flicked a page. 'Juliet McCree—my question—"Did you
steal that nectarine? My Red Roman?" "*No, Uncle Peter*"—That was your
answer!'

He snapped the elastic band back and put the book away.

'I said, "Remember, child, your hope of Heaven hangs on your
answer. Speak the truth! *Did you speak the truth?*" You again answered,
"Yes, Uncle Peter!" What perfidy! To rob your dear Aunt of my gift! The
fruit I had watched from the bud up! What do you mean, wretched liar,
in saying you did not know it was not my nectarine? It grew on my tree.'

'There are so many things everywhere, and I don't quite know who
owns everything. It's all so puzzling, Uncle Peter, because, when I filled
my bucket with sand no one said I had stolen it, and when I dipped my
mug in the river, no one said I was not to steal the Lane Cove River,
Uncle Peter, and when we pick blackberries, and mushrooms along the
roads or in the paddocks, no one calls us thieves, and I'm only a little girl,
Uncle Peter, and I don't rightly know the way to get things that don't
belong to me for nothing, Uncle Peter, the way you and Dr Phantom do,
and I don't know whose sea-gulls those are, neither.'

She again had recourse to her basin.

'What! Dreadful child! Do you accuse *us* of theft!'

'Oh, no, Uncle Peter, it's not quite like that. But you can get the things
you want without stealing them, and you know what things belong to
other people, and I don't yet! But I will try to learn, indeed I will.'

'What a depraved mind.'

'But you see, you know what is free and I don't! And you know what
you must *pay* for, and I don't! I did hear the sound you were making with
your words, Uncle Peter, but I did not understand what the noise you
made really meant; and if you could please explain to me how you got the
fruit in the baskets and didn't pay for it, and didn't really steal it, I mean,
if it was someone else's, and you did not have to pay for it? Will you teach
me how to get things that are someone else's and not pay?'

She suffered an attack of dry retching that was quite spectacular.

The six other children had filled their black basins and waited, white
of face and wet of eye.

'Empty your basins in the river, my bairns, and then wash your hands and faces and go into the dining-room for tea. Since you have been proved to be innocent you may each have two pieces of the birthday cake Cook Jane has made for James. But, before you go, take leave of your cousin, Juliet McCree, for this is the last time that—with my approval or permission—you will ever speak to her. If God spares me, she shall never darken my doors again. Wicked, wicked child!'

'Good-bye, Juliet,' the children murmured, awe-struck, walking uncertainly past her, their black papier-maché basins carefully carried in their weak hands; they had all been very sick—the emetic had been a powerful one, though perhaps slow in starting.

Juliet went dutifully down to the water's edge and emptied her basin into the Lane Cove River, and, in going up to the house to wash, she lagged well behind her cousins, not that she suffered any sense of guilt, but because she appreciated the drama of the occasion.

While awaiting Juliet's return, Dr Boisragon remarked genially to his companion: 'It is an extraordinary thing that the expulsion of food—with us—should require so much effort. I believe that the Romans, before they had a banquet, tickled the backs of their throats and emptied their stomachs. They must certainly have practised regurgitation as an art, for they were a civilised people and I imagine that the hall of Augustus, the house of Maecenas, the villas of Horace and Cicero, could hardly have presented such unbridled scenes as those we have just witnessed! They must have had some nicer system of their own in the method of vomiting!'

Dr Phantom ran an eye over the row of lace curtains that draped the windows of the square, yellowstone house behind them.

'The ladies of your household?' he enquired, 'How is it they were not present?'

As a matter of fact he had several times noticed the agonised faces of Dr Boisragon's younger step-sisters, Miss Loveday, Miss Tabitha, and Miss Matilda, peeping through the lace of upstairs windows.

'I can't understand,' he mused, 'why his womenkind left those unhappy children to my friend's untender mercies! They must, by this time, know what he is like!'

He said this to himself, but as if replying to him Dr Boisragon broke off from his classical conjectures to say, 'My dear wife was prostrate! She was inclined to be hysterical, so I ordered her off to her room to lie down for an hour or two. My sisters, too, attempted to gloss over an incident they regarded as trivial. Poor, silly women! I ordered them indoors, and I will thresh out the question with them tonight after dinner.'

Juliet here came back, her face shining with tears and soap, her red hair, so wet that it looked dark, drawn off her forehead with two combs; she had tried to hide the stains on her apron by rolling it up round her elbows, with the result that the unfaded patch on her green cotton checked dress showed how old and worn it was.

The child looked peaked and hungry.

She had left her brother, Donalblain (who was four), happily eating bread and butter masked with 'hundreds and thousands', and she could see the glow of the candles, round the birthday cake, and the six other children laughing and talking round the table, with its sweets and bon-bons, crackers and toys, and sugar animals, while the three aunts, having, as it were, come into their own, were busy 'making it up' to the infant martyrs.

Juliet's straw hat (from China) was swinging from her arm by a green ribbon, and her reddening curls, which, as they dried resumed their gloss, were seen against a background of pale river-water and the brackish hillside of the further bank; the salt seemed to have cured the hanging leaves of the grey-boled trees; and it encrusted, too, the pool-brightened rocks. The sky was purely Tuscan as Dr Phantom had already noted.

Dr Boisragon, as Juliet joined them, at once returned to the pursuit of Truth.

'Do you not realise, Juliet, that if I had not hit on the expedient of interrogating Nature herself, six innocent children might, all their lives, have lived under the stigma of theft—of being *thieves*! And *this* for your crime. Do you not realise the enormity of your crime against society?'

'But, don't you see, Uncle Peter, it is only *you* who see anything wrong in it? When Papa used to go shooting duck—whose ducks did he shoot? And when you go catching fish—whose fish do you catch? And you know perfectly well that when God gave Adam the earth—as for all I can learn He did—He gave him every blessed thing! And I have never heard anyone say that what belonged to Adam does not belong to me. And whether I took a Red Roman, or whether any of my cousins, or my brother Donalblain (who is four) took a Red Roman, it is only a person like you, who thinks so much of owning a thing, who makes a sin of it. It is just the natural thing to do.'

'Then, being naturally a thief, you are, naturally, a liar?'

'Oh, no, Uncle Peter, I did not think I was a thief. So, of course, I was not a liar. Don't you see, there is no such thing as sin, it is only that some men, who don't understand God or what God said, begin to make their own rules to suit themselves, and they invent sin, Uncle Peter. I expect, if you thought a little about it, you would soon grow to see that this is the truth. It is just grown-ups who invent wickedness, and then accuse innocent children of it.'

'Hopelessly casuist. Irreclaimably evil. A dangerous liar, a thief! I see, Juliet, that no Christian teaching I can give is likely to reclaim you! I shall write a letter for you to take back to your mama and grandmama—what sort of home life you have at Mallow's Marsh Vicarage, I tremble to think!

It baffles my imagination. Wait, wicked girl, wait! Phantom, watch her, if you please! Be careful to allow her no intercourse with any member of my family.'

Dr Boisragon walked majestically up the tree-dotted slope to his four-square yellow stone house, where a shaded lamp in Mrs Boisragon's bedroom showed that she was still 'resting', and where flickering candles in the dining-room, reddening still more gaily the crimson rep of the curtains, showed that the birthday party was still in full swing.

As soon as Dr Boisragon's back was turned Juliet slapped her flat stomach and said, conversationally, 'I'm like a tympanum! I'm as empty as a drum—just you listen!'

She twanged her thin body again. It certainly gave out a hollow moaning sound.

Dr Phantom gave her a very cool, direct look from eyes that hitherto avoided any direct encounter with her own brightly sparkling copper-coloured glance. It was, perhaps, rather the squirrel's tanny coat than its wildwood eye that (as he had at first considered) her lively regard had evoked.

'Not quite hollow,' Dr Phantom rejoined with meaning.

Juliet blushed. She really looked quite lovely, her small, Titian-bright head set trimly against a skyey nimbus of Tuscan gold.

'What do you mean?' she asked cautiously.

Dr Phantom leant towards her and took, from a fold in her bib, two or three carraway seeds and a few cake crumbs.

'Dry,' he explained. 'They were not there when you went up to the house to wash.'

'Oh, those? Oh, I just asked Cook Jane for a piece of cake! I was simply starving!' After considering her companion for a few minutes in silence she asked, 'Don't you think I took the best line with Uncle Peter?'

'I thought it clever enough.'

Looking relieved, Juliet drew closer.

'I just didn't have a chance of thinking it out! We were playing at murdering the Duke, when James suddenly caught sight of the nectarine we'd been hearing so much about, and called out—"First in gets the Holy Globe!" And we all started running down the slope and shouting out, "Bags I the Holy Globe!" It was a great lark, really, and I got there first; I only beat Victoria McMurthie by the edge of a hair-ribbon as you might say; so I had it, but of course we all shared it. Everyone had a bite! But I had the skin, mostly, and of course that showed more.'

'Then all the children were equally guilty?'

'But, don't you see, we don't think it guilty!'

'The fact remains that since you stole something—took what did not belong to you—you have committed a sin against society, and you will have the whole world against you. People think theft the meanest of crimes.'

'But Mama brings back a few hairpins every time she goes to her Club, and Papa used to carry home some envelopes and note-paper every time he visited *his* Club, in Sydney, and I wouldn't mind betting, Dr Phantom, that I could catch you out in a theft of some sort if I gave my mind to it.'

A mere flutter of dismay, a fraction of alarm, passing across his face as swiftly as the shadows made by the sea-gull's wings on the darkening waters (for the sun was now due west and as red as an apple) told Juliet that she might, as she put it, 'be on to something'.

Jumping up and down and clapping her hands, the dreadful child pressed home her advantage.

'Will you let me search you? That would be a perfectly fair test!'

She sprang towards him.

He kept her at bay with a grip of iron.

'No! No! I never heard of such a thing! What cheek!'

Dr Phantom shed ten years of his assumed dignity at least, as, laughing and red in the face, he struggled with the lively Juliet.

'A prize! A prize!' shouted that exasperating child, wild with excitement. 'I shall find a spoon! One of Lady Mary's salt-cellars!'

The tussle was really incredibly brisk! Juliet's darting attacks, first at one pocket, then at another, were quite spectacular in their success.

'A case book!'

'Mine!'

'A purse!'

'Mine!'

'A pencil!'

'Mine!'

'Bitten at the end!' gasped Juliet, breathlessly, putting it back as she whirled, wriggled, twirled.

'A key! Two keys! Three keys!'

'Mine! Mine! Mine!'

'A love letter!'

'No! No! *A bill!*' he clutched it.

'Ah, ha!' Juliet wrenched herself free, doubled up with laughter, 'A prize! A prize! Whose pocket handkerchief is this, you wicked thief?'

As Dr Phantom rushed after her she doubled and dodged round the saplings.

'Whose? Whose?'

'You dreadful child! Give me that handkerchief this instant!'

Catching a moment when her hardly less agile opponent had side-slipped in skimming too quickly round a juniper, Juliet read the name embroidered on the bit of scented lawn, her treasure.

'"Aminta Wirraway!" Oh! Dr Phantom. Oh, you wicked thief! Bad,

bad man! I shall tell your mother! Does that poor girl know you have stolen her new Irish linen?'

'Do I understand,' asked Dr Boisragon, joining the struggling pair and judging as usual by appearances, 'that this depraved child has actually stolen your handkerchief?'

Silence.

Dr Phantom pulled down his waistcoat and re-buttoned his hip-pocket. He looked blankly at Juliet.

'No, of course she hasn't,' he blurted out, getting back his breath.

He looked appealingly at Juliet.

She sniffed at the scented square of pink lawn.

'I was just guessing what kind of scent Dr Phantom uses,' she said, meekly, 'I think it must be Opopomax or Alderman's Bouquet.'

'The only perfumes allowable for male use are Florida Water and Eau de Cologne. I myself use Florida Water.' He addressed himself entirely to Dr Phantom, ignoring Juliet. 'As a bachelor, you might conceivably be permitted a sprinkling of Verbena; it is slightly astringent and not too tropical.'

Juliet put the handkerchief back in Dr Phantom's breast pocket.

'Over your heart,' she whispered.

Dr Boisragon turned his attention to her.

'Juliet McCree,' he announced, portentously, 'I have in this letter informed your widowed mother and grandparents of your incredible perfidy. That you, a girl of eleven or twelve, should steal in a house where your lightest request, if not granted, would at least have been sympathetically considered, that you should, when detected in that theft, lie, and that, having lied in the most bare-faced manner, in the plain proof of your falsehood, that you should persist in the most Jesuitical casuistry, in asserting your *innocence*, has so shocked me, so outraged my feelings, that I feel compelled to forbid you ever to enter my house again. My house, or my *grounds*,' he looked meaningly at Juliet.

With a humble and gentle expression his niece stepped forward and took the letter he extended to her, at an arm's length.

'Good-bye, Uncle Peter,' she said, sadly, and she dropped him a curtsey, the charity bob she had been taught to use when greeting or saying good-bye to her elders.

'If Dr Phantom would be so kind as to send you home in his Hyde Park—should the murderer not object to your company—I should be much obliged to him.'

'Oh, certainly, certainly.' Dr Phantom was all complaisance. 'I will remove everything of value and give my coachman due warning of her weakness. There is a second basket of fruit—'

The trio walked across the shadowed lawn to the Hyde Park which drooped by the kerb in the warm, windless air, for the sea-breeze had expended its energy and a glowing sun, cut across the middle by the twin towers of the church, was pouring its hot rays through the valance and neatly tied-back curtains. Juliet was surprised to find 'First Murderer' asleep in the driving seat; she had hardly expected that murderers could sleep, but it was still oppressively warm, and even the piebald Waler in his straw hat snuffled his nostrils and stamped his hooves and whisked his cream tail with less than his usual verve.

'I am sending a duplicate letter by post,' Dr Boisragon mentioned to Dr Phantom, intending Juliet to hear. 'Should anything happen to my first missive, her poor relatives will hear of her wicked conduct by the first post on Monday morning.'

'I think you are so wise,' Dr Phantom rejoined, also intending Juliet to hear. 'What a disaster it would be for her family if they did not learn what a hardened criminal the child is!'

And in the most ostentatious manner he removed the basket of pears from the vehicle. Their aroma was almost as heady as wine, the heat had brought out their delicious, yet not cloying, fragrance.

'A pear, perhaps, is the most delicate of all fruits.' Dr Boisragon's elegant hand hovered. 'A *Beurré du Roi*?' He tasted. 'Yes, I thought I could not be mistaken! The skin paler than the finest champagne! The shape, symmetrical, but slightly squat, if one could apply so bald a word to so desirable a form! Pipless! Indeed the faultless fruit.'

With a grave propriety, settling her green checked skirts and folding her hands in her lap, Juliet crossed her neat ankles, in the white culottes, and, at last assuming her straw hat (from China), she settled herself on the box beside 'First Murderer', in the Hyde Park, while he, having saluted his master with two fingers, and flicked the piebald Waler's back with his whip, urged that animal to the pace which was, in those days, described as 'a spanking trot'.

As they were moving off Dr Phantom heard Juliet saying in an easy and conversational manner to 'First Murderer': 'I am not quite in your class, of course, but this afternoon I have been proved to be both a thief and a liar, and, as one criminal to another, I should very much like your advice, as a more experienced—'. He heard no more. He was, however (since he did not care for children), rather surprised to find himself envying 'First Murderer'.

'At this time of the evening,' Dr Boisragon took Dr Phantom's arm, 'it is pleasant to sit on the steps facing the water, where one occasionally gets a puff of sea air, and since the children's party is in full swing in the house, let us linger here for an hour before going indoors.'

The partners took their places on the step where the basket of mixed fruits still adorned the parapet. Dr Phantom, having set down his own basket of pears by his side, made an incision in a Golden Pear of Xaintonge with thirty-two sharp white teeth.

'I have been thinking over that depraved girl's case,' Dr Boisragon murmured, having embarked on a second pear. 'I see that her first sin— *theft*—was the cause of her second sin—*lying*—but, delving more deeply into the cause of her crimes, I am of the considered opinion that the child's inability to control her carnal appetite was the primal reason for her downfall. *That girl is a glutton!* Did you notice the way she kept eyeing these grapes?'

'Yes, I did,' Dr Phantom rejoined, averting his eyes.

KATHARINE SUSANNAH PRICHARD

N'Goola

Stumbling and swaying, the old man climbed the sandy track. It wound through thin scrub and thorn bushes covering a low hillside.

Mary passed him as she came from work in the nearby township. The old man called after her. She stopped and he shambled wearily towards her. The bare toes with broken nails sticking out of shoes, thick with red dust, told her that he had come a long way.

'N'goola!' he cried. 'D' y' know a girl called N'goola in the native camp, missus?'

'Never heard of her,' Mary said and went on.

It was Saturday afternoon and she was in a hurry to get home. Her string bag, full of meat and vegetables for the week-end, slung her wiry figure to one side as she plodded with bare feet up the track, carrying her shoes. A woman of forty or thereabouts, wearing a neatly made dress of floral cotton, she had met the old man's eyes with the beautiful brown eyes of an Aboriginal, but her hair was brackish brown, and there was a yellowish tinge in her skin.

The old man was a stranger, she guessed. A derelict from the remnants of tribes all over the country who had wandered into the settlement of native huts on the far side of the hill. A place of refuge, it was, for the outcasts of his people, and hers—the men and women of mixed blood who were still regarded as aborigines.

Mary had little to do with the wild, gypsyish crew which foregathered there, although she was friendly with most of the older men and women. She lived on the outskirts of the settlement. Her husband, a man of her own colour, often sneered at her for trying to live like a white woman: keeping her home clean and tidy and herself respectable, as she had been taught to in a mission school.

Her home was not far off: a humpy, squat and dark, built of rusted kerosene tins and old scraps of timber, with a roof through which the rain poured in winter. But the land where the humpy stood belonged to her. Mary prided herself on that. She had bought it with money earned doing washing and scrubbing in the township: money hidden and saved for years. Her children had grown up and drifted away from her. She lived and worked now to get a house built on her land: a small wooden house with a roof of corrugated iron.

A few geraniums and tomato plants wilted in the dry sand of what she called her garden. Mary's eyes lingered on them lovingly before she opened the door and went into the one room of the humpy.

Vexed to find her husband had left scraps of food and unwashed dishes littering the table, she put down her shopping bag and cleared them away; lit a fire on the open hearth, swept the floor, washed the dishes, cut-up the meat and vegetables she had bought to make a stew, and put them in a pot on the fire. Ted would be coming in soon for a meal, she expected, although often on a Saturday night he was too drunk to do more than sprawl on the bed and sleep until morning.

Her tidying done, Mary went to the door, wondering whether the old man she passed on the track had gone down into the settlement. She wished she had not been so sharp with him. Glancing back along the track, she saw that he had made himself a little fire on the brow of the hill. She could hear him singing to himself in a dreary, monotonous voice.

Why had he asked about a girl by her native name? No one would know that. Most of the girls in the settlement would not remember if they ever had a native name. They were all Jeans and Janeys, Kittys and Dulcies, these days.

'N'goola.' Mary was disturbed by something vaguely familiar in the name. She seemed to have heard it before, but when and where she could not remember.

Sunset was searing the sky. Mary sat down on a box near the door, tired after her day's work. Her thoughts strayed over the many evenings she had sat like this watching the sun set and soothed by the quiet, despite a vile smell which filled the air, coming from the dilapidated building on the hill top where the filth of the district accumulated for treatment.

Because of it, Mary reflected bitterly, a stretch of arid country was the only place, in all the hundreds of miles this side of the ranges, where people of the native race were permitted to meet and live together. Here on the low hillsides surrounding a depression which was a swamp in winter but dry and hard in summer, a score or so of families had built shacks like her own. For the most part, mere hovels of rusty tin and bagging, they looked like rotten mushrooms thrust up from the ground.

Mary could see a twist of smoke rising from some of them and children running about the huts; toddlers quite naked, and other young-sters in coloured rags. Half a dozen women squatted beside a clump of bushes playing cards. Round the two-up ring on the flat, a crowd of men and women milled crazily, making their last bets before the light failed.

'N'goola! N'goola!'

The word was like a fly in Mary's brain. Hauntingly, irritatingly, it clung to her, making her feel uneasy, stirring confused memories. Who was she? Where had she come from? She had no idea—unless there was something in what an old woman said when she was visiting sick natives in hospital. The old woman had been delirious and dying when Mary stood beside her.

'*Yienda* Port Hedland girl,' she exclaimed. 'Bulyarrie, same me.'

'How do you know?' Mary asked.

The old woman had mumbled a word or two about ants and a mark on her forehead. Afterwards, in the settlement, Mary was pleased to say that she came from Port Hedland and belonged to the Bulyarrie group in tribal relationship, but she never mentioned to Ted, or any white people, the secret elation it gave her to think she belonged somewhere, and to somebody.

Dull red, like the ochre used in rock drawings, was burning out behind the rim of the hills. Dusk gathered and lights sparkled from huts on the hillside.

'N'goola! N'goola!'

Mary was startled to hear the old man singing in a southern dialect. She had learnt many words of it from Blind Nelly: hearing her talk, listening to her songs and stories about the birds and animals which were once men of the *nyoongar*.

> *Little one, Little one,*
> *Little lost one,*
> *Child of my dreaming,*
> *Where are you?*
> *Long and far has Gwelnit wandered,*
> *Calling and searching.*
> *Now his bones are weak,*
> *His eyes dim,*
> *The end of the journey is near.*

Like that, it went, the weird crooning and wailing, on and on, over and over again. Mary listened intently as the old man droned away. His voice was muffled, then it rose, crying so piercingly: 'N'goola! N'goola!' that Mary jumped to her feet.

She walked quickly to where the old man was sitting beside his fire. He looked at her with dazed, bleary eyes when she stood before him in the firelight.

'Who is she, this N'goola?' she asked.

'My daughter.'

The old man stared at her, his face heavy with the grief that had gone into his singing.

'*Yienda?*'

'Mary. I live with my husband, over there.'

'*Wongi* woman?'

'Yaller-biddy.'

The old man caught the rasp in her voice.

'N'goola, yaller-biddy,' he murmured.

'Tell me about her.' Mary sat down on the ground opposite to him. '*Bulyarrie*, me.'

The old man nodded, deep lines in the worn leather of his face relaxing to her respect for tribal custom as if it were a bond between them.

But she wanted no bond with this dirty old man, Mary told herself, in a quick revulsion of feeling. She had lived too long among white people to go back to Aboriginal ways and ideas. Why had she mentioned her tribal group? Was it in case they might be in a forbidden relationship? To put him at his ease? Or on an impulse she could not restrain?

A more aloof dignity in the old man's bearing intimated that he understood what she was thinking. Instinctive awe crept into Mary's sympathy as she looked at the broad, dark face in its dejection and sorrow.

Light from the fire glimmered in his eyes as they met hers. It struck a dull red band under the shaggy grizzled hair standing up from his forehead. Tattered his shirt might be, and his faded dungarees might show patches sewn on with black shark's teeth; but Mary knew he was a man of importance in the tribe from which he had come.

'N'goola is my daughter—and not my daughter,' the old man said. 'I am a man of the Wabarrie tribe, *waich bronga* Gwelnit, the name my fathers gave me. Jo Moses, what the white people called me. They found me in the reeds of a creek after a fight with white men. Many of my people were killed. The *boujera* of my people lies in the far south, along the Kalgan River!'

Gwelnit could speak the language of the white people as if he had known no other, Mary realised; but he reverted now and then to his own dialect, or to the slipshod half-and-half way the natives of various tribes spoke in the settlement.

This was the story he told her with many meanderings into the past.

The wife of a pioneer in that southern district had taken the native baby who was one of the few survivors of his tribe and reared him with her own son. The lads grew up together learning to be horsemen and stockmen. When young Jack Winterton went north to take up land beyond Port Hedland, Gwelnit went with him. He had become head stockman on Djeeral cattle station, won a woman of the tribe there in a fight with spears, and lived with her in the native camp.

Old men of the tribe were hostile to white people. Although they clung to the belief that the spirit of a child came to its mother through a rock, pool or animal, impregnated with the vitality of remote ancestors, they had decided that the association of their women with white men weakened the tribe. They foresaw that it would die out, as so many tribes had done, if they did not safeguard their women. Experience had taught the old men that light-coloured babies resulted from intercourse between native women and white men, and light colour was considered a sign of weakness in a child. For this reason women of the tribe were forbidden to give their bodies to white men.

With fierce pride the women showed-off their babies, delighting in the glossy darkness of their skin. None had been more fierce in her pride than Mittoon, Gwelnit's woman, when she bore him sons whose skin was as deeply bronze as his and her own.

Then she gave birth to a daughter. The old women tending her were suspicious when they saw the child, and Mittoon overwhelmed by shame and rage. Gwelnit knew she had done what was forbidden when he, too, saw the baby. His anger rose because his woman had brought this disgrace upon him, a stranger in the tribe, yet of pure blood; a man her kinsmen had come to trust and admitted to all rights. But Mittoon's anger had been greater than his.

' "It was the Boss," Mittoon said.' The old man's voice trembled to the shock of remembering. ' "When you were away on the bullock muster, Gwelnit, I went to the big house for stores. He took me into the store-miah and shut the door. Nothing would come of it. No one would know, he said. Now there is this child to shame me. Aie! Aie!" '

Gwelnit had spent happy years with his woman. She had been slight and girlish when he practised throwing spears to win her from the man of another tribe to whom she was promised. She grew full-bosomed and handsome; he never doubted her loyalty to him and to the tribe. What disturbed him most was that the man he had served faithfully for many years should have brought this trouble upon them.

' "The child will not live," Mittoon said in her anger,' the old man mourned. ' "Our people must know I was forced by the white man. Soon they will forget what has happened".'

Gwelnit had stood looking at the baby in the *coolamon*; its delicate limbs of yellowy-brown, the black lashes curled up from sleeping eyes, tiny hands. He remembered that once he had been a little creature like this—and as helpless. His anger left him.

'She is my daughter,' he told the old women. 'See that she is well-cared for.'

The old women knew what that meant. A man had the right to claim any child born by his woman. They dared not disobey Gwelnit.

Mittoon brooded sullenly over his decision. She refused to take any notice of the baby. Her breasts were heavy with milk but she would not feed the child.

In the evening when Gwelnit returned from work on the run or in the stockyards, he would find Mittoon squatted on the ground outside the *wurley*. Inside, the baby wailed fretfully. He would lift her, wash her, and stand over Mittoon while she suckled the little one. Every morning and night, he did that; and every morning and night he and Mittoon quarrelled about the child.

N'goola, he called her, because she was like a small brown and yellow flower which grew along the creeks and in the swamps of his *boujera*.

Gwelnit warned Mittoon that if she did not feed and care for N'goola he would take the child away. Mittoon's anger and jealousy smouldered because Gwelnit's eyes glowed when he looked at the child, and darkened as they turned to her, Mittoon, his woman.

When Gwelnit returned from work, one evening, there was no wailing in the *wurley*. Mittoon sat outside, as usual, sullen and brooding.

Gwelnit looked into the *wurley*. The *coolamon* was empty.

'Where is N'goola?' The fear that moved him then vibrated in the old man's voice.

' "The ant people have got her",' Mittoon had said. ' "The yellow one will disgrace me no more".'

Gwelnit seized her in his fury.

'Where did you put her?' he demanded.

Mittoon would not say. Not until she was terrified and bleeding from his blows, did she cry:

' "On the ant nests . . . near the Big Rock".'

Gwelnit dashed away through the scrub. Darkness had fallen and he had to find a track through the mulga and thorn-bush which led to the Big Rock ten miles away. Then he ran, ran with the speed of his emu brothers. His brain was bursting; his breath could hardly drive him along when he came to the open country on which the Big Rock stood, with the dumps of ants' nests scattered out from it.

The moon was rising as he searched among them, stopping now and then to listen for any sound; but there was no frail cry to guide him. At last he found her, lying on her back; a little yellow body to which swarms of black ants were clinging, sucking at her eyes and mouth, every moist hidden fold of her limbs.

Gwelnit took her in his arms. She was still alive, still breathing, but so faintly that he could not believe the ant people had not already taken her spirit. He brushed them from her, plucked them from her eyes and mouth, and from the broken skin on her forehead into which they were burrowing. He had nothing to revive her except his own spittle. He put that in her mouth.

Quickly, carefully, he carried her back along the track, stopping again and again to put his mouth to hers and listen for the sound of her breathing.

When he confronted Mittoon with the child in his arms, he said:

'If N'goola does not live—Mittoon will not.'

Mittoon took the baby. Its mouth was too weak to suck. She squeezed her nipples so that the milk fell drop by drop into N'goola's mouth. The madness which had come over her man, Mittoon could not understand.

His pity and tenderness for the little one were strange also to Gwelnit. Was there some magic within her that had melted the marrow of his bones? Had the spirit of by-gone ancestors in her eyes won him?

Gwelnit watched to see Mittoon did everything necessary for the child. There was no need to watch, he realised after a while, because Mittoon feared he would kill her if N'goola died.

The old women exclaimed because the ants had not eaten the little one's bones dry; and because she had not perished of thirst lying out in the sun all day. But she was strong, his N'goola, Gwelnit exulted: she had the will to live. He rejoiced as she grew. When she was a little girl, she had been as quick and graceful as a bird, N'goola. He was proud of her: proud when she could run to him and call him *mumae*.

With a quivering under her skin, and a quickening of her senses, Mary heard the old man describe how, when N'goola was playing with other children in the camp, sometimes, they would call her 'the yellow one'; and how she would fly at them, scratching and shrieking, until the mothers came and tore her away.

N'goola burnt quandongs, mixed the black dust with grease, and rubbed it over her body. But it was no use. The other children laughed and teased her more than ever for trying to look like them.

Mary could see it all, the little girl smeared with greasy black dust, and the naked, dark-skinned children dancing round her, jeering and driving her to a frenzy; then a big man coming out from the trees, shouting angrily at them, taking the little girl in his arms and washing the black stuff from her body. What was it he had told her? That colour of the skin did not matter. She must laugh and have courage to be a good member of the tribe. Then everybody would forget that an evil spirit had frightened her mother and stolen some of the baby's skin colour before it was born.

There was a song he had sung to comfort the child; a song about a flower, brown and yellow, which grew in far-away country. Blind Nelly, too, sang this song. It told about two children who had wandered away into the bush and were lost, until their mother found them, following the scent of the *n'goola* they had picked and carried about with them.

'N'goola was six years old when a mounted trooper rode into the camp and took her away.' The old man's voice drew Mary's attention back to his story.

Gwelnit was mustering cattle in the back hills when it happened. N'goola had been accepted by the tribe, then. Her gaiety and nimble grace were pleasing to the old men. They had given her a place in tribal organization. When Gwelnit returned, Mittoon wept and howled because she thought Gwelnit would blame her for letting the trooper take the child; but every man and woman in the camp was angry and indignant at the way the trooper had seized N'goola, tied her hands together, bound a handkerchief over her mouth, and ridden away with her.

Gwelnit saddled a horse in the Boss's yards and rode off to the police station in the Port.

The policemen laughed when he told them he had come to enquire why they had taken away his daughter.

'She's not your daughter,' the tall trooper said. 'You're black as the ace of spades, and she's a half-caste. Our instructions are to remove half-caste children from the native camps and send them south to learn the ways of white people in government institutions and mission schools.'

Gwelnit cursed the white people in his rage and grief.

'Where have you sent her?' he asked.

The police would not tell him.

'The idea is,' the trooper said, 'to keep the kid away from natives so that she can forget she ever had anything to do with them.'

Gwelnit left the police station distraught by the disaster which had befallen him and N'goola. From other natives in the township he learnt that she, with other little girls like her, had been put on a boat going south the day after she had been brought to the police station. Gwelnit was on the next boat going south.

On the boat he talked to one of the seamen. It would be hard to discover where the child had been sent, this man said. There were Roman Catholic, Salvation Army, Methodist and other 'homes,' in outlying suburbs of Perth, which received a subsidy from the government for looking after half-caste children.

Gwelnit made the rounds of all of them, enquiring for N'goola; but no one would tell him anything about her. Nowhere could he find her.

Mary's mind seethed with the conflict which had arisen within her. Had the old man made her see and feel what his will contrived for her to see and feel? Or was it true that she was 'the little yellow one' other children had jeered at in the native camp? Even if it were true she would not admit it, she told herself. She was sorry for the old man; but, after all, she was half white. He was not her father; her father had been a white man.

People in the settlement said she was 'a crawler to the whites.' But she crawled to nobody, Mary thought resentfully; neither to them nor to the whites.

Her sympathies were all with the dark people. She had learnt hymns and poetry at school, but they did not move her like Blind Nelly's songs, or the fragments of corroboree songs and stories old Aboriginal men and women told in the settlement.

Yet she had struggled so long to win for herself the right to live like a white woman in a real house, and to be regarded as a decent person, and she could not give up the struggle now. It had taught her to be stubborn and independent. So far nothing else had come of it. She could not get permission even to build a new house on her block of land. It would never be granted, she was sure, if she allowed this old man to call her his daughter and took him to live with her.

Gwelnit's voice drew and held her again.

He had wandered to the north and to the east in his search for N'goola; to the cities and townships white men had built everywhere. On gold-mining camps and out-back stations, on native reserves and in ports along the coast, he had begged for news of N'goola. Nobody could tell him anything about her.

For twenty-five years he had wandered, up and down, all over the country, looking for her, calling her name. Now he was old; he could walk no further. This settlement near what had once been a corroboree ground for south-west tribes, he feared, was the last place he would reach.

'If no one has seen or heard of N'goola, here,' he said from the depths of his weariness and despair, 'I will return to the *boujera* of my people, and wait for the spirits of my fathers to come for me.'

The old man moved back from the embers of his fire when he had no more to say. Their glow touched the deeply furrowed, weather-beaten bronze of his face.

His eyes went past Mary, unwilling to meet hers. He gave no sign of having sensed what he had done to her, lifting a shroud from her mind, and stirring in her that conflict between her desire to live like a white woman and her loyalty to the traditions of the dark people.

She knew, all the same, he was aware of her desire to leave him without a word which would unite her with him and his quest.

Silence hung between them: a silence, heavy and oppressive.

Mary broke it.

'You need wander no further, *mumae*,' she said. 'I am N'goola.'

GLOSSARY

boujera	tribal territory
Bulyarrie	a tribal group
coolamon	scooped wooden utensil for carrying food and babies
mumae	father
n'goola	wild boronia
nyoongar waich	black people
bronga	emu totem
wongi	native
wurley	shelter of bark and brushwood
yiena	you

MARJORIE BARNARD

Dry Spell

I walked because there was no reason for stopping, because it was more intolerable to stay still, and because I wanted to reach the sea. I wanted to wade out into the water and perform some ritual act—like the Doge wedding Venice to the Adriatic, or William the Conqueror with his hands full of symbolic mud, or Cuchulain, or McDouall Stuart rushing into the Indian Ocean when he had crossed the continent, or Cortes greeting the Pacific—but was that Pisarro, or was it somebody else altogether, Drake perhaps? My mind caught painfully on the doubt like a plane running on a knot of hardwood. It upset me. I began rubbing my hand across my chin again, and listening to my footsteps. The things I had not been thinking came closer.

I was coming into the city along Anzac Parade. It was late and quiet. Occasionally a tram passed, an empty, illuminated box, leaping on the rails under a crackle of blue sparks. The trees were black, and their leaves made a little dry sound like ghostly butter pats. There were no soft, rounded, sounds in the night, only dry brittle ones, and the pavement was gritty under my feet. My lips tasted of dust as they always did. The torrid street lamps were like sores on the night.

Walking alone at night always stimulated my imagination and now I was exalted as if with fever. But it was the city's fever, not mine. Images, like the empty, lit tram, ran through my mind and I was aware, with a febrile intensity, of my surroundings, immediate and remote.

It was the third waterless summer, and the heat had come down like a steel shutter over the city. The winters between had been as bad. Dry, with a parching, unslacked cold; westerly winds that drove and drove, bringing such clarity to the air, that a hill five miles away looked near enough to touch. The drought was in everything now, penetrating and changing life like blind roots at work upon a neglected pavement. The colours and quality of the world had been altered in the long months of desiccation. The pattern of existence was pulled awry.

Around the city there was a great fan of desolation. The sun had beaten the Emu Plains to a black brown on which the isolated houses and the townships themselves drifted like flotsam on a dead sea. The mountains were not blue but purple, a waterless ridge of rocks and shadows with the vegetation, except in the deepest seams of the valleys, mummified and black. Beyond again the Bathurst Plains were like a petrified sea, and very quiet. Further west, in an eternity of their own, were the iron-hard, fissured Black Soil Plains. There was no green anywhere. The stock had been driven away to agistment over the border long ago. Or had died.

There was nothing even for the crows, who last year had had their saturnalia.

The country with its endless, aching death pressed in on the city, the drought and the heat pressed on both. In the city and its environs its stamp was no less clear. The bush on the outskirts was more than half dead. Even the deep feeders, the black butts and the like, were dying. The life that was left was drawn in and banked down, muted and secret. The scrub was shabby and colourless. Fire had licked through it, leaving patches of black and sharp red-brown. Where there were houses, wide fire breaks had been cut as the only protection. Water could no longer be relied on to combat the fires. These breaks were raw scars, even on the devastated country. They looked like the trail of vengeance. Orchards were long since dead, and the trees fallen on the eroded ground. On the eastern slopes around Dural the orange trees were burnt black. The flats that used to be vegetable gardens were bare, the last dried stalks blown away. Even Chinamen could make nothing grow.

In the wealthy suburbs of the North Shore and Vaucluse a change had taken place too. It was as if the earth had been squeezed so that all the fine houses that had nestled so comfortably in the contours and in the greenery, were forced up into the light. They bulged out, exposed, and the sun tore at them. The gardens that had embowered them were perished. Tinder dry, fire had been through many of them, scorching walls and blistering away any paint that remained. Most of these houses were empty or inhabited as if they were caves, by people who had come in from the stricken country. The owners had fled, not so much from present hardship, as from the nebulous threat of the future, the sense of being trapped in a doomed city. The shores of the harbour were lion-coloured or drab grey. Sandhills showed a vivid whiteness. Only the water was alive and brilliant. And it was salt.

In the crowded districts, there was less to perish, but light and air were equally abrasive, changing all surfaces, fading and nullifying all colour. There was no pleasure of touch left anywhere, for the dust was undefeatable. It pulled down pride and effort. The suburbs sagged under an intolerable burden.

I was perpetually aware of all this. It cumulated into a black wave which hung over me in threatening suspense. Nothing that I knew had escaped. From my windows I looked over the golf course and that had taken, because it was defenceless, the clearest print of all. Its silvery green hills were stripped to pale brown and tawny purple. The earth was like starved, sagging flesh on an iron skeleton. Here and there a fire had run for a few yards before it died for lack of tinder, and left a black smear with a little edging of white ash. I used to think that the desert of Arizona looked like that. Now I know that heat and drought can bring even the gentlest country to it.

There was a man walking in front of me that I hadn't noticed before. When he passed a lamp I saw that he was a different shape from the pedestrians you'd expect to see about there. He was a swaggie all right with his roll of old blue blanket across his shoulders, and his quart pot dangling from it. I overhauled him.

'Good-night, mate.'

'Night, mate,' he answered, as a bushman answers the gate-crashing townsman. He was an old-timer, might have been a fossicker, short and spare, with a wealth of grey whiskers and clothes subdued to use and want as only a bushman's can be.

'Come far?' I asked him.

'Middlin' far.'

'Where's that?' I felt an insatiable curiosity.

'Back o' beyond.'

I'd seen hundreds like him but here there was a sort of long range persistence that was impressive. His gaunt and bristling dog at heel was cut out of the same stuff. My imagination took a leap.

'Did you ever do a perish on the Diamantina?'

'Aye, there and more places besides.'

'And now the track runs through the city?'

He didn't answer. So that was the way of it. I felt coldly sick. Looking back over my shoulder I saw that there were others, many of them, moving singly among the trees, all with the same intent, converging, persistence. It would be the same on all the other highways. I took to the middle of the road and, almost, to my heels.

I reached Taylor Square ahead of them. The neon signs were sizzling, and a few shop windows still bulged with light on the indifferent night. There were hardly any people about, but in the narrow, crowded streets at the bottom of the hill there were plenty, sitting on door steps or on chairs dragged out on to the pavement. Children were playing languidly in the street because it was too hot to go to bed. There was a queue at the pump, with buckets and kerosene tins and even jugs.

There was still water in the pipes, brownish stuff with a smell, but the pressure was so poor that it didn't reach the higher levels, so the pumps had been put in where people could come and get it. The city hadn't been used to queues, and they were changing people's outlook. They made new channels for rumour, perhaps for thought.

So many things were different, and the men's minds with them. Unemployment was general either directly from scarcity, or from its by-product of apathy. Idleness was everywhere and the people were differently distributed. Whole districts were almost depopulated whilst others were overcrowded to suffocation. Practically all the food had to be brought in. The Government was distributing it as a ration. There was enough, and yet it didn't slake the public appetite. There was a sense of famine. Even those who were eating better than ever before, felt it. The whole of our civilization was piled up like a pyre waiting for the fire to consume it.

The city seethed with rumours and with the promulgators of fantastic schemes, but everyone was fatalistic about the drought. They didn't expect it to break, they even took an inverted pride in it. It, at least, relieved them of the responsibility of living their own lives. There was always a crowd at the General Post Office reading the bulletins that were posted hourly, but no one believed the jargon of lows, depressions and tropical disturbances, any more than they believed in the bona fides of the clouds that often blanketed the sky—as on this night—with their barren oppression. Yet nothing else mattered. All interest in outside events had been discarded, as if it were the most obvious of luxuries. It was obvious that something must come sooner or later of this mass tension, but no one knew what. It was like a long thunderstorm that did not break. Apathy and exasperation were racing one another.

I followed the tramline out of the hot and odorous streets. The open space beside the Blind Institute and the Domain beyond were crowded with people in search of air. They were quiet, bivouaced for the night, but never quite still. There was no grass to sit on, only dusty earth. The Botanic Gardens were the same, ruined between the drought and the trampling people. Authority had long ago given up the thankless task of conserving them.

I no longer wanted to get to the water. These febrile cravings died easily. I was just drifting. Did it matter what I did, or where I went with those old-timers closing in? The narrow canyons of the city offered no relief. There was nothing for the mind to feed on but nostalgia. I remembered Macquarie Place, and had a vision of it as it used to be, the three-cornered garden, the giant Port Jackson figs, dark against the pale soaring buildings, the zinnias, the cushiony buffalo grass, the statue (I forget its original), declaiming to the street, the anchor of the Sirius on a pedestal, Macquarie's obelisk in its bear pit . . . In the early days the officers and the higher officials lived round there. It was their compound where the children romped in safety, and in the evening the regimental band played under those same trees, lovers counted the southern stars between the leaves, and the gaiety of exiles flourished by candlelight. It was the outpost of something that had had to fall, and it might be again. It was a goal, a place with significance in a meaningless desert, a spot where we might turn at last and resist the invasion, the perishing men who came so quietly and surely through the dust. I hastened my steps like a hungry man who half remembers some forgotten fragment of food, and hurries back to ransack his belongings once more. Down I went through narrow, twisting streets, between buildings glowing with heat, but dead to light.

At first sight Macquarie Place did not seem to be greatly changed. The trees still stood, and the lights showed the dark labyrinth of their leaves scarcely breeched. It was, like all these places, crowded with people. I had the good fortune to find a seat on one of the benches. I was shaking with fatigue. All about me were points of light from cigarettes, and a murmur of talking. Those crowds had their fits of talking and their fits of silence. I turned to my neighbour and was surprised to see that he was apparently in fancy dress, white breeches, a tail coat, and a three-cornered hat. He was small and sharp, but fine too. Before I could speak to him he addressed me.

'This is nothing new, Sir, it happened before, and worse.'

'Indeed?' said I, not feeling comfortable.

'Not so much the drought—though that was bad enough, even the parrots were dropping dead out of the trees at Rose Hill—but the scarcity. You have no conception, Sir, of what it was like then.'

'Was that long ago?' I asked, trembling.

'Some time ago. There was the same talk then of abandoning the settlement but I didn't listen to it. I hope no one listens now. Of course I've no authority these days. But if I could hang on surely you could. It was two and a half years before ships came from England that time. I'd grieve to see my work thrown away now.'

I got up hurriedly. 'Good-night, Captain,' I said.

'Captain-General.' he corrected me.

A man buttonholed me. 'I've been to the Observatory every day but no one will listen to me. In the Book of Revelations . . .'

I broke from him. I hoisted myself on to the pedestal and leaned against the anchor. That was something solid. Two men below me were quarrelling quietly. I tried to speak to them to tell them what would be happening to all of us soon. They both fell silent.

'That's right, mate,' said a man beside me, whom I had not noticed. 'What we want's solidarity.'

I tried to see his face. 'Are you real?' I asked.

He laughed, and called down to a friend, 'Here's a poor cove gone balmy.'

There was a roar of laughter, and a screech came up. 'Don't laugh, you fools, repent.'

I sat trembling with rage. Let it happen to them, whatever it was. I wouldn't warn them.

Two men were talking over my head.

'There's a change coming.'

'I've heard that before.'

'It's true this time.'

'I don't hold with this metterology. It never did anything for us.'

'I don't neither. I know this myself. Smell it, see? You listen, it'll begin anytime.'

'I'll wait.'

'Feel that?'

'Nope.'

The country was coming to take its vengeance on the city. Climax. Apotheosis. Then nothing. Come quickly. Come quickly. All ugliness, all corruption will be burned away.

'Feel that?'

'Something fell on my bald pate.'

'Rain.'

'Go on.'

LISTEN

Silence fell. There was a crepitation among the leaves. Everybody stood up, stock still. I slid from the pedestal and stood with them. I felt the drops on my face. I was furious, nothing could hold me.

'No,' I shouted. It couldn't come now. It was too late. Our fate was on us. We were going up in fire, consummated. It was agony to turn back now with the end we had toiled so long to reach in sight.

There were people holding me. 'It isn't true,' I cried. 'It won't happen. No rain ever.'

Someone forced me to my knees. There was a great silent ring of people around me. A match was struck and held in a cupped hand. I stared at the asphalt. Great black drops were falling on it, drying, disappearing, coming again, faster and faster, making a pattern like the leaves against the light, then coalescing and defacing itself. I stared and stared. Out on the roads, that pattern was tangling the feet of the perishing men, turning them back. Nothing would come of it now. Nothing would save us. We must take up the burden of remaking our world.

ELEANOR DARK

'Hear My Prayer'

I

It was an old convict-built house; of weathered stone, close to the street, and shut off from it only by a row of dusty shrubs, it took you back with rather disconcerting abruptness into another generation.

Looking along the verandah you could (if you had enough imagination to forget the street outside) persuade yourself that you saw the tall, frock-coated figure of the old Canon walking there before church, his high, broad forehead, his side-whiskers, his long Irish upper lip clean shaven above his grim mouth, his big Bible with its gold-engraved inscription held firmly in both hands.

You could imagine that you heard from one of the rooms hidden by the long green shutters the subdued whispering of the children as they collected their prayer books and manœuvred to be last out, and so less obvious to the parental eye; and you could see them come forth sedately—Fanny first, because she knew very well that even extreme godliness was not altogether proof against such devastating prettiness as hers; and then William, lanky and earnest; and then little Beatrice, dark and demure, so that you would think she couldn't possibly know anything about the pin so cleverly arranged in the seat of poor Richard's Sunday knickerbockers; and lastly Richard himself, my father, the bad boy of the family, who led its inconsiderable rebellions and endured its not so inconsiderable punishments . . .

Well, they are only ghosts. The Canon's old church still stands there across the road, with green grass about it, and iron railings guarding it from the street; but between the church and the Rectory the years have rushed like a flood, bringing petrol and concrete and electricity, so that it is only in odd moments of receptiveness—in the early morning, sometimes, or late at night when the traffic is over—that one can realise how closely bound they once were by queer strong bonds of something that we may call by many different names, but which we don't really understand any longer.

It was Aunt Maggie, the earnest virgin whose good works my Uncle William married with such chaste enthusiasm, who first told of 'Stony-cross.' It was no longer the Rectory, you see, but a boarding-house, kept by two old ladies who, once upon a time, went, in their best bustles, to hear my grandfather preach. When they learned that I proposed to board with them their happiness was pathetic and embarrassing, but their joy in me, as time went on, was not unmixed with anxiety. At first they would smile rather nervously and say that of course I was dear Richard's son. And then they would say that times had changed and one must be broad-minded. And then they would say, very timidly, didn't I *ever* go to early Communion? And wouldn't I like to see the tablet erected to my grandfather's memory in the church?

This sort of thing bothered me so much that I began to think I should have to look for other quarters. It was not that I minded their gentle proddings, but that my unchristian ways obviously distressed them so terribly. All the same, the thought of telling them that I was leaving was more than I could face. I imagined their anxious questionings: 'Was the rent too high?' 'Wasn't I comfortable?' . . .

Feeling worried and oppressed, I did wander over to the church one day and look for the memorial tablet. I had seen my own name inscribed on various things before now—on school honour boards and rowing oars and cups for boxing—but it gleamed suddenly and rather accusingly at me now out of the silent semi-darkness—'BRIAN RICHARD O'BRIEN . . . *true servant of the Lord . . . his grateful and devoted parishioners . . .*'

I turned and came out into the sunlight with a queer, panicky, relieved feeling that I was rescuing myself from some unspecified danger. And when I got back to 'Stonycross' there was the letter from Aunt Maggie waiting for me.

My instant thought was that it solved my problem.

> 'I am so happy to tell you,' wrote Aunt Maggie, 'that Martin has made up his mind that he wishes to enter the Church, thus fulfilling what I am sure you know was the dearest wish of your poor Uncle William and myself. It adds greatly to my happiness that he should have so desirable a place to stay during his studies in Sydney, and that you, my dear Brian, who are older and more experienced, will be at "Stonycross" to keep an eye on him. The Misses Barlow will, I am sure, make him comfortable for his dear grandfather's sake. I feel that with the great tradition . . .'

Well, certainly I was 'older,' but that only made me twenty-two. I let out a whoop of joy, and slid down the banisters on my stomach in my haste to spread the good news.

The old ladies trembled with delight. *Two* grandsons of the Canon! Such felicity! And the dear boy studying for the Church! Here, in the very house where his grandfather had lived so long and righteously! They crooned and cooed. Already, with deep satisfaction, I thought I could see the focus of their attention shifting from me, a mere Med. III, to Martin, the Student of Divinity.

II

I awaited my cousin in a glow of benevolence, but my first sight of him damped me rather. I had not seen him for years, and then only briefly, and his uncouthness as he stood there in the hall of 'Stonycross' was rather startling.

I began:

'Oh—er—you're Martin, of course. How are you?'

His voice was quite the best part of him—a very youthful and rather charming voice.

'I'm all right, thanks. Er—mother sent her love.'

'Oh, thanks—er . . .'

I was beginning to feel that all this was going to be a bit beyond me, when he smiled. Of course, he had been smiling in a way before—the conventional grimace that arrives automatically when you greet any-one—but now his eyes flashed into life behind his clumsy spectacles, and I saw that they were blue like my own, like his father's and my father's and the Canon's, and that he had the family nose and the long Irish upper lip.

'I'm glad you're here,' he explained. 'I don't know anyone in Sydney yet.'

After a few days I found myself liking him. I don't know why, for we really hadn't a thing in common except our eyes and our upper lips, and for sheer genius in being irritating I have never met his equal. His gift for doing and saying the wrong thing would have made him completely insufferable to any ordinary person if it hadn't been for some quality in him that only became apparent when he smiled. What was it, so deeply buried and yet, indomitably, still so very much alive? A streak from some remote forbear of the true Irish scallywaggery? A hint of the demure lawlessness that had landed my poor Aunt Beatrice in the terrible position of being no longer spoken of by the family? Whatever it was, it's dead now—safely, decently, blessedly dead, for it would never have done in a Bishop . . .

He fell instantly and passionately into the tradition of Canon worship. 'Stonycross' was holy ground to him; he was never tired of hearing which room the Canon had slept in, where he had prepared his sermons, where he had received the poor and needy of his parish who came to ask and receive aid for their worldly needs and thundering rebuke for their spiritual transgressions. I was inclined to think, sometimes, that as far as religion was concerned he was actually a little bit unbalanced—and yet haven't I admitted myself to seeing ghosts, to feeling vaguely at odd moments the pull of some mysterious unity between Brian Richard O'Brien, holder of boxing trophies, and that other O'Brien, 'true servant of the Lord'? For what is it, after all, this need for religion? An emotional urge? A light from Heaven to the Chosen? An inheritance? I don't know, and to be quite truthful I find other problems in life more worth considering. But whatever it was that drove Martin—godliness or super-stition, inspiration or weakness, emotional need or mild lunacy—I had it myself in a lesser degree. If I hadn't I should never have been able to stand him as the months went on, and he became paler and more devout, clumsier and more earnest, everlastingly getting in my way and being trodden on, and apologising, and then reprimanding me with extra-ordinary courage and sincerity when I swore. He did, in fact, wake a sort of devil in me. Whether it was him I was defying or some streak of generations-old Irish devoutness, I don't know, but I stayed out later than ever at night and came home smelling of whisky simply to shock him and to assert myself. As a matter of fact, being in training, my evenings were always most blamelessly spent, and the smell of whisky practically nothing but a smell.

It was quite inevitable, I suppose, that he should, at last, begin an effort at conversion. If he had left me alone I should have left him alone, and our queer association (it could never have been called a friendship) might have lasted for ever. I remember the evening it began quite clearly.

He had come out on to the balcony where I slept, and was sitting on the edge of the stretcher, being, it seemed to me, more than ordinarily revolting.

I said snappishly at last:

'Look here, you're trying to convert me, aren't you?'

He swallowed nervously and made one of his wandering, futile gestures.

'It is the duty—I mean—we have to—if you believe in the Lord Jesus Christ you want to bring others to believe in Him too.'

I sat up with a bounce that nearly sent him flying, and poked him impressively in the ribs.

'I, too, have my faith,' I proclaimed.

Even in the uncertain light from the street lamps I saw the sudden pinkness of his face, the earnest joy that woke behind his spectacles; and, realising that to him 'faith' meant only one thing, I felt rather contrite, and hurried on:

'If you're going to try and convert me to your faith, I claim the right to try and convert you to mine. That's fair enough, isn't it?'

He peered at me mistrustfully.

'What is your faith?' he asked.

Sitting there in my pyjamas, I explained to him. When one is twenty-two and in the thick of a medical course, one rushes in very blithely where angels fear to tread. I had delved into philosophy, physics, com-parative religion, psychology, economics, socialism, and all the rest of the 'ologies' and 'isms' that I had been able to discover. There were quite a lot of good things that I was only too ready to say about them.

To this day my faith is the same that it was then, but I see now that it was really the same that Martin was trying so gropingly to teach me—the same that Buddha preached in India, and Confucius in China, and

Mohammed in his Arabian deserts, and that Shakespeare finally boiled down into the six all-sufficient words: 'To thine own self be true.'

But at nineteen and twenty-two words are a very potent wizardry. Six? What niggardliness! Six thousand having failed to express the vastnesses of our respective creeds, Martin, pale and really tired with his spiritual wrestlings, went at last, anxiously, to bed.

III

Of all his annoying qualities, his earnest sentimentality was the hardest to endure. The old ladies, certainly, aided and abetted him in that. It was their suggestion, for instance, that he should have the little downstairs room with the long window opening on to the verandah for his bed-room. It had been, in bygone days, the Canon's study; there was actually an ancient armchair that had been there in his time, and a copy of 'The Light of the World' in a vast and gloomy frame. The old ladies, full of awed enthusiasm, were even able to produce from some forgotten lumber-room an old and rather rickety desk at which (it was only reasonable to suppose) the Canon might have written a sermon or, at the very least, addressed an envelope.

'The atmosphere . . . !' they murmured raptly from the threshold. 'The never-fading influence of a saintly life . . . !'

Well, if there was anything in that, it may have been, perhaps, the never-fading influence of my father's anything but saintly life which goaded me into telling that wickedly delicious little story of the Canon's famous *faux pas* . . .

I had a couple of friends—fellow-students of my own year—who dropped in sometimes to have dinner and spend the evening yarning in my bedroom. Martin used to come occasionally, when I suggested it, and sit on the edge of a chair looking acutely unhappy over our godless conversation. The talk, one night, had turned to the architecture of the old house, and from that it swung very naturally to its history and its former inhabitants. Martin, steeped in Canon lore, was on much firmer ground than I was here. He was able to give us the fact we wanted, but he didn't stop at that. After a while I couldn't stand it any longer, and I said:

'You know the old chap's famous sermon on the Sunday School picnic, don't you, Martin?'

He looked at me in surprise and pleasure.

'I don't think I do. It isn't in the collection, is it?'

'Well—no.'

While I told them the tale I could almost see it happening. There was the long, dim stretch of the cathedral, and the sunlight, turned by the stained-glass windows into pools of scarlet and blue and amber, lying motionless on the floor. The choir-boys, fidgeting hotly under their white surplices. The congregation sitting very still with upturned faces, and in the pulpit my most formidable grandparent. His anger, his disgust, his genuine distress and horror made him formidable; his fine figure, his lean, handsome face, with its smouldering blue eyes and its grim Irish mouth, made him impressive. There was not a sound, not a breath while they waited for him to speak again. For he had made them see as vividly as he saw it himself how the Devil might work silently while none suspected; how a good Christian must never rest, but be always vigilant; how, in the very midst of a harmless pleasure sanctioned—nay, organised—by the Church itself, sin might creep stealthily, like a thief, and strike at virtue. Their own Sunday School picnic—and at it no less than three innocent girls had been seduced . . . !

Very still the congregation sat, awed, chastened, waiting for him to speak again.

If only he hadn't . . . !

'Now, *the Dean* was at that picnic, . . .' he said.

The yell of laughter from my two friends swept over Martin's bewildered head and left him thinking—hard. I was watching him. I saw the flood of colour that marked his sudden realisation, and I saw, for one fraction of a second, the irrepressible gleam of laughter that fled madly, like an escaping prisoner, across his face, with outraged anger in close pursuit. Whatever it was that he said, standing there with hot cheeks and fierce, disgusted eyes, we didn't hear it. It was only a sentence, and it was lost in our helpless abandonment of mirth. Then he was gone, and after a little while we pulled ourselves together and forgot about him.

But that evening, I believe now, was his turning-point. It was not the story itself that mattered, nor the fact that his idol had been made, for a moment, ludicrous. Not even our unregenerate hilarity impressed him very much. It was that infinitesimal second when he felt his own laughter bubbling wickedly inside him, when some other Martin whose existence he had never suspected frightened him with a wild and almost successful bid for liberty.

The next morning I was momentarily startled to see how ill he looked, but I was too busy with my own concerns to think of it for long. The old ladies were different. It was about a week later that they brought their anxieties to me. Hadn't I noticed how pale he was? How little he ate? How seldom he spoke? And, most staggering of all, didn't I know that he had not been to church last Sunday?

That did sober me. I made it my business to see a good deal of him in the next few days, and he was undoubtedly changed. It is hard to say exactly what the change was; he gave me an odd impression of being temporarily suspended—like a pair of scales exactly balancing, like an empty house in the gap between two tenancies, like a tennis ball wobbling on a net, before you know which side it is going to fall. He was waiting.

For what? I didn't know, but for some reason my conscience pricked. I asked him to come and sit with me and my friends that night, and warned them beforehand that Canon-baiting was to be barred. He came, and was very silent—so silent that we forgot he was there. I don't remember now what we talked about, but to medical students there are no taboos. I only know that suddenly, without a word, Martin got up and walked out of the room, and we, looking at each other in bewilderment, felt his disapproval fall unpleasantly upon what had been, to us, a perfectly commonplace discussion. I was annoyed. Russell, who had been speaking at the moment, flushed uncomfortably and made a little movement of exasperation.

The next morning I tackled Martin.

'What did you walk out for like that last night? Damned rude, it was!'

He looked at me steadily.

'I thought the conversation offensive.'

'Very good,' I said shortly. 'It was an ordinary conversation on an ordinary subject, and until you created it there was no thought of offence in our minds. If you don't like our conversation you can keep away.'

I turned to go, but he called me back.

'I will come again if you don't mind.'

'All right,' I said, shrugging. 'Come any time you want to, but leave your pruderies outside.'

After that he came regularly, for weeks. He hardly said anything at first, but there came a night when he joined in one of our interminable discussions. They might begin, say, with the art of Oscar Wilde and finish with the theory of reincarnation, but they were always lively, and, I think I may say, always logical. Martin found, to his amazement and ours, that he had the true Irish 'gift of the gab.' He could thrust and parry; he, who had dreamed of no greater verbal attainment than to preach, found, intoxicatingly, that he could argue! And, from the harmless shoals where it had started. I could see the debate drifting rapidly into deeper waters. I could see rocks ahead, and Martin making for them merrily; there was, to me, an instant of true drama when he saw them too—he hovered for one dreadful second, and then crashed, winning his argument, but denying something which had been for all his life a categorical imperative—an article of faith.

For the rest of the evening he was dumb. The next day was Sunday, and I came down to breakfast in flannels and sand-shoes. The old ladies only looked at me sorrowfully as I passed their table, but Martin, crumbling his toast opposite me, said presently:

'Tennis?'

'No,' I said. 'Russell's taking his boat out on the harbour. I'm going with him.' And added teasingly: 'Will you come?'

He said 'Yes,' and I stopped with my coffee cup halfway to my mouth to gape at him. His face was white, and his eyes bluer than I had ever seen them. I said, stammering:

'My dear chap, I'm awfully sorry, but, really, I was only joking. I—I'm going as soon as I've finished my breakfast; I couldn't wait till after church. And anyhow...'

'I'm not going to church any more.'

'But...'

'You set out to convert me, didn't you?'

Shocked, alarmed, but, more than anything else, irritated by his colourless face and his queer, intense stare, I said roughly:

'In pure self-defence; I don't care a damn what you believe. My advice to you is to wrap yourself up safely in your nice comfortable dogmas; otherwise you'll probably get hurt.'

And I walked out, too jarred and angry to finish my excellent poached eggs.

Several times during the day I thought of him. Several times I found myself seeing the last glimpse I had had of his face across the white tablecloth—again that waiting look, but now with a hint of fear in it, as though something he had expected had failed him—a listening, holding-his-breath look, that seemed to say: 'Dare I go on? Can I go back?'

We stayed out fairly late, and I went home to dinner with Russell. It must have been after eleven when I set out from Rose Bay in the brilliant moonlight to walk home. I like walking at any time, but particularly on a moonlight night, and I was in a warm glow both mentally and physically when I came in sight of 'Stonycross' and the tall spire of the church. I thought again, for the first time in several hours, of Martin.

In those days the jargon of Freud and his disciples was unknown, but though I had no effective words to express my knowledge, I did have enough native intelligence to realise that my cousin was, psychologically speaking, in danger. If it were true that I had, however indirectly and unintentionally, taken his faith from him, it was up to me to give him something in its place. But what? I began to see now that a robust paganism is a thing born in one and not acquired. Martin, at all events, would never acquire it—Martin, with his innate faculty for worship, for reverence, for faith...

Feeling thoroughly bothered, I pushed open the little iron gate, which always stood ajar, and stepped up on to the verandah with my latchkey in my hand.

What I heard can only be described as a wail. It was very low and very brief, but it held me there with my hand halfway to the keyhole, stiffened with an unreasoning dread. It came, without any doubt, from Martin's room, and my first rational thought was that he was asleep and wrestling with a nightmare. Half satisfied with this explanation, my key was almost in the lock, when he began to talk. Then I was really alarmed, for there was no light in his room, and it didn't sound like the incoherent babblings of a sleeper. I went quickly along the verandah, and my sand-shoes made no sound on the stone flags. Outside his window I paused uncertainly, for the room was silent now. The shutters were wide open, but the heavy serge curtains hung closely together, and I could see nothing, hear nothing.

I thought:

'Confound it! he *must* have been asleep!' And, uneasily: 'Poor kid . . . !'

I took two steps back towards the door.

His voice burst out again—a fierce, desperate undertone, pleading, begging, beseeching—*praying* . . .

That was it—praying . . .

My skin went hot and cold, my spine crept, my hair seemed to bristle on the back of my neck like an animal's. I felt sick, panicky, with no thought but to get away—to escape . . .

And then I remembered how he had walked out of the room when Russell was talking. Was *his* skin hot and cold then? Was his skin creeping, and his whole being shrinking as mine was now, from something that outraged his every conception of dignity—decency . . . ?

I thought wildly: 'What can I do? Something . . . ! I *must* . . . !'

I put my hand on the serge curtains.

The lost, dreadful whispering went on:

'O God, I have sinned—I have left the path . . . I'm afraid—I'm not sure any longer . . . O God, help me, help me—give me a sign . . . ! O Christ, hear my prayer . . . !'

Where my fingers had separated the curtains a shaft of moonlight fell across the room like a bar of white fire. The figure of the Christ in 'The Light of the World' blazed out dramatically; in the surrounding blackness He shone there above poor Martin's adoring eyes—sorrowful, forgiving, serene . . .

I stood rooted, holding my breath. I could not see Martin's face, but I had heard his voice break on a little gasp—and then silence. Dazed with nervousness, I stood there waiting for him to realise that the light was moonlight, that the curtains must have parted, that there was not a breath of wind to part them—that *something* must have done it . . . and so to discover me there.

It took me several moments of silence, and then the sound of his voice again, quiet now, rapt and bemused with awe and gratitude and adoration, to realise that a mind half-crazed with fear, demanding nothing less than a miracle for the preservation of its sanity, will not boggle when a miracle is clearly offered. He had said: 'O God, give me a sign! O Christ, hear my prayer!' and somewhere, deeply buried beneath his miseries, had been the faith that the sign would be vouchsafed.

And it had.

Taking my fingers from between the curtains, I found myself looking at them rather curiously; discovered in myself an irrational feeling of shame that I, in Martin's place, could not have been so gloriously deluded; wondered, rather feverishly, seeing the church spire black against the silver sky, whether it might not be possible that I, Brian Richard O'Brien, had been really the chosen instrument of a manifestation of God . . .

Those things are very long ago. The emotional stress being over, I don't wonder about them any more. My cousin the Bishop is a good man, a useful man, a likeable man (though he doesn't approve of me), and in a fair way to become a legend, as his grandfather was before him. So I'm content now when I meet his austere gaze to feel glad that there was a moon that night, that I wore sand-shoes, and that a picture happened to hang just exactly where it did.

CHRISTINA STEAD

A Harmless Affair

Everything went right in this love affair from the beginning. It began just after Lydia had thought, 'It's spring and an empty spring; it's years since I felt really in love, I must be getting stupid—never looking outside my eyes, never longing for anything else.' The next day she went to a party and there met a lot of distinguished people, people who had all arrived at their destinations. Lydia hated this sort of party—to be with people who were famous made her feel that life had stopped and there was nothing more to live for, whereas she wanted to keep on living, and for that reason preferred people who had not arrived, at the top, or anywhere else, but who still nourished impossible ambitions and desires. There had been some unpleasantness about the invitation, on that account. The woman invited her: she wrote and accepted the invitation and she had not known the woman was famous: she only found it out after. And then the woman had not invited Lydia's husband. Lydia was known as 'Miss Parsons' in the laboratory and so she often used the name outside. This woman was a doctor, a simple ordinary woman, and after accepting the invitation, Lydia had discovered that she was not only Dr Brown, but also Mary Cohoet, a great social light and humanitarian, and one who was so far above the battle that she believed in meeting people from all strata of society— radicals, conservatives, revolutionary artists, writers in society papers and so on. Lydia had been invited because she had done some work in bacteriology and was still a young woman, and had travelled—she had some social graces in fact, although her parents were very poor.

Lydia put on a French dress and shoes and arrived late: the studio room in the duplex apartment was nearly full, people were drinking sherry and cocktails, and yet there was a flat, round-shouldered air in the room, which revealed, at a glance, that the guest of honour had not yet arrived. He was a man who had lived in China a long time and was going to make a plea for aid for the Chinese people.

Lydia felt very much at her ease, for a wonder, that day. It was an early spring day: thin sunlight slanted through the great studio windows and made the scattered people look untidy. Lydia saw she was the best-dressed woman there—not the richest dressed, but the woman with the best cut frock. The hostess was even a little surprised at her appearance, evidently, and began to introduce her to the people there. Lydia tried to remember the names, but only seized one here and there. There was a line-up of young men more or less ill dressed standing in the sun, an accidental line-up—they had been standing in a group and the circle had opened out into a parade line when the distinguished hostess appeared. Dr Brown named them.

'Dr Lyall, my cousin, Dr West, Roy Finch, Captain Paul Charters, Herr von Wirtz . . .' and so on. After one or two more introductions they had reached the other end of the room. Lydia received a cocktail and was left to herself. Seeing no-one there she knew and everyone awkward, she turned back to the group, which again opened into a parade line when she approached and going straight to a tall young man with a black thicket of hair, said, 'Did Dr Brown say Paul Charters, or Paul Charteris?' He laughed, 'Well, she says Charters, but *I* call it Charteris.'

'Then you're the journalist and soldier,' Lydia said confidently. He laughed, 'Yes. I'm the journalist and soldier.'

The other men had discreetly moved away by this.

'We have all your books at home,' said Lydia. She bubbled with uncommon good spirits.

'All,' she went on: 'so if you ever find one's missing, come and get it at our place. My husband's a great admirer of yours.' Charteris was in a good temper: for some reason, she beamed at Charteris, she felt idiotic and yet delighted. Dr Brown tore them away from each other to introduce the guest of honour, Mr Henri Lafargue. Lydia began to chat with Lafargue in an inspired fashion: she became terrified, for fear that this singular animation would leave her in the middle of a sentence and Lafargue would find her stupid. But no, Dr Brown tore Lafargue away from her, with something of a frown; she had no right to hog the guest of honour, she knew, but she was in a very strange exhilarated state and did not wish to come back to earth.

Later in the evening, Dr Brown came back, 'I did not know you were married. How stupid you must think me not to have invited your husband too. Please forgive me.' Lydia was puzzled, then remembered she had mentioned her husband to Paul Charteris.

She was different that evening from any time in her life. She liked a lot of the people immensely: she invited at least half a dozen of them to come to their apartment and meet her husband. She came away by herself and walked a long way by herself in the dark, missing several subway entrances on purpose. There was plenty of time to go home and take up the cordial connubial relations she enjoyed with her husband.

About a week later, Charteris telephoned at ten o'clock in the morning, asking if she had really meant her invitation and if he could come and see them. Suddenly the same confident exhilarated mood took her and she answered, 'Yes, of course, whenever you like,' but in a voice and mood quite unlike herself.

'Can I choose my own date?' asked Charteris.

'Of course.'

'Any time?'

'Any time.'

'Thanks,' said Charteris and rang off.

She told her husband that the famous Paul Charteris was really coming to see them. But he did not telephone again and she almost forgot him. Then a month later, he telephoned again, 'Hello Lydia,' he said coolly: 'can I come and see you today?'

'Yes, of course.'

'At three o'clock?'

'Yes.'

'Thanks,' said Charteris, and rang off.

Lydia scarcely gave a second's thought to his coming, although generally she fussed round the house, tidied herself up for hours before even the most uninteresting visitor arrived.

Charteris came at four o'clock. 'I'm sorry,' he said. 'I was with Anna Brown, getting things ready for Lafargue's lecture. How are you Lydia?'

Lydia felt herself trembling with joy. 'This is my husband, Tom Dunne,' she said. It was with a vague disappointment that she saw the two men take an immediate liking to each other.

Charteris' coat was greasy and old, his hair uncombed and his skin was bad: she could see he was not living well and that he was over-tired. Just as they sat down, and her husband had begun some question about Charteris' work in China, the telephone rang and Tom said, 'I know that's for me, that's my broker,' with the good natured parade of influence he sometimes made, and he dashed to the telephone and began chaffing the broker, calling him by his first name and putting on a wonderful variety show for the benefit of Charteris and herself. She sat down in his vacated chair and said to Charteris, 'You have been over-working, haven't you?' Charteris looked straight at her, and said,

'Oh Lydia, I never had any of the luck in life,' he hung his head and then suddenly looked again and smiled softly.

'How do you mean, Paul?' She felt towards him as towards Tom in their quieter marital moments.

'I have no luck,' he said looking at her with meaning. What meaning? She could not quite believe that he meant what he seemed to mean, that is, that she was already married. Tom had suddenly ceased his jokes and cutting-up at the telephone and was finishing his conversation in brief businesslike words.

'I didn't know you were married,' said Charteris. 'Anna Brown didn't know either.' He said it very coolly, with wide open eyes on her face and he seemed cunning to her, for it was impossible to tell whether this followed from his first words, or not.

'No,' said Lydia.

Paul smiled into her face with a look of humble affection, and yet there was a cunning in his coolness, that made her speechless. However, she was thinking very fast, weighing her chances with him, his chances with her, the outcome of love between them.

All this happened in the first five minutes. Their conversation had been carried on in a low, but natural tone, and Tom had hurried back from the telephone, as if intrigued, all the same. Thereafter Tom, of course, led the conversation on to China. Lydia had always admired Tom's brilliance and scholarship and was very surprised to see that not only was Paul equal to him in brilliance and scholarship, but seemed cooler, surer of himself, and moreover had exactly the same kind of thinking as Tom. Tom talked, talked, Paul answered him, argued with him, opulently showered him with his own ideas, and every few minutes would turn on her a golden smile, the kind of smile, Lydia had always thought up to now, that was only exchanged between lovers. And she felt herself giving him, too, those rare golden smiles: she felt very happy, at ease, as if floating on an inland brook, in midsummer in full sunlight. She had never felt at ease with a man like that in her life before, except with Tom, but in a different, more maternal way, with Tom. She had no maternal feeling towards this stranger, but no sinful nor vulgar adulterous feeling either. Only a feeling as if the love of the ages of gold existed between them and would never be disturbed.

Presently, because she could take no part in their conversation, which had become 'a feast of the intellect', she retired to her own workroom and went on with a monograph in bacteriology she was doing. This did not please Tom very much: he always liked her to be there, to listen to his brilliance, and to love and admire him; so he called her, 'Lydia! Make us some coffee.' She came out at once, as she was used to doing, and as she passed the door, Paul smiled at her and said, 'Well, if you come like that when people call you'll never get your work done. *I* wouldn't do it.'

Everything about him was natural and sweetly audacious. When she gave him the coffee, he smiled at her as if he were absolutely sure of her love. 'What a strange thing,' she thought: 'I must be seeing things! I'm just mad, that's all. He's being pleasant.' But she saw he smiled at her husband coolly, carelessly, with the faint air of an adversary, and would turn from one of those rather crisp looks, to give her one of those smiles that was slowly dissolving her out of herself, out of her wifehood, back into her childhood, into the romantic and rapturous child she had been. She felt that Paul knew instinctively the kind of child, girl and woman she had been up till now—the kind of family life she had had, all about her, her secret thoughts were the most open things in nature to him. She was obsessed by him, but it was a kind of dream: and when the door closed on him, she rushed into Tom's arms with a quiet rapture. Standing there, thinking of Tom's goodness and their happiness, she found herself looking at the hall mirror.

'Tom,' she said slowly, 'who does Charteris remind you of?' Tom looked into the mirror too, 'Of someone,' he said thoughtfully.

'Of someone we know very well?' said Lydia, puzzled.

'Yes: someone we see often,' Tom continued.

'Tom,' Lydia continued in a low voice, 'look at me.'

'Yes,' her husband answered, after a scrutiny: 'you are right. He is so like you that you might be twins.'

She looked closer at the glass, 'All the time, I had an odd feeling that I had known him for many years. But it was only myself!' She laughed: and noticed on Tom's face a baffled expression.

It happened that soon after that Tom and Charteris began to work together on a textbook, and all their meetings were at some office in town. Lydia encouraged this and even refused to go with Tom: 'Why? I just sit there while you two gas.'

And again shortly after this, Tom got an appointment in another state, for two years. They returned to New York at the end of that time, on a Sunday evening and went straight to Broadway to see a movie in the 'stinkoes' along Forty-Second Street. At the corner of Broadway, Lydia saw Paul, looking very pale and untidy, and with a young woman.

'Why, there's . . .' she began.

But Paul hastily turned right about and crossed to the Times building. Lydia said 'Tom, there's Paul, there's Paul . . .' and dragged him with her. At the bus stop Paul, with a tired and almost frightened expression was standing, with a badly dressed and tired, but pretty girl who had also a timid expression.

'Hello Lydia,' he said so awkwardly, that she knew he had seen them and turned away purposely. She looked at the young woman with a friendly smile.

'This is Rosetta—Rosetta Myria,' he said.

The girl seemed glad that they were friendly.

'Let's go and have a drink,' proposed Lydia. She felt masterful, confident. She wondered why Paul had wanted to avoid them, but did not care. They went to one place after another and found them nearly all crowded. At last they found a 'tavern' that had booths and almost no-one there. They sat down and looked at the gallant frescoes, ordered wiener schnitzels and beer and Paul, very ill-at-ease, conscious of his dirty collar, untidy hair and greasy coat (the same as two years before) began cracking bad jokes. Rosetta and he had been to France since they had met, and in fact, this evening had only just got off the boat with only ten cents between them and had not even tipped the stewards. This made Tom feel very jolly and he urged them to eat and drink and lent them some money. Paul easily accepted the money, Rosetta looked relieved. Lydia invited them to come and see them and they accepted for the next Saturday. Paul put on a bold air as soon as he had eaten and told some broad jokes. He was always a frank fellow and tonight he seemed to want to appear as rollicking as they had known him before. What had happened to make him so blue?

Lydia looked at him curiously. 'This is the man I nearly lost my head over.' He certainly looked very like her, when she was looking tired and blue: his reactions were just the same, except that he was a man. When she felt 'scraggy' she tried to avoid people and then she tried to be bold, laugh it off, be vulgar. She looked at him feature by feature—he seemed miserable and ordinary, and yet very comprehensible and she was ready to defend him against the world, as one is a member of one's family. She was careful not to offend the girl Rosetta, by showing the affection she had for him. Paul sought her eye and her smile once or twice pitiably, without confidence.

She did not wait for the Saturday night and had no feeling against Rosetta. 'I don't want him,' she thought, 'and I'm glad he got someone to console him for his unhappy married life of the other year.' When Paul came, she spent the whole time talking to Rosetta. Rosetta was an agitator, conscientiously going from factory to factory where she was not blacklisted, organising the girls. Once or twice, she looked at Paul: Paul was not so talkative, he was letting Tom talk and, rather discouraged and tired was sitting back, stretched out in the comfortable armchair, with his eyes fixed strangely and quietly on Rosetta. 'He loves her,' thought Lydia. They gave her their address: she was to come and see them. 'He was never really mine,' thought Lydia.

A fortnight later, he rang up and asked if he could come at once to see them. When he came, an hour later, Lydia craning in the darkness of the passage, at the woman behind him, saw his wife. 'I am so glad you came, Mrs Charteris.'

The woman, plain, unhappy and tempestuous, looked round the flat. 'It's very small,' she said, 'and you can see the bedroom so plain.'

'It is,' said Lydia: 'we can't do a thing here.'

'It's hard to find,' complained the woman: 'I don't know how anyone finds you.'

'Oh,' said Lydia, 'we leave the lamp in the window, and then Paul was here before.'

'Yes,' the woman gave them all a bitter look: 'he was here before of course.'

Some other people came—among them, a friend of Paul's, a journalist equally brave and famous, and with him his wife, one of the most beautiful women alive, delicate, slant-eyed, porcelain-faced. Mrs Charteris and she discussed the Spanish and Chinese wars and Lydia, who knew nothing of them, worked on an embroidered bedspread she had begun years before. She had begun it superstitiously, 'She would not marry Tom till it was finished'—but she had married Tom long before. The three men talked: when she looked up she saw Paul, stretched out as before in the very same chair, looking as bitter as old age at his wife. When they went, they all heard them begin to argue bitterly immediately outside the window and down the lane.

Their new place was in the centre of the city, near Paul's place of work. Paul dropped in several times with a manuscript he wanted Tom's advice on, and once or twice he ate there before going home to his wife. They were very poor and lived a long way out of town: he did not get home till eight in the evening. Once Paul spoke of Rosetta 'Yes, I left her and went back to my wife: it's my own fault I suppose.' Rosetta? Lydia was sure she loved him. That evening, she noticed how seedy Paul was, how a little beer paunch was developing on him, and crows' feet round his eyes, although he was not much older than herself. The hard, discouraging and dissipated life was drying him.

He began to drop in. Once she spoke of some young poet she knew and lent him the book of poems: 'This one is splendid,' she said: 'it's his finest.' He took it unwillingly, but politely. Afterwards she repeated the poem to herself: a glorious but stirring and sensual poem. She felt ashamed and yet thought, 'He will understand I meant nothing by that.'

He came in one afternoon about two o'clock to return the book. It happened that Tom was off from work early that day and he was in the apartment. She answered the door and there stood Paul, tall, wind-flushed, with his curly dark hair and a certain timidity, 'I came to return to you your books.'

'Come in, Tom is here.'

'No, no.'

'Yes, he would love to see you.'

She forgot everything that had intervened: it was as if they stood there, meeting awkwardly in a doorway in the first flush of a love affair. He entered. A journalist was there who hated Paul Charteris, a political opponent: he instantly went out, crushing on his hat, scarcely muttering 'Hullo'.

Charteris looked surprised, gained his full manhood in a moment, but merely said, 'I don't think he likes me!'

He was amiable and full of ideas after all. He went promising to come soon. He came the next day, at four o'clock. No-one was there, but Lydia. She was nervous. She sat on the edge of the couch, with her whole body hidden behind an armchair, her arms and chin resting on it and began to talk. She could not stop herself talking. He listened, looked at her, in an alien way, never answered a word. She went on feverishly talking, in a high squeaky voice, as it seemed, that she detested. Suddenly, 'What is the use?' she thought and fell silent, and frowned. It was too bad of him not to answer at all. At the frown he jerked and began to talk—about himself, his brothers, his idea of writing a novel of his youth. When Tom came they were both relieved. Paul came the next day. She gave him liquor, which he liked very much. They talked about parties—she had given one which had fallen flat. 'Why?' he asked: 'give them rough liquor and beds to make love on, and no party falls flat.' He laughed tipsily. She was hurt. When Tom came home early, she was glad, and sat down in the deep armchair doing her bedspread. When he went Tom had some stories to tell. He had been talking to friends of Paul's. Paul was a heartbreaker, a Don Juan and so on: he had a new flame every five months and everyone was disgusted with him. Lydia excused him to herself, but she observed that Tom was capable of pinpricks. (And Tom had once said 'If another should love you, I'd be proud to know this lover: I would never stoop to jealousy.') A day rarely passed without Tom getting in a gentle hint about Paul's lovemaking, some little joke 'the ladykiller'. It ended by Lydia forgiving Paul entirely in her heart: 'So he is, and I love him for what he is.' She didn't know when she began speaking thus of the tender feeling she had for the erring Paul.

Paul began to drop in every day. When he went one day, she would say, 'Come tomorrow if you can, Paul: Tom will be home about five.' Paul would always come at the time mentioned and have wine or cocktails. He liked drink and Lydia always had it for him now. Tom was always there and there would be a long session of political discussion. Lydia would say nothing—just do her work and look at them both. Winter was approaching and the evenings drew in soon: in the semi-darkness Paul sat, with his legs stretched out, resting back, with a fatigued look in the deep armchair. Sometimes answering Tom and sometimes letting his inspiration flow. When he answered him, it was always pungently, with a personal philosophy. Paul had studied a long time abroad, and was an original. Lydia watched them and in these few evenings, the tender and familiar feeling she had for Paul, changed: she fell in love with him. When the lamp was lighted, he shaded his fine almond shaped eyes and listened still. At first he came two or three times a week, then every day. When they were out of liquor, she left them talking and ran out to get it. The cloak hooks stood in view of the chair he always sat in. Neither of the men made a move to go out and get the things. As she got into her things, she could look in and see Paul stretched out there: whenever he saw her he would turn and give her that melting smile of his and she would smile back from the depths of her heart, a smile that was the fulfilment of romantic love almost, something dreamed about in poetic youth. And so when she came back. Tom saw little or nothing of this, which was the only interchange they made all day, except when she asked him a question 'A little more port? Another glass of beer?' He never refused. One day, when she was going out, Tom asked her to go up the street and get some carbon paper too. Paul, at this, gave her a quaint tender smile, one of those he was a past master in. She was as happy as a schoolgirl to whom a professor has smiled in the street. Her heart beat fast and cheerfully going along the lane. She got into the street in a high state of mind. In the shop waiting for the boy to wrap up the carbon paper, a dark storm rushed on her, and for a few seconds, everything in the room whirled round in a glorious delirium: the dark wind rushed on, but left, where had only been a joyful excitement, the surge of adult passion. This was not like her earlier crushes with their blind rages and aches: she had been living happily with a man for a long time and she knew what happy passion was, and this that was left with her now was the night-darkened heavenly garden of love. She desired, with every sense, Paul of the tender smile and understanding heart: and joy rushed over her too, 'I thought I would never feel it again, and God be praised I am madly in love: what splendid joy.' She went back soberly, but like someone to whom glorious tidings have been announced in the street. 'I have won the lottery, yes, really,' she thought. She hastened out of her coat and hat, did not look at any of them when she came in, but began pulling corks and so on.

When she came in to give him his drink, Paul was saying, 'Yes, I'm going to China again and I'm never coming back this time: what have I to stay here for?'

No-one tried to dissuade him: that was his business, and everyone felt it was his fate. He was not happy here: the reconciliation with his wife was a torment for both: stories were being whispered about his affairs and people were turning against him for no good reason, chiefly because of his wife's unhappiness. But it was a long way off. Lydia saw him as always to the door and asked him to come again tomorrow, 'Tom will be home at five.' 'All right,' he said, in his sweet manner.

When he came the next day, she had been through hours of desire— the first time she had ever waited for him to come, or deeply desired it. He sat there this time, in the lamplight of the early fallen day very silent, hardly saying a word, and she kept looking at him, quietly, little glances that no-one could notice.

'How is it possible,' she thought 'that I am so madly in love with this man I've seen so often, and who is after all, like me, if rather handsomer and sweeter?' She began to look at him, 'Is it the mouth? Is it the eyes?' She found that each item gave her a pang and that in fact, it was each item that she had not, and then had, fallen in love with. She went out silently, unnoticed by the others and looked at herself in the mirror in the bathroom—pulling her eyes up and down, trying to get the sweet expression Paul got so easily. Her smile did not seem much like his: but in her happiness thinking about him, she caught herself looking rather like him when he smiled. This made it nearly all pure joy. She came back and stole fresh glances at him—she began to notice the parts of his body. He seemed so potent, full of manly strength that she felt like fainting: she seemed to get a little delirious although she had not drunk very much, and began to think that he was all honey, all roses, and so on. She found that she had moments of absence, when she heard nothing of what was going on, but only heard beautiful words about him, 'His limbs gather passion as the bees honey and I am the hive . . .' Her feeling this evening was so powerful that she could not believe he did not feel it, that Tom did not feel it, it seemed to have thickened and made fluid the air. He said very little, shading his eyes with his hands and looking through them, while Tom went on about Ethiopia.

When she saw him to the door that evening in the usual polite and indifferent fashion, she thought suddenly 'Oh, if I could only walk in the street with him a few minutes.' The moment of greatest joy had passed and she was already beginning to feel the pains and aches of desires, but very much more powerful than before because of her marriage, and almost uncontrollable, as convulsions or childbirth are a giant revolutionary spasm. She thought at once, 'I must not see him again.' She had to control her thought and face during the evening with Tom and have his caresses from which she had never once turned away, but all the time she was realising with more plainness the gulf of passion and drama on which she stood. 'Another moment,' she acknowledged 'and I would have walked out into the street with him, without a hat or coat, without a penny or in my slippers: and it wouldn't have mattered how long the street was— even if it was as long as the country—that's how I felt. If he had asked me, would I have had the heart to refuse? I would follow him barefoot: I would not have the heart to refuse him.' She never had the smallest idea of leaving Tom nor of hurting him, and she loved Tom deeply and wholesomely. She then realised that she was in danger, and thought 'I must never see him again.' She began to think how she could manage this without arousing Tom's suspicions or Paul's. She could be absent, once or twice—but not more than that. 'What am I to do?' The conflict had begun: it was not a conflict between one man and another, for her relations to each of them had never changed from the beginning, she loved one because of their marriage and the chances of their coming together, but in Paul was some secret command from her own destiny, he was destiny, and they both knew it. In his wilful wayward and incon- siderate way, if he cared to ask her to do something (he would plead, with an appearance of weakness), she would do it without a second's thought: it was foretold from the earth's youth that she would meet him. She was his equal, she knew her own powers, she knew she was like him, she did not grovel before him, she knew his nature without any blindness and the things she thought of obeying him in were—following him in his many wanderings more than anything else, for as to the result of desire, she knew that he was made this way—he adored love for its own sake and if she mentioned her love to him he would love her, for the sake of love. So there was no unhappy crushed desire in her feeling, only this singular feeling of destiny which came upon her with a sure ferocity. It was the strangest and most perfect of loves. 'O, Gods,' she kept thinking 'I have known it: this is it, perfect, spotless, boundless love: how lucky I am.' To her he seemed the most imperfect of mortals, with a godlike power over her. And naturally, when she realised this, she knew she could never see him again. She feared him.

The next morning he telephoned to say that he had an immediate assignment to go to China and that once there he would never return: he would die there. These were his strange words. 'I have nothing to live for here nor there,' he said.

He could only come twice before he went, because he had so much to do. He came for one or two hurried visits then and the whole time was taken up by the journalist who was politically his opponent and who almost lived with Tom and Lydia, in the hope of gibing at Paul before he went out. They had no last moments with him at all. He went on a Monday night.

Lydia felt little that night: 'He has gone—well, fate's relieved me of him.'

The next morning she was so deeply in love with him that she could do nothing. Tom went to work and instead of starting her work herself, she pulled down the blinds and thought about her lost love, about his face, limbs and sexual beauty, his charming smile and tenderness: it was as if a smouldering fire had been poured into her flesh and she had no bones or sinews. She could do nothing, eaten up with tenderness and cruel desire. About twelve she roused herself and put on her hat to go and buy some envelopes, thinking 'Why does this happen when he's gone?' when the doorbell rang and she opened it to see Paul standing there. She took two steps forward and murmured in a low voice 'I thought you had gone.'

'It's put off till Saturday,' he said.

He came in and talked in a low, inconsequential way, almost in a low fever, of various things, but had not been there more than ten minutes when the talkative journalist, who was his political enemy, rang up and said he would be over.

'Shall I put him off?' asked Lydia, her hand over the receiver.

'He doesn't like me,' said Paul.

But she could think of no reason for putting him off: he only wanted to come over for a cup of coffee and a chat. She said, 'Paul Charteris is here.'

'Well, I won't come then' said the journalist nastily. 'You don't want me if that red is there.'

'Don't be silly, Edgar.'

'No, I won't come,' said the journalist in a pet.

'All right.'

The journalist suddenly relented: he couldn't pass up his gossip. 'Well, if you want me?'

There was no way to put him off decently. He arrived and began a sharp discussion with Paul and after that, in came Tom again, not working in the afternoon. It was really odd that, at whatever time Paul came, they could never have a minute alone. And yet she had nothing to talk to him about: she hadn't the faintest idea what she would talk to him about if she had no interruptions. She had got so used to Tom taking up every conversation and engaging everyone's attentions, that she had got out of the way of rousing herself. Perhaps Paul thought she did not care for him.

Paul came every day that week, although he was very busy—and always at different times, just when he was free, but every day that week the gossipy and touchy Edgar was there too, and every day that week also Tom was home incredibly early from work—in fact, one day he did not go at all. He liked Paul and he wanted to see him as often as he could before he went away for ever.

'It's unlikely I'll ever get to China to see you,' he told Paul.

'Oh, I'll die there this year,' said Paul, rather bitterly.

'You won't.'

'Why not? Yes, I will.'

Lydia said nothing, sitting there wondering about him. Why was he going? Why did he want to die? Why did he come so often? She knew he was going and so she quietly gave herself up to contemplation of him: she would never see him again. No-one noticed anything. When he came to see them for the last time, Edgar was still there. Paul said nothing the whole evening but let Edgar rail against him and his cause and the Chinese: Paul sat with his face covered with his hand and drank everything he was given. Lydia drank a lot too: whenever she gave Paul a drink, she drank too. Tom was not much of a drinker and Edgar preferred to talk and was slow getting through his drinks. She felt herself presently very drunk, but very cool too. Paul stayed as long as he could but presently had to go home to have his last meal with his wife. Everyone offered him gifts—a pair of fur-lined gloves, socks, marching boots, a fountain pen and the like, but he turned them all down but the boots and gloves.

Edgar relented at the last moment and offered the gloves. He had always said that that rat would never go off to China and now he saw him going he felt ashamed but he still said, 'He'll only sit in Hong Kong or Canton in a cosy café and send home despatches, he'll never fight.' Paul said nothing to all this. It was very strange. Lydia knew why Edgar was so biting—he was jealous that they had become so friendly with Paul: he wanted to be their bosom friend alone, himself. That was why he had been there every day that week—to be sure that she and Tom didn't get sessions alone with Paul and to find out what Paul had to say that interested them so.

Presently Paul got up to go, got his hat, and everyone said 'Goodbye and good luck.' Paul was to meet Tom on the next day to get the measurement of the boots and the gloves, but this was the last time he would call. Lydia was very jolly, took him to the door, then decided to go out to the lane with him. Paul was silent, surprised that she went to the lane with him. He was surprised that she had drunk so much. At the lane she stopped, 'Well, goodbye, Paul.'

'Goodbye,' he said indifferently. She held out her hand and he took it, when suddenly she grasped his hand in both hers and pressed it hotly. He lifted his face with an expression of great surprise and smiled in delight: he searched her face and waited for what she would say.

'I'll go with you.'

'Will you?'

'I haven't got the money yet.'

'Can you get it?'

'I don't know. No.'

'No,' he said shaking his head.

'Well, goodbye, anyhow.'

'Goodbye,' he said smiling. He went off and she ran up the stairs.

It had only taken a minute and a murmur and no-one would notice her absence. Tom was rattling away, but Edgar laughed and said, 'Here comes Lydia all excited.' Jealousy makes him say that, that's all, she thought: he's so glad Paul has gone. Heaven above, she thought, I actually said I'd go with him: I nearly walked out into the street after him. I must be careful she thought: I could never never let Tom down, never. But I forget everything in the world beside the imperative Paul. She got their dinner ready and no-one remarked anything. Paul had gone, but she was not sorry, she was inflated, ecstatic. Paul knew she loved him now. What a cool customer, she thought smiling to herself. She would have been ashamed to let any other man know she loved him, but not Paul. To Paul love was an autonomous thing with its own rule, the creator of life; he admired it for its own sake. A man able to get women from other men by sleight of hand, without struggle.

But Paul did not keep his appointment with Tom the next day. Instead he came early and to lunch. For lunch they had a visitor, a young boy who hero-worshipped Paul and who would not take their hints that they wanted to see Paul alone at the last minute. He wanted to see the famous Captain Charteris himself, especially as he was leaving for China. He stayed through lunch and after lunch: and only after a painful silence on everyone's part did he take the hint and go. It was then late, within five minutes Charteris himself was leaving. The men put on their hats to go and buy the boots and then Lydia noticed that Tom came into the passage looking rather pale and startled.

'He wonders if I am going to kiss Paul goodbye,' she understood by this. She was too rollicking with Paul and it was not a farewell at all. Tom stood at the door staring at them both, still with that startled look. She tried to think of something to ask him to do so that he would leave them for a moment, but she could think of nothing rational. 'Goodbye, Paul.'

'I'll try to come back for a moment later,' said Paul gently.

She was so surprised that she answered stiffly 'Oh?'

Paul was discomforted, 'I don't know if I'll have time.'

'No, no,' she said: 'no, no, you'll be busy...'

She was worried by the staring pale face of Tom, minutely observing the two of them.

'And so goodbye.'

'Goodbye.'

Paul hesitated again, worried, 'And you do my work for me.'

'I can't do that.'

'Try, Lydie.'

'Until you come back.'

'Oh, I don't think I'll come back.'

He was gone. She was so astonished by everything that she could not collect her wits. What did it mean? She saw in an instant that she had never really understood him, how clever he was.

It was a long time till Tom came back, and she thought, 'He will come back from China of course, and by then we must be out of the way: I must never see him again.' For the conflict had arisen now between the two men. The angelic, patient and deserving Tom who had been faithful to her for ten years was there, and also the undeserving but imperative Paul. Who would win? She envisaged all the consequences of going with Paul. She and Paul were too close to have any great surprises for each other — there might simply be the amusement of being with your twin for a while: after a while, Paul would have another flame — and she would get angry with him, she was sure — his dilatoriness, his flames, even his beer parties and his little paunch, which had disappeared at present, but would come back when he returned to ordinary life. Also she could sense that Paul had given up most of his ambition and hope in life: while she had not, she was still mad with it and she hoped always would be. She would make Paul laugh and Paul would seem dull to her. 'It would never work,' she thought 'and I would hurt Tom forever and for no good reason.' But she knew that if Paul said in his yearning and understanding way, 'Come to me,' she would find it hard, perhaps impossible to resist him. 'That's the end,' she said: 'if he comes back twice as large as life, I will never see him again.'

She was so resolved, that she did not miss Paul, and never thought of writing to him, although she knew other people were—Anna Brown and all the friends he had worked with in causes. Why? She and Paul understood each other: that was all there was to their friendship. It would always be so. She regretted that she had not known Paul's love, that would have been she was sure the revelation of love: and she bitterly regretted not having in her body a child of this dear and intimate man: that was what she really wanted of him, a child of him, a child like him, a child to be her perfect joy for ever, of which he would be the distant father. She wanted to love him but not live with him. She felt that she had already been married to him and lived with him for years. But with Tom, life was a constant excitement and pleasure: she felt she had only lived with Tom a few weeks, even after all this time.

Three months later, they had a telephone call late at night, telling them that Paul had been killed in action. She said nothing, a feverish activity began in her soul, she began to lament like a woman in a Greek play, in long rhythmic phrases: her heart began to slowly weave Paul's funeral dance and in her ears rang long phrases of lament. When the light was turned out, she lay in bed with Tom seeing night for the first time.

'How dark it is when the lamp is turned out,' she said. Tom listened and after a moment asked 'What do you mean by that?'

'I never noticed before.'

At that moment the church bell began to strike the hour.

'Listen to them ringing,' she said: 'Why do they ring for the hours that are gone: all the ages that are dead and they still ring the hours: it's so little—such a little sound in the night. Even the dead hour just past doesn't hear it: the people dead the past hour don't hear it and what do we care? We live tomorrow—not an hour or two, but endless days of life.'

'Lydie?' he asked in a small voice, curiously.

'Oh, Tom, let's leave here. What is there here? I don't like it.'

'Why do you say that?'

'I don't know. My heart isn't in it here.'

He was silent. She realised what he might take this to mean and hastened to talk a lot about their circumstances. Meanwhile she was realising what it had all meant that she had said, and that Tom perhaps guessed too—she turned away from his affectionate hands. A light from another window fell on the pillow: it was a fine pale yellow light. Among the words in her ears, she heard ones she recognised, 'Oh, Jonathan, Oh my brother Jonathan—very pleasant was thy life unto me, . . .' The words went on repeating themselves. Suddenly a great sob shook her and she began to cry uncontrollably.

'Lydie, Lydie,' said the good Tom, 'Lydie what is it?'

'I never knew anyone who died before. I'm so silly, it's just new to me,' she said.

But she spent three days in uncontrollable sorrow, in tides of regrets that came and went: Tom could not help knowing that it was more than shock and he became angry on the third evening. On the third night he made love to her and she who had never refused him in her life didn't dare refuse him now.

Tom began to talk to everyone cheerfully about Paul saying 'Yes, I knew him, he was a great friend of mine,' and 'The last time I saw Paul he hardly listened to what I was saying: I guess his mind was on some girl: he was a great lover of the ladies,' and 'Oh, yes, I knew Paul intimately, I collaborated with him, but Lydie knew him even better than I did.' After a little while, this seemed very comic to Lydia, and whenever they began to talk about Paul's death and Tom said this, 'Yes, we were very close to him just before his death but Lydie knew him better than me, didn't you Lydie?' she would say 'Yes,' and begin to laugh. Everyone always looked astonished, but Tom's little gag continued to strike her as very funny. Meanwhile for quite a long time, perhaps two years or three, she knew that if the choice had been between lying in his Chinese grave with Paul or living her happy, unclouded and fertile life with Tom, she would have taken a long time to choose and what would have been the choice?

Paul had said 'Do my work for me,' but no-one can do another's work for him and who cares to? We only want to do our own work. She thought, though, 'I will work till I do a very fine piece of work—that will be in memory of Paul although no-one will know it (and it's better that they don't, they'd laugh at both of us, the three of us)—and then I won't mind what happens.'

And whenever she went out into company, she dressed very carefully, tried her hair various ways, wondered if tonight, or next week, she would meet the other Paul that the contemporary world probably held.

ALAN MARSHALL

Trees Can Speak

I heard footsteps and I looked up. A man carrying a prospector's dish was clambering down the bank.

'This man never speaks,' the store-keeper in the town three miles away had told me. 'A few people have heard him say one word like "Hullo" or something. He makes himself understood by shaking or nodding his head.'

'Is there something wrong with him?' I asked.

'No. He can talk if he wants to. Silent Joe, they call him.'

When the man reached a spot where the creek widened into a pool he squatted on his heels and scooped some water into the dish. He stood up and, bending over the dish, began to wash the dirt it contained by swinging it in a circular motion.

I lifted my crutches from the ground and hopped along the pebbles till I stood opposite him across the pool.

'Good day,' I said. 'Great day.'

He raised his head and looked at me. His eyes were grey, the greenish grey of the bush. There was no hostility in his look, just a searching.

They suddenly changed their expression and said, as plainly as if he had spoken, 'Yes.'

I sat down and watched him. He poured the muddy water into the clear pool.

It rolled along the sandy bottom, twisting and turning in whorls and convolutions until it faded into a faint cloud, moving swiftly with the current.

He washed the residue many times.

I crossed over above the pool and walked down to him.

'Get anything?'

He held the dish towards me and pointed to three specks of gold resting on the outer edge of a layer of sand.

'So that's gold,' I said. 'Three specks, eh! Half the troubles of this world come from collections of specks like those.'

He smiled. It took a long time to develop. It moved over his face slowly and somehow I thought of an egret in flight, as if wings had come and gone.

He looked at me with kindliness and, for a moment, I saw the bush, not remote and pitying, but beckoning like a friend. He was akin to trees and they spoke through him.

If I could only understand him I would understand the bush, I thought.

But he turned away and, like the gums, was remote again, removed from contact by his silence which was not the silence of absent speech, but the eloquent silence of trees.

'I am coming with you,' I said.

We walked side by side. He studied the track for my benefit. He kicked limbs aside, broke the branches of wattles drooping over the path that skirted the foot of the hill.

We moved into thicker timber. The sun pierced the canopy of branches and spangled our shoulders with leaf patterns. A cool, leaf-mould breath of earth rose from the foot-printed moss. The track dipped sharply down into a gully and ended in a small clearing.

Thin grass, spent with seeding, quivered hopelessly in a circle of trees.

In the centre of the clearing a mound of yellow clay rose from around the brink of a shaft. A windlass, erected on top of the mound, spanned the opening.

A heavy iron bucket dangled from the roller.

'So this is your mine!' I said.

He nodded, looking at it with a pleased expression.

I climbed to the top of the mound and peered down into darkness. A movement of air, dank with the moisture from buried rocks and clay, welled up and broke coldly on my face. I pushed a small stone over the edge. It flashed silently from sight, speeding through a narrow darkness for a tense gap of time, then rang an ending from somewhere deep down in the earth.

'Cripes, that's deep!' I exclaimed.

He was standing beside me, pleased that I was impressed.

'Do you go down that ladder?' I asked. I pointed to a ladder of lashed saplings that was wired to a facing of timber.

He nodded.

'I can climb ladders,' I murmured, wondering how I could get down, 'but not that one.'

He looked at me questioningly, a sympathetic concern shading his face.

'Infantile paralysis,' I explained. 'It's a nuisance sometimes. Do you think you could lower me down in that bucket? I want to see the reef where you get the gold.'

I expected him to demur. It would be the natural reaction. I expected him to shake his head in an expressive communication of the danger involved.

But he didn't hesitate. He reached out across the shaft and drew the bucket to the edge. I placed my crutches on the ground and straddled it so that my legs hung down the sides and the handle lay between my knees. I grasped the rope and said, 'Righto,' then added, 'You're coming down the ladder, aren't you?'

He nodded and caught hold of the bucket handle. He lifted and I was swung out over the shaft. The bucket slowly revolved, then stopped and began a reversing movement. He grasped the windlass, removed a chock. I saw him brace himself against the strain. His powerful arms worked slowly like crank-shafts. I sank into the cold air that smelt of frogs.

'What the hell did I come down here for?' I thought. 'This is a damn silly thing to do.'

The bucket twisted slowly. A spiralling succession of jutting rock and layers of clay passed my eyes. I suddenly bumped the side. The shaft took a turn and continued down at an angle so that the opening was eclipsed and I was alone.

I pushed against the side to save my legs from being scraped against rocks. The bucket grated downwards, sending a cascade of clay slithering before it, then stopped.

A heavy darkness pressed against me. I reached down and touched the floor of the shaft. I slid off the bucket and sat down on the ground beside it.

In a little while I heard the creak of a ladder. Gravel and small stones pattered beside me. I was conscious of someone near me in the dark, then a match flared and he lit a candle. A yellow stiletto of flame rose towards his face, then shrank back to the drooping wick. He sheltered it with his hand till the wax melted and the shadows moved away to a tunnel that branched from the foot of the shaft.

'I'm a fool,' I said. 'I didn't bring my crutches.'

He looked at me speculatively while candle shadows fluttered upon his face like moths. His expression changed to one of decision and I answered the unspoken intention as if it had been conveyed to me in words.

'Thanks very much. I'm not heavy.'

He bent down and lifted me to his back. Beneath his faded blue shirt I could feel his shoulder muscles bunch then slip into movement.

He crouched low as he walked so that my head would not strike the rocks projecting from the roof of the tunnel. I rose and fell to each firm step.

The light from the candle moved ahead of us, cleansing the tunnel of darkness.

At the end of the drive he stopped and lowered me gently to the ground.

He held the candle close to the face and pointed a heavy finger at the narrow reef which formed a diagonal scar across the rock.

'So that's it!' I exclaimed.

I tried to break a piece out with my fingers. He lifted a small bar from the ground and drove it into the vein. I picked up some shattered pieces and searched them in the light of the candle. He bent his head near mine and watched the stone I was turning in my fingers. He suddenly reached out his hand and took it away. He licked it then smiled and held it towards me. With his thumb he indicated a speck of gold adhering to the surface.

I was excited at the find. I asked him many questions. He sat with his hands clasped around his drawn-up knees and answered with eloquent expressions and shakes of the head.

The candle flame began to flutter in a scooped stub of wax.

'I think it's time we left,' I said.

He rose and carried me back to the foot of the shaft, I tied my knees together with string and placed my legs in the bucket this time. I had no control over the right leg, which fell helplessly to one side if not bound to its stronger neighbour. I sat on the edge of the bucket clasping the windlass rope and waited. The candle welled into sudden brightness then fluttered and died. I could hear the creaks of the tortured ladder, then silence.

In all the world only I was alive. The darkness had texture and weight like a blanket of black. The silence had no expectancy. I sat brooding sombrely, drained of all sunlight and song. The world of birds and trees and laughter was as remote as a star.

Without reason, seemingly without object, I suddenly began to rise like a bubble. I swung in emptiness; I moved in a void, governed by planetary laws over which I had no control.

Then I crashed against the side and the lip of the bucket tipped as it caught in projecting tongues of stone. The bottom moved up and out then slumped heavily downwards as the edge broke free.

I scraped and bounced upwards till I emerged from a sediment of darkness into a growing light. Above my head the mouth of the shaft increased in size.

I suddenly burst into dazzling sunlight. An arm reached out; a hand grasped the handle of the bucket. There was a lift and I felt the solidity of earth beneath me. It was good to stand on something that didn't move, to feel sun on your face.

He stood watching me, his outstretched arm bridging him to a grey box-tree that seemed strangely like himself.

I thanked him then sat down on the rubble for a yarn. I told him about myself and something about the people I had met. He listened without moving, but I felt the power of his interest drawing words from me as dry earth absorbs water.

'Goodbye,' I said before I left him, and I shook his hand.

I went away, but before I reached the trees I turned and waved to him.

He was still standing against the grey box like a kindred tree, but he straightened quickly and waved in return.

'Goodbye,' he called, and it was as if a tree had spoken.

JUDAH WATEN

Mother

When I was a small boy I was often morbidly conscious of Mother's intent, searching eyes fixed on me. She would gaze for minutes on end without speaking one word. I was always disconcerted and would guiltily look down at the ground, anxiously turning over in my mind my day's activities.

But very early I knew her thoughts were far away from my petty doings; she was concerned with them only in so far as they gave her further reason to justify her hostility to the life around us. She was preoccupied with my sister and me; she was for ever concerned with our future in this new land in which she would always feel a stranger.

I gave her little comfort, for though we had been in the country for only a short while I had assumed many of the ways of those around me. I had become estranged from her. Or so it seemed to Mother, and it grieved her.

When I first knew her she had no intimate friend, nor do I think she felt the need of one with whom she could discuss her innermost thoughts and hopes. With me, though I knew she loved me very deeply, she was never on such near terms of friendship as sometimes exist between a mother and son. She emanated a kind of certainty in herself, in her view of life, that no opposition or human difficulty could shrivel or destroy. 'Be strong before people, only weep before God,' she would say and she lived up to that precept even with Father.

In our little community in the city, acquaintances spoke derisively of Mother's refusal to settle down as others had done, of what they called her propensity for highfalutin day-dreams and of the severity and un-reasonableness of her opinions.

Yet her manner with people was always gentle. She spoke softly, she was measured in gesture, and frequently it seemed she was functioning automatically, her mind far away from her body. There was a grave beauty in her still, sad face, her searching, dark-brown eyes and black hair. She was thin and stooped in carriage as though a weight always lay on her shoulders.

From my earliest memory of Mother it somehow seemed quite natural to think of her as apart and other-worldly and different, not of everyday things as Father was. In those days he was a young-looking man who did not hesitate to make friends with children as soon as they were able to talk to him and laugh at his stories. Mother was older than he was. She must have been a woman of nearly forty, but she seemed even older. She changed little for a long time, showing no traces of growing older at all until, towards the end of her life, she suddenly became an old lady.

I was always curious about Mother's age. She never had birthdays like other people, nor did anyone else in our family. No candles were ever lit or cakes baked or presents given in our house. To my friends in the street who boasted of their birthday parties I self-consciously repeated my Mother's words, that such celebrations were only a foolish and eccentric form of self-worship.

'Nothing but deception,' she would say. 'As though life can be chopped into neat twelve-month parcels! It's deeds, not years, that matter.'

Although I often repeated her words and even prided myself on not having birthdays I could not restrain myself from once asking Mother when she was born.

'I was born. I'm alive as you can see, so what more do you want to know?' she replied, so sharply that I never asked her about her age again.

In so many other ways Mother was different. Whereas all the rest of the women I knew in the neighbouring houses and in other parts of the city took pride in their housewifely abilities, their odds and ends of new furniture, the neat appearance of their homes, Mother regarded all those things as of little importance. Our house always looked as if we had just moved in or were about to move out. An impermanent and impatient spirit dwelt within our walls; Father called it living on one leg like a bird.

Wherever we lived there were some cases partly unpacked, rolls of linoleum stood in a corner, only some of the windows had curtains. There were never sufficient wardrobes, so that clothes hung on hooks behind doors. And all the time Mother's things accumulated. She never parted with anything, no matter how old it was. A shabby green plush coat bequeathed to her by her own mother hung on a nail in her bedroom. Untidy heaps of tattered books, newspapers, and journals from the old country mouldered in corners of the house, while under her bed in tin trunks she kept her dearest possessions. In those trunks there were bundles of old letters, two heavily underlined books on nursing, an old Hebrew Bible, three silver spoons given her by an aunt with whom she had once lived, a diploma on yellow parchment, and her collection of favourite books.

From one or other of her trunks she would frequently pick a book and read to my sister and me. She would read in a wistful voice poems and stories of Jewish liberators from Moses until the present day, of the heroes of the 1905 Revolution and pieces by Tolstoy and Gorki and Sholom Aleichem. Never did she stop to inquire whether we understood what she was reading; she said we should understand later if not now.

I liked to hear Mother read, but always she seemed to choose a time for reading that clashed with something or other I was doing in the street or in a near-by paddock. I would be playing with the boys in the street,

kicking a football or spinning a top or flying a kite, when Mother would
unexpectedly appear and without even casting a glance at my companions
she would ask me to come into the house, saying she wanted to read to
me and my sister. Sometimes I was overcome with humiliation and I
would stand listlessly with burning cheeks until she repeated her words.
She never reproached me for my disobedience nor did she ever utter a
reproof to the boys who taunted me as, crestfallen, I followed her into the
house.

Why Mother was as she was only came to me many years later. Then
I was even able to guess when she was born.

She was the last child of a frail and overworked mother and a bleakly
pious father who hawked reels of cotton and other odds and ends in the
villages surrounding a town in Russia. My grandfather looked with great
disapproval on his offspring, who were all girls, and he was hardly aware
of my mother at all. She was left well alone by her older sisters, who with
feverish impatience were waiting for their parents to make the required
arrangements for their marriages.

During those early days Mother rarely looked out into the streets, for
since the great pogroms few Jewish children were ever to be seen abroad.
From the iron grille of the basement she saw the soles of the shoes of the
passers-by and not very much more. She had never seen a tree, a flower,
or a bird.

But when Mother was about fifteen her parents died and she went to
live with a widowed aunt and her large family in a far-away village. Her
aunt kept an inn and Mother was tucked away with her cousins in a
remote part of the building, away from the prying eyes of the customers
in the tap-rooms. Every evening her aunt would gaze at her with startled
eyes as if surprised to find her among the family.

'What am I going to do with you?' she would say. 'I've got daughters
of my own. If only your dear father of blessed name had left you just a tiny
dowry it would have been such a help. Ah well! If you have no hand you
can't make a fist.'

At that time Mother could neither read nor write. And as she had
never had any childhood playmates or friends of any kind she hardly knew
what to talk about with her cousins. She spent the days cheerlessly
pottering about the kitchen or sitting for hours, her eyes fixed on the dark
wall in front of her.

Some visitor to the house, observing the small, lonely girl, took pity
on her and decided to give her an education. Mother was given lessons
every few days and after a while she acquired a smattering of Yiddish and
Russian, a little arithmetic, and a great fund of Russian and Jewish stories.

New worlds gradually opened before Mother. She was seized with a
passion for primers, grammars, arithmetic and story books, and soon the
idea entered her head that the way out of her present dreary life lay

through these books. There was another world, full of warmth and interesting things, and in it there was surely a place for her. She became obsessed with the thought that it wanted only some decisive step on her part to go beyond her aunt's house into the life she dreamed about.

Somewhere she read of a Jewish hospital which had just opened in a distant city and one winter's night she told her aunt she wanted to go to relatives who lived there. They would help her to find work in the hospital.

'You are mad!' exclaimed her aunt. 'Forsake a home for a wild fancy! Who could have put such a notion into your head? Besides, a girl of eighteen can't travel alone at this time of the year.'

It was from that moment that Mother's age became something to be manipulated as it suited her. She said to her aunt that she was not eighteen, but twenty-two. She was getting up in years and she could not continue to impose on her aunt's kindness.

'How can you be twenty-two?' her aunt replied greatly puzzled.

A long pause ensued while she tried to reckon up Mother's years. She was born in the month Tammuz according to the Jewish calendar, which corresponded to the old-style Russian calendar month of June, but in what year? She could remember being told of Mother's birth, but nothing outstanding had happened then to enable her to place the year. With all her nieces and nephews, some dead and many alive, scattered all over the vastness of the country only a genius could keep track of all their birthdays. Perhaps the girl was twenty-two, and if that were so her chance of getting a husband in the village was pretty remote; twenty-two was far too old. The thought entered her head that if she allowed Mother to go to their kinsmen in the city she would be relieved of the responsibility of finding a dowry for her, and so reluctantly she agreed.

But it was not until the spring that she finally consented to let her niece go. As the railway station was several miles from the village Mother was escorted there on foot by her aunt and cousins. With all her possessions, including photographs of her parents and a tattered Russian primer tied in a great bundle, Mother went forth into the vast world.

In the hospital she didn't find that for which she hungered; it seemed still as far away as in the village. She had dreamed of the new life where all would be noble, where men and women would dedicate their lives to bringing about a richer and happier life, just as she had read.

But she was put to scrubbing floors and washing linen every day from morning till night until she dropped exhausted into her bed in the attic. No one looked at her, no one spoke to her but to give her orders. Her one day off in the month she spent with her relatives who gave her some cast-off clothes and shoes and provided her with the books on nursing she so urgently needed. She was more than ever convinced that her deliverance would come through these books and she set about swallow-ing their contents with renewed zest.

As soon as she had passed all the examinations and acquired the treasured diploma she joined a medical mission that was about to proceed without a moment's delay to a distant region where a cholera epidemic raged. And then for several years she remained with the same group, moving from district to district, wherever disease flourished.

Whenever Mother looked back over her life it was those years that shone out. Then she was with people who were filled with an ardour for mankind and it seemed to her they lived happily and freely, giving and taking friendship in an atmosphere pulsating with warmth and hope.

All this had come to an end in 1905 when the medical mission was dissolved and several of Mother's colleagues were killed in the uprising. Then with a heavy heart and little choice she had returned to nursing in the city, but this time in private houses attending on well-to-do ladies.

It was at the home of one of her patients that she met Father. What an odd couple they must have been! She was taciturn, choosing her words carefully, talking mainly of her ideas and little about herself. Father bared his heart with guileless abandon. He rarely had secrets and there was no division in his mind between intimate and general matters. He could talk as freely of his feelings for Mother or of a quarrel with his father as he could of a vaudeville show or the superiority of one game of cards as against another.

Father said of himself he was like an open hand at solo and all men were his brothers. For a story, a joke, or an apt remark he would forsake his father and mother, as the saying goes. Old tales, new ones invented for the occasion, jokes rolled off his tongue in a never-ending procession. Every trifle, every incident was material for a story and he haunted music-halls and circuses, for he liked nothing better than comedians and clowns, actors and buskers.

He brought something bubbly and frivolous into Mother's life and for a while she forgot her stern precepts. In those days Father's clothes were smart and gay; he wore bright straw hats and loud socks and fancy, buttoned-up boots. Although she had always regarded any interest in clothes as foolish and a sign of an empty and frivolous nature Mother then felt proud of his fashionable appearance. He took her to his favourite resorts, to music-halls and to tea-houses where he and his cronies idled away hours, boastfully recounting stories of successes in business or merely swapping jokes. They danced nights away, though Mother was almost stupefied by the band and the bright lights and looked with distaste on the extravagant clothes of the dancers who bobbed and cavorted.

All this was in the early days of their marriage. But soon Mother was filled with misgivings. Father's world, the world of commerce and speculation, of the buying and selling of goods neither seen nor touched, was repugnant and frightening to her. It lacked stability, it was devoid of ideals, it was fraught with ruin. Father was a trader in air, as the saying went.

Mother's anxiety grew as she observed more closely his mode of life. He worked in fits and starts. If he made enough in one hour to last him a week or a month his business was at an end and he went off in search of friends and pleasure. He would return to business only when his money had just about run out. He was concerned only with one day at a time; about tomorrow he would say, clicking his fingers, his blue eyes focused mellowly on space, 'We'll see.'

But always he had plans for making great fortunes. They never came to anything but frequently they produced unexpected results. It so happened that on a number of occasions someone Father trusted acted on the plans he had talked about so freely before he even had time to leave the tea-house. Then there were fiery scenes with his faithless friends. But Father's rage passed away quickly and he would often laugh and make jokes over the table about it the very same day. He imagined everyone else forgot as quickly as he did and he was always astonished to discover that his words uttered hastily in anger had made him enemies.

'How should I know that people have such long memories for hate? I've only a cat's memory,' he would explain innocently.

'If you spit upwards, you're bound to get it back in the face,' Mother irritably upbraided him.

Gradually Mother reached the conclusion that only migration to another country would bring about any real change in their life, and with all her persistence she began to urge him to take the decisive step. She considered America, France, Palestine, and finally decided on Australia. One reason for the choice was the presence there of distant relatives who would undoubtedly help them to find their feet in that far-away continent. Besides, she was sure that Australia was so different from any other country that Father was bound to acquire a new and more solid way of earning a living there.

For a long time Father paid no heed to her agitation and refused to make any move.

'Why have you picked on Australia and not Tibet, for example?' he asked ironically. 'There isn't much difference between the two lands. Both are on the other side of the moon.'

The idea of leaving his native land seemed so fantastic to him that he refused to regard it seriously. He answered Mother with jokes and tales of travellers who disappeared in balloons. He had no curiosity to explore distant countries, he hardly ever ventured beyond the three or four familiar streets of his city. And why should his wife be so anxious for him to find a new way of earning a living? Didn't he provide her with food and a roof over her head? He had never given one moment's thought to his mode of life and he could not imagine any reason for doing so. It suited him like his gay straw hats and smart suits.

Yet in the end he did what Mother wanted him to do, though even on the journey he was tortured by doubts and he positively shouted words of indecision. But he was no sooner in Australia than he put away all thoughts of his homeland and he began to regard the new country as his permanent home. It was not so different from what he had known before. Within a few days he had met some fellow merchants and, retiring to a café, they talked about business in the new land. There were fortunes to be made here, Father very quickly concluded. There was, of course, the question of a new language but that was no great obstacle to business. You could buy and sell—it was a good land, Father said.

It was different with Mother. Before she was one day off the ship she wanted to go back.

The impressions she gained on that first day remained with her all her life. It seemed to her there was an irritatingly superior air about the people she met, the customs officials, the cab men, the agent of the new house. Their faces expressed something ironical and sympathetic, something friendly and at the same time condescending. She imagined everyone on the wharf, in the street, looked at her in the same way and she never forgave them for treating her as if she were in need of their good-natured tolerance.

Nor was she any better disposed to her relatives and the small delegation of Jews who met her at the ship. They had all been in Australia for many years and they were anxious to impress new-comers with their knowledge of the country and its customs. They spoke in a hectoring manner. This was a free country, they said, it was cultured, one used a knife and fork and not one's hands. Everyone could read and write and no one shouted at you. There were no oppressors here as in the old country.

Mother thought she understood their talk; she was quick and observant where Father was sometimes extremely guileless. While they talked Father listened with a good-natured smile and it is to be supposed he was thinking of a good story he could tell his new acquaintances. But Mother fixed them with a firm, relentless gaze and, suddenly interrupting their injunctions, said in the softest of voices, 'If there are no oppressors here, as you say, why do you frisk about like house dogs? Whom do you have to please?'

Mother never lost this hostile and ironical attitude to the new land. She would have nothing of the country; she would not even attempt to learn the language. And she only began to look with a kind of interest at the world round her when my sister and I were old enough to go to school. Then all her old feeling for books and learning was re-awakened. She handled our primers and readers as if they were sacred texts.

She set great aims for us. We were to shine in medicine, in literature, in music; our special sphere depended on her fancy at a particular time. In one of these ways we could serve humanity best, and whenever she read to us the stories of Tolstoy and Gorki she would tell us again and again of her days with the medical mission. No matter how much schooling we should get we needed ideals, and what better ideals were there than those that had guided her in the days of the medical mission? They would save us from the soulless influences of this barren land.

Father wondered why she spent so much time reading and telling us stories of her best years and occasionally he would take my side when I protested against Mother taking us away from our games.

'They're only children,' he said. 'Have pity on them. If you stuff their little heads, God alone knows how they will finish up.' Then, pointing to us, he added, 'I'll be satisfied if he is a good carpenter; and if she's a good dressmaker that will do, too.'

'At least,' Mother replied, 'you have the good sense not to suggest they go in for business. Life has taught you something at last.'

'Can I help it that I am in business?' he suddenly shouted angrily. 'I know it's a pity my father didn't teach me to be a professor.'

But he calmed down quickly, unable to stand for long Mother's steady gaze and compressed lips.

It exasperated us that Father should give in so easily so that we could never rely on him to take our side for long. Although he argued with Mother about us he secretly agreed with her. And outside the house he boasted about her, taking a peculiar pride in her culture and attainments, and repeating her words just as my sister and I did.

Mother was very concerned about how she could give us a musical education. It was out of the question that we both be taught an instrument, since Father's business was at a low ebb and he hardly knew where he would find enough money to pay the rent, so she took us to a friend's house to listen to gramophone records. They were of the old-fashioned, cylindrical kind made by Edison and they sounded far away and thin like the voice of a ventriloquist mimicking far off musical instruments. But my sister and I marvelled at them. We should have been willing to sit over the long, narrow horn for days, but Mother decided that it would only do us harm to listen to military marches and the stupid songs of the music-hall.

It was then that we began to pay visits to musical emporiums. We went after school and during the holidays in the mornings. There were times when Father waited long for his lunch or evening meal, but he made no protest. He supposed Mother knew what she was doing in those shops and he told his friends of the effort Mother was making to acquaint us with music.

Our first visits to the shops were in the nature of reconnoitring sorties. In each emporium Mother looked the attendants up and down while we thumbed the books on the counters, stared at the enlarged photographs of illustrious composers, and studied the various catalogues of gramophone records. We went from shop to shop until we just about knew all there was to know about the records and sheet music and books in stock.

Then we started all over again from the first shop and this time we came to hear the records.

I was Mother's interpreter and I would ask one of the salesmen to play us a record she had chosen from one of the catalogues. Then I would ask him to play another. It might have been a piece for violin by Tchaikowsky or Beethoven or an aria sung by Caruso or Chaliapin. This would continue until Mother observed the gentleman in charge of the gramophone losing his patience and we would take our leave.

With each visit Mother became bolder and several times she asked to have whole symphonies and concertos played to us. We sat for nearly an hour cooped up in a tiny room with the salesman restlessly shuffling his feet, yawning and not knowing what to expect next. Mother pretended he hardly existed and, making herself comfortable in the cane chair, with a determined, intent expression she gazed straight ahead at the whirling disc.

We were soon known to everyone at the shops. Eyes lit up as we walked in, Mother looking neither this way nor that with two children walking in file through the passage-way towards the record department. I was very conscious of the humorous glances and the discreet sniggers that followed us and I would sometimes catch hold of Mother's hand and plead with her to leave the shop. But she paid no heed and we continued to our destination. The more often we came the more uncomfortably self-conscious I became and I dreaded the laughing faces round me.

Soon we became something more than a joke. The smiles turned to scowls and the shop attendants refused to play us any more records. The first time this happened the salesman mumbled something and left us standing outside the door of the music-room.

Mother was not easily thwarted and without a trace of a smile she said we should talk to the manager. I was filled with a sense of shame and humiliation and with downcast eyes I sidled towards the entrance of the shop.

Mother caught up with me and, laying her hand upon my arm, she said, 'What are you afraid of? Your mother won't disgrace you, believe me.' Looking at me in her searching way she went on, 'Think carefully. Who is right—are they or are we? Why shouldn't they play for us? Does it cost them anything? By which other way can we ever hope to hear something good? Just because we are poor must we cease our striving?'

She continued to talk in this way until I went back with her. The three of us walked into the manager's office and I translated Mother's words.

The manager was stern, though I imagine he must have had some difficulty in keeping his serious demeanour.

'But do you ever intend to buy any records?' he said after I had spoken.

'If I were a rich woman would you ask me that question?' Mother replied and I repeated her words in a halting voice.

'Speak up to him,' she nudged me while I could feel my face fill with hot blood.

The manager repeated his first question and Mother, impatient at my hesitant tone, plunged into a long speech on our right to music and culture and in fact the rights of all men, speaking in her own tongue as though the manager understood every word. It was in vain; he merely shook his head.

We were barred from shop after shop, and in each case Mother made a stand, arguing at length until the man in charge flatly told us not to come back until we could afford to buy records.

We met with rebuffs in other places as well.

Once as we wandered through the university, my sister and I sauntering behind while Mother opened doors, listening to lectures for brief moments, we unexpectedly found ourselves in a large room where white-coated young men and women sat on high stools in front of arrays of tubes, beakers and jars.

Mother's eyes lit up brightly and she murmured something about knowledge and science. We stood close to her and gazed round in astonishment; neither her words nor what we saw conveyed anything to us. She wanted to go round the room but a gentleman wearing a black gown came up and asked us if we were looking for someone. He was a distinguished looking person with a florid face and a fine grey mane.

Repeating Mother's words I said, 'We are not looking for anyone; we are simply admiring this room of knowledge.'

The gentleman's face wrinkled pleasantly. With a tiny smile playing over his lips he said regretfully that we could not stay, since only students were permitted in the room.

As I interpreted his words Mother's expression changed. Her sallow face was almost red. For ten full seconds she looked the gentleman in the eyes. Then she said rapidly to me, 'Ask him why he speaks with such a condescending smile on his face.'

I said, 'My mother asks why you talk with such a superior smile on your face?'

He coughed, shifted his feet restlessly and his face set severely. Then he glared at his watch and without another word walked away with dignified steps.

When we came out into the street a spring day was in its full beauty.

Mother sighed to herself and after a moment's silence said, 'That fine professor thinks he is a liberal-minded man, but behind his smile he despises people such as us. You will have to struggle here just as hard as I had to back home. For all the fine talk it is like all other countries. But where are the people with ideals like those back home, who aspire to something better?'

She repeated those words frequently, even when I was a boy of thirteen and I knew so much more about the new country that was my home. Then I could argue with her.

I said to her that Benny who lived in our street was always reading books and papers and hurrying to meetings. Benny was not much older than I was and he had many friends whom he met in the park on Sunday. They all belonged to this country and they were interested in all the things Mother talked about.

'Benny is an exception,' she said with an impatient shrug of her shoulders, 'and his friends are only a tiny handful.' Then she added, 'And what about you? You and your companions only worship bats and balls as heathens do stone idols. Why, in the old country boys of your age took part in the fight to deliver mankind from oppression! They gave every-thing, their strength and health, even their lives, for that glorious ideal.'

'That's what Benny wants to do,' I said, pleased to be able to answer Mother.

'But it's so different here. Even your Benny will be swallowed up in the smug, smooth atmosphere. You wait and see.'

She spoke obstinately. It seemed impossible to change her. Her vision was too much obscured by passionate dreams of the past for her to see any hope in the present, in the new land.

But as an afterthought she added, 'Perhaps it is different for those like you and Benny. But for me I can never find my way into this life here.'

She turned away, her narrow back stooped, her gleaming black hair curled into a bun on her short, thin neck, her shoes equally down at heel on each side.

HAL PORTER

First Love

My paternal grandfather was English, military and long-nosed. He married twice, and had seven sons and four daughters. My maternal grandfather, Swiss, agricultural and long-nosed, married once but had six sons and six daughters. As a child, therefore, I was well-provided not only with ancestral aunts and uncles but also with the uncle-husbands and wife-aunts they had married. Since each of these couples were abundantly productive, long-nosed cousins of all ages, from braggart striplings and chatterbox young women to india-rubber babies like tempestuous Queen Victorias with bonnets awry congested my boyhood. It seems to me now that what my grandparents imported to Australia along with fecundity and long noses was largely noise. Noise, in their case, can be enlarged to cover vivacity bordering on uproar, devil-may-care wildness, a febrile intensity about issues of great unimportance. From the most feckless uncle to the most social aunt, from bread-line-treading aunts to rich uncles, all were afflicted by this rowdy insouciance. My mother, essentially provincial, was nevertheless giddy as a porpoise, and lived like a windmill rotating to alternate gusts of temper and charm.

In this uproarious tribal whirlpool I was odd boy out. A throwback inheritance of some less mettlesome blood braked me. I had the same passion for decorous behaviour as they had for fits-and-starts behaviour, for conversations at full pitch, for gambling and gipsying about. This perversity of self-restraint caused me to lag behind, to be a some-time observer rather than a full-time participant. Yet, oddly enough, I also had maximum *esprit de corps*. Nor was I niminy-piminy and stand-offish. Japan-shaped scabs blotched my fruit-stealer's country boy knees; my bare soles were as rind-like as fire-walkers'. I could swim like a toad, swear like a cow-cocky and smoke like a *débutante*. These abilities and simulated ferocities were, however, strictly conventional. In their execution I went just so far. I drew a line. Other members of the family always went farther and further. I would not, for example, kill snakes as Uncle Foster and cousins and brothers did by cracking them like whips. Sticks did me. As well as affecting protective discretions such as this, and making withdrawals from hereditary bravura, I often broke the wrong rules. My brothers and country cousins each had a dog, usually a bossy fox-terrier or a smart-alec mong with lots of heeler in it. I had a cat. I found its relative muteness and disdainful independence preferable to the ostentatious servility and noisily neurasthenic demands of dogs. Need I say that I wore spectacles and spoke in polysyllables?

Not only did I violate the clan code by visible nonconformity but I was mentally and invisibly rebellious. This was harder to swear at. I believed, as all we youngsters did, that broken-backed snakes could not die until the sun set, that warts grew where dogs licked one, that to gash the skin linking thumb with forefinger caused lockjaw which we translated as instant and eternal dumbness. Along with the mob I circumspectly believed in ghosts, the end of the world and Spring-heel Jack. Then I ran off the rails. As logic's advocate I believed, for longer than was deemed orthodox or manly, in Father Christmas: his leavings were evidence. I did not believe in God who had let me down in the matter of prayers for a Meccano set. To the terror of the others, I said so piercingly enough for the vast ear in the sky to take in the blasphemy. I became the tree for believers not to stand by when lightning flashed.

More disconcerting and shaming than even blasphemy was my most eccentric trait. I cherished the family caprices and florid behaviour so much that I came out of my comparative silence to exult—in public— over what my kith and kin accepted as one does a birthmark better hidden. I let out, to the dirt-rimmed and contemptuous sons of the washerwoman, that Swiss grandfather's daughters, in order of birth, were named Rosa Bona, Adelina, Sophia, Maria, Meta and Ida. I explained that each name, besides ending in A, had, sequentially, one letter less. My brothers, failing to shut me up or divert interest from my humiliating treason, looked bleakly down their noses. I continued to rattle on, chattily revealing my disappointment that there had not been two more aunts born—a final aunt, a fabulous creature called Aunt A, would have exhilarated me more than my favourite Sago Plum Pudding. The family, boorishly I thought, instead of these cunningly graduated names, used Bon, Addie, Sophie, Ria, Min Min and Doll. It irked my senses of order as much as my sense of possession to hear my mother called not Aunt Ida but Auntie Dolly. As a gesture, although Aunt Rosa Bona and Aunt Adelina were mouthfuls, I prissily insisted on using the full names. I was inflexible in not saying Uncle Whit, Uncle Gat and Uncle Tini to my paternal uncles who had been christened Whitworth, Gatling and Martini-Henry after firearms. My military grandfather's other sons were Lancaster, Enfield, Snider and Mauser.

Though pointing an attitude, my delight in these absurdities of baptism was a little only of the magnetism my flamboyant relatives had for me. Even a porcupine regards its own as soft and sleek. I overdid it: my blood-porcupines were powder-puffs and satin to me.

Each aunt and uncle had at least one dashing foible which still, now, years later, enchants my nostalgic middle age as much as it then enchanted me. I know now, alas, that behind the screen of levity and animal spirits lay concealed human imperfections, guile, improvidence, stupidity, mendacity, anguishes of every variety and even downright tragedy. In those days, however, I gaped at everything I heard or overheard of their vivid and forthright doings. These legends, which they dramatically recounted of themselves and of each other, so magnified them that they swaggered and swept by, heroes and Amazons, along the rim of my mind's horizon, casting miles-long shadows as blinding as searchlight rays. When these nobilities appeared before me in the flesh I could still gape, for I was not yet ready for disillusion. Reality matched imagination. About the family, anyway, I was the Three Wise Monkeys.

I was stimulated by Uncle Martini-Henry's waxed moustache, and malacca, and watch-chain with its shark-tooth *breloque* as much as by the saga of his earlier bush-whacking adventures, by Uncle Whitworth's plush-lined pipe-cases, by Aunt Rosa Bona's garden gorged with flowers so large and crisp as to appear edible. I was captivated by their houses which smelt variously of strawberry jam cooking, or furniture polish and Brasso, or cut lemons, or Eau de Cologne, or boiled-over milk, or cats and cigars. Because, indeed, the mind and its shadow senses do preserve a detailed past, I still recall the smell of Uncle Mauser's Turkish cigarettes or Aunt Sophia's glycerine soap, the exact disposition of Mazzawattee tea-canisters and gilt-handled vases long destroyed, still feel the Greek key pattern embossing the rim of Aunt Adelina's fruit-plates, still hear Melba hooting *Home, Sweet Home* through the toffee-coloured, convolvulus-shaped horn of Aunt Meta's gramophone.

I seized every opportunity to stock a granary of impressions. I picked up whole and wonderful sentences thrown carelessly down among cake-crumbs and tea-slopped saucers; tucked away luminous smiles released in happy-go-lucky flights at picnics; carried off, as it were, armloads of cuttings from virile and showy plants in a garden where summer seemed perfect and unending. How cruelly endless now seems a deadlier season.

As children in a spread-out but gregariously inclined sept, my cousins and brothers and sisters and I, during school holidays, were always anywhere but in our own rowdy nests. We were interchanged like home-made tokens of affection. Those of us who were suburban were bundled off to country aunts and uncles; those who were country bumpkins went citywards. Children are pickers-up. Each child returned home bearing objects that, almost valueless otherwise, were sacred mementoes, and doubly sacred as being something for nothing. I remember my sisters bringing back shoe-buckles, wildernesses of embroidery silks, bone cro-chet needles, Piver's powder boxes, raped-looking dolls, and fans still releasing from their broken wings shadows of a scent long out of fashion and the name of which nobody knew. At one time or another, my brothers brought back wilting lizards in jars of spirits, cigar-boxes of cigar-bands, a carved emu's egg, tortoise-shell pen-knives with broken blades, a rectangular tennis-racquet and, on a notable occasion, Uncle Snider's elderly banjo. These things were rubbish but, like tourist souvenirs, retained enough glamour just long enough to garnish the short interval before, coach into pumpkin, holiday turned back to workaday.

As the one child in this riotous shuffling to and fro who was family-obsessed and a born archivist, I was a magpie of a different colour. I wanted more of Uncle Snider's past than an unplayable banjo. I wanted facts, dates, the how and why and where, all possible information about the pasts of the living gods and goddesses I paid homage to. My eyes must have glittered as much as my spectacles when I was given dated menu cards of P & O dinners, Masonic dinners, mayoral dinners, or old theatre programmes, ball programmes, invitations to exhibitions and weddings. It steadied the spinning world to fix an eye on the fact that Aunt Adelina had gone to a wedding on June 24, 1911. It added depth and richness to my knowledge that she was still going to weddings. Postcards were special grist to my enthusiastic mill. Since my aunts and uncles had been young in the late nineteenth century and early twentieth century, that era of postcard-sending and postcard-collecting, I had many reefs to mine. It was a fascinating find, say, that, in Victoria Street, North Williamstown, on February 13, 1913, Uncle Gatling received a certain message on a postcard which showed a ragged negro Topsy, her head spiked like a battle-mace with plaits, submerging her face in a monster semi-lune of water-melon under the words AH'S UP TO MAH EARS IN IT. Below her toes which were splayed out like pianist's fingers, the sentence finished AT ST KILDA. Written on the back in violet ink was:

> Dear Gat,
>   Take a gander at the coon on the other side!!!! Just a line to say all the Jokers will be foregathering at the White Hart next Sat. about 3. Expecting a hot time!! Don't wear that bokker!!!! Harry.

I begged postcards of all sorts: *Sunset on the Nile, Miss Billie Burke, Miss Zena Dare,* cards of padded velvet roses, cards garishly illustrating boarding-house and mother-in-law jokes. I was, nevertheless, really hunting photographs—footballer uncles striped like barbers' poles; Aunt Sophia under a cartwheel hat of ostrich feathers, and horse-collared by a boa; Uncle Enfield, whom I knew as a well-tailored sphere with an eye-glass, as a cock-eyed skinamalink in Little Lord Fauntleroy velvet; Aunt Meta, with unpainted lips, bare shoulders and a cumulus of hair, emerging glass-eyed as a hairdresser's wax model from a nest of chiffon.

So feverish did I become, repeating my overtures as monotonously as creation, that I exhausted family teasing into recognition of my fervour. I was understood to be some sort of notary. Spring-cleaning aunts sent me packets of photographs; uncles put aside for me dim, henna-coloured snapshots (*Me at Leongatha Woodchop,* 1920) or postcards of magenta-nosed drunks with crayfish semaphoring from their hip-pockets which they had dug out of drawers holding the treasures of a lifetime . . . sovereign-cases, insurance policies, opal tie-pins, wives' first love-letters, and the halves of pairs of cuff-links. Proff became my nickname, and my bottom was pinched affectionately. On my behalf, archaeology into their own racy and cluttered pasts became an accepted pastime of my aunts and uncles.

Alas!

At the height of my miniature fame, at the unornamental age of ten, a bee-keeper stung by his own bee, I fell in love with a photograph. I fell deeply, unfalteringly and hauntedly in love.

The photograph came in a packet of postcards from Aunt Meta. Had I not been alone in the house, with nobody peering over my shoulder, I could have been saved a long ecstasy and a savage destruction. Alone I was, however, when the postman came; alone I unwrapped my gift and, among postcards of Gaiety Girls, and snapshots of bowler-hatted uncles in jinkers, and ant-waisted aunts leaning on or being leaned on by bicycles, alone I came upon my fate. Nothing can undo what was done that instant, that day.

I saw the photograph. The door of the one addled world I had known closed softly behind me. I was in the ante-room to Paradise. Its bejewelled throne was mine. I perceived that all loves experienced in the back-room past were imaginary, were delusions, were nothing. I had been wastefully librating above shadows—however spirited; visions—however cock-a-hoop; hollow beings; deceptive shapes; creatures of gauze; dresses empty of women; names without men to them. I had had merely a bowing acquaintance with love.

The photograph was of a girl about my own age. She was dressed in Dolly Varden-ish costume. Since she held a shepherd's crook feminized by a large bow I gathered she was being Bo Peep for a fancy dress party. Or was she Bo Peep herself? There was nothing on the photograph to tell. The tilted oval of hat with its rosebuds and ribbons, the black hatching of the elbow-length mittens, the crisscross-laced bodice, all excited me romantically. What flooded into my being, however, to reveal inner depths and expanses never revealed before, was the illumination from the smile and the eyes. It did not occur to me that what really confronted the smile and the eyes was a camera like half-a-concertina on a tripod which was concealed with a nameless human under a black cloth. No! That faintly scented smile was for me. Those eyes, bottomless, and yet of dark sharpness, were looking into me. A gale of voices whirled through the galleries of my consciousness, aromatizing them, purging them of all former presences, and calling out deliciously, 'Thou!'

'Thou!'

I was eavesdropping on eternity.

Eternity is time's victim.

Eternity had scarcely begun when I heard my mother at the front door. With the unflurried movements of a master criminal I put the photograph in an inside pocket. I was aware that the pocket was on the left, and the divine face deliberately turned inwards. The eyes looked directly into my heart which I imagined crimson as a playing-card heart, plump as an artichoke, and composed of a material with the texture of magnolia petals. I extinguished the lights in my face, swept up the other photographs with a gambler's gesture and, as my mother entered, cried out ... oh, perfect imitation of a frank and guileless boy ... 'Look what Aunt Meta sent!' Not a word about the divinity staring into my heart, not a word. I said nothing then. I kept the photograph and my love hidden for seven years. I said nothing ever.

Because my pockets and chest-of-drawers were subject to maternal investigation it was necessary to be on guard against discovery. I cannot remember, now, all my love's hiding-places when I could not carry her with me. When I had to desert her under the paper lining a boot-box of silkworms, behind a loose skirting-board or in the never-read bible, heavy as a foundation-stone, I believed the subtle smile to dissolve away and those unflinching eyes to be in sleep.

That my idolatry persisted and became more intense was—still is—astounding for, too violently soon, I was, in years, older than she. In all else but my worship I changed. She did not change, although her beauty took on other meanings; her eyes displayed truths that, at one and the same time, vacillated like the opalescence on black oil, and remained steady and mystifying as infinity.

I changed. The family changed. Their lustihood, animation, over-large gesturings and vitality, if one took a quick look, were unabated. Closer examination showed the gilt flaking off, or a hair-fine crackle of flaws. Like plates left too long in the oven some older aunts and uncles illustrated that they had been long enough in the oven of life. As wrinkles darned themselves more closely around eyes, as hair wore away or became margined with white, as figures broadened or became juiceless, curving downwards towards the earth that was their destination, perhaps what I noticed most was an increase of braggadocio and hullabaloo. High spirits were larded with slangy defiance; hilarity was so constant that cause and effect were lost sight of, and no longer had value. No one seemed to dare to ask, 'Why are we laughing?' but went on defiantly laughing. All those epic suns that had warmed my earlier boyhood were declining in a sky flushed with stubborn anger.

Most gaudy of these declines was Aunt Maria's. For years the family had called her the Merry Widow: singular title to hold among so many married couples. Maria's husband had been, I endlessly kept on over-hearing and was endlessly told, handsome, rich, gifted, charming, and so on. I concluded that the dead were inevitably possessed of all the attributes the living have few or none of. Luxuriance of graces seemed a necessary qualification for death. It was a tragedy, they all said, that he should have died two months after marriage. He and dear Ria, they all said, had been a perfectly matched couple, madly in love. At first, I gathered, Maria had sought consolation in travel; later, in travel and port wine; ultimately, in less travel, more port wine, and—they lowered their voices so that I listened harder and heard more—and young men.

I saw her rarely. She was sensationally made-up. Her sardonicisms were hoarsely outrageous. Scent breezed from her furs wherein glittered the mean eyes of foxy faces chiselling snouts into their own expensive bodies; rings bulged her kid gloves; she smoked baby-blue, primrose and lilac cigarettes tipped with gold. She was the clan scandal. She belonged to the family, but she belonged in the manner of some elaborate pet with unusual vices. These were understood to age her. Virtues, nevertheless, aged the virtuous others as inexorably: simplicities aged to idiosyncrasies, habits to affectations, lovable quiddities to boring eccentricities.

As for myself, I reached the stage of rubbing vaseline on a breath of moustache. I started brilliantine which my parents regarded in much the same light as opium-smoking. I whined for adult caste-marks such as cuff-links and a wristlet watch. I was, evanescently, of that self-loving, self-pitying, unbearable race which invents loneliness and boredom, and in which all the major evils of humanity are in powerful bud. I was an adolescent of sour seventeen.

From the arrogant, dirty-minded, unaesthetic and altogether unworthy side of my nature, I found absolution only in my photograph. Since I was insufferably older and in my first long trousers, mother no longer, without fair warning, rifled my pockets with cries of 'How long have you been using this revolting handkerchief?' The photograph, therefore, was able to stand constantly at my heart in a morocco wallet Uncle Lancaster had given me. The eyes I had looked into so often during seven years still offered me, from the midst of their dark moonlight, a prophetic truth; the smile seemed still that of one whispering 'Thou!' and promising all affirmations, all peace, all wisdom, all love.

At this stage, my moustache still unawakened, brilliantine still anathema to my mother, my wrist still watchless, and the days a passion of ennui, Aunt Maria came to the country town we lived in.

One night, while we were at dinner, the telephone rang. Mother left the table and the room to answer it. We heard her squeal ecstatically in the distance. She returned looking younger, and had gone rosy under the eyes. That rosiness said to us children, '*Rattled!*' Father was away. Mother was at our mercy. The six of us stared at her in a certain manner. Mother stared bravely back.

'Aunt Ria's here,' she said at last, over-nonchalantly and not sitting down again. 'And stop that. Immediately. I'll tell your father. Take that smug expression off your smug faces.'

'Sit down, mother *dear*,' we said. 'Relaxez-vous. Collect your thoughts. Don't be shy. Speak out. Give us the dirt, mama. Or *we'll* tell papa.'

She remained standing, and said, 'Stop that. Immediately. Or I'll scream the house down.' She looked at the clock with a pretence of vagueness. 'She's travelling through to Sydney. She's staying overnight at the Terminus.'

'Ah, *ha*!' It was my twelve-year-old sister. 'Is she dee-ah-you-en-kay? Is she coming to see her poor relations?'

'No,' said mother, and 'How dare you, miss?' and sat down as if there were nothing else to do. 'She says she's too tired.'

'She *is* dee-ah-you . . .'

'Stop that,' cried mother. 'How dare you suggest that Ria . . . how dare you, miss? She's had a very tragic life.' Her eyes hinted tears, but she finger-tipped her just-marcelled shingle with gratification. Her inward eye was riffling through her wardrobe.

'What's the time? Is that clock fast or slow or right? I have to go down and see her.'

Have meant, we knew, *am so excited I can hardly wait.*

As eldest son and deputy man-of-the-house, I went with mother.

The Terminus Hotel was a hive of inactivity. The Guests' Drawing-room, to which several palms gave the atmosphere of a down-at-heel Winter Garden, contained only Aunt Maria and a young man. They sat, deep in moquette armchairs, with the air of people who have been sitting for a long time. Between them a Benares-brass-tray table held their drinks, and a whisky-advertising ash-tray fuming like a rubbish-tip with butts bloodstained by lipstick.

'My loves!' cried Aunt Maria huskily, hoisting herself upright. Scarcely less loudly, out of the corner of her mouth, she also said, 'Get up, you lout, when a lady enters the room.'

From under the horizontal single eyebrow which served both eyes the young man spat a glance at her which I recognized for I had ejected just such a glance at my mother when she had publicly revealed that I wrote poetry or bit my fingernails. The young man, handsome in an unlit fashion, brutally stood.

Most of what happened after does not matter.

Aunt Maria was fairly drunk. For a woman of fifty she had kept enough of her figure. Her dress and shoes were in the safely faultless taste that costs money. Her hair, of dead black, was astrakhan-crinkled, and had obviously also cost, colour and design, much money.

We were an unmatched quartette but, whatever lay under the surface of the evening, Aunt Maria and my mother gave no apparent thought to it. My aunt's one rebuke to the young man had vibrated instantly to silence. She introduced him as Ivan Something but, with a kind of marital mockery, addressed him as Ee-fahn. She disregarded him but not pointedly. One felt she might, later in the evening, as she walked much too carefully bedwards, have to stop and say, 'My God! My Ee-fahn! I nearly forgot him!' as of an umbrella. She had, so to speak, already walked away leaving a number of umbrellas.

The conversation was overlapping gabble between the two sisters, and was family, family, family. They giggled, they shrieked. Diagonally across their chit-chat Ee-fahn reconnoitred me with monosyllabic information about weight-lifting. It was Urdu to me. I sat egg-faced wishing his eyebrow on my lip. He lowered this eyebrow like a perambulator-hood, and withdrew under it to drink brandies. Aunt Maria drank port after port. Saying 'No, *no*, Ria! Not one more drink. I'll be featherstitching!' mother had two, three and then four Drambuies. I was permitted two beer-shandies.

My adoration of family personalities and goings-on having subsided with puberty, I was not merely uninterested in Aunt Maria, but bored, shamed and revolted. Before me, I thought, were the classic lineaments of immorality. Its surface moved as though lined with decayed elastic, it grimaced, it winked, it pleated itself to laugh, and yet was dead. Its lips, from which the lipstick had worn centrally off to reveal a naked mauve, writhed about. The eyes seemed to flash darkly but that was an illusion fostered by restlessness. They dared not tarry moveless under their glistening blue lids.

So, utterly fed-up, attempting to buy escape by startling mother into awareness of me and the late hour, I took out my wallet and opened it in a manly way. This gesture stopped mother in her tracks.

'I should like to buy . . .' I could not think of the word for a number of drinks '. . . to buy some drinks.'

'The naughty love!' cried Aunt Maria. 'You know, Doll, he's going to be quite a good-looker, even with the gig-lamps. Dear boy, you mustn't waste your substance on filthy-rich aunts.'

She reached and took the wallet from me, took it between forefinger and thumb by one corner, and held it up, and waggled it. This was no more than old-fashioned, ex-girlish playfulness, Lily Langtry skittishness, but was earthquake and annihilation to me. From the wallet on to the brass table fell my secret, my silence, my peace, my dreams, my seven years of devotion, the photograph with its undefiled gaze and smile, the smile of my first love.

I was too stricken to snatch, to save, to conceal.

'A dark horse, Doll,' said Aunt Maria, taking up the photograph. 'A Casanova. The girl friend!' Focusing, she held the photograph at arm's length.

'Who? Who is that? Who?' said mother, hand outstretched.

There is a moment when, for the first time, Life is no longer seen in exquisite profile.

Life turns full-face to one, swiftly and savagely, and unshutters her eyes. There is nothing to be seen in their recesses but the evidence of destruction, of negation, perspectives of nullity. Peace, one sees, is perjury. The gods are down-and-out. The jewelled throne one slumbered on is no more than a rock in wasteland. The flowers one thought to have been thrown at one's feet are seen to be not flowers but the rotting wings of shapes that flew ecstatically into emptiness, and circled in emptiness, and starved there, and fell. One is, for the first time, aware of mortality, and learns in a flash that death is the one sure possession.

'Who?' said Aunt Maria, horribly smiling and smiling at the photograph. 'Look, Doll. Look at the sweet, quaint little sobersides.'

'Where *did* you get this?' said my mother.

'Found it. I found it,' I said, my voice thick with lies and hate. 'I found it in the drawer. Where the old photographs used to be. This afternoon.'

'Remember, Doll?' said Aunt Maria, knocking over her wine. 'Lolly Edward's party? My God, I shouldn't care to shout from the rooftop how long ago that was. You were Miss Muffet. Remember, Doll? Show Eefahn what a serious duck of a Bo Peep I was.'

And the drunken woman with wine-scummed eyes agitated the dying muscles of her loose and painted mouth, and began to laugh hoarsely, and I heard what I heard, and saw what I saw, and my heart broke.

DAL STIVENS

The Man who Bowled Victor Trumper

'Ever hear how I bowled Victor Trumper for a duck?' he asked.

'No,' I said.

'He was a beautiful bat,' he said. 'He had wrists like steel and he moved like a panther. The ball sped from his bat as though fired by a cannon.'

The three of us were sitting on the verandah of the pub at Yerranderie in the Burragorang Valley in the late afternoon. The sun fell full on the fourteen hundred foot sandstone cliff behind us but the rest of the valley was already dark. A road ran past the pub and the wheeltracks were eighteen inches deep in the hard summer-baked road.

'There was a batsman for you,' he said.

He was a big fat man with a chin like a cucumber. He had worked in the silver mines at Yerranderie. The last had closed in 1928 and for a time he had worked in the coal mines further up the valley and then had retired on a pension and half an inch of good lung left.

'Dust in my lungs,' he said. 'All my own fault. The money was good. Do you know if I tried to run a hundred yards I'd drop dead.'

The second man was another retired miner but he had all his lungs. He had a broken nose and had lost the forefinger and thumb of his right hand.

Before they became miners, they said, they had tried their hand at many jobs in the bush.

'Ever hear how I fought Les Darcy?' the big fat man asked.

'No,' I said.

'He was the best fighter we have ever had in Australia. He was poetry in action. He had a left that moved like quicksilver.'

'He was a great fighter,' I said.

'He was like a Greek god,' said the fat man reverently.

We sat watching the sun go down. Just before it dipped down beside the mountain it got larger and we could look straight at it. In no time it had gone.

'Ever hear how I got Victor Trumper?'

'No,' I said. 'Where did it happen?'

'It was in a match up at Bourke. Tibby Cotter was in the same team. There was a man for you. His fastest ball was like a thunderbolt. He was a bowler and a half.'

'Yes,' I said.

'You could hardly see the ball after it left his hand. They put two lots of matting down when he came to Bourke so he wouldn't kill anyone.'

'I never saw him,' I said, 'but my father says he was very fast.'

'Fast!' says the fat man. 'He was so fast you never knew anything until you heard your wicket crash. In Bourke he split seven stumps and we had to borrow the school kids' set.'

It got cold and we went into the bar and ordered three rums which we drank with milk. The miner who had all his lungs said:

'I saw Tibby Cotter at the Sydney Cricket Ground and the Englishmen were scared of him.'

'He was like a tiger as he bounded up to bowl,' said the big fat man.

'He had even Ranji bluffed,' said the other miner. 'Indians have special eyesight but it wasn't enough to play Tibby.'

We all drank together and ordered again. It was my shout.

'Ever hear about the time I fought Les Darcy?' the big fat man asked me.

'No,' I said.

'There wasn't a man in his weight to touch him,' said the miner who had all his lungs. 'When he moved his arm you could see the muscles ripple across his back.'

'When he hit them you could hear the crack in the back row of the Stadium,' said the fat man.

'They poisoned him in America,' said the other miner.

'Never gave him a chance,' said the fat man.

'Poisoned him like a dog,' said the other.

'It was the only way they could beat him,' said the fat man. 'There wasn't a man at his weight that could live in the same ring as Les Darcy.'

The barmaid filled our glasses up again and we drank a silent toast. Two men came in. One was carrying a hurricane lantern. The fat man said the two men always came in at night for a drink and that the tall man in the raincoat was the caretaker at one of the derelict mines.

'Ever hear about the kelpie bitch I had once?' said the fat man. 'She was as intelligent and wide awake as you are. She almost talked. It was when I was droving.'

The fat miner paid this time.

'There isn't a dog in the bush to touch a kelpie for brains,' said the miner with the broken nose.

'Kelpies can do almost anything but talk,' said the fat man.

'Yes,' I said. 'I have never had one but I have heard my father talk of one that was wonderful for working sheep.'

'All kelpies are beautiful to watch working sheep but the best was a little bitch I had at Bourke,' said the fat man. 'Ever hear how I bowled Victor Trumper for a duck?'

'No,' I said. 'But what about this kelpie?'

'I could have got forty quid for her any time for the asking,' said the fat miner. 'I could talk about her all day. Ever hear about the time I forgot the milk for her pups? Sold each of the pups later for a tenner.'

'You can always get a tenner for a good kelpie pup,' said the miner who had all his lungs.

'What happened when you forgot the pups' milk?' I said.

'It was in the bucket,' the fat miner said, 'and the pups couldn't reach it. I went into the kitchen and the bitch was dipping her tail in the milk bucket and then lowering it to the pups. You can believe that or not, as you like.'

'I believe you,' I said.

'I don't,' said the other miner.

'What, you don't believe me!' cried the fat miner, turning to the other. 'Don't you believe I bowled Victor Trumper for a duck? Don't you believe I fought Les Darcy? Don't you believe a kelpie could do that?'

'I believe you bowled Victor Trumper for a duck,' said the other. 'I believe you fought Les Darcy. I believe a kelpie would do that.'

The fat miner said: 'You had me worried for a minute. I thought you didn't believe I had a kelpie like that.'

'That's it,' said the miner who had all his lungs. 'I don't believe you had a kelpie like that.'

'You tell me who had a kelpie like that if I didn't,' the fat miner said.

'I'll tell you,' said the miner with the broken nose. 'You never had a kelpie like that but I did. You've heard me talk about that little bitch many times.'

They started getting mad with each other then so I said:

'How did you get Victor Trumper for a duck?'

'There was a batsman for you,' said the fat man. 'He used a bat like a sword and he danced down the wicket like a panther.'

PADDY ROE

Lardi

Yeah--
I can tell story, that whatname (Rasping) you know-----
that two--
man?----
you know that---
Lardi Lardi-----
that man---
they used to camp in Anna Plains, station you know--
he had two, mate belongta him too-
in the outcamp[1]--------
and these two boy used to go alla time days 'n' days you know-
eeevery day they trouble these, brolga-
brolga----
the bird want to come for drink (Stops rasping)--
but (Laughs) they humbug all the time you know[2]--
they go there (Tap tap)-
they had shotgun too--
you know from boss--
boss used to give them shotgun to kill bullock er, oh anything
    kangaroo[3]--
(Tap tap, rasping)---

so this old fella---
see he said to these two young fellas-
oh good friend old, friend (Laugh)----
he used to tell them 'Don't humbug these birds let-em come for drink'-
you know (Rasping stops, tap tap)---
they couldn't get chance to come in for drink (Rasping starts)-----

so one day---(Rasping stops)
this old man he went--
he went bush-
'nother place (Tap tap) not very far--
jus' walkin' round-
an' he left these two blokes, behind they waiting for---
for this brolga--
they made shade this time in the trough---

all right ---
this old fella went bush --
all right an' when they look hello they see one brolga coming -
one, ooh straight-up -
jus' lookin' round you know what kine Brolga he's looking this way that
    way he's coming straight for well[4] -
straight for the trough -
an' when they come close to the trough he jus' stand up straight -
right alongside -
an' this two bloke gettin' ready with the gun -
with the shotgun you know --
BANG got 'im knock 'im down --
'nother bloke run pick-im up --
pick-im up take-im back home (Rasping starts) -----
they know --
they can tell if he's fat or skinny --
you know they open his --(Rasping stops)
wing you know like this they feel ooh they can see that big lump here you
    know his fat -
(Clap) oooh proper fat --

all right they say --
well we only got one they say -
'Before that oldman come you better clean-im up an' we'll cook-im an'
    have a feed' (Laughs) -
this two bloke -
before that oldman come -
this nearly, oh long way yet time for 'im he won't be back yet -
'So we'll have to clean' they clean im up make fire everything make hole
    for im everything finish -
all right when they, when they finish -
when they finish --
then they --
to pull-im out from fire -
tupella start to eat-im now -
ooh big feed, fat -
ooh very fat -
they eat-im (Rasping) aaaall up --
nothing left -
they eat the lot -
an' they couldn't leave-im because he's too fat -
they didn't want to leave-im for the oldfella too -
I dunno what made them --
to think --

because they can--(Rasping stops)
one brolga is not enough for, lotta people you know-
they want to get a good feed two man-
so they did-------
yeah--

so that oldfella come back---
mmm 'Did you fella get any, anything?'-
'Yeah we got one'--
'Where that thing now?'-
'Oh finish, we bin finish-im'--
'Ohhh mus' be fat eh?'-
'Yes yes oh yes' they tell-im-
'We thought you not goin' to come back you know--
we thought you gone to station Anna Plain--
come little bit late eh?'-
'Yes'-
'Ahh'-
'Ah well tha's right then' he say (Laugh)-

so when they finish--
(Rasping starts)--
'All right' he said-
'Mm, he fat eh?'-
'Yeah'-
'Ahh--
I think you tupella might get sick soon' (Rasping stops) say-
'He be too fat you know-
might be you tupella get sick soon'--
'Yeah?'-
'Yeah'-
'Ah--
oh well, too late now we bin eat-im' (Laughs)-
'nother fella off now straight away--
they start to spew you know--
eeeegh eeeegh 'nother fella--
'nother one gone again straight up *beeeegheeegh* one fella there
      eeegheeeeeeegh shit come out he go *bbbbbbbbbbb* (Laughter)-
eeeeeeaaagh bbbbbbbbb everything come out one time same time everything
      come out, you know-
two of them-
same--
oooh they bin, musta spew about five times 'till nothing left inside that
      thing I s'pose they mighta spew everything out-
but that fat too, made-im come this end (Laughs)--

so 'nother fella start again this side you know *beeeeeeegh bbbbbbbbb*
 (Laughter) -
'nother one again *eeeeeeagh bbbbbbbb* -
ahh finish he say 'Oh, that old fella coming -
oh you better see us' -
he's *maban* too that man oh proper *maban* -
'You better see us' -
'All right' he tell-im 'We got a whatname here --
you better --
have a look at us must be something wrong' -
'Yeah --
yeah' he say -
come up he rubbed these two fella you know[5] --
oh finish they stop now no more -
nobody spew now finish -
stop -
oh everything stop-im everything one time -
maban man that fella too -
Lardi Lardi --

'All right' he tell-im 'well --
yeah --
you tupella right now?' he ask-em -
'Yeah we all right --
yeah' -
'You know what you pella bin eating?' -
'No -----
oh yes' they say 'Yeah we bin eat that, bird -
yeah -
yeah' -
'You tupella reckon that's that bird you pella bin eating?' -
'Yeah' -
'Well that's me' he tell-im (Laughs) -
you know -
'You tupella bin humbuggin' round all the time in that trough --
these birds never come for drink you know, hunt-im out all time -
yeah --
I only bin jus' play-play with you tupella you know' he say -
and tha's -
'We bin eat YOU?' they bin tell-im -
'YEAH, I bin turn meself into whatname --
ah brolga *gurdurwayin*' you know we say gurdurwayin --
'that's me' -
'Ahhh' Oh they know-im too oh everybody know him -

this oldfella he's a proper *maban* too--
dis man--
so that's the finish--
you know--
Lardi Lardi--
(Rasping)

NOTES

1   These men had the job of keeping a windmill and trough in order.
2   'humbug' means 'cause a nuisance'.
3   A lot of trouble was caused by the mismatch of economic systems in the early days of European colonisation of the area. Aborigines who were used to hunting anything on their land didn't understand, initially at least, the whites accumulation of animals for sale at distant markets. Spearing of cattle by Aborigines led to disputes between them and settlers and sometimes to punitive expeditions (massacres) of Aborigines by police patrols.
4   'kine' means 'kind'; the way the brolga walks.
5   Massage as trauma therapy.

NOTE ON THE TRANSCRIPTION

This technique of transcription was designed to reproduce the poetic effects of storytelling in Aboriginal English. The texts are divided into lines whenever the narrator pauses, and each line usually lasts as long as a breath. The length of the pauses is indicated by about one dash per second of pause. Kimberley Aboriginal English is also grammatically different from Standard English. Here readers will notice, for instance, lack of plurals in some nouns and lack of gender marking in pronouns. (S. M.)

PATRICK WHITE

Clay

For Barry Humphries and Zoe Caldwell

When he was about five years old some kids asked Clay why his mother had called him that. And he did not know. But began to wonder. He did, in fact, wonder a great deal, particularly while picking the bark off trees, or stripping a flower down to its core of mystery. He too, would ask questions, but more often than not failed to receive the answer because his mother could not bring herself to leave her own train of thought.

Mrs Skerritt said: 'If only your father hadn't died he'd still be putting out the garbage the bin is too much for me the stooping not to mention the weight in anyone short of breath but you Clay I know will be good to your mum and help when you are older stronger only that is still a long way off.'

So that it was Clay's turn not to answer. What could you say, anyway?

Mrs Skerritt said: 'I wouldn't ask anything of anyone but there are certain things of course I wouldn't expect a gentleman to stand up for me in the tram while I have my own two legs only it's the sort of thing a gentleman ought to do and ladies take Mrs Pearl for instance what she expects of her husband and him with the sugar-diabetes too.'

Clay mooned about the house listening to his mother's voice boring additional holes in the fretwork, for fretwork had been Dadda's hobby: there was fretwork just about everywhere, brackets and things, even a lace of fretwork hanging from table-top and doorway. Stiff. Sometimes while his mother's voice bored and sawed further Clay would break off pieces of the brown fretwork and hide it away under the house. Under the house was full of fretwork finally.

Or he would moon about the terraces of garden, amongst the collapsing lattices, flower-pot shards crackling underfoot, legs slapped by the straps of dark, leathery plants, lungs filled with suffocating bursts of asparagus fern. He would dawdle down to the harbour, with its green smell of sea-lettuce, and the stone wall, scribbled with the white droppings of gulls. The house itself leaned rather far towards the harbour, but had not fallen, because some men had come and shored it up. There it hung, however.

So Clay mooned. And would return often to the photograph. It was as though his childhood were riveted to the wedding group. There was his father, those thick thighs, rather tight about the serge crutch (unlike the Dadda he remembered lying Incurable in bed), and the influential Mr

Stutchbury, and Auntie Ada, and Nellie Watson (who died), and someone else who was killed in action. But it was to his mum that Clay was drawn, before and after all, into the torrential satin of the lap, by the face which had just begun to move out of its fixture of fretted lace. And the shoe. He was fascinated by the white shoe. Sometimes its great boat would float out from the shore of frozen time, into the waters of his imagination, rocking his cargo of almost transparent thoughts.

Once Mrs Skerritt came into the room and caught him at it, though she did not exactly see Clay for looking at herself.

'Ah dear,' she said, 'in the end things is sad.'

She would often half cry, and at such moments her hair would look more than ever like so many lengths of grey string, or on windy days, a tizz of frayed dish-cloth.

On this particular day when she caught Clay looking at the photograph, his throat swelled, and he dared to ask:

'Why is my name Clay, Mum?'

Because by that time he was seven, and the kids were asking worse than ever, and bashing him up (they were afraid that he was different).

'Why,' she said, 'let me think your father wanted Percival that is after Mr Stutchbury but I could not bring myself I said there are so many things you don't do but want take a name a name is yours take pottery I said I've half a mind to try my hand if I can find some feller or lady you never know I may be artistic but didn't because well there isn't the time always so much to do the people who have to be told and who have to be told and then Dadda's incurable illness so I did not do that only thought and thought about it and that I believe is why you was called Clay.'

Then she went out the back to empty the tea-pot on a bed of maidenhair which tingled perpetually with moisture.

So the kids continued to bash Clay up, and ask him why he was called that, and he couldn't tell them, because how could you even when you knew.

There were times when it got extra bad, and once they chased him with a woman's old cast-off shoe. He ran like a green streak, but not fast enough in the end—they caught him at the corner of Plant Street, where he had been born and always lived, and the heel of their old shoe bored for ever in his mind.

Later, when he had let himself in, into the garden of the leaning house, lost amongst collapsing lattices and the yellow fuzz of asparagus fern, he cried a bit for the difference to which he had been born. But smeared his eyes dry at last, and his nose. The light was rising from the bay in all green peacefulness, as if the world of pointed objects did not exist alongside that of the dreamy bridal shoe.

But he did not embark. Not then. His ribs had not subsided yet.

Once Clay dreamed a dream, and came down into the kitchen. He had meant to keep the dream to himself. Then it was too late, he heard, he was telling it to his mum. Even though his mouth was frozen stiff he had to keep on, to tell.

'In this dream,' he said, 'the steps led on down.'

His mum was pushing the rashers around, which went on buckling up in the pan.

'Under the sea,' said Clay. 'It was beautiful.'

He was sorry, but he could not help it.

'Everything drawn out. Hair and things. And weeds. The knotted ones. And the lettucy kind. Some of the fish had beards, Mum, and barked, well, like dogs.'

His mum had put the fried bread on a plate to one side, where the little squares were already stiffening.

'And shells, Mum,' he said, 'all bubbles and echoes as I went on down. It felt good. It felt soft. I didn't have to try. But just floated. Down.'

He could see his mother's behind, how it had begun to quiver, and he dreaded what might happen when he told. There was no avoiding it, though, and his mum went on prodding the bacon in the pan.

'When I got to the bottom,' he said, 'and the steps ended, you should have seen how the sea stretched, over the sand and broken bottles. Everything sort of silvery. I don't remember much else. Except that I found, Mum,' he said.

'What?' she asked.

He dreaded it.

'A cloud, Mum,' he said, 'and it was dead.'

Then Mrs Skerritt turned round, it was dreadful, how she looked. She opened her mouth, but nothing came out at first, only Clay saw the little thing at the back. Raised. When suddenly it began to act like a clapper. She began to cry, she began to create.

'Whatever are you gunna do to me?' she cried, as she pummelled and kneaded the moist grey dough of her cheeks.

'On top of everything else I never ever thought I'd have a freak!'

But Clay could only stand, and receive the blows her voice dealt. It was as though someone had taken a stick and drawn a circle round him. Him at the centre. There was no furniture any more.

The bacon was burning in the pan.

When Mrs Skerritt had thought it over, and used a little eau-de-Cologne, she took him up to McGillivray's. It was late by then, on a Saturday morning too. All the way Clay listened to her breathing and sometimes the sound of her corset. McGillivray was already closing, but agreed to do Mrs Skerritt's lad. McGillivray was kind.

'We want it short short Mr McGillivray please,' Mrs Skerritt said.

As the barber snipped Clay could hear his mum breathing, from where she sat, behind his back, under the coloured picture of the King.

Mr McGillivray did his usual nice job, and was preparing to design the little quiff when Mrs Skerritt choked.

'That is not short Mr McGillivray not what I mean oh no oh dear but it is difficult to explain there is too much involved and I left school when I turned fourteen.'

McGillivray laughed and said: 'Short is not shorn!'

'I don't care,' she said.

Clay could only look at the glass, and suck his cheeks in.

'Short is what I said and mean,' Mrs Skerritt confirmed. 'I was never one for not coming to the point.'

McGillivray was a gentle man, but he too began to breathe, he took the clippers, and shore a path through his subject's hair. He shore, and shore. Till there Clay was. Exposed.

'That suit?' McGillivray asked.

'Thank you,' she said.

So meek.

Then they went home. They crunched over the asphalt. They were that heavy, both of them.

As they went down the hill towards the turn where the milko's cart had plunged over, Mrs Skerritt said:

'There Clay a person is sometimes driven to things in defence of what we know and love I would not of done this otherwise if not to protect you from yourself because love you will suffer in life if you start talking queer remember it doesn't pay to be different and no one is different without they have something wrong with them.'

Clay touched his prickly hair.

'Let me remind you,' she said, 'that your mum loves you that is why.'

But Clay could no longer believe in love, and the kids bashed him up worse than ever, because his no-hair made him a sort of different different.

'Wot was you in for?' the kids asked, and did windmills on his stubble. 'Old Broad Arrer!' they shouted, and punched.

Actually Clay grew up narrow. He was all knuckle, all wrist. He had those drawn-out arms. He had a greenish skin from living under too many plants. He was long. And his eyes overflowed at dusk, merged with the street lights, and the oil patches on lapping water.

'Are you lonely, Clay?' Mrs Skerritt asked.

'No,' he said. 'Why?'

'I thought perhaps you was lonely you should get out and meet other young people of your own age you should get to know nice girls otherwise it is not normal.'

Then she drew in her chin, and waited.

But Clay stroked his prickly hair. For he went to McGillivray's every so often since it was ordained. When his voice broke the others no longer bashed him up, having problems of their own. The blackheads came, the pimples and moustaches.

Sometimes Mrs Skerritt would cry, sitting on the rotten veranda overlooking the little bay in which cats so often drowned.

'Oh dear Clay,' she cried, 'I am your mother and have a responsibility a double one since Dadda went I will ask Mr Stutchbury but cannot rely totally do you know what you want to do?'

Clay said: 'No.'

'Oh dear,' she moaned worse than ever, 'how did I deserve a silent boy who loves what I would like to know himself perhaps himself.'

In fact Clay did not know what he loved. He would have liked to think it was his mother, though it could have been Dadda. So he would try to remember, but it was only cold yellow skin, and the smell of sick sheets. When he had been forced to approach his father, lying Incurable in the bed, his heart could have tumbled down out of the belfry of his body.

Once his mother, it was evening, clutched his head against her apron, so that she must have pricked her hands.

'You are not my son,' she clanged, 'otherwise you would act different.'

But he could not, did not want to. Sometimes, anyway, at that age, he felt too dizzy from growing.

'How?' his voice asked, or croaked.

But she did not explain. She flung his long body away.

'It's not a matter,' she said, 'that anybody can discuss I will ask Mr Stutchbury to see what we must do and how.'

Mr Stutchbury was so influential, as well as having been a mate of Herb Skerritt's all his life. Mr Stutchbury was something, Mrs Skerritt believed, in the Department of Education, but if she did not clear the matter up, it was because she considered there was not all that necessity.

She bought a T-bone steak, and asked him round.

'What,' she asked, 'should we do with Clay I am a widow as you know and you was his father's friend.'

Mr Stutchbury drew in his moustache.

'We will see,' he said, 'when the time comes.'

Then he folded his moist lips over a piece of yellow fat from the not so tender T-bone steak.

When it was time, Mr Stutchbury thought up a letter to some fellow at the Customs and Excise.

> Dear Archie (he composed)
>   This is to recommend the son of an old friend. Herb Skerritt, for many years in the Tramways, died in tragical circumstances — of cancer to be precise . . .

(Clay, who of course opened the letter to see, got quite a shock from a word his mother never on any account allowed to be used in the home.)

. . . it is my duty and wish to further the interests of the above-mentioned boy. In brief, I would esteem it a favour if you could see your way to taking him 'under your wing'. I do not predict wonders of young Skerritt, but am of the opinion, rather, that he is a decent, average lad. In any event, wonders are not all that desirable, not in the Service anyway. It is the steady hand which pushes the pen a lifetime.

I will not expatiate further, but send you my
Salaams!

The young lady whom Mr Stutchbury had persuaded to type the letter had barely left the room, when his superior called, with the result that he forgot to add as he intended: 'Kindest regards to Mrs Archbold.' Even persons of influence have to consider the ground they tread on.

But Clay Skerritt started at the Customs, because Mr Archbold was not the sort to refuse Mr Stutchbury the favour he asked. So Clay took the ferry, mornings, in the stiff dark suit his mother had chosen. His long thin fingers learned to deal in forms. He carried the papers from tray to tray. In time he grew used to triplicate, and moistened the indelible before writing in his long thin hand the details, and the details.

Clay Skerritt did not complain, and if he was ignored he had known worse. For he was most certainly ignored, by the gentlemen who sat amongst the trays of papers, by the young ladies of the Customs and Excise, who kept their nails so beautifully, who took their personal towels to the toilet, and giggled over private matters and cups of milky tea. If they ever laughed at the junior in particular, at his tricky frame, his pimples, and his stubble of hair, Clay Skerritt was not conscious of it. Why should he be? He was born with inward-looking eyes.

That all was not quite in order, though, he began to gather from his mother.

'When I am gone Clay,' she said—it was the evening the sink got blocked up, 'you will remember how your mother was a messer but found she only scraped the dishes into the sink because her mind was otherwise engaged with you Clay your interests always some practical young lady will rectify anything your mother ever did by good intention I would not force you but only advise time is not to be ignored.'

But on days when the wind blew black across the grey water Mrs Skerritt might remark, peering out from the arbours of asparagus fern:

'Some young woman clever with her needle lighter-handed at the pastry-board will make you forget your poor mum well it is the way.'

Her son was bound to ignore what he could not be expected to believe. He would take a look at the wedding group. All so solidly alive, the figures appeared to announce a truth of which he alone could be the arbiter, just as the great white shoe would still put out, into the distance, for destinations of his choice.

His mother, however, continued in her mistaken attempts to celebrate the passing of reality. There was the day she called, her voice intruding amongst the objects which surrounded him:

'Take my grey costume dear up to the dry cleaner at the Junction tomato sauce is fatal when a person is on the stoutish side.'

Clay acted as he had been told. Or the streets were acting round him, and the trams. It was a bright day. Metal sang. The brick homes were no longer surreptitious, but opened up to disclose lives. In one window a woman was looking into her armpit. It made Clay laugh.

At the cleaner's a lady finished a yarn with the young girl. The lady said from alongside her cigarette:

'I'll leave you to it, Marj. I'm gunna make tracks for home and whip me shoes off. My feet are hurting like hell.'

Then the bell.

Clay was still laughing.

The young girl was looking down at the sheets of fresh brown paper, through the smell of cleaning. She herself had a cleaned, pallid skin, with pores.

'What's up?' she asked, as the client continued laughing.

She spoke so very flat and polite.

'Nothing,' he said, but added: 'I think perhaps you are like my mother.'

Which was untrue, in a sense, because the girl was flat, still, and colourless, whereas his mother was rotund, voluble, and at least several tones of grey. But Clay had been compelled to say it.

The girl did not reply. She looked down at first, as though he had overstepped the mark. Then she took the costume, and examined the spots of tomato sauce.

'Ready tomorrow,' she said.

'Go on!'

'Why not?' the girl replied. 'We are a One-day.'

But flat and absent she sounded.

Then Clay did not know why, but asked: 'You've got something on your mind.'

She said: 'It's only that the sink got blocked yesterday evening.'

It sounded so terribly grey, and she looking out with that expression of permanence. Then at once he knew he had been right, and that the girl at the dry cleaner's had something of his mother: it was the core of permanence. Then Clay grew excited. For he did not believe in im-permanence, not even when his mother attempted to persuade, not even when he watched the clods of earth tumble down on the coffin lid. Not while he was he.

So he said: 'Tomorrow.'

It sounded so firm, it was almost today.

Clay got used to Marj just as he had got used to his mum, only differently. They swung hands together, walking over the dead grass of several parks, or staring at animals in cages. They were already living together, that is, their silences intermingled. Each had a somewhat clammy palm. And if Marj spoke there was no necessity to answer, it was so flat, her remarks had the colour of masonite.

Marj said: 'When I have a home of my own, I will turn out the lounge Fridays. I mean, there is a time and place for everything. There are the bedrooms too.'

She said: 'I do like things to be nice.'

And: 'Marriage should be serious.'

How serious, Clay began to see, who had not told his mum.

When at last he did she was drying the apostle spoons, one of which she dropped, and he let her pick it up, on seeing that it was necessary for her to perform some therapeutic act.

'I am so glad Clay,' she said, rather purple, after a pause, 'I cannot wait to see this nice girl we must arrange some we must come to an agree there is no reason why a young couple should not hit it off with the mother-in-law if the home is large it is not so much temperament as the size of the home that causes friction.'

Mrs Skerritt had always known herself to be reasonable.

'And Marj is so like like you, Mum.'

'Eh?' Mrs Skerritt said.

He could not explain that what was necessary for him, for what he had to do, was a continuum. He could not have explained what he had to do, because he did not know, as yet.

All Mrs Skerritt could say was: 'The sooner we see the better we shall know.'

So Clay brought Marj. Their hands were clammier that day. The plants were huge, casting a fuscous tinge on the shored-up house.

Mrs Skerritt looked out of the door.

'Is this,' she said, 'I am not yet not yet ready to see.'

Clay told Marj she must go away, for that day at least, he would send for her, then he took his mother inside.

Mrs Skerritt did not meet Marj again, except in the mirror, in which she saw with something of a shock there is no such thing as permanence.

Shortly after she died of something. They said it was her ticker.

And Clay brought Marj to live in the house in which he had been born and lived. They did not go on a honeymoon, because, as Marj said, marriage should be serious. Clay hoped he would know what to do as they lay in the bed Mum and Dadda had used. Lost in that strange and lumpy acre Clay and Marj listened to each other.

But it was good. He continued going to the Customs. Once or twice he pinched the lobe of Marj's ear.

'What's got into you?' she asked.

He continued going to the Customs. He bought her a Java sparrow in a cage. It was a kind of love poem.

To which Marj replied: 'I wonder if it's gunna scatter its seed on the wall-to-wall. We can always spread a newspaper, though.'

And did.

Clay went to the Customs. He sat at his own desk. He used his elbows more than before, because his importance had increased.

'Take this letter away, Miss Venables,' he said. 'There are only two copies. When I expected five. Take it away,' he said.

Miss Venables pouted, but took it away. She, like everybody, saw that something had begun to happen. They would watch Mr Skerritt, and wait for it.

But Marj, she was less expectant. She accepted the houseful of fretwork, the things the mother-in-law had put away—sets of string-coloured doilies for instance, once she came across a stuffed canary in a cardboard box. She did not remark, but accepted. Only once she failed to accept. Until Clay asked:

'What had become of the photo?'

'It is in that cupboard,' she said.

He went and fetched out the wedding group, and stuck it where it had been, on a fretwork table. At least he did not ask why she had put the photo away, and she was glad, because she would not have known what to answer. The bits of your husband you would never know were bad enough, but not to understand yourself was worse.

So Marj stuck to the carpet-sweeper, she was glad of the fluff under the bed, she was glad of the pattern on the lino, the cartons of crispies that she bought—so square. Even light is solid when the paths lead inward. So she listened to the carpet-sweeper.

All this time, she realized, something had been happening to Clay. For one thing his hair had begun to grow. Its long wisps curled like feather behind his ears. He himself, she saw, was not yet used to the silky daring of hair, which formerly had pricked to order.

'Level with the lobes of the ears, Mr McGillivray, please,' Clay would now explain.

McGillivray, who was old by this, and infallibly kind, always refrained from commenting.

So did the gentlemen at the Customs—it was far too strange. Even the young ladies, who had been prepared to giggle at first, got the shivers for something they did not understand.

Only when the hair had reached as far as Mr Skerritt's shoulders did Mr Archbold send for Clay.

'Is it necessary, Mr Skerritt?' his superior asked, who had the additional protection of a private office.

Clay replied: 'Yes.'

He stood looking.

He was allowed to go away.

His wife Marj decided there is nothing to be surprised at. It is the only solution. Even if the fretwork crackled, she would not hear. Even if the hanging basket sprouted hair instead of fern, she would not see. There were the chops she put in front of her husband always so nicely curled on the plate. Weren't there the two sides of life?

One evening Clay came up out of the terraced garden, where the snails wound, and the sea smells. He stood for some considerable time in front of his parents' wedding group. The great shoe, or boat, or bridge, had never appeared so structural. Looking back he seemed to remember that this was the occasion of his beginning the poem, or novel, or regurgitation, which occupied him for the rest of his life.

Marj was certain that that was the evening he closed the door.

She would lie and call: 'Aren't you gunna come to bed, Clay?'

Or she would stir at the hour when the sheets are greyest, when the air trembles at the withheld threat of aluminium, Marj would ungum her mouth to remark: 'But Clay, the alarm hasn't gone off yet!'

From now on it seemed as though his body never stayed there long enough to warm the impression it left on the bed. She could hardly complain, though. He made love to her twice a year, at Christmas, and at Easter, though sometimes at Easter they might decide against—there was the Royal Agricultural Show, which is so exhausting.

All this is beside the point. It was the sheets of paper which counted, on which Clay wrote, behind the door, of that little room, which his wife failed to remember, it was soon so long since she had been inside. One of the many things Marj Skerritt learned to respect was another person's privacy.

So Clay wrote. At first he occupied himself with objects, the mysterious life which inanimacy contains. For several years in the beginning he was occupied with this.

> '. . . *the table standing continues standing its legs so permanent of course you can take an axe and swing it cut into the flesh as Poles do every once in a while then the shriek murder murder but mostly nothing disturbs the maps the childhood journeys on the frozen wave of wooden water no boat whether wood or iron when you come to think satin either ever sails from A to B except in the mind of the passenger so the table standing standing under an electric bulb responds unlikely unless to determination or desperation of a Polish kind . . .*'

One night Clay wrote: '*I have never observed a flower-pot intimately until now its hole is fascinating the little down of green moss it is of greater significance than what is within though you can fill it if you decide to if you concentrate long enough. . . .*'

Up till now he had not turned his attention to human beings, though he had been surrounded by them all his life. In actual fact he did not turn his attention to them now, he was intruded on. And Lova was not all that human, or not at first, a presence rather, or sensation of possession.

That night Clay got the hiccups, he was so excited, or nervous. The reverberations were so metallic he failed to hear his wife Marj, her grey voice: 'Aren't you gunna come to bed, Clay?'

Lova was, by comparison, a greenish-yellow, of certain fruits, and plant-flesh.

'*Lova Lova Lova,*' he wrote at first, to try it out.

He liked it so much it surprised him it had not come to him before. He could have sat simply writing the name, but Lova grew more palpable.

> '. . . *her little conical breasts at times ripening into porepores detachable by sleight of hand or windy days yet so elusive fruit and shoes distributed amongst the grass . . .*'

In the beginning Lova would approach from behind glass, her skin had that faint hot-house moisture which tingles on the down of ferns, her eyes a ferny brown that complemented his own if he had known. But he knew no more than gestures at first, the floating entanglement of hair in mutual agreement, the slight shiver of skin passing over skin. She would ascend and descend the flights of stone steps, inhabiting for a moment the angles of landings of old moss-upholstered stone. The leaves of the *monstera deliciosa* sieved her at times into a dispersed light. Which he alone knew how to reassemble. On rare occasions their mouths would almost meet, at the bottom of the garden, where the smell of rotting was, and the liquid manure used to stand, which had long since dried up. She was not yet real, and might never be. No. He would make her. But there were the deterrents. The physical discords.

Marj said: 'My hands are that chapped I must ask Mr Todd's advice. You can enjoy a chat with a chemist, doctors are most of them too busy pushing you out.'

And Lova got the herpes. Clay could not look at her at first. As she sat at her own little table, taking the fifteen varieties of pills, forcing them into her pig's snout, Lova would smile still, but it was sad. And soon the sore had become a scab. He could not bring himself to approach. And breath, besides.

For nights and nights Clay could not write a word. Or to be precise, he wrote over several nights:

> '. . . *a drying and a dying . . .*'

If he listened, all he could hear was the rustle of Lova's assorted pills, the ruffling of a single sterile date-palm, the sound of Marj turning in the bed.

Then it occurred to his panic the shored-up house might break open. It was so rotten, so dry. He could not get too quickly round the table, scattering the brittle sheets of paper. Motion detached itself from his feet in the shape of abrupt, leather slippers. Skittering to reach the door.

Clay did not, in fact, because Lova he now saw locking locking locked it, popping the key afterwards down between.

Lova laughed. And Clay stood. The little ripples rose up in her throat, perhaps it was the cold key, and spilled over, out of her mouth, her wet mouth. He knew that the private parts of babies tasted as tender as Lova's mouth.

He had never tried. But suspected he must.

She came to him.

'Bum to you!' Lova said.

She sat in his lap then, and with his free hand he wrote, the first of many white nights:

'At last my ryvita has turned to velveeta life is no longer a toast-rack.'

'Golly,' said Lova, 'what it is to be an educated feller! Honest, Clay, it must be a great satisfaction to write, if only to keep one of your hands occupied.'

She laughed again. When he had his doubts. Does every face wear the same expression unless it is your own? He would have liked to look at the wedding group, to verify, but there were all those stairs between, and darkness. All he could hear was the sound of Marj breaking wind. Marj certainly had said at breakfast: 'It is the same. Whatever the manufacturers tell you, that is only to sell the product.'

But Lova said: 'It is different, Clay, as different as kumquats from pommygranates. You are the differentest of all perhaps. I could lap up the cream of your genius.'

She did, in fact, look at moments like a cat crouched in his lap, but would close at once, and open, like a knife.

'I would eat you,' she repeated, baring her pointed teeth, when he had thought them broad and spaced, as in Mum or Marj.

Although he was afraid, he wrote with his free right hand:

'I would not trust a razor-blade to any but my own . . .'

When Lova looked it over.

'Shoot!' she said. 'That is what I am!'

He forgot about her for a little, for writing down what he had to write.

'. . . Lova sat in my lap smelling of crushed carrot tops she has taken the frizz out of her hair but cannot make it smell less green I would not trust her further than without meaning to cast aspersions you can't trust even your own thoughts past midnight . . .'

'Chip Chip Chip chipped off his finger,' Lova said. 'Anyway it begins with C.'

'Oh dear,' C began to cry. 'Oh dear dear dear oh Lova!'

'When does D come in?' she asked.

'D isn't born,' he said, 'and pretty sure won't be. As for A, A is in bed. No,' he corrected. 'A am not.'

Suddenly he wished he was.

He realized he was eye to eye with Lova their lashes grappling together in gummy agreement but melancholy to overflowing. They were poured into each other.

After that, Clay finished, for the night at least, and experienced the great trauma of his little empty room, for Lova had vanished, and there were only the inkstains on his fingers to show that she had ever been there.

There was nothing for it now but to join Marj in the parental bed, where he wondered whether he would ever be able to rise again. He was cold, cold.

Actually Marj turned over and said: 'Clay, I had an argument with Mr Tesoriero over the turnips. I told him you couldn't expect the public to buy them flabby.'

But Clay slept, and in fact he did not rise, not that morning, the first in many years, when the alarm clock scattered its aluminium trays all over the house.

Clay Skerritt continued going to the Customs. They had got used to him by then, even to his hair, the streaks in it.

He realized it was time he went to McGillivray's again, but some young dago came out, and said:

'Nho! Nho! McGillivray gone. Dead. How many years? Five? Six?'

So Clay Skerritt went away.

It was natural enough that it should have happened to McGillivray. Less natural were the substances. The pretending houses. The asphalt which had lifted up.

Then he saw the pointed heel, caught in the crack, wrenching at it. He saw the figure. He saw. He saw.

When she turned round, she said:

'Yes. It's all very well. For you. With square heels. Bum bums.'

Wrenching at her heel all the while.

'But Lova,' he said, putting out his hands.

She was wearing a big-celled honeycomb sweater.

'Oh, yes!' she said.

And laughed.

'If that's how you feel,' he answered.

'If that's how I *feel*!'

His hands were shaking, and might have caught in the oatmeal wool.

'I'm not gunna stand around exchanging words with any long-haired nong in the middle of Military Road. Not on yours!'

'Be reasonable,' he begged.

'What is reasonable?' she asked.

He could not tell. Nor if she had asked: what is love?

'Aren't you going to know me then?' he said.

'I know you,' she said, sort of flat—two boards could not have come together with greater exactitude.

'And it is time,' she said, 'to go.'

Jerking at her stuck heel.

'I've come here for something,' he remembered. 'Was it bird-seed?'

'Was it my Aunt Fanny!'

Then she got her heel free and all the asphalt was crackling up falling around them in scraps of torn black tinkly paper.

If he could only have explained that love cannot be explained.

All the while ladies were going in and out, strings eating into their fingers together with their rings. One lady had an alsatian, a basket suspended from its teeth, it did not even scent the trouble.

It was Saturday morning. Clay went home.

That evening, after they had finished their spaghetti on toast, because they were still paying off the Tecnico, Marj said:

'Clay, I had a dream.'

'No!' he shouted.

Where could he go? There was nowhere now.

Except on the Monday there was the Customs and Excise. He could not get there quick enough. To sharpen his pencils. To move the paper-clips the other side of the ink eraser.

When what he was afraid might happen, happened.

Lova had followed him to the Customs.

The others had not spotted it yet, for it could have been any lady passing the day at the Customs in pursuit of her unlawful goods. Only no lady would have made so straight for Mr Skerritt's desk, nor would she have been growing from her big-celled oatmeal sweater quite so direct as Lova was.

She had those little, pointed, laughing teeth.

'Well,' she opened, 'you didn't reckon on this.'

She was so certain of herself by now, he was afraid she might jump out of her jumper.

He sat looking down, at the letter from Dooley and Mann, Import Agents, re the Bechstein that got lost.

'Listen, Lova,' he advised. 'Not in here. It won't help find the piano.'

'Pianner? A fat lot of pianner! You can't play that one on me.'

'You may be right,' he answered.

'Right!' she said. 'Even if I wasn't. Even if I was flippin' wrong!'

She put her hand-bag on the desk.

'If anyone's gunna play, I'm the one,' she said.

Sure enough the old black upright slid around the corner from behind Archbold's glassed-in office, followed by the little leather-upholstered stool, from which the hair was bursting out. Lova seemed satisfied. She laughed, and when she had sat down, began to dish out the gay sad jazz. Playing and playing. Her little hands were jumping and frolicking on their own. The music playing out of every worm hole in the old, sea-changed piano.

Clay looked up, to see Archbold looking down. Miss Titmuss had taken her personal towel, and was having trouble with her heels as she made her way towards the toilet.

When Lova got up. She was finished. Or not quite. She began to drum with her bum on the greasy, buckled-up rashers of keys of the salt-cured old piano.

'There!' she shouted.

She came and sat on the corner of his desk. She had never been so elastic. It was her rage of breathing. He was unable to avoid the pulse of her suspender, winking at him from her thigh.

One or two other of the Customs officials had begun to notice, he observed, desperately through the side-curtains of his hair.

So he said: 'Look here, Lova, a scene at this stage will make it well nigh impossible for me to remain in the Service. And what will we do without the pension? Marj must be taken into account. I mean to say, it is the prestige as much as the money. Otherwise, we have learnt to do on tea and bread.'

Lova laughed then.

'Ha! *Ha!* HA!'

There is no way of writing it but how it was written on the wall. For it was. It got itself printed up on the wall which ran at right angles to Archbold's office.

Clay sat straight, straight. His adam's apple might not endure it much longer.

'Scenes are so destructive,' he said, or begged.

So his mum had told him.

'If that is what you want,' said Lova, 'you know I was never one for holding up procedure for the sake of filling in a form.'

And she ripped it off the pad from under his nose. Her hands were so naked, and could get a whole lot nakeder. He was afraid he might be answerable.

'I would never suggest,' she shouted, 'that the pisspot was standing right end up when it wasn't.'

But he had to resist, not so much for personal reasons as for the sake of public decorum, for the honour of the Department. He had to protect the paper-clips.

Because their hands were wrestling, troubling the desk. Him and Lova. At any moment the carton might burst open. At any. It happened quite quickly, breathily, ending in the sigh of scatteration.

'I will leave you for now,' she said, getting off the corner of the desk, and pulling down her sweater, which had rucked up.

Almost every one of his colleagues had noticed by this, but all had the decency to avoid passing audible judgment on such a very private situation.

When it was over a little while, Miss Titmuss got down and gathered up the paper-clips, because she was sorry for Mr Skerritt.

He did not wait to thank or explain, but took his hat, treading carefully to by-pass the eyes, and caught the ferry to the other side.

Marj said: 'Aren't you early, Clay? Sit on the veranda a while. I'll bring you a cuppa, and slice of that pound cake, it's still eatable I think.'

So he sat on the veranda, where his mother used to sit and complain, and felt the southerly get inside his neckband, and heard the date-palm starting up. Sparrows gathered cautiously.

Marj said: 'Clay, if you don't eat up, it'll be tea.'

You can always disregard, though, and he went inside the room, which he did not even dread. There she was, sitting in the other chair, in the oatmeal sweater. Her back turned. Naturally.

'Lova,' he began.

Then she came towards him, and he saw that she herself might sink in the waters of time she spread before him cunningly the nets of water smelling of nutmeg over junket the steamy mornings and the rather shivery afternoons.

If he did not resist.

She was just about as resistant as water not the tidal kind but a glad upward plume of water rising and falling back as he put his hands gently lapping lapping. She was so gentle.

Marj began to knock on the door.

'Tea's getting cold, Clay,' she announced.

It was, too. That is the way of things.

'I made you a nice devilled toast.'

She went away, but returned, and held her ear to the dry rot.

'Clay?' she asked. 'Don't you mind?'

Marj did not like to listen at doors because of her regard for privacy.

'Well,' she said, 'I never knew you to act like this.'

It could have been the first time in her life that Marj had opened a door.

Then she began to scream. She began to create. It was unlike her.

She could not see his face because of all that hair. The hair and the boards between them were keeping it a secret.

'This is something I never bargained for,' she cried.

For the blood had spurted out of the leg of the table. Just a little.

And that old shoe. He lay holding a white shoe.

'I never ever saw a shoe!' she moaned. 'Of all the junk she put away, just about every bit of her, and canaries and things, never a shoe!'

As Clay lay.

With that stiff shoe.

'I don't believe it!' Marj cried.

Because everyone knows that what isn't isn't, even when it is.

PETER COWAN

Requiem

Down below the sharp, steep slope of the limestone cliff the beach was clearly white and the waves pushed down and rushed in on it, and he looked at the colours of the shallow water and the shifting deeps out beyond, and then his eyes went along the steep coastline to where it sloped and the high brush gave place to low stunted wind-sloped scrub, and the haze that held the distance blotted it out and he came back to where he was. He leaned over and pulled the girl's dress up, and he said why don't we go for a swim. She rolled over and he looked as he always looked, and it was as though it were new. I'd rather sleep, she said. Why don't we swim and have a sleep after. She didn't say anything, and he slapped her and said you're lazy. Well, we'll go, she said. They got up and took their towels from the bushes outside the small natural cavity the bushes formed. Then carefully they went down the cliff face where they had cut the path, and reaching the sand he ran over it and he wanted to cry out, and he felt the strength in him and the sea and the sand and the timeless place about him so that when the water closed on him he felt, yes, I have lived, if they smash me tomorrow I have lived in these things that are of more reality and of more worth than us in our meanness and filth and proud smallness. He pushed from the water and ran to the girl, and because of the strength that was in him because he was joined to the natural the real things he grabbed her arms and held her hard, and she understood, yet he hurt her so that she cried out don't, you hurt me, and he let her go, and the marks of his fingers were strong on her arms like the hard visibleness of his desire that now was for her only as much as it was for all the things of unity and reality to which he was attuned. He looked at the bare body of the girl, the shoulders and arms, the insloping back and the balanced rounds of her generous buttocks that quivered as she moved and hesitated and could not bring herself to dive, and he thought, you fit, you are a part of the natural, but here I see you best, where I can see all things. And when they had swum they walked up the beach and dried themselves, and were warm in the sun. They climbed back up the cliff, and in their place in the bushes the girl lay down, and for a time he stroked her thighs and the flesh that spread now and was different to when she was standing, and then he sat still and listened to the sound of the sea, gaining, and saw the sloping coast in the afternoon light, and he felt that all time had halted there, in the middle of the afternoon, and that as it was now so it must be always. Yet I shall not know it, he thought. When we go from here it is to be dragged to the madness of unreality. I am not really part of this, else I would stay here, else this time would be all time. But we go, and these steep cliffs, the sea coast scrub, the sloping dunes and the white beach and the sea and the rocks are here. My eyes have seen these things and something, the last real part in me, has gone out and become part of this, and has felt that alone which endures. For a time I have been a part of reality, for a time I have been fitted to this scene, have been one with the things which gave me being. Then in the madness which has triumphed over the ages I go and become engulfed and am no more.

JUDITH WRIGHT

The Weeping Fig

' . . . only condensed milk, I'm afraid, Mr Condon. When you live in a place like this you have to expect that,' the woman was saying. She held the teapot stagily suspended, waiting for his answer.

'Oh—no, no milk, thank you.' Looking out into that uninviting landscape he had momentarily forgotten her. But he drew up his chair now and made an effort at conversation. Though it was really too hot to try to keep up her tea-party foolishness. Good Lord, the woman had actually changed her dress; she was wearing some frilly affair—chintz, was it? The word sounded right, brittle and foolish.

'Have you always lived here, Mrs Hastings?'

'Oh, goodness, no. Harold came here as manager two years ago—that was before we had met. I always tell him I would never have married him if I had had any idea! But we hope for a city job as soon as we can find a house—so difficult, you know. Of course, the pay *is* good, I have to admit that. But seventy miles from the nearest town—and such a town! And frankly, Mr Condon, I don't feel myself cut out for country life. Now my old home—well, it makes me miserable to think of it here; down on the river-bank you know, quite close to the city shops—right in the swim as you might say. But Charlotte Downs is really beyond words—now, isn't it? I have a phrase for this kind of country—the abomination of desolation. Don't you think that's appropriate?'

He found some polite formula. 'Who really owns this place, then?'

'Oh, it's run by a company—most of these old places are now, you know. No one would live here for choice, would they? I don't know how long they've had it. We get a director's visit now and then—big cars, you know, and good clothes—they make something out of it. But they only come in the cool season.' She laughed rather viciously. 'They don't have to know what the rest of the year is like, now do they?'

'You don't know, then, whether any of the original buildings are still standing?'

She looked bored, she pouted. 'Well, I don't. I've never asked, to tell you the truth. But Bertha might. She's the old housekeeper, you know. Her father was a stockman here all his life, she tells me; and Bertha never married—you'll see why, if you'd like to ask her.'

'Well, yes, I should like to know. I have a special reason,' he began to explain; 'you see, this place—'. But she was not interested in his reasons.

'Bertha,' she called to the dim back regions beyond the broad verandah. 'Come here a minute.'

There was a pause at this summons, then a shuffle. The door leading off the verandah behind him opened, and he turned. Bertha advanced— any age over thirty, deeply coffee coloured, bare-footed and hideously dressed, she half-limped, half-hopped on a withered leg.

'Yes, Missus?'

'Mrs Hastings, please, Bertha,' the woman corrected. 'This gentleman, Mr Condon'—(Condon half-bowed anxiously, as at an introduction, but Bertha's eyes did not move) 'would like to know something about the buildings here.' She took out a cigarette and turned impatiently away towards the tea-table.

Bertha waited.

'I was just asking Mrs Hastings'—Condon could not help feeling foolish—'whether any of the original buildings, the first that were built on the station, are left.'

Bertha raised a sinewy arm. 'Out there, by the big green tree, you see?'

'Yes,' Condon answered.

'That the old homestead, my father tole me years ago. See, made of split slab. Roof used to be bark, now tin. They use that one for store— timber, paint, that kind of thing. Nearly fallen down, you see.'

'Did your father know—did he ever tell you anything about the people who built that hut? You know the name of Condon?'

Bertha looked vague, uninhabited. 'No, didn't say. I got scones in the oven, Missus—Hastings. Think I better go and look.'

Mrs Hastings, swinging a brilliant earring (good God!) looked at Condon wearily. 'Are there any more questions you'd like answered, Mr Condon?'

Condon shook his head and thanked Bertha. The wall was blank, of course. Little enough had ever been written on it. The years, the dust of the dry seasons, the wet of the monsoons, had washed out names, persons, all that had been. But he would like to look at that building, just the same, before he went.

'Tell me,' Mrs Hastings asked now with a pallid interest, 'how long ago were your people here?'

'My great-grandfather left here in eighteen sixty-five.'

'My goodness,' Mrs Hastings murmured, dismissing the subject. 'Fancy being still interested in it. Would you care to go and look at the building, perhaps?'

Condon rose with relief. 'I should, thank you. I'll have to be going shortly, though. I have an appointment in the town tonight.'

'Please consider the place your own,' Mrs Hastings invited. 'I shan't come out; it's really too hot. But do call back to say goodbye. We don't get so *many* people dropping in for a chat, do we?' Her eyes said plainly that this one had been a sore disappointment.

Condon made his way down the side steps and turned towards the old building. As he left the shade of the verandah the heat took him by the shoulders and the dry air burned into his lungs. November was no month to travel in north-western Queensland; he would not take this on again for the firm if he could help it. It was the name of the town that had arrested his attention—Hambleton. So it still existed, he had thought, that name that had come into the old diaries, written in rusty pale ink like dried blood. So the places were real. He would go and see.

The little building, crooked, tottering against a support like an old grey staggerer on a crutch, had yet been honestly built, he could see. He remembered the progress of the work, noted in the diary over months; the choosing of trees, the felling, the splitting of slabs, the dressing of them, the mortising; then the roof was on, the ant-bed floor smoothed. 'Ellen and the children moved into the house yesterday. A great change from the wagon and they are rejoicing accordingly. All now looks fair for our new venture, and cattle so far doing well.' He bent down to examine that mortising, nearly a century old—yes, old Stephen had known his job. 'As far as I can tell,' he said to himself bitterly. For it seemed to him suddenly that there was a pride in that work that he himself had never known.

Inside, the house was stacked with all the cast-off and left-over material accumulated over the years by various owners and managers. Two old wagon-wheels leaned in a corner; slabs, fencing-posts, coils of rusted wire, nameless pieces of iron, branding-tools, cobwebs, dusty odd stirrup-irons, buckles, lengths of chain—all deeply silted with the whitish choking dust. The inside of the house, such as it had been, was hidden behind the piles of rubbish.

He could see the window-space, empty now and hung with old hides; there Ellen (he could not think of her as his great-grandmother, so real had she become to him in his absorption in that old diary) had sat and sewed; had leaned shaking with ague, the two children burning hot in their stringybark bunks had endured her loneliness and known her fears and joys—Ellen, the Devonshire girl, seventeen when she married, twenty when she came here, twenty-two when she died, who had loved birds and fed them with scanty crumbs, who had hated snakes and lost her daughter through snakebite. And there by the timber chimney stood a rough-sawn table which he fancied must have been hers. Stephen must have made that.

But the heat in the little hut drove him back to the door. It was inhuman, that heat, like a climate from another world. He leaned gasping on the outside of the door and looked out beyond the homestead buildings to the thin ragged trees that clung to the earth, an earth that burned the hand.

Pioneers, o pioneers. A lot of rot was talked about them. As though they had not been ordinary human creatures, as though they had been nobler, more equipped with endurance and virtue, as though they had been—clichés. One didn't put up with this unless one had to, said Mrs Hastings dimly in his mind. Or had they indeed been different? Was there something in them of faith, of vitality, that Mrs Hastings and he, John Condon, never had known? Nonsense to ask—one couldn't know, more than the diary said.

And what did it say, of this crazy hut that sagged beside him? Death, death and again death; hope lost, revived again; loneliness, ugliness, semi-starvation; and at last the cry in a handwriting almost unrecognizable. 'My wife is dead.' Not her name; no more was said; the diary ended.

It was by chance he had found out the rest, down in the hot northern port, in the crumbling earliest file of that old newspaper in the news-paper office, consulted more in idleness than hope. So Stephen Condon had deserted his venture, leaving nothing but graves behind, fanned by monsoon winds and dried by burning heat. One son, the eldest child, remained; Stephen had ridden, carrying him in a pack-saddle, those three hundred miles to the northern port, and died there. Of what had happened after that, John Condon had no idea. Only the diary remained, washed up on the shore of John's life when his own father died, lying unexplained among irrelevant papers. On it his father had written, among scrawls of sums, pounds, shillings and pence that had probably never added up to the advantage of the Condons who had lived on hope and the three-thirty next Saturday; 'Diary of my grandfather?' So sank Stephen Condon behind question-marks into a lost past.

And what on earth had brought him, John Condon, here, at any rate? Nothing had come out of this but a headache. Did he want to come back here, to this disastrous oven of a place, which had already set every nerve throbbing behind his eyes? Even if he could afford to buy the place—and certainly he couldn't—no, he certainly did not. He leaned giddily against the door-post and looked round for shade. He would go as soon as he had had another drink, as soon as he could find that woman and say goodbye. Death! The place was full of it.

But round the wall of the hut there was shade. Seeing it only as a darkness in the terrible attack of a world-wide light, he made for it thankfully. Not until he looked up did he see the thick green depth of swaying leaves, the blessing of that cool cave, the living fact of it. A weeping-fig tree.

'Today Ellen planted the Port Jackson fig. She has kept it alive all the way in the wagon, I must say almost miraculously. We plan for our old age a bench and table under it, though it is now just one foot in height. It will make a splendid shade for the garden.'

'A bitter day for us both. Today we buried little Jane near the fig-tree. Ellen says she cannot bear to have her any farther from the house.'

'Ellen last night bore a son, which died at birth. She is grief-stricken and very weak. The child is buried near little Jane. One son remains to us . . .'

A sentimental journey. A crazy journey. Yet he could not help feeling, as he looked up into the fig-tree's blue-green shadows, a sense of triumph. 'Well,' he said to himself, hardly knowing why; 'that was worth coming for.' Yes, that fig-tree. It was an achievement of some kind. It was alive, it was green; in that waste unlikely landscape it triumphed. And in it, he said to himself, those dead Condons probably had some part—their red blood had gone to feed its green. It was taller than anything he could see. The Condons and the landscape—here they met. It was a root—it was what he had wanted.

Mrs Hastings came delicately across the baked grassless waste; her enormous hat was feathery, shiny pink straw.

'Do come and have a drink before you go, Mr Condon. Do you know, you've been here nearly an hour! I quite thought you had a sun-stroke or something.'

He indicated the tree on impulse. 'My great-grandmother and two of her children are buried under that tree.' Now why had he said that? For it was a boast, he realized.

Mrs Hastings screamed a little. 'But how dreadful! That just puts the finishing touch on the place for me. You don't know how creepy graves make me feel. Do come back to the house. My husband will be in in a little while; he would so much like to meet you, I'm sure.'

Driving away, John Condon was the business-man again. He had not much time to get to the town for that appointment. Tall and triumphant in the withering landscape the weeping-fig swayed its leaves, but he did not look back. He had got what he had come for.

OODGEROO NOONUCCAL

Carpet Snake

He was a beauty, that ten-foot carpet snake we had as a pet. My father belonged to the Noo-muccle tribe of Stradbroke Island, and the carpet snake was his totem. He made sure he looked after his blood-brother. My mother belonged to a different tribe. The carpet snake was not her totem. She hated old Carpie, because of his thieving ways. She was proud of her fowl-run and of the eggs our hens provided. Carpie liked the fowl-run too; every time he felt hungry he would sneak in, select the choicest fowl in the run, and swallow it. He could always outsmart Mother, no matter what she did to keep her chooks out of his ravenous belly. But, somehow, Mother never was game enough to bring down the axe on Carpie's head. We all knew she was often tempted to do just that. I think two things stopped her: her deep respect for the fact that Dad's decisions were final around the house, and the thought that if she killed in anger, Biami the Good Spirit would punish her.

We all loved Carpie except for Mother—and the dog. The dog kept well out of Carpie's way, because he was scared stiff of him. He seemed to know that a ten-foot carpet snake can wind itself around a dog and in time swallow it whole.

Whenever Mother thought none of us kids was around, she would swear at old Carpie—and Mother's swearing could outmatch that of any bullocky anywhere in Australia.

One day Mother went away for a short while to hospital. She came home with a brand-new baby sister for us. The day of her homecoming, we were rather overawed as we watched the baby sleeping in her cot. The big black dog looked at the baby, too, and obviously approved of the new arrival. After a while, Mother shooed us out to play, placed the cover gently over the sleeping baby, and went to make herself a cup of tea. Some friends, tribal neighbours, called to welcome her home; playing in our summer-house of tea-tree bark that Dad had built to catch the cool breezes blowing from the bay, we heard the women gossiping and the clink of teacups. When the neighbours left, Mother peeped in with pride on her new baby.

Suddenly we heard Mother's voice raised in a terrible screech as she raced outside, calling to Dad. Dad read the urgency of that screech, dropped his hammer, and ran.

Mother looked as though she were having a fit. She was jumping up and down, running to snatch up the long-handled broom, swearing like a bullocky. We knew something terrible must have happened for Mother to carry on like this. She behaved differently in different sorts of emergencies. We knew this one was serious.

'Stop shouting, woman!' Dad ordered. 'What's wrong?'

Mother pointed a shaking finger towards the bedroom. 'Get that gluttonous reptile out of my bedroom!'

Dad went into the bedroom. There, curled up in the cot with the baby, now wide awake and crying, was old Carpie.

Carpie seemed to sum up the situation in no time flat. He quickly slithered off the bedclothes, down onto the floor and out of the door.

The dog was trying to do the right thing by the family, taking menacing steps towards the snake and making growling noises in his throat. He was very happy to obey Dad, however, when he called him off.

Finally Mother found her composure, once Carpie had disappeared. 'But you mark my words, you stubborn fellow, that snake could have swallowed my baby,' she told Dad.

'Don't be silly, woman, why would he want to swallow your baby when he can swallow your chooks any time he wants to?' Dad retorted, and shot out of the door before Mother could think up a reply.

After that old Carpie carried on exactly as before, roaming about the house wherever he pleased. He went on stealing fowls and eggs, and slept anywhere he liked—though he never again tried to get into my baby sister's cot. I used to like it when I went off to the lavatory and found him holed up there. He would stretch himself right out across a beam in the ceiling. I used to sit in the lavatory for hours and tell him my innermost secrets, and it was very satisfying the way old Carpie would never interrupt the conversation or crawl away. Mother often accused me of dodging chores by going off and spending such a long time in the lavatory. This wasn't quite true; all I wanted to do was to share my secrets with Carpie.

When Dad died, we lost Carpie. He just seemed to disappear. We never found out what happened to him. Perhaps Biami the Good Spirit whispered to him: 'Your blood-brother has gone to the shadow land. Your days are numbered. Get lost.'

I like to think he still roams somewhere. Maybe he found a better fowl-run. I hope so. Funny thing about women. When my father died and Carpie disappeared, Mother decided to give away her fowl-run. She seemed to lose interest in it, somehow.

THELMA FORSHAW

The Widow-maker

We had always lived within the sound of a crowd's roar. I first recall a terrace hard by the Roxana Dance Hall, in Bondi, where talent quests were held with much timpani and percussion. Later, a lane that swarmed on Saturday nights with patrons of the Leichhardt Stadium. And then—at the time the following trauma took place—we lived within cooee of Harold Park, where three nights a week the Trots and Greyhound Races were run.

Whaaahhoo WHAAAHH! Like the surf it thundered, with aspirates huffing and sibilants hissing through it. The vast sigh of collective ecstasy. Or the giant groan of collective dismay. And triumph roaring upward through the funnels of a thousand throats. Our people at play. The honourable grime of toil showered away; the open-neck sports-shirts; the breath relaxingly beery; the entrance-fee sweaty within the fist; and the feeling of essentiality to the great collective entity of the queue.

I grew up in a ferociously recreational atmosphere. Polarizing my mother's worn Missal was a tattered booklet—*The Rubaiyat of Omar Khayyam*. Which *he* spouted in frisky mood, or parodied, as is our nature:

> *Tickets for the fight, a jug of beer and Thou*
> *Beside me in the wilderness . . .*

Thou—usually the mate. The china-plate. The cobber. And—let us be fair—sometimes the love-and-kisses. Almost as sporty as he. No nonsense. No slop: 'Come *kick* me, sweet-and-twenty', rather. The Missus.

Joyfully he exuded our national ethos, his hand on the *Rubaiyat* swearing eternal good times. But he had a dangerous edge, a prancing nervousness that may have been the festering of the young athlete he had killed off with hedonism. Or, might he have been a throwback? Saxon-descended, there blared out of him a personal splendour, a blond radiance, a body-worship (ah, God, how he scrubbed and oiled and scented, and watched the paunchless waistline, and consulted regularly the mirror of women's eyes:

> *Woman, woman on the wall,*
> *Who is the fairest of us all?*)

Hellenic body. Gladiatorial mind. Vital, violent, sudden. A wife-beater. A mountain swooping to leather his child. That hardly mattered. But *her* bleeding mouth, the bruised eye. *That* mattered to the social-worker I tried later—and failed—to become. Lover of the poor. Protector of the weak. Righter of wrongs. Lady Galahad falling off the unfoolable white horse of vocation. Trying to be splendidly redemptive as he was splendidly vicious. Perhaps I laughed too much ever to be a 'proper' social worker. *Not sound*, I believe they call it.

I was an eerie-minded child. I saw through a glass darkly. But not—exactly—*glum*. I made people nervous with my oddly timed laughter. I laughed wherever I was not supposed to. In church, for instance. In school. With the wrong visitor. I had to grow up before I knew why I laughed, and was surprised to find it warrantable. Obviously, my wisdom lay in my funny-bone. Jolt that, and instead of an angry howl, you got a scream of laughter. A scream . . . of laughter.

I realize now I should have laughed at my father. Too late. He was my blind spot. His quality numbed my funny-bone. I am a sucker for splendour. Lo, the Blond Beast and I present the 'Hippocratic countenance'—the gaping mouth and staring eye—that stasis which the dead share with the amazed, the enchanted, and the idiot. Ah, yes—see the Beautiful Brute, moving like a thoroughbred, flashing his golden teeth. The stammer that gave his mouth alluring shapes, and provided that soupçon of pathos without which no man is truly irresistible.

I ought to have laughed at Golden Boy the Anachronism in a time and place that made him absurd—as an actor out of the context of his stage is often a fool, and a dictator among democrats a loony fanatic. Dressed to kill in a society where it was queenish to 'dress'. Seeking anarchy as the chum of a Darlinghurst razor-gang. Game as Ned Kelly, or, as someone said, 'gallant about nothing'. A warrior without a war. A gladiator aching for the marathon he had missed. Therefore beating men up for pleasure. Torturing his wife, inculcating in that fittest survivor with the metronome of fist or terrorist's razor the Nietzschean anthem of the superman. And when he grinned and his hand clasped a most passionate mateship—people forgetting to remember. Therefore, an 'ecstatic', rapt in the contemplation of his effect on others.

A man should not die because he is a self-glorifier, a womanizer, an athlete-gone-bad. Thugs should die. Rapists. Razor-wielders. Gangsters' chums. When I was a woman I fitted together the smashed fragments of his beauty, brutality, and absurdity and knew no woman could ever have killed him. Only a child.

I'm the lucky one, I am. My chance came. I felt as people do when the unbelievable, the despaired-of chance plops straight down in front of them. The Immortal fell ill! An attack of 'flu combined with a sprained ankle softened him up for the Mills of the Little One to begin grinding. In the night he put a wet sock on the precious sprained ankle, and awoke, delirious, to rave through the house, sobbing and striking out, shadow-boxing. The ambulance wailed to the door at dawn, and away he went on a stretcher to the hospital. His grey eyes, as he passed me, oddly fine and candid in fever.

Now for peace, peace, peace. But first—*delenda est Carthago!*

I knew precisely how it was done. It was not culled from aboriginal lore, for I knew none. How then shall a city child know what needs knowing? Why, radio-serials and Saturday afternoon movies! At that time, an hilarious radio-serial called *Mrs 'Obbs* was convulsing the nation. Mrs 'Obbs, played by a male actor, was quite a character. She was a great believer in Positive Thinking. When she took a ticket in the lottery, Mrs 'Obbs would mutter fervently, 'I *will* win the lottery. I *will* win the lottery.' I became indoctrinated with Mrs 'Obbs's philosophy of Positive Thinking, and I put it into action.

'My father *will* die! My father *will* die!'

I did not know that Mrs 'Obbs was merely making use of an ancient ritual of the impotent yet implacable desirer. I 'sang' my father in the city where I lived, like the aboriginal who 'sings' his enemy in the inland places I have never seen.

My father died . . . naturally?

The dogs were racing at Harold Park when they told us the gladiator was dead. He had had a bet placed on Sweet and Lovely, which came home at ten to one. *He* didn't.

Now my mother was safe. Now my hair would not turn white as I had feared when I waited throughout those nights for him to finish with her. The Reign of the Razor was over.

We went away from the roar of the crowd, to live with my mother's brother and his wife in a quiet street where, on the day following a rare party, the local citizenry would stare at the sheepish roisterer as he collected his newspapers from the lawn, and count his empties with comptometer-eyes. Clickety-click-zing! Clickety-click-zing! Total: 'Without a word of a lie—*seven dozen!*' That sort of street.

But all was not well with the young Nemesis. Utopia was uncommonly slow in coming. The pressure off, there sprang up changes I had not envisioned. For instance, it had not occurred to me that my surly, sad-eyed mother might be someone I did not know. Now, with a job, and in a less hectic environment, she began to put forth blooms I had never seen on the hardy weed of her wifehood. She went in for being a Gay Mad Thing—'flung roses, roses riotously with the throng'. The new matiness she offered shocked me and I would not respond to it. I missed the familiar mother-figure, her rough, self-comforting embraces. I was *not* her contemporary, her sister, her chum. I did not want her winks across the table, her pally grins. Her renascence made her a stranger. I was an orphan. It seemed I had killed two birds with one stone.

Among the visitors, one soon began to take shape for me—he whom she jocularly referred to as 'Snakeface'. He who, from being one of the poker-players, began to come to dinner, to accompany us all on Sunday outings to Manly, or, if it rained, shuffled with us through the echoing

Museum, staring at stuffed gorillas and the bones of extinct monsters, offering us peanuts. He who finally showed his hand the Saturday afternoon they swayed in together after a morning in town at Usher's Hotel, and, laughing, bent to present me with a comic, and a warm paper-bag containing a Sargent's pie. So ... he came bearing gifts, did he?

'Old Snakeface!' my mother would gibe, laughing (the Gay Mad Thing) in our bedroom. 'He's a card, that Snakeface.'

Uh-uh! She didn't fool me with her nickname. 'Snakeface' was a shield, like other people's reticence, or stoicism, or angry denials—but, in her mooning, his image might well be, I knew, princely and tender. 'Snakeface' did not reassure me, if such was what she slyly hoped. Nor the grin in her bright, curving eyes, her wry, scornful mouth as she talked about him. I am not a fool, I tell you.

One may love passionately and say to one's intimates, 'That idiot!'— give an indifferent shrug. Jeer, 'So what!' when the leaping, magic syllables of his name are uttered. That is the way of our country, where 'you old bastard' is a declaration of deep affection, and 'Hullo, Stupe!' can be spoken with the beating heart and dry lips of passion, the hoarseness of the voice masked with a heavy cynicism. That is our way in love. 'Snakeface' is the smoked glasses through which we may confront the dazzle of the beloved in comfort, shielded from the derision of observers. I would have preferred a stilted 'Mr Riley'. A 'Mr' or 'Mrs' prefix with my mother inexorably set people among the respected, the awesome, or the detested.

'Snakeface' had the lineaments of a man. Any man. He seemed oddly suited to my pastel-coloured mother (when she would cease to call for madder music and stronger wine). He seemed manageable. I would not have given twopence for his chances in the hands of a woman who had been forced to evolve, in a rugged environment, all the subtle strategies of the weak. He had no aura to speak of. He was not a man for whom crowds might roar. You could not visualize him in an arena tearing a lion's jaws apart.

Contemptuously, I grabbed the comic and the pie and sauntered off. Rid of me, were they? Bought off, eh? That's what *they* thought. I bided my time.

My aunt and uncle were poring over the race-guide in the kitchen, trying to pick winners with a few friends. On the radio, Cyril Angles's strident, nasal voice trumpeted the fates of punters from Randwick racecourse. The sitting-room began to emit faint sounds of its own. Music! *Giggling*, by God!

I ran soft and soundless down the hall, my heart intent and deadly as a black-tracker's. The door was slightly ajar, and to this aperture I applied an eye that Edgar Allan Poe might have envied. The gramophone was playing selections from *Balalaika*, and they were hip-to-hip, moving to the music. Pah! Clumsy she was, trying-to-be-romantic! Her sensory centres firing off messages her limbs could never decode with a natural warmth and grace. Or had I, perchance, seen too many movies? Expected the cliché'd mummery of cinema romance, the intense shorthand the actress sketches smoothly with every delicate muscle, the amorous choreography of a screen vamp? He—for sure—lacked the style I had seen in Nelson Eddy and Robert Taylor! Not even the barbaric brio of Tarzan. Nor did he bend her backwards, as a revival of *The Sheik* had shown Valentino to be so adept in doing. His legs just shuffled meekly after hers, sort of *obedient!*

Was it their pathetic clumsiness that proclaimed them uninvited strangers in Paradise—vandals, forsooth!—in some *fata-morgana* world behind my forehead? Could that nickering giggle be the morse of passion? What sense of outrage brought my fury boiling red behind my eyes? If they had joined with the eloquence and truth of the heart, might I not—I say, *might I not*—have let them be, fallen back before a right to be as undisturbed as coupling swans? Was this only the simple fury of jealousy? Or did I become no more than the spillway of some bursting reservoir as I hurtled forward and, with fists clenched to bone, pummelled his back, howling, 'Leave her alone, pig! She is not yours! Get out, you rat! I did not kill him for *you!*' Pummelling, thumping small hard rage-powered fists against his spine.

Lizard-mouth agape, he reeled with shock, broke away from my mother, who was pealing with laughter, and he ran—yes, *ran*—for the front-door. I streaked after him to hasten him on his way: 'Get out! Get out!' The door slammed on his flying heels almost in my maddened face.

My mother stood, still leaning against the table to support her gust of laughter. 'You shuh-shouldn't have—have told Mr R-Riley you'd kuk-kill him.' She could hardly speak for laughing. 'Did you see—see him—arckh, arckh, arckh—*run?*'

Mr Riley, she'd said.

When she had stopped laughing, she wiped her eyes and sighed, then said dryly, 'Well, it's easy to see *you* don't want a new daddy.' And she went out to the kitchen to relate, amid great hilarity, how I had put her suitor to headlong flight. She was proud of my despotism. She enjoyed my fury. She was her old self, the need to 'watch her step' restored, no longer, in fact, entirely widowed.

'Streak of the bloody killer like her ole man,' my uncle hooted with wry amusement. 'She'll be a handful for you, sis. Hey, Killah, come on out here an' show us what yer did to ole Snakeface!'

I stood where she had left me, my fingers wrung together, crying. Crying, at last. Mourning the good old days.

CHARMIAN CLIFT

Three Old Men of Lerici

The day, after all, had remained hot. It was nearly evening when the car flung itself over the hill—Freiburg's thumb was jammed irritably on the horn: he had had enough of damned lunatic Italian motorists for one day—and under the deepening sky, still strewn with those big lazy whoofs of cloud that had, after all, come to nothing, they hurtled down on Lerici.

'Wake up, Ursula! We've arrived!' Freiburg felt more cheerful suddenly. He liked arrivals.

Down they swooped, down through the villas and the red and purple vines, and Ursula, who had been slumped apathetic against the sticky plastic upholstery for the last hour—eyes closed behind her dark glasses in a stupor of heat and misery—straightened her back and reared her long neck questioningly. Freiburg took a corner with tremendous dash, leaning with the car, rejoicing childishly in its power, showing off a bit for the benefit of the basking villas. He had a queerly ecstatic vision of the car leaping from one of the hilltops and sailing on through the evening, right over Lerici and into the Gulf of Spezia. There it was, spinning round beneath them, a great breadth of wrinkled peacock silk, flecked all over with tiny moving scraps of white and crimson and blue, and with white towns edging it.

Ursula took off her glasses and peered down, blinking. It was too bright! Too agonisingly bright! It hurt her eyes to look at it. Three squashy little yellow stars leapt on the dusty windscreen in front of her. Really, she ought not to have discouraged him from buying one of those plastic deflector things, even at the risk of pandering to his tendencies towards vulgarity. But those insects! She picked another tiny stunned body off her crumpled skirt and began rummaging in the big Florentine straw bag for comb and mirror. The wind-scoops had been open all day, and the burning blasts of air had whipped her hair into a dry, frizzy tangle, and caked her make-up into a gritty mask that pulled her muscles down and down. Oh why, why had she let Pierre perm her hair? It was too light, too fine. And why in heaven's name did she go on making up her face every morning! She knew well enough what these long hot days in the car did to it. She ought to just scrub well and slap some astringent on, and a touch of lipstick. Then she would still look fresh at the end of the day instead of . . . instead of . . . oh, damn this clear, harsh Italian light! *You don't dare any more*, the face in the mirror said sullenly, and the strained, dust-rimmed eyes welled with tired tears.

Lerici shimmered and wavered, and Freiburg eased his foot off the accelerator as it rushed up to meet them. They crawled in through a voluble, admiring populace and nosed along beside the sea, Freiburg's thumb still on the musical horn.

'Oh, my God!' Ursula breathed shakily. 'The Shelley Restaurant!' A *plage*! A casino! It was a *resort*!

'Look, darling,' Freiburg said, darting a quick, concerned glance at her, 'I'll run up a bit and turn and work back to that market place. Looks like the old town there.'

It was Ursula who negotiated for their room, rocking backwards and forwards on her heels between the dusty potted shrubs, sick with tiredness. Like a marionette the *padrone* bowed, twirled, flicked his fingers, darted an oblique bright glance, hopped back a pace or two, considered Ursula, rocking rocking, and behind her the dusty silver-grey car with the gleaming club badges and the radio aerial, and Freiburg, who couldn't get the hang of languages, pretending to adjust the windscreen wipers, vaguely ashamed that Ursula always had to do this sort of thing.

Chattering groups detached themselves from the swarms under the market awnings and came to stare, to discuss, to conjecture. Children gathered, grouped about the car like ragged bunches of flowers. Beyond a stone parapet the clear waters of the bay slapped and sighed against gay little boats: 'Only two fifty *lire*, mister' . . . a blue-jerseyed boy grinned hopefully. . . 'Right around the bay. . .'

Freiburg tried a smile at the children. '*Bella*, eh?' he said, patting the car.

'All right,' Ursula said shortly, returning. 'We can't have a private bath. They're full up, or pretty well.'

'Garage?' Freiburg asked, quite humble.

'Damn!' She clenched her fists with exasperation. Really! Why, in heaven's name? She had to think of everything. Everything . . . while he stood around showing off to a pack of kids she was expected to . . . It was too much!

The *padrone* watched from the cavernous doorway, showing all his teeth, and past him a thin dark sliver of a boy, wrapped all about in a snowy apron that was crossed over his narrow buttocks, cleaved through the sunlight in two leaps and stood beside them, smiling extravagantly.

'Give him the bags,' Ursula said wearily, closing her eyes against the brutal light and all the curious dark glances fixed upon her. 'I'll ask about the garage later.'

Freiburg handed out two pigskin cases, and after a moment's deliberation he took both cameras as well, and the leather briefcase that contained their passports, and the roadmaps and pamphlets. It was a bit late for photography today perhaps, but Ursula might feel better after a wash and brush-up, and the market would compose quite well, with that queer, crumbly little clock-tower in the background. Need a filter, though, to get the best out of it; and then there was the question of the light. He rummaged for the leather accessory bag and stowed it in the briefcase, rather furtively. Well, it wasn't safe to leave things like that in cars, anyway. He'd known fellows who'd had cameras lifted while they were having lunch.

'Americano?' a voice piped winningly, and the children broke and clustered around him, grinning and holding out their little brown claws. 'Shewing gum? Cigaret?'

'My *God*!' Ursula said, and stalked off into the hotel behind the boy with the bags. Horribly, right in the centre of her shoulder-blades, she could feel the dispassionate scrutiny of the still group of men clustered in the open doorway pasted all round with Communist posters. The men were black and unmoving, like part of the posters, printed against the red lettering, watching her.

Freiburg looked after her uneasily. But then a bell clanged surprisingly from the weed-grown clock-tower, and clanged again, swinging its big grey mouth so heavily away that it seemed as if the tower, already tilting dangerously, must inevitably collapse into a mound of old tired dust. The clock showed six forty-five. Freiburg stared at it, his jaw fallen in surprise, but the bell was still, the last of its two single echoes hanging metallically in the high excited buzz of the market. Freiburg laughed. Crazy! Wonderfully crazy!

'Here!' He called suddenly to the children, and held out a handful of small coins. Funny little beggars . . . eyes like pansies! Prettiest kids in the world!

Ursula, flinging up the window of their room, looked down to see Freiburg, hung ridiculously with his cameras, smiling down with a queer, tender sort of joy at a score of ragged children who clamoured around him screeching. She turned back into the cool dark room, shaking.

At the head of one white bed the boy glimmered like a taper, erect above the pigskin bags, waiting expectantly.

'You may go,' she said curtly. 'The signor,' she added, puckering her eyes to see him in the darkness, and speaking very slowly to make sure he understood, 'the signor will see to your tip, and the registration.'

Let him damn well do it himself for once. That long curious scrutiny of the passports, the speculative glance from her to Freiburg, Freiburg hovering behind her, humming carelessly, oblivious—how many times had she writhed? 'But why do you *care*, darling girl?' he would say. '*They* don't. They adore it, don't you see?' Well, if he didn't mind let him muddle through it himself for a change.

But when the boy had gone she ran to the door of the room and called after him down the long cool corridor:

'And if you would show the signor where to put his car?'

The boy turned at the stair-well and looked back at her, ears pricked like a faun's.

'The signor worries,' Ursula called softly, as if an explanation were necessary. 'It is a valuable car.'

But she was tired, tired. Weary to the bone. Somehow the Shelley Restaurant had been just too much. *Lines Written in the Bay of Lerici.* Was there nowhere in all the world beyond the reach of vulgarity and commercialism any longer? In some queer way she had high hopes of Lerici—as though the name and its associations could somehow break down the barriers of irritability and misunderstanding that had been building up between them ever since they had set out—as though, even now, it might be possible to . . .

She kicked off her shoes viciously—those fine flat Venetian shoes, soft and smooth as gloves, extravagantly simple. She had winced translating the price to him. If only, afterwards, he had not so obviously yearned for a gondola, forcing her to suggest it: all the ancient, remote magic of Venice spoilt, ruined utterly, irretrievably, by that horrible touristy ride, and the gondolier—hard, crafty, oh so contemptuous!—waiting until they slid by the crowded Rialto steps to suddenly throw back his Latin-lover head and pour out a ridiculous cascade of song. And Freiburg smiling at her so tenderly, so happily, quite unable to see how humiliating it was.

Stealthily she paddled over the worn tiles—arching her feet against the wonderful coolness. The huge, gilt-framed mirror caught her, and she looked at herself for a while, sullenly, with no sense of recognition. *I shouldn't have come with him.* She turned away from the tired caricature of herself and began unpacking. Everything rumpled, everything travel-stained. She wanted to cry. Hesitantly she unfolded the narrow linen trousers and the white poplin shirt he had bought for her in Rome. She had been saving them—her last reserve of elegance. The shirt would never survive more than two wearings. She stood by the case, smoothing them over and over. *I'm too old*, she thought with sudden bleak honesty, *for this sort of thing.*

And yet the prospect had been so charming. Freiburg lolling at her feet in front of the blazing February fire, and the rubbed velvet curtains drawn against the Chelsea mist. Pouring tea from the lovely Rockingham pot she had picked up for a song in the Portobello Road, and the firelight dancing on the glowing surfaces of her few perfect pieces of furniture, and the red and blues and golds of her books glinting like a very old tapestry spread against the wall. Freiburg's chestnut eyes—*like a very intelligent fox terrier's*, she used to think, with tender amusement—eager and ardent, yet humble, and his sensitive freckled hand stroking her instep while her voice murmured on wistfully, bringing the sunshine of Italy into the room, and the splendour of the Renaissance, San Gimignano's towers, the flag-dancers of Siena, the taste of sunwarmed grapes. She could hear herself sighing, and see the half-rueful smile curving her mouth.

'Oh, damn!' she said loudly to the jaded creature sulking in the mirror; and laid out the linen pants, the poplin shirt.

When Freiburg came, sidling cautiously into the room, his eyes wary but his face on the brink of a beam of sheer happiness, she had finished with her make-up case and was brushing a touch of brilliantine into her hair to soften the curls.

'Darling!' He moved towards her. 'Turn around. You look like George Sand! Lovely! Absolutely lovely! No wonder the old boy downstairs slapped me on the back.'

Outside a bell tolled, once, and then a series of small bells broke in with an unrelated clamour.

'That clock!' Freiburg laughed. 'That crazy, wonderful clock!' He pushed his head and shoulders through the window. 'Come and see, darling,' he called. 'The market's packing up. And there's an old woman with a basket scaling fish on the sea wall. And a ferryboat going out— bursting at the seams with trippers.'

Broken threads of song drifted across the bay from the gaudy pleasure boat. In the dusky golden light that filled the market place the crowds swirled and eddied, and above them the scarlet and blue and yellow awnings swayed and collapsed and were borne away wrapped tight about their poles. A frieze of men and women carrying on their heads trays of shoes and clothing moved in stately procession around the base of the clock-tower. The old Mother Carey on the sea wall plunged and dipped and rose again in the blinking red eye of the sun, dappled all over with silver, and in her wicker creel the heaped fish glittered like jewels.

Ursula put down her brush, and hung two tiny silver hoops in her ears. In the mirror George Sand watched her aloofly, and then smiled, mollified.

She curled up gracefully on the window-ledge beside Freiburg and rubbed her pointed chin into his shoulder. How nice he smelt, always, and how absurdly young was that soft drake's tail of chestnut hair on the brown nape of his neck.

'If you'll suspend your enchantment for long enough to wash that grubby face of yours,' she said, 'you can take me for a little walk up to the *castello* before dinner.'

'Of course,' Ursula continued, 'the plain fact is Shelley was too highly original for his contemporaries. You must remember that. Pure intellect made them uncomfortable. And then practising idealism as well as preaching it. I suppose if he had stayed at home and gone mad with silly little Harriet and that awful harpy Eliza they would have found it easier to forgive him. Don't you think?'

Freiburg nodded acquiescence and smiled sidelong at the women peeling vegetables in the dark, narrow doorways. They were like pigeons, he thought: plump and soft and quiet except for the alert movements of their smooth heads as they called to each other. The steep, dirty little canyons seemed to be filled with a liquid murmuring that paused as they passed, and welled up again behind them.

'. . . to avoid actuality,' Ursula concluded, and pulled his sleeve lightly to emphasise her point. Freiburg turned his warm, credulous face to her and captured her hand in his. He was so happy he could . . . he didn't care who was looking . . .

'Oh, do look at the fishwives,' Ursula said. 'I'll swear they've been sitting on those same doorsteps since Shelley walked past. Queer, isn't it, how insensitive the human animal can be? How anyone could loll there in that appalling stench! Shall we go back and ask *them* what they thought of Mary Godwin?'

Freiburg earnestly turned Mary Godwin over in his mind, trying to see her, but all that emerged was a picture of Ursula's thin clever face pointed disdainfully over some sort of rich trailing dress, and all the fishwives bobbing curtsies. He felt vaguely ashamed of his own romanticism of a moment before. *Pigeons!*

Above them the warm castle walls lifted against the dark sky. They climbed the last flight of slippery steps out of the old town, panting a little, Ursula's hand still caught tight in his.

'Pitched betwixt heaven and the *plage*,' Ursula said. 'At least they haven't turned it into a casino.'

Below them the purpling bay was brushed with gold. Two black-rigged fishing boats slid like shadows into the crowded anchorage, and a ferryboat left the wharf, pricked all over with pale lights, irritably spitting steam. The daytime trippers were leaving, the fishermen coming home. Freiburg, watching the lights moving across the water, was filled with a soft, beautiful melancholy. Ursula prowled about with her slow, graceful stride, pleasantly conscious of her own angular black and white elegance moving in the dusk. There was, she thought, something quite sublime about heights. If only one need never descend to the neon lights! A breeze tugged her hair, gently, and Freiburg's arm stole about her shoulders and turned her to him. *Why*, she thought, in sudden surprised happiness, *this is* . . .

A plump red-headed girl with a flowered seersucker skirt sticking damply to her wet bathing costume heaved over the railings and disappeared around the castle wall.

'Veronica! Ron-n-n-ie!' They could hear her high voice wailing. 'Chuck us a towel, do! I'll drip through the hall otherwise!'

'Good heavens!' Ursula said, 'What do you suppose . . . ?'

Two very hefty young men wearing leather shorts and boots strode across the courtyard, and with a cursory glance at Freiburg and Ursula marched off down the steps into the old town, arguing as they went. Their thick German voices rumbled all the way down the narrow street.

'Of *course*!' Freiburg said. 'The castello must be a youth hostel. Lucky young beggars! . . . What's the matter, darling? Ursula?' But Ursula was striding off down the steps, and when he caught her she refused his arm and thrust her hands into the pockets of her pants, dragging the seams. They returned to the hotel in silence, walled about by their separate miseries.

In front of the hotel, behind the dusty potted shrubs, twelve tables had been pushed together, and the white-aproned boy flickered around them like a moth, touching bowls of fruit, wicker-cradled bottles of Chianti, carafes of rough wine, shallow baskets heaped with bread. The *padrone* appeared, twirling, bowing. *The signor and the signora had had a pleasant walk? The castello was fine, was it not? And the view? Their table? Quite ready . . . if the signor and signora would follow him to the dining-room.*

'We prefer to dine outside,' Ursula said coldly.

He was desolated. On any other night . . . but as the signor and signora saw—all the outside tables . . . tonight there was to be a celebration, a reunion . . .

'What is he saying?' Freiburg asked.

Ursula explained with tight control. The *padrone* smiled and smiled, and the white-aproned boy regarded them softly with his velvet eyes.

'Tell him we'll dine somewhere else, then,' Freiburg said gently.

'Tell him yourself!' Ursula grimaced, and she fixed Freiburg with a wide cold stare that might at any moment be blurred with tears. 'Tell him anything you damn well please! *I* intend to have a tray sent up.' And halfway up the stairs she turned and looked down on him, as he stood smiling foolishly and apologetically at the *padrone*, 'Why don't you go and eat at the Shelley?' she called shakily. 'I'm sure you'd love it.'

She had been standing at the darkened window for a long time. She didn't know how long. She never wore a watch; the thin threadlike pointers frightened her somehow, spinning so fast. Like wearing one's death on one's wrist.

In the square the evening promenade had thinned out to a few gossiping fishermen, loath to relinquish the warm night, and two small boys, who, in spite of repeated shooing from the *padrone*, continued to loiter, watching the party assemble self-consciously around the tables beneath her window. In the lighted window of the Communist office a man in shirt sleeves sat hunched over a typewriter, picking out the letters with two fingers.

The bell on the ludicrous tower tolled again, maddeningly, swinging its great open mouth up to the stars, and all the little bells set up an insane clamour. A jazzy orange moon shot up into the sky and hung among the jangling echoes, lighting the square like a Chinese lantern. The clock on the tower had stopped at nine minutes past seven.

The chubby carafes moved across the white cloth below. White napkins fluttered and opened their folds over anonymous, dark-suited knees. The glass and the silver winked on the whiteness with an intolerable glitter; the mountains of fruit exploded with colour. Behind a great platter of scampi the *padrone's* smile stretched into a wide, winking arc, tilted up to her window. The little bells began to peal again, with irritable haste.

Ursula moved back from the window slyly, one foot behind the other, letting the curtain fall from her fingers fold by fold. The room leapt back to bright normality, and she stood by the light switch, blinking uneasily at her nightclothes laid out on the high white bed that seemed so isolated on the vast checkerboard of tiles. The light from the naked bulb pendant among shadowy cupids was clear and harsh. A clinical light. Alone in the bare bright room she felt somehow . . . *exposed*.

The thing was, of course, that she must not allow herself to become so tired in future. Everything got out of proportion. She would tell Freiburg in the morning—very gently, of course—that she simply could not go on at this pace. 'It isn't fair, my dear,' she would point out, 'to either of us.'

With an air of decision she unfolded her nightgown and walked briskly across the room to the window. Very firmly she closed the shutters.

But in bed in the dark the sheets were cold and slippery. She slid her toes up and down. A roughened piece of skin caught and rasped against the sheet and she twisted in sudden exasperation. Something *else* to be attended to tomorrow. Her feet were always as smooth and well-tended as her hands. Details like that were so important. You couldn't let up on all the little things, and lately there hadn't been time. How many dusty sightseeing miles had she tramped in the past weeks? No, she would have to be firm with Freiburg in the morning.

He *must* have had dinner by this time. Probably he was down by the water somewhere, mooning about. Lonely, humiliated . . .

A great shout of laughter buffetted the shutters. The big bell began to toll again, and all the little ones, utterly demented with the warm air and the full-blown moon.

With her eyes closed she tried to relax from the forehead down as she had been taught by Dr Heinrich. Frown and then relax the muscles; the frown smooths out and the muscles become limp. Next the eyes. Roll the eyeballs downwards as if you were looking at an imaginary black spot on your toes. A rough piece of skin there. And her eyes felt horribly puffy. She *must* get to sleep before Freiburg returned. Those swollen throbbing eyes put her at such a disadvantage. He would think her hideous. *Old*. No. No. He adored her. Worshipped her. With my body I thee worship . . .

Tension is muscular contraction . . . relaxation is muscular limpness . . . black skin on her toes . . .

Suppose he was not mooning. Suppose he had picked up a girl, a soft Italian girl with great shivery breasts and a milky bloom to her skin, and was worshipping her with his body in the moonlight. Oh, it wasn't fair! It wasn't fair! He'd have been nothing without her guidance and encouragement. Nothing! She had taught him everything he knew of sensitivity, appreciation, all the finer things. She tossed, desperately, and a tear trickled down the side of her nose.

Clench your teeth together . . . let go. Feel the weight of your lower jaw as it sags. Sags. Sagging jaw. No. No. He was sulking. That was it. Small boy sulking. Rather sweet. Exasperating, of course, but forgivable. I can't sleep . . . *I can't sleep* . . . the noise . . . those damned bells . . . *I can't sleep* . . .

Yet she did sleep, for when she first heard the pipe it was very thin and far away, and so high it was almost beyond the threshold of sound. There was nothing else, neither laughter nor bells, but after a time a faint thrumming rose and fell behind the reed, like the beating of innumerable tiny wings over a summer pond. Ah, don't! Ursula cried silently, don't hurt me like that. But the little wings were beating in her head, and the pipe pierced her like sunlight. But it's too bright, too agonisingly bright, she protested. It hurts me terribly! And her eyes were so swollen, too. It wasn't fair.

She awoke stumbling across the room to the shutters to put it out. To fling the shutters wide and put it out.

'Oh, my God!' she thought hysterically, leaning against the window and looking down into the square. 'There's a variety turn as well!'

The square was white with moonlight and wild with music. She looked down on broken bread and spilt wine and scraps of food congealing on oily plates and ashtrays spilling butts over the soiled tablecloth; and now all the diners were leaning forward, quite still, each dark head immobilised at the very moment of attention, turned towards a lively triangle at the head of the table. There, ludicrous in their age and poverty, three very old men in round-crowned hats and shabby coats bent bobbing shoulders over pipe and strings, jigging out a measure to their own music. Their thin old legs bent, fragile and brittle-looking as twigs beneath their flapping rags, shuffling out a spritely parody of youth, and as they shuffled they tilted their heads, each in a listening attitude, as if they were translating some secret thing they heard in the night.

Shuffle to the right, shuffle to the left . . . the strings thrummed and the pipe rose and lingered and fell and rose again effortlessly . . . a reedy sound, bubbling, pithy, a reed still wet with the river . . . the mouth curved over it wide, flat, fleshy, and the eyes above the mouth flat too, hooded, lashless, with a thick fold of skin at the outer corners.

But she couldn't *see* their faces! It would not be so awful if she could see the old men's faces! Lewd old men, jigging obscenely to their indecent music! It hurt—it hurt so terribly! She wanted to summon up a picture of her glowing books, her rubbed velvet curtains, her Rockingham pot, the cool conversations among the thin old china teacups. Her barriers. But the unseen face intervened, wide, flat, curving, white as the moon, tender over the reed, and now the wet bubbling sound of the reed was everywhere in the night: it ran along the cobbles, gushed from the clock-tower, it lapped with the waves against the seawall, it welled from the tiles under Ursula's feet. The old men whirled among the potted shrubs, grotesque in their age and stiffness, blown rags in a wild wind of their own making. Ursula felt—she ought to feel—outraged. It seemed an outrageous thing was happening to her. As if . . . *why*, she thought, groping feverishly on the outskirts of memory, *I know* . . .

But just as her mind stumbled in surprised recognition the strings twangled into silence and the last high gurgling note of the pipe floated out over the sea and was gone. And now the still figures around the table were moving, raising their hands, clapping, the old men were bowing stiffly, their knees bent outwards. The diners leaned towards each other, shouting ribaldries. The old men accepted wine and, drinking it, huddled together among the shrubs, as if for reassurance. A fat Italian lurched to his feet and began making a speech. The top buttons of his trousers were undone and there were stains on his shirt front. It was over.

In the window Ursula shivered, as though the impersonal coldness of the moon had seeped through to her bones, and stumbled back to the high white bed. She was cold now, stretched out empty and desolate in the sterile moonlight, colder than she had ever been. She would always be cold now. Because Freiburg would not come back. She thought of him with the warm girl on the sand, and she knew that his eyes would hold no wariness, and his forehead would no longer be puckered with vague puzzled shame. He would not even have heard the extraordinary music.

But then, she thought, with an old familiar envy stirring tiredly, *Freiburg hears it all the time.*

He heard it all the time. But that was *it*, of course! That was this thing about Freiburg. That was what she had resented in him all this time—and envied—calling it vulgarity. She was always distracted by the discordant notes, but Freiburg was simple and humble enough to hear them as part of the pattern. And it seemed suddenly to her that if one could only hear it the pipe played always—if one knew how to listen, as Freiburg did. Perhaps, after all, there was nothing grotesque or impious in the raucous shouts of drunken laughter that had succeeded the old men's music. The grotesqueries were part of it. The laughter went on fluting up and up . . . one peal of laughter and another chasing it . . . and another . . . and the bells mixed up in the laughter . . . or was it the pipe again? All the bells pealing with laughter at the ironical pipe . . . yes, it *was* the pipe, leading them on with the most absurd and delirious comments . . . ever higher, ever clearer . . . up and up and up . . . The bells all crashed together with discordant chimes—three—and were quiet.

When she awoke again the music was fading. The strings thrummed and the reed danced on three notes, lightly, lightly sadly fading. The room was moon-grey and Freiburg was there, sitting on the window ledge and gripping it as if for support as he stared out into the square. When she crossed the room to his side she saw that his face was puffy and sagging and even his clothes reeked of cheap wine.

Only the wreckage of the feast remained at the table below. The chairs were empty. Across the deserted square the three old men were receding. Three thin backs, three round-crowned hats. The very tall old man was still in the middle, and as they played they bent their knees and shuffled from side to side in time to their music. Their legs looked so very thin . . . so very infirm . . . old men's legs . . .

Freiburg reached unsteadily for Ursula and laid his head against her. She held him there, watching over his warm drunken chestnut head the three old men shuffling away into the dark shadows. Shuffle to the right, shuffle to the left. Like old bent sticks their legs seemed. Past the clock-tower . . . into the shadows . . . gone . . .

Still she stayed in the window, holding Freiburg against her, listening, until she could no longer be sure whether she still heard the vibration of a thin, high note. (. . . how the wide mouth pursed suddenly tight over the reed . . . and the heavy curved eyelids opened, wide, over eyes rolled back in agony or ecstasy . . .)

Freiburg's maudlin tears had soaked through her nightgown. She could feel them spreading hot and wet across her bosom, as if her heart had burst.

ELIZABETH JOLLEY

Poppy Seed and Sesame Rings

Tante Bertl collapsed and died without my being able to do anything about it on the steps of the Art Gallery and Museum. It was on the way home from a short afternoon visit to Grossmutti.

We sat, all three together, in the watery green light of her small apartment, the room opened into a conservatory and the winter sun, fading, made a delicate pattern of fern shadows on the coffee coloured lace table cloth. Tante Bertl sighed repeatedly.

'Das schmeckt mir,' she said, taking a third cream filled pastry. 'Wirklich gut!' Tante Bertl's voice was contented.

'Only try and walk,' I implored her, pulling at her plump hand. It was such a public place though, at the time, no one was walking there or sitting on the benches. She had insisted on getting off at the Museum. A light rain was falling.

'Let us make a little rain walk,' she said and, clambering on her short fat legs from the tram, she sank down on to the bottom step of that wide flight which seemed to reach up behind her to the sky.

As if I were the cause of her difficulties I felt ashamed and embarrassed. I glanced round quickly and nervously, anyone could see us there, even the pigeons could notice us in our trouble. I was afraid she was going to be sick there on the pavement.

I tried to pull her from the step but she only sighed and, making no attempt to get up, she simply leaned forward and died. I ran straight home leaving her there with the pigeons and the coming darkness.

'Tante Bertl wanted to walk,' I told them so they did not expect her for a time.

I thought I heard Mother crying in the night, her subdued sighs followed my father creaking on bent legs about the shop. I knew Tante Bertl was dead. All night long I pictured her huddled all alone on the steps of the Museum with its strange and grotesque treasures piled up behind her. Would the pigeons come to her I wondered, or would they avoid a dead old lady smelling of the vague warm sweetness of old age and so stuffed with pastries.

'Go to sleep, it's all right, go to sleep,' in the candle light my father crawled flickering across the ceiling crouching doubled on the cupboard, 'it's nothing, it's all right, everything's all right, go to sleep.' Flickering and prancing he moved up and down the walls big and little and big and I heard Mother crying and crying.

Next day Mother had to go to the mortuary. My father said to me, 'You go with her and comfort her.' I did not want to go but my father could not leave the shop he said, and I knew this was so. Mother felt so strange in the New Country and she tried to make friends with the few customers we had. She was always giving away packets of groceries or bars of chocolate and washing soap.

'Take ziss too, but take ziss,' she said, trying to imitate the tone and the accent of the people who were now her neighbours. She wanted to be accepted by these people and she pushed the presents my father could not afford to give into the spaces in their shopping baskets.

There were not many corpses in the mortuary. Tante Bertl's body looked so small as if it had been cut in half. I wondered if there would be a mess of blood and pastry, a body cut in half would be a terrible sight unless there was some clever method that I didn't know about. While Mother was being led away towards the white enamelled door, I hurriedly lifted the bottom end of the cloth.

Tante Bertl's unexpected feet gave me a shock. I had never seen her bare feet before, they were plump and neat and very clean. They were wide apart. I supposed this was because of her fat thighs.

It seemed then, that a person was very small in death.

At once Grossmutti came to stay. With her tin trunk and wicker-work baskets, she sat in the back room and disapproved of Mother's marriage to a shopkeeper. When Grossmutti came she usually stayed for several weeks, her disapproval mounting daily until, after a series of small explosions, she entered into a grand packing and a departure, after which things went on as before. Except that this time there would be no Tante Bertl to nudge Mother softly and whisper with her in the back room.

Mother wept aloud and wished for Bertl.

'Recha!' said Grossmutti. 'Stop sniffing and get my bed made up in the spare room and send Louise up with some hot coals, the room's sure to be damp.'

The night was long and I heard my father creaking to and fro over the floorboards.

'Who's that!' Grossmutti's voice crackled in the darkness, she always kept her door open keeping an unasked for vigil over her son-in-law and his house.

'It is only me,' he replied softly. 'I am looking for fly spray. Mosquito.'

'No mosquito this time of year. More likely vermin!' And then she called, 'What for is Recha crying?'

'It is all right,' my father patiently explained. 'She is homesick that is all.' Grossmutti made a sound of scorn and disbelief.

I often heard Mother crying in the night. When I called out my father always explained in a soft voice, 'She is homesick, that is all.' So I always knew what was the matter. Sometimes, after those times, Mother sent me

out for fillet of veal cut in thin slices, she hammered the meat on the red
tiles of the kitchen floor and sang,

'Mein' Schätzlein ist sauber ist weiss wie die Schnee—'

And after dinner, when the shop was closed, my father got up from the
table, slapped his thighs and leapt across the room, and Mother, with a
demure expression, danced sedately round and round the dinner table
with him.

My poor mother was always homesick. She longed for the scenery and
the smells and for the people of her homeland. She blamed her marriage
for all that she was suffering.

'Why are you crying so?' my father, perplexed, would ask her. 'We
have a nice house and a shop and a good life safe here in the New
Country. What you wanted isn't it? You and your sister and your mother.
Really it is as if I have married all three of you to bring you here, all safe,
and you are not satisfied,' he scratched his fine sandy hair. 'And,' he said,
'And I bring Louise too because you are used to her even though she will
soon be too old to work,' his voice climbed in indignation. 'Really it is as
if I marry four women to bring out,' he said. He looked at me, 'But five,'
he said and shrugged helplessly.

Mother longed for the bread she had been used to all her life at home.
Though we had poppy seed bread and sesame rings, she said they were
not the same at all. Often she took a small roll from the glass sided
cupboard where the bread was kept and she broke the bread and sniffed
it and dipped it in her coffee.

'It is not the same,' she moaned softly.

I too liked to break the fresh bread and sniff it and pile it into my coffee
and pick up the succulent fragrant lumps with a spoon. But with Mutti
in the back room we had to refrain from these habits only fit for
shopkeepers.

At school I learned the alimentary system of the rabbit. I knew the
rabbit from the pinna to the tail. I learned all the Latin names of the
human skeleton by heart and all the details of internal combustion and
gaseous interchange. I sorted out in my mind the mingling and exchanging of the various juices involved in the process of digestion. And when
we had examinations I was always top of the class.

Because of old age, Louise had to leave us and then Grossmutti died.
No catastrophe, she just fell asleep quietly like a doll in the little bedroom.

And the years went by one after the other.

'Your mother has no one,' my father said to me in his soft concerned
voice. He was so busy in the shop, his skin was paler than ever from being
indoors all the time. He never went anywhere and the shop did not
change. It did not prosper and it did not give up. The same foods were
there and the same customers starting at half past seven in the morning

wanting small purchases until nine o'clock at night. The shop was only closed on Good Friday and on Christmas Day. Our own holidays and feasts were pushed aside left in a bygone life. I had been too young when we left to remember this other life but Mother continued to weep alone in the dingy room at the back.

'She is alone all the time. You might try and come and see her more often,' my father said at the end of one of my rare visits. He was in the closed shop with me, the smell of mixed delicatessen and spices seemed sharper because of the dark. I had to be back at the hospital for the night.

'I'm pretty busy these days,' I made the excuse.

'Yes yes but your mother is always waiting for you to come,' he made a movement of self effacing apology with his hands in which, even his shoulders and neck and head, even his whole body, took part.

'Your father is working all the time,' Mother reproached me during the short visit. 'He has never a holiday, always working and working so that you can study and pass your exam.'

She always spoke as if I had only one examination to pass. My whole life had become a series of tests and examinations and the only friends I had were books and scalpels and test tubes and dry dead bones. My father toiled so that I could study so that is what I did.

I promised my father I would come home more often and I ran like a thief, with nothing stolen except some hours from my studying, through the empty streets all the way to the hospital.

I resolved to find a friend and to take her home with me the very next week to end my loneliness and to please Mother.

Of course it took longer than I expected and I did not go home for a whole month.

'Go in to her!' my father was just closing the shutters. 'Every day she waits and waits hoping you will come.' She was sitting in the back behind the shop, that was all she had to do, just sit. There was scarcely enough work for two people in the shop.

I explained quickly I was coming on Sunday.

'I'm bringing Marion,' I said trying to make it sound like a treat.

'Who is Marion?' Mother asked. 'Who is this Marion?'

'She is my friend from the hospital,' I explained nervously.

'Does she study too for exam?' Mother asked.

'She works in the hospital,' I said.

'How can she work there and not study?' Mother wanted to know.

'There is other work,' I said, 'all kinds of work.'

'Sunday, you close the shop,' Mother said to my father, 'we have a visitor coming.' She seemed pleased. 'Sunday afternoon, we close the shop,' she said.

'So!' my father said. 'Good! good!' he rubbed his pale soft hands together. I hoped Marion would be a success, but at the back of my mind were some grave doubts.

As soon as we arrived Mother made it very clear that she had not rested, that she had worked without stopping for some days. The table was covered with dishes, bean salad, herring salad, potato salad, even cabbage salad, the air was heavy with their various dressings. There was a large flat plate of cold meat, veal coated with sauce, liver sausage and salami slices and hard boiled eggs, enough for a dozen people. There were cakes too, pastries filled with jam and cream and little heart shaped biscuits.

'She has not made these things for years,' my father said happily. But he had not yet noticed Mother's face as I brought in Marion. I hardly knew my new friend. I had chosen her because she looked healthy and very clean and was the nearest one to speak to at the counter in the hospital administration department. She had seemed pleased to be invited to my home on Sunday. She was a big girl, bigger than all of us, I had not noticed this before. Her pink blouse filled our living room. She kept talking too, from the minute we entered, trying to be well behaved and say the right things. Mother's face was dark with disapproval and it became worse especially as Marion couldn't pronounce our name. She kept calling Mother Mrs Mosh.

'I love the embroidered cushions Mrs Mosh, did you make them?' and 'That's a dream of a dress you have on Mrs Mosh.'

'Nothing but personal remark!' Mother snapped at me in the scullery.

'She is only trying to be friends,' I whispered uneasily.

'She is not any friend for you, she is not ours!' she said so vehemently, I knew she could never receive anyone for me from this New Country as she still thought of it. Just then the radio came on. Mother flew into the living room.

'In this house I switch on or off the wireless!' she said grimly. Years of unhappiness had made her like this I knew but I wished she would try to be agreeable.

Marion blushed.

'It's a lovely radio,' she said. 'Pardon me! but I just love music. Do you like classical music Mrs Mosh?' There was a silence after Mother had switched off, Marion hummed quietly.

'Tell your friend she is not Beethoven,' Mother said coldly. And then she helped Marion to a big plateful of meats and salads even though Marion protested,

'Oh no more thank you Mrs Mosh! If I eat all that I'll be like the side of a house!' She was buried in egg and salami.

In his embarrassment my father stood up and passed plates to Marion all in the wrong order.

'Cake?' he said in his gentle voice. 'Biscuit? All home-made!' I wanted to ask him to wait. I felt it was all my fault this terrible afternoon.

'Oh very nice I'm sure,' Marion thanked him, 'But I'll have to refuse. I'll be putting on pounds. I've got a spare tyre already!'

'Look such waste!' Mother snatched Marion's plate from me angrily in the scullery. 'You see she does not like our food even!' she scraped the plate noisily into the pail under the sink.

I felt I couldn't face the impossible evening which lay ahead but Marion solved this.

'Well,' she said smiling all round the table, after the meal. 'I'll just have to be going now. I have enjoyed myself really I have Mrs Mosh. Thank you so very much Mrs Mosh for having me and thank you Mr Mosh.'

My father, who was already on his feet, gave a little bow which seemed to involve his whole body, and I jumped up gratefully.

'I'll go with you,' I said, and I fetched our rain coats. At the bus stop Marion said there was no need to go all the way with her, she would be all right, she said. She waved to me from inside the bus and, from the wet pavement, I waved to her.

I thought I ought to go back home.

I ran straight back and Mother was quite different. There was a smell of fresh coffee and she had put some stale poppy seed rolls and a sesame ring from the shop into the oven. All her photograph albums were on the table. Not a word was said about Marion. It was as if she had never been there. We spent the evening in another world with Tante Bertl, Grossmutti and Louise and myself when I was a child. At intervals my father exclaimed in his gentle voice,

'Ach so! Look at this one!' and, 'this is a good picture, take a look at your mother in this picture she has not changed has she.' It was just as if we were looking at the photographs for the first time. Mother talked and laughed and recalled the materials and the colours of our dresses, and the various occasions. One happy time after another, she described them all.

Then she busily packed up some cold meats and pastries and I had to run all the way to catch the last bus to the hospital. The hard boiled eggs were coming through the wet paper, so I left the parcel in a deserted waiting room on the ground floor.

Upstairs I sat at my table and tried to read and write and study but I kept writing Marion's name everywhere.

I thought about her. I kept thinking about her without being able to do anything about it.

Because of her it seemed that the diagram of the systemic circulation was all wrong. Suddenly it was clear to me that blood flowed in all directions at once. The twelve pairs of cranial nerves, I knew them all by heart, were said to govern the special senses but now I knew these special senses had no government. I thought I would write about the lymphatic system, but instead I began to write about quiet lakes and deep pools which have no reflection and no memory; I wrote too about the excitement of the secluded places where land and water meet.

In my thoughts I found I had an unknown store-house of feelings and I wrote them into half remembered sunsets and half known ways leading through secret woods and along hidden river banks. As I wrote during the night of these strange and grotesque treasures it seemed as if the fragrance of fresh grass came from somewhere not far beyond the hospital and the roof tops and the chimneys. Somewhere in the world I knew there were mountains and more mountains. I wanted a whole mountain to myself. In the night I wanted to be on the mountain climbing up to reach the clear air and the magic place on the peak just when the first sunlight would reach it too.

In the morning I wrote Marion's name again and again on every piece of paper on my study table. And in my hand my pen had an innocence I did not quite understand.

ELIZABETH HARROWER

The Beautiful Climate

The Shaws went down to the cottage on Scotland Island every week-end
for two years. Hector Shaw bought the place from some hotel-keeper he
knew, never having so much as hinted at his intention till the contract was
signed. Then he announced to his wife and daughter the name of a certain
house, his ownership of it, its location, and the fact that they would all go
down every Friday night to put it in order.

It was about an hour's drive from Sydney. At the Church Point wharf
they would park the car, lock it up, and wait for the ferry to take them
across to the island.

Five or six families made a living locally, tinkering with boats and
fishing, but most of the houses round about were week-enders, like the
Shaws' place. Usually these cottages were sold complete with a strip of
waterfront and a jetty. In the Shaws' case the jetty was a long spindly affair
of grey wooden palings on rickety stilts, with a perpendicular ladder that
had to be climbed getting in and out of the boat. Some of the others were
handsome constructions equipped with special flags and lights to summon
the ferry-man when it was time to return to civilisation.

As Mr Shaw had foretold, they were constantly occupied putting the
house in order, but now and then he would buy some green prawns,
collect the lines from the spare-bedroom cupboard, and take his family
into the middle of the bay to fish. While he made it obligatory to assume
that this was a treat, he performed every action with his customary air of
silent, smouldering violence, as if to punish misdemeanours, alarming his
wife and daughter greatly.

Mrs Shaw put on her big straw sun-hat, tied it solemnly under her
chin, and went behind him down the seventy rough rock steps from the
house. She said nothing. The glare from the water gave her migraine.
Since a day years before when she was a schoolgirl learning to swim, and
had almost drowned, she had had a horror of deep water. Her husband
knew it. He was a difficult man, for what reason no one had been able to
discover, least of all Hector Shaw himself.

Del followed her mother down the steep bushy track, not speaking,
her nerves raw, her soundless protests battering the air about her. She did
not *want* to go, nor, of course, could she want to stay when her absence
would be used against her mother.

They were not free. Either the hostage, or the one over whom a
hostage was held, they seemed destined to play for ever if they meant to
preserve the peace. And peace had to be preserved. Everything had always

184

been subordinated to this task. As a child, Del had been taught that happiness was nothing but the absence of unpleasantness. For all she knew, it was true. Unpleasantness, she knew, could be extremely disagreeable. She knew that what was irrational had to be borne, and she knew she and her mother longed for peace and quiet—since she had been told so so often. But still she did not want to go.

Yet that they should not accompany her father was unthinkable. That they should all three be clamped together was, in a way, the whole purpose of the thing. Though Del and her mother were aware that he might one day sink the boat deliberately. It wasn't *likely*, because he was terrified of death, whereas his wife would welcome oblivion, and his daughter had a stony capacity for endurance (so regarding death, at least, they had the upper hand): but it was *possible*. Just as he might crash the car some day on purpose if all three were secure together in it.

'Why do we *do* it?' Del asked her mother relentlessly. 'You'd think we were mental defectives the way we troop behind him and do what we're told just to save any trouble. And it never does. Nothing we do makes sure of anything. When I go out to work every day it's as if I'm out on parole. You'd think we were hypnotised.'

Her mother sighed and failed to look up, and continued to butter the scones.

'*You're* his wife, so maybe you think you have to do it, but I don't. I'm eighteen.'

However, till quite recently she had been a good deal younger, and most accustomed to being used in the cause of peace. Now her acquiescence gnawed at and baffled her, but though she made isolated stands, in essence she always did submit. Her few rebellions were carefully gauged to remain within the permitted limits, the complaints of a prisoner-of-war to the camp-commandant.

This constant nagging from the girl exhausted Mrs Shaw. Exasperation penetrated even her alarming headaches. She asked desperately, 'What would you do if you *didn't* come? You're too nervous to stay in town by yourself. And if you did, what would you do?'

'*Here*. I have to come *here*, but why do we have to go in the boat?' On a lower note, Del muttered, 'I wish I worked at the kindergarten seven days a week. I dread the night and week-ends.'

She could *think* a thing like that, but never say it without a deep feeling of shame. Something about her situation made her feel not only, passively, abused, but actively, surprisingly, guilty.

All her analysis notwithstanding, the fishing expeditions took place whenever the man of the family signified his desire for some sport. Stationed in the dead centre of the glittering bay, within sight of their empty house, they sat in the open boat, grasping cork rollers, feeling minute and interesting tugs on their lines from time to time, losing bait and catching three-inch fish.

Low hills densely covered with thin gums and scrub sloped down on all sides to the rocky shore. They formed silent walls of a dark subdued green, without shine. Occasional painted roofs showed through. Small boats puttered past and disappeared.

As the inevitable pain began to saturate Mrs Shaw's head, she turned gradually paler. She leaned against the side of the boat with her eyes closed, her hands obediently clasping the fishing-line she had been told to hold.

The dazzle of the heavy summer sun sucked up colour till the scene looked black. Her light skin began to burn. The straw sun-hat was like a neat little oven in which her hair, her head and all its contents, were being cooked.

Without expression, head lowered, Del looked at her hands, finger-nails, legs, at the composition of the cork round which her line was rolled. She glanced sometimes at her mother, and sometimes, by accident, she caught sight of her father's bare feet or his arm flinging out a newly-baited line, or angling some small silver fish off the hook and throwing it back, and her eyes sheered away.

The wooden interior of the boat was dry and burning. The three fishers were seared, beaten down by the sun. The bait smelled. The water lapped and twinkled blackly but could not be approached: sharks abounded in the bay.

The cottage was fairly dilapidated. The walls needed painting inside and out, and parts of the veranda at the front and both sides had to be re-floored. In the bedrooms, sitting-room and kitchen, most of the furniture was old and crudely-made. They burned the worst of it, replacing it with new stuff, and what was worth salvaging Mrs Shaw and Del gradually scrubbed, sanded and painted.

Mr Shaw did carpentering jobs, and cleared the ground nearby of some of the thick growth of eucalyptus gums that had made the rooms dark. He installed a generating plant, too, so that they could have electric light instead of relying on kerosene lamps at night.

Now and then his mood changed inexplicably, for reasons so unconnected with events that no study and perpetuation of these external circumstances could ensure a similar result again. Nevertheless, knowing it could not last, believing it might, Mrs Shaw and Del responded shyly, then enthusiastically, but always with respect and circumspection, as if a friendly lion had come to tea.

These hours or days of amazing good humour were passed, as it were, a few feet off the ground, in an atmosphere of slightly hysterical gaiety. They sang, pumping water to the tanks; they joked at either end of the saw, cutting logs for winter fires; they ran, jumped, slithered, and laughed till they had to lean against the trees for support. They reminded each other of all the incidents of other days like these, at other times when his nature was in eclipse.

'We'll fix up a nice shark-proof pool for ourselves,' he said. 'We own the water-frontage. It's crazy not to be able to cool off when we come down. If you can't have a dip here, surrounded by water, what's the sense? We'd be better to stay home and go to the beach, this weather.'

'Three cheers!' Del said. 'When do we start?'

The seasons changed. When the nights grew colder, Mr Shaw built huge log-fires in the sitting-room. If his mood permitted, these fires were the cause of his being teased, and he liked very much to be teased.

Charmed by his own idiosyncrasy, he would pile the wood higher and higher, so that the walls and ceiling shone and flickered with the flames, and the whole room crackled like a furnace on the point of explosion. Faces scorching, they would rush to throw open the windows, then they'd fling open the doors, dying for air. Soon the chairs nearest the fire would begin to smoke and then everyone would leap outside to the dark veranda, crimson and choking. Mr Shaw laughed and coughed till he was hoarse, wiping his eyes.

For the first few months, visitors were non-existent, but one night on the ferry the Shaws struck up a friendship with some people called Rivers, who had just bought a cottage next door. They came round one Saturday night to play poker and have supper, and in no time weekly visits to each other's house were established as routine. Grace and Jack Rivers were relaxed and entertaining company. Their easy good-nature fascinated the Shaws, who looked forward to these meetings seriously, as if the Rivers were a sort of rest-cure ordered by a specialist, from which they might pick up some health.

'It was too good to last,' Mrs Shaw said later. 'People are so funny.'

The Rivers' son, Martin, completed his army training and went down to stay on the island for a month before returning to his marine-engineering course at a technical college in town. He and Del met sometimes and talked, but she had not gone sailing with him when he asked her, nor was she tempted to walk across the island to visit his friends who had a pool.

'Why not?' he asked.

'Oh, well . . .' She looked down at the dusty garden from the veranda where they stood. 'I have to paint those chairs this afternoon.'

'*Have* to?' Martin had a young, open, slightly-freckled face.

Del looked at him, feeling old, not knowing how to explain how complicated it would be to extricate herself from the house, and her mother and father. He would never understand the drama, the astonishment, that would accompany her statement to them. Even if, eventually, they said, 'Go, go!' recovering from their shock, her own joylessness and fatigue were so clear to her in anticipation that she had no desire even to test her strength in the matter.

But one Saturday night over a game of cards, Martin asked her parents if he might take her the next night to a party across the bay. A friend of his, Noel Stacey, had a birthday to celebrate.

Del looked at him with mild surprise. He had asked her. She had refused.

Her father laughed a lot at this request as though it were very funny, or silly, or misguided, or simply impossible. It turned out that it *was* impossible. They had to get back to Sydney early on Sunday night.

If they *did* have to, it was unprecedented, and news to Del. But she looked at her father with no surprise at all.

Martin said, 'Well, it'll be a good party,' and gave her a quizzical grin. But his mother turned quite pink, and his father cleared his throat gruffly several times. The game broke up a little earlier than usual, and, as it happened, was the last one they ever had together.

Not knowing that it was to be so, however, Mrs Shaw was pleased that the matter had been dealt with so kindly and firmly. 'What a funny boy!' she said later, a little coyly, to Del.

'Is he?' she said indifferently.

'One of the new generation,' said Mr Shaw, shaking his head, and eyeing her with caution.

'Oh?' she said, and went to bed.

'She didn't really want to go to that party at all,' her mother said.

'No, but we won't have him over again, do you think? He's got his own friends. Let him stick to them. There's no need for this. These fellows who've been in army camps—I know what they're like.'

'She hardly looked at him. She didn't care.' Mrs Shaw collected the six pale-blue cups, saucers and plates on the wooden tray, together with the remnants of supper.

With his back to the fire, hands clasped behind him, Mr Shaw brooded. 'He had a nerve though, when you come to think of it. I mean—he's a complete stranger.'

Mrs Shaw sighed anxiously, and her eyes went from one side of the room to the other. 'I'm sure she didn't like him. She doesn't take much interest in boys. You're the only one.'

Mr Shaw laughed reluctantly, looking down at his shoes.

As more and more of the property was duly painted and repaired, the Shaws tended to stop work earlier in the day, perhaps with the unspoken intention of making the remaining tasks last longer. Anyway, the pressure was off, and Mrs Shaw knitted sweaters, and her husband played patience, while Del was invariably glued to some book or other.

No one in the district could remember the original owner-builder of their cottage, or what he was like. But whether it was this first man, or a later owner, *someone* had left a surprisingly good library behind. It seemed likely that the builder had lived and died there, and that his collection had simply been passed on with the property from buyer to buyer, over the years.

Books seemed peculiarly irrelevant on this remote hillside smelling of damp earth and wood-smoke and gums. The island had an ancient, prehistoric, undiscovered air. The alphabet had yet to be invented.

However, the books *had* been transported here by someone, and Del was pleased to find them, particularly the many leather-bound volumes of verse. Normally, in an effort to find out why people were so peculiar, she read nothing but psychology. Even after she knew psychologists did not know, she kept reading it from force of habit, in the hope that she might come across a formula for survival directed specifically at her: *Del Shaw, follow these instructions to the letter! . . .* Poetry was a change.

She lay in a deck-chair on the deserted side-veranda and read in the mellow three o'clock, four o'clock, sunshine. There was, eternally, the smell of grass and burning bush, and the homely noise of dishes floating up from someone's kitchen along the path of yellow earth, hidden by trees. And she hated the chair, the mould-spotted book, the sun, the smells, the sounds, her supine self.

And they came on a land where it was always afternoon.

'It's like us, exactly like us and this place,' she said to her mother, fiercely brushing her long brown hair in front of the dressing-table's wavy mirror. 'Always afternoon. Everyone lolling about. Nobody *doing* anything.'

'My goodness!' Her mother stripped the sheets off the bed to take home to the laundry. 'I thought we'd all been active enough this week-end to please anyone. And I don't see much afternoon about Monday morning.'

'Active! That isn't what I mean. Anyway, I don't mean here or this week-end. I mean everyone, everywhere, all the time. Ambling round till they die.' Oh, but that wasn't what she meant, either.

Mrs Shaw's headache look appeared. 'It's off to the doctor with you tonight, Miss!'

Del set her teeth together. When her mother had left the room with her arms full of linen, still darting sharp glances at her daughter, Del closed her eyes and raised her face to the ceiling.

Let me *die.*

The words seemed to be ground from her voiceless body, to be ground, powdered stone, from her heart.

She breathed very slowly; she slowly righted her head, carefully balancing its weight on her neck. Then she pulled on her suede jacket, lifted her bag, and clattered down the uneven stone steps to the jetty. It always swayed when anyone set foot on it.

When the cottage had been so patched and cleaned that, short of a great expenditure of capital, no further improvement was possible, Hector Shaw ceased to find any purpose in his visits to it. True, there was still the pool to be tackled, but the summer had gone by without any very active persuasion, any pleading, any teasing, from his wife and daughter. And if *they* were indifferent, far be it from him . . .

Then there was another thing. Not that it had any connexion with the place, with being on Scotland Island, but it had the side-effect of making the island seem less—safe, salubrious, desirable. Jack Rivers died from a heart-attack one Sunday morning. Only fifty-five he was, and a healthier-looking fellow, you couldn't have wished to meet.

Since the night young Martin Rivers had ruined their poker parties, they had seen very little of Jack and Grace. Sometimes on the ferry they had bumped into each other, and when they had the Shaws, at least, were sorry that it had all worked out so badly. Jack and Grace were good company. It was hard not to feel bitter about the boy having spoiled their nice neighbourly friendship so soon before his father died. Perhaps if Jack had spent more time playing poker and less doing whatever he did do after the Saturdays stopped . . .

On a mild mid-winter night, a few weeks after Jack Rivers's funeral, the Shaw family sat by the fire. Del was gazing along her corduroy slacks into the flames, away from her book. Her parents were silent over a game of cards.

Mr Shaw took a handful of cashew nuts from a glass dish at his side and started to chew. Then leaning back in his chair, his eyes still fixed on his cards, he said, 'By the way, the place's up for sale.'

His wife stared at him. 'What place?'

'*This* place.' He gave her his sour, patient look. 'It's been on Dalgety's books for three weeks.'

'What for?' Del asked, conveying by the gentleness of her tone, her total absence of criticism. It was dangerous to question him, but then it was dangerous not to, too.

'Well, there isn't much to do round here now. And old Jack's popped off—' (He hadn't meant to say that!) Crunching the cashew nuts, he slid down in his chair expansively, every supra-casual movement premeditated as though he were playing *Hamlet* at Stratford.

The women breathed deeply, not with regret, merely accepting this new fact in their lives. Mrs Shaw said, 'Oh! . . .' and Del nodded her comprehension. Changing their positions imperceptibly, they prepared to take up their occupations again in the most natural and least offensive ways they could conceive. There was enormous potential danger in any radical change of this sort.

'Ye-es,' said Mr Shaw, drawing the small word out to an extraordinary length. 'Dalgety's telling them all to come any Saturday or Sunday afternoon.' Still he gazed at his handful of cards, then he laid them face down on the table, and with a thumb, thoughtfully rubbed the salt from the cashews into the palm of his other hand. It crumbled onto his knees, and he dusted it down to the rug, seeming agreeably occupied in its distribution.

'Ye-es,' he said again, while his wife and daughter gazed at him painfully. 'When and if anyone takes the place, I think we'd better use the cash to go for a trip overseas. What do you say? See the Old Country . . . Even the boat trip's pretty good, they tell me. You go right round the coast here (that takes about a week), then up to Colombo, Bombay, Aden, through the Suez, then up through the Mediterranean, through the Straits of Messina past some volcano, and past Gibraltar to Marseilles, then London.'

There was a silence.

Mr Shaw turned away from the table and his game, and looked straight into his wife's grey eyes—a thing he rarely did. Strangers were all right, he could look at them, but with relations, old acquaintances, his spirit, unconscious, was ashamed and uneasy.

'Go away?' his wife repeated, turning a dreadful colour.

He said, 'Life's short. I've earned a holiday. Most of my typists've been abroad. We'll have a year. We'll need a year. *If* someone turns up on the ferry one day and *wants* the place, that is. There's a bit of a slump in real estate just now, but I guess we'll be okay.'

And they looked at each other, the three of them, with unfamiliar awe. They were about to leave this dull pretty city where they were all so hard to live with, and go to places they had read about, where the world was, where things happened, where the photographs of famous people came from, where history was, and snow in cities, and works of art, and splendour . . .

Poetry and patience were discarded from that night, while everyone did extra jobs about the cottage to add to its attractiveness and value. Mrs Shaw and Del planted tea-trees and hibiscus bushes covered with flowers of palest apricot, and pink streaked with red. Mr Shaw cemented the open space under the house (it was propped up on columns on its steep hillside) and the area underneath was like a large extra room, shady and cool. They put some long bamboo chairs down there, fitted with cushions.

Most week-end afternoons, jobs notwithstanding, Del went to the side-veranda to lean over the railing out of sight and watch the ferry go from jetty to jetty and return to Church Point. She watched and willed, but no one ever came to see the house.

It was summer again, and the heatwave broke records. Soon it was six months since the night they had talked about the trip.

Always the island was the same. It was scented, self-sufficient; the earth was warm underfoot, and the air warm to breathe. The hillside sat there, quietly, rustling quietly, a smug curving hillside that had existed for a long time. The water was blue and sparkled with meaningless beauty. Smoke stood in the sunny sky above the bush here and there across the bay, where other week-end visitors were cooking chops, or making coffee on fuel stoves.

Del watched the ferries and bargained with fate, denying herself small pleasures, which was very easy for her to do. She waited. Ferries came and went round the point, but never called at their place.

They lost heart. In the end it would have been impossible even to mention the trip. But they all grieved with a secret enduring grief as if at the death of the one person they had loved. Indeed, they grieved for their own deaths. Each so unknown and un-understood, who else could feel the right regret? From being eaten by the hillside, from eating one another, there had been the chance of a reprieve. Now it was evidently cancelled, and in the meantime irretrievable admissions had been made . . .

At the kindergarten one Tuesday afternoon Miss Lewis, who was in charge, called Del to the telephone. She sat down, leaning her forehead on her hand before lifting the receiver.

'Hullo?'

'Del, your father's sold the cottage to a pilot. Somebody Barnes. He's bought the tickets. We've just been in to get our cabins. We're leaving in two months.'

'What? . . . A pilot?'

'Yes. We're going on the *Arcadia* on the 28th of November. The cabins are lovely. Ours has got a porthole. We'll have to go shopping, and get injections and passports—'

'We're *going*?'

'Of course we are, you funny girl! We'll tell you all about it when you get home tonight. I've started making lists.'

They were going. She was going away. Out in the world she would escape from them. There would be room to run, outside this prison.

'So we're off,' her mother said.

Del leaned sideways against the wall, looking out at the eternal afternoon, shining with all its homey peace and glory.

'Oh, that's good,' she said. 'That's good.'

MENA ABDULLAH &
RAY MATHEW

Because of the Rusilla

The whole day—the trip to town, the nigger word, the singing kettle—was because of the Rusilla. It had flown away.

It was a small bird and of no use to the farm, but it was Lal's and its loss was a tragic thing.

It was Rashida who found it, though, Rashida and I. It was in the grass by the creek, shining red and green and fluttering to get out of the long creek grass. I saw it first and I pointed to it. But Rashida stalked it and caught it. Then we carried it back to Father. That's to say, Rashida carried it. I wanted to and I had the right because I saw it first, but Rashida didn't offer it and I couldn't ask her. She was older than I was and she had the right to decide. And besides, even though we were children on the banks of the Gwydir, we were still Punjabis and Punjabis do not beg. Even a little child like Lal knew that. And so did I. Rashida carried it.

Father looked at the bird. 'Young and weak,' he said. 'Young and weak. It will mostly die.'

'Yes,' said Rashida in a proud voice, holding herself up to look at life as a Punjabi should. 'It will die.'

She gave the bird to me then and I took it gladly. I held it tightly, too tightly probably. Its wings flapped at my hands and I could feel, under the wings and the feathers, a wild beating like the noise you hear at night when your ear is on the pillow, and I knew it was the bird's heart beating.

So I held it more gently than before, in a cage of fingers. 'What bird?' I said. 'What sort of bird? What name?'

Father looked at me and frowned. I was always asking names, more names than there were words for. I was the dreamy one, the one he called the Australian.

'Rusilla,' he said at last. 'It is a bird called Rusilla.'

'Rusilla?' I said. 'Rusilla.' It was a good name and I was satisfied.

I took it home and showed it to Lal, who was only four. 'I have a Rusilla,' I said. 'It is a very strange bird, young and weak, and it will mostly die, but you can help me feed it. Get grass-seeds and blackberries. Grass-seeds like these.'

He pottered away gravely while I put the bird in a chicken-coop that had been left by some accident in the garden. And from that day Lal and I hunted the garden, gathering and sorting, to feed the Rusilla.

The garden was a strange place and lovely. It was our mother's place, Ama's own place. Outside its lattice walls was the farmyard with its fowls and goats (Sulieman the rooster and Yasmin the nanny), and beyond that was Father's place, the wool-sheds and the yards, and beyond that the hills with their changing faces and their Australianness. We had never been to them, and Ama—that was our word for 'mother'; *ama* means love—Ama told us they were very strange. But everything was strange to Ama, except the garden.

Inside its lattice walls grew the country that she knew. There were tuberose and jasmine, white violets and the pink Kashmiri roses whose buds grew clenched, like baby hands. The garden was cool and sweet and full of rich scent. Even the kitchen smell of curry and of ghee was lost and had no meaning in that place. There was Shah-Jehan the white peacock, too. And other birds came there, free birds of their own will, the magpie day and night to wake us at morning and to bed us at night, and a shining black bird that Indians call 'kokila' and Australians call 'koel'. But these were singing birds that came and went, came and went. For the Rusilla, the garden was a cage.

It was a cage for Lal, too. He was gentle and small and the only son because another, an elder one, had merely opened his eyes to die. Ama and Father were afraid for Lal; they kept him in the garden. Rashida and I could run mad by the creek, bare feet and screaming voices, but Lal could not go out without a grown-up. He had to live in the garden with the baby, Jamila, who was only six months and who spent all her day sucking her fist and watching the rose-leaves move on the sky or in sleeping and sleeping. She was not much good for a boy to play with, even a delicate boy of four. To Lal the Rusilla was a bird, a friend, from heaven.

And it was entirely his. As soon as it was well I lost interest in it and grew sick of the garden. I told him he could have it, that it was no use anyway, and that it would never do anything but walk round in its cage and make whistling noises. Lal didn't care. He loved it and watched it for hours.

And then one morning, just like any other morning, we woke up and it was gone. The door of the cage was open and Salome the cat had disappeared. The magpies went on singing as on any other morning and Lal shook his fist at them as he'd seen Father shake his fist at the sun. And he cried.

How he cried! Tears down his face, and no sound. And all the time he ran round the garden—now quick, now slow—looking, looking. He didn't even speak.

'Ama,' said Rashida, 'let Lal come to the swamp with us.'

'We'll show him the ducks,' I said. 'Baby ones, Lal. Learning to swim.'

But it was no good. Ama told Father it was no good, and Father, smiling a little, nursed Lal for a long time. But the tears were still there and all afternoon Father went round the paddocks with a net trying to find a

Rusilla. But the bird from heaven had gone and it seemed that there was no other like it in the world. It was just as Lal had said.

We children slept in the same room and that night Rashida and I lay for a long time listening to Lal, waiting for him to cry himself to sleep. But it was no good. We climbed out of the big bed and went over to him.

'Lal-baba,' said Rashida. 'Don't cry. Don't cry,' she said again, and I saw that there were tears on her cheek and I began to sniffle and to feel my eyes filling.

'Don't cry, don't cry, don't cry,' I said. And then I was crying, very loudly, and Rashida, with tears on her face, was disgusted with me, and Ama, as she always was when we needed her, was suddenly there with a lamp. She picked up Lal and held him like a very little baby.

'What noise!' she said. 'Go to bed.' And when she had seen us safely in, she sat on a chair with Lal and talked to him in her soft Indian voice, so soft that the words were hardly words they seemed so true. And yet we heard them. 'My son,' she said. 'My son, no tears. Allah makes birds to fly. No tears. It is cruel, it is cruel to stay in a cage when you have the wings and the heart to fly. No tears. You cannot hold a bird. You cannot hold things, anything, my son.'

Lal leant against her. I could tell that his face was hot from crying by the way Ama rubbed her cheek on him. Her face was creased and tired, but suddenly she smiled and looked beautiful.

'Tomorrow,' she said, 'Seyed can take you in the wagon and you can see the town.'

'Me, too, Ama? Me, too?' Rashida and I jumped up in bed. None of us had ever been to town. Lal stopped crying.

'Yes, sleepers,' said Ama. 'All of you.' And she took Lal in her arms into her own room while Rashida and I whispered excitedly about Uncle Seyed, the Rusilla, and the town.

Uncle Seyed came the next day with the wagon. It was always used on town days, but it was very old. It belonged to the time when father first came to Australia. He had nothing but the clothes he wore and the Koran tied in a red handkerchief which he used for a prayer mat. With the money from his first jobs he bought the wagon. Faded, but still proud, the letters on the side said: MUHUMMAD DIN—LICENSED HAWKER.

We'd been in it lots of times, but never to go to town, never to go to town. We hopped about in the back like birds while Seyed worried about us falling out and eventually tried talking to us in an effort to keep us still.

'Good land that,' he said. He always spoke to us in English, his sort of English. 'Long time ago I want your father to buy it, but no. He want go back home, get marry. I tell him he too young get marry, but no.' Seyed shook his head and Rashida laughed. She knew that father was forty when he married. Seyed shook his head again. 'Always your father wanting to get marry.'

'When will you get married, Uncle Seyed?' asked Rashida.

'Plenty time yet,' said Seyed, who was in his fifties. 'Plenty time yet.'

'I will marry you,' I said. And then I thought a bit. 'Soon,' I added, and Rashida laughed.

And so the talking, the good time, went while the sun got big and the paddocks got small and the houses came closer to one another. By the time we drove into the town we had no words to say.

Seyed stopped the wagon in the grass at the side of the road and lifted us down.

'Better you wait in shade,' he said. 'No run on road. Back in few minutes.' He shook a warning finger and left us.

It was only a small town and we looked at it, looked hard.

'What's that?' I said pointing to a high, high, brick building.

'Only a Jesus-house,' said Rashida knowledgeably, but she looked at it as curiously as Lal and I.

'Look!' said Lal suddenly. 'Rusilla.'

We looked. It was a stone rooster near a stone man on the side of the building. It seemed very wonderful to us and we stood staring at it while Lal crowed quietly about Rusilla, the bird from heaven, and how it lived on a house.

It was because of the Rusilla and the stone man that we saw no one approaching. Suddenly they were there, white children—a big boy, a middle-sized girl, and a little boy. We stared at them. They stared at us.

'What y' wearin' y' pyjamas in the street f'r?' said the big boy.

'What y' wearin' y' pyjamas in the street f'r?' said the girl.

We stared at them and I kept saying the question over in my head like a song. I didn't know what it meant except that it meant our clothes. We were all dressed alike in the sulwakameez, a sort of loose tunic and baggy cotton trousers caught in at the ankles, serviceable, cheap to buy and easy to make. It was easy to wash, too. And Ama had washed them as white as anything. Why were they pointing, and singing, and saying such sharp pointy words?

'Nigger,' sang the big boy. 'Nigger, nigger, pull the trigger.'

'Nigger, nigger, pull the trigger,' said the others. They were all saying it, singing it, like a game.

'Game!' cried Lal. He ran forward. He lived in a world of women, an only son, and here were boys. He ran to meet them.

The big boy caught him around the waist and gave him a throw that sent him backwards to the ground. I saw him there and looked at him sitting up surprised and felt my legs shaking and my eyes sore.

'*Sur ka bucha!*' said Rashida. '*Sur ka bucha!*' she screamed and flung herself at the boy, her clenched fists banging at him. I was horrified because that means 'son of a pig', and it was a terrible phrase to us, but I followed her, crying, '*Sur! Sur!*' And, jumping at the girl, I grabbed two handfuls of hair.

We were all there fighting—thumping and kicking and scratching, with Lal sitting amazed on the ground—when Seyed came back.

'*Ai! Ai!*' he cried as he turned the corner and broke into a run. At the sound of his voice and the sight of his turban, the fighting stopped and the strangers ran away. Rashida stood looking after them, still shaking with anger and strength, but I looked towards Seyed wanting him to come to us.

He asked us what had happened and I held up a fist that had some blonde hair in it and started to cry. And, of course, that set Lal off; he couldn't let any of us cry alone. Seyed was distraught, but tried hard to be calm. He picked Lal up and dusted him. He retied the ribbon in my hair, a clumsy bow, but I loved him for it. And he told Rashida, who was being too proud to cry, to wipe her nose.

'Wipe good,' he said.

'Take us home,' commanded Rashida. 'Take us home now.'

'Business at bank. No go home yet.' Even as he said it he must have seen that Rashida would begin to cry, too, so he hurried us back into the wagon and drove us down the street. We none of us looked out. We crouched in the back.

'Where are we going?' I said, but in a very little voice that Seyed couldn't hear. Rashida sat up and looked.

'We are not going home,' she said and her voice trembled. But she stayed sitting up, looking proud, and as I lay there crying into Lal's hair I thought that she looked very like father and wondered if anyone would ever think that about me.

Seyed took us to a cottage on the other side of town where a white lady lived. He told us to stay with her and to give her no trouble because she was a friend, and that if we were good he would come back and take us home soon. Then he went away, into the town, while we stood stock-still in the garden and looked at the ground.

'I don't know your names,' said the lady.

Rashida was the eldest. 'I am Rashida Bani. This is my sister, Nimmi Kushil. And this is my brother—the only son—Lal Muhummad. We come from Simla Farm.'

'I know it,' said the lady. 'I knew it, and I knew your father before you were thought of.' We stared at her with respect; she must be very old. We could not imagine a time when father and Ama had not thought of us, and longed for us.

She took us into the house and like a very wise woman indeed went on with her work and left us alone. We walked round slowly, in sight of one another, and looked at everything. Then we decided.

Rashida stood by the piano. She struck a key. A miracle happened. A note came loud and clear. Then it died away till no matter how carefully you listened it was gone. Only you knew that it would never go because you had it in your mind and in your heart. She struck another one and, after the note started, sang with it. There were two notes then, the same and different, but again the piano note faded away into your mind. Lal laughed and I stood listening and Rashida, sure of herself, sat by the piano and began picking at the keys. High notes some of them were and some were low, and she sang with all of those she could. She was always singing at home and she knew all of Ama's songs.

I sat on the floor near her and turned over the pages of a magazine I'd taken from a big pile of papers. The pages shone and the ink smelt beautifully. There were big pictures, and I put my head close to them to see them and smell them and know them properly.

Lal began talking to a black cat that was sleeping under the table. He talked happily for a long time, but the cat woke up and arched his back and stretched himself and walked off into another room. Lal went after him.

Suddenly there was a whistling noise and a shout from Lal. Such a shout! Rashida and I jumped up and ran after him. He was in the kitchen, standing in front of the stove. On it was a kettle, a kettle that sang. He pointed to it.

'Look,' he said. 'Listen.' We were astounded. We stood wide-eyed as Lal. A kettle that sang, sang high and shrill!

'Like a locust,' said Rashida. 'Like a bird.'

'Magic,' said I.

'Rusilla,' said Lal.

The lady came in and took the kettle off the stove. 'It sings to say that it is boiling,' she said. 'I saw Seyed coming up the street and put it on to make some tea.'

So we all sat down to tea and scones and chattered like relations. We loved the lady now, the kind lady with the piano and the papers, the cat and the kettle. We told her about the farm and the three kangaroos that Ama fed, about the Rusilla and the garden where Lal lived, about Jamila the baby and the long time she was asleep. We told her everything and she listened and laughed and smiled while Seyed drank cups of black tea full of sugar. And when Lal could get a word in, he talked, too. He talked to Seyed and told him, very gravely, about the wonderful kettle that sang like a bird.

Then we all went out to the wagon. We stood for a moment in the garden to say good-bye and the lady, picking a rose from each bush, gave a strong red one to Rashida and a dear pink one to me. 'For good girls,' she said. Then she looked at Lal and shook her head. 'I can't give flowers to a man.'

Lal's face fell and we were all afraid he would cry, but he just looked sad and Seyed lifted him into the wagon.

'Don't go,' said the lady. 'Wait.' And she went inside.

We were all in the wagon ready to go when she came out. She was carrying the kettle.

'This is for you,' she said and held it towards Lal. 'I have two others for myself.'

Lal took it, but Seyed was frowning at him and he half held it out for her to take back. Even Lal knew that Punjabi men do not accept gifts easily.

'Let him take it,' said the lady. 'A friend gives you what is already your own.'

Seyed thought about it and then smiled, a huge grin. 'You Punjabi lady,' he said.

So the kettle was Lal's. All the way home we held on to our presents, even when we fell asleep as we all did. But we woke up near home, not because of any sound or any difference, but only because of the nearness of home. We climbed up on to the seat near Seyed, who worried about us falling off and prayed loudly that we'd stay on until he got us to our father.

The sun was going down as we sighted home. It was the time that Father called the Glory of Allah. The day was burning itself out. The crows cawed and flapped their way towards the trees. There was a night noise of animals, drowsy and faint. There was a smell—growing stronger all the time—of wood-smoke and curry cooking. There was a white gleam down near the cowbail that was Father's turban and there, there in the doorway, with the baby on her arm and a lamp in her hand, was Ama.

'No more,' said Seyed Muhummad solemnly and untruthfully as he helped us down from the wagon. 'No more as long as Allah let me live will I take these devils in town.'

We laughed at him, and we held our roses up for Ama to smell. But Lal pushed between us.

'Look, Ama,' he said holding up his kettle. 'Rusilla.'

BARRY OAKLEY

Father Carroll

Someone must have finally protested about Father Mangan's tortuous and interminable sermons, because when we came back to Middleton after the long Christmas holidays, he was gone. The new man's name was Carroll, but until the Sunday I wasn't sure whether it was my old schoolmate of ten years ago at the Christian Brothers—the driving, extrovert Carroll, the Carroll who'd been both one of the boys and a ladies' man until he'd disconcerted everyone by giving it all up for God. But at Mass that stifling January morning there was no mistaking him as he strode from the sacristy, a dark rubicund colossus with attendant altar boys—thicker in the neck and body though he was.

I had in mind going round afterwards and making myself known to him until, after powerfully intoning through the Epistle and Gospel, he got into the pulpit. Its rail didn't seem to go much higher than his knees. The preliminary trivia of the pilgrim statue of Our Lady of Fatima and the Catholic Women's Social Guild were as chaff before him. What he really wanted to talk about, he rang out, after a measured sign of the cross which reverberated noiselessly round the walls in two hundred similar actions, was the Holy Name Society. Tight-lipped, bull-shouldered, he paused for a moment; then said slowly, giving each word its due emphasis:

'My aim is to have every man—every man that's really a man—in the Holy Name Society within the next four weeks.'

From his great height he surveyed us, arrayed there helpless in the worn pews, glared at the latecomers cowering in the porch: mere prime matter for the potter's hand we were, sweating there hardly daring to move, sicklied over by the yellow light from the tall windows.

'The Holy Name Society', he went on, as if it pained him to bring the obvious before us, 'happens to be Christ's own society, it's not for the élite, but for each and every one of us.' In that final first-person pronoun he linked us with him irrevocably: Father Mangan, who cared as much for his bowls as his apostolic mission, had been a luxury we had never been really able to afford.

His finale was impressive. He had a knack, we later discovered, of stopping dead at the most vehement moment, turning his back on us in a flash, and going straight back to the altar. 'Get this into your Catholic heads,' he'd bellow. 'It's a life-and-death struggle we're engaged in; are *you* going to fight in Christ's army, or don't you think it's worth the trouble?'

After this even the Consecration came as something of an anti-climax, and it was thus probably his fault that, when to the ringing of bells he blessed, genuflected, and finally, with arms stretching up like a marking footballer, he elevated the Host, I couldn't get the Jack Carroll of old out of my mind: Jack the captain of the football and cricket, Jack the head prefect, Jack the masculine cadet-lieutenant who had abused me, a thin-voiced stripling, for not having my webbing clean, Jack—sweet memory this—whom I'd beaten at tennis, if at nothing else. Was there anything, we used to murmur against him, that he couldn't do? Even then he'd been one set apart, with plenty of mates but no close friends—and the girls I'd seen him scorn at dances! By the time he turned to us to distribute Communion, I'd faced up to the fact that he'd been a hero to me.

It struck me how subdued the congregation were afterwards, badgered by the recruiting officers he'd enrolled. It didn't matter how far the shirt-sleeved farmers had come in their big Fords and Plymouths—they knew they were marked men. Listen, I felt like saying to them all, he's no St Paul sent to prick and goad you from on high—he's not thirty, I went to school with him; I can remember the time when he told me a dirty story.

A meeting was inevitable in a town as small and introverted as Middleton, and it took place a fortnight later when he came to take the Catholic pupils at the Technical School for their weekly half-hour of religious instruction. He saw me from afar off along the long low corridor, and recognized me at once. All affability, his hand enveloped mine.

'I didn't know you were teaching here,' he said, a little reproachfully.

'It took me a fair while before it dawned on me myself,' I answered, letting him know I was quite equal to the occasion; one profession to another, so to speak.

'You're a family man by now, I suppose?'

I nodded, giving the necessary numerical details.

He listened with close enough attention, but I had the feeling his interest wasn't personal—perhaps it never really had been—but just so he could get the picture straight before he planned his mode of attack. He paced up and down the sunlit porch, intensely black, showing the gold in his teeth, hands behind his back, unable to rest, a dynamo working ceaselessly within him. I felt limp and feeble, grist already to his apostolic will. When he turned to go into his class, he had my address neatly noted in a little black book, rather like the one the English inspector used.

A week later he came uninvited, at an awkward time, when my wife was ill. Not to be deterred, he asked my permission to go in and see her. What could I say in the face of someone who had apparently never known shyness? Permission granted, he thrust back the curtain that hung in the doorway and introduced himself to her, while she lay there as though stunned, in her blue nightdress, breasts clearly discernible over the blanket. It was here, not at the school, that our vocations squarely confronted one another, and her embarrassment and his unbreakable urbanity seemed to have no doubt which was the superior. 'Yes father,' she said, 'no father,' in an abject submissive way that drove me mad.

Finally he sprawled in an armchair in the living room and had a beer with me, apparently oblivious of the Klees and Picassos that seemed to flaunt their modernism before him on the surrounding walls. Black legs extended, looking a little out of place in the promiscuous domesticity of nappies, cot, and feeding-bottle, he came quickly to his purpose.

'I've only been here six weeks and I still can't believe it,' he said, exhaling smoke, his one concession to the world, in twin plumes.

As he spoke of the job to be done, I felt myself subsiding gently: my comfortable relationship with provincial Middleton wasn't much longer for this world.

'They're a pretty parochial lot up here,' I said, 'and Father Mangan fitted them only too well. The redemption—not of Christ but of the parish debt.'

Father Carroll frowned slightly. He was either registering disapproval of my lack of respect, or fighting the temptation to agree with me.

'After all, he was an old man. One has to make allowances—'

'He'd been the same for twenty years, apparently.'

He downed his beer, politely refused another glass, and said he'd have to be on his way, pausing only to mention that he was planning to form a little study group for the professional men of the town in the very near future. Would I be interested?

'Of course,' I said, though my spirits sank. It had been my own fault, for being hypocritical. For though I'd been ready to criticize the genial Father Mangan, I'd enjoyed the comfortable consequences only too well.

The following Thursday Father Carroll for some unknown reason failed to turn up for his religious instruction class, and the headmaster asked me to take them instead. I was at a loss, and the kids soon sensed it, and bombarded me with complaints about him: how he roared and boomed, how he threatened to strap them if they didn't know their catechism, how he had them up and down for prayers.

I felt as if every Catholic in this huge extended parish was bemoaning the loss of the ancient, comfortable order of things. Amidst protests I gave them an essay to write, then moved abstractedly amongst them, happening to notice as I did so the first page of Church History they'd each noted down in their books, with obvious pains. 'The Church and the Modern World' was the heading.

'Stripped to its essentials,' I read, in a crabbed and uncomprehending schoolboy hand, 'today's war is a life-and-death struggle between two basic views of life: atheistic Communism and Catholicism. Between these there can never be any agreement in any form. Co-operation, co-existence and other communist slogans are but snares and traps for the unwary soul.

'Communism is reaping the harvest sown at the Reformation and nourished at the French Revolution. A harvest of weeds, nettles and briars which have managed to dim the consciences of men. We call this poison by the general name of Secularism.'

I stopped reading, lost in a mixed thicket of metaphor. I felt brambled, pricked, a fire burned inside me, flushed my cheeks, made my voice quaver when I told them to leave off and take down some notes. But as I started to write on the blackboard about the personal freedoms that had sprung from this demon secularism, I knew I didn't really care whether the class fully understood my proud radical sentiments or not. I was challenging Carroll—showing him the schoolboy power of my serve.

He took exactly one week to rush the net. That Thursday I managed to avoid him, but there was no gainsaying the note he'd left for me on the staff-room table.

'I would like to see you tonight at the presbytery, if I could.' That was all. One single volley under an impressive cruciform crest.

By eight o'clock, when I stood nervous on the tiles of the presbytery verandah, the first chill wind of autumn was blowing. I heard the thin needle of the bell I'd pressed insert itself into the cool repose of the dark hall. There were footfalls; a lobby light went on, and a shadow, like a great fish, moved in the depths behind the coloured glass round the door. But it was only the housemaid, a truculent, buxom woman with a moustache.

She led me along a dark hallway into the parlour. It was barely furnished: a large, now-tell-me-what's-worrying-you cedar table; some hard chairs, as unrelenting as dogma; and a statue of Our Lady of Fatima in coloured barley sugar on the mantelpiece. But the room, warmed by what was probably the first fire of the year, had a kind of ascetic cosiness more sensual than genuine luxury. Father Carroll (perhaps he was ill) looked paler than I'd ever seen him before. He sat down at once at the head of the table, motioning me to a chair uncomfortably close: I could smell his breath, sour, celibate, recalling the intimacy of the confessional.

'Well,' he said, brusque as a doctor tending an ailment that his patient had hitherto managed to keep hidden, 'what have you got to say for yourself?'

The suddenness of his attack left me nonplussed. As if to ease my discomfiture, he offered me a cigarette.

'I don't get you, Jack. What is this, a meeting of the Inquisition?'

'Not so, not so. I'm just a little bit surprised about two things. First that you saw fit to do my job for me. Second, what you actually got those kids to write. D'you think they understood it?'

'As much as they understood what went before. No more and no less.'

'If you stand four-square against Communism, certain things naturally follow. Right?'

'Right. But it doesn't automatically follow that it should be fought through cells of dedicated Catholic laymen.'

He inhaled deeply. He was now a little flushed, the way he got in the pulpit when he was building up to a climax. He tapped the table briskly, a ghostly white finger rising rapidly from the depths to meet his own.

'The Church can't afford the luxury of individualists in times like these.'

'It's a question of principle, of my right to choose the way I think best. That's not a luxury.'

'In a time of crisis, a united front is what we want.'

The old apocalyptic note! But he wasn't preaching now, and it didn't sound quite so alarming; though his dark expression told me the end of his patience was near.

'These are no special times. The Church is always at war. And if we'd had a few more individualists in the past, we wouldn't have backed the wrong horse so often.'

Father Carroll again tapped the table. It was his fist-thump in the pulpit scaled down to a congregation of one.

'The Church is guided by the Holy Spirit. You ought to know that.'

'I do. But that doesn't mean it hasn't made mistakes.'

'The Church is also human, if that's what you mean. But as an institution it cannot err.'

'That's not much consolation to the heretic burned, or the class of society abandoned.'

'It's easy enough to stand off and pick faults. You want a perfect Church before you'll act with it.'

'No I don't. I merely want one honest enough to admit it's made mistakes. Take Australia for example. Controversy horrifies it.'

He stood up; class dismissed.

'The split in the Church in Australia has been a catastrophe.'

I stood up too.

'On the contrary, it's done a lot of good. It's made me realize what's involved when one prays for a Catholic Australia.'

He regarded me with a kind of pained squint, as though trying to focus me through the incredulity he felt.

'I'm sorry to say this after all these years. But I think you're lacking in good faith.'

He didn't even show me out, but left me to grope my own way down the darkened passage. Then at the last moment, he switched on the lobby light. A large oleograph of Christ stared down at me from beside the door: handsome, aristocratic, with an incandescent heart. Under its reproachful, sorrowing gaze (had I lost? was I the guilty one?) I opened the door and went out into the cold.

RUDI KRAUSMANN

The Street of the Painters

'Ladies and gentlemen, may I draw your attention to something, although it is not on the program,' said the guide. 'You are entering the street of the painters, a sightseeing spot which may one day surpass the Opera House. From the outside you will not notice anything, a street like any other. But behind the venetian blinds more than a hundred painters are at work. And what you probably would not believe, is the fact that all these painters belong to the same school, the school of the "concrete expressionists." It is typical of that school to work only on the grand scale, and to say the minimum by using the greatest amount of colour. A factory near by is busy day and night to produce colour only for them I may add, and this too may be unexpected, that behind these insignificant looking houses you can find huge backyards, where the studios are situated. Generally they consume four to five times the space of the living quarters. These painters, having little sense for life and giving everything to art, belong unfortunately to the poorest part of the community. To top it all, the little money they have is spent almost totally on material and this brings them naturally to the brink of starvation. Yet seen from another angle, one could also without embarrassment say, they are the only members of society who are going to have a bright future. Although unknown to the public and not being able to sell their products yet, the prominent critics have already recognised the talents of individuals and the aims of the school. Articles in national and international magazines have appeared from time to time not only showing the avant garde minds and perception of the critics, but the quality that is apparent in the concrete abstractionists. A quality so subtle of course that in the beginning it can be noticed only by experts, but later no doubt it will also become visible to the masses. Admittedly the degree of expression is relatively small in relation to the huge canvasses, nevertheless owing to the skilled technique a balance is preserved. Let us say in ten years time when the spirit of the Opera House will have been dulled by routine performances and manipulation and its creator becomes less than a shadow on the eternal waves of the harbour, the quality of the paintings of the concrete expressionists will throw its brilliance over Sydney, coming from the backyards of this suburb. Ladies, and gentlemen, for the sake of truth I must not forget another though regrettable aspect. Competition between the painters is carried to the razor's edge. Having so many members in one school whose scope of expression is minimal has occasionally led to an outbreak of violence rare in the realm of art. Recently one painter was killed by another, using as a weapon his own work of art which could have been a masterpiece. But considering the history and background of the country a corpse must be considered as trivial in relation to the achievement and importance of the school in the future.

'I regret that I am not allowed to take you through the studios, not even my own, apart from the fact that what you would see is too abstract and obscure for the pleasures of tourism.'

DAVID MALOUF

The Only Speaker of His Tongue

He has already been pointed out to me: a flabby, thickset man of fifty-five or sixty, very black, working alongside the others and in no way different from them—or so it seems. When they work he swings his pick with the same rhythm. When they pause he squats and rolls a cigarette, running his tongue along the edge of the paper while his eyes, under the stained hat, observe the straight line of the horizon; then he sets it between his lips, cups flame, draws in, and blows out smoke like all the rest.

Wears moleskins looped low under his belly and a flannel vest. Sits at smoko on one heel and sips tea from an enamel mug. Spits, and his spit hisses on stone. Then rises, spits in his palm and takes up the pick. They are digging holes for fencing-posts at the edge of the plain. When called he answers immediately, 'Here, boss,' and then, when he has approached, 'Yes boss, you wanna see me?' I am presented and he seems amused, as if I were some queer northern bird he had heard about but never till now believed in, a sort of crane perhaps, with my grey frock-coat and legs too spindly in their yellow trousers; an odd, angular fellow with yellow-grey side-whiskers, half spectacles and a cold-sore on his lip. So we stand face to face.

He is, they tell me, the one surviving speaker of his tongue. Half a century back, when he was a boy, the last of his people were massacred. The language, one of hundreds (why make a fuss?) died with them. Only not quite. For all his lifetime this man has spoken it, if only to himself. The words, the great system of sound and silence (for all languages, even the simplest, are a great and complex system) are locked up now in his heavy skull, behind the folds of the black brow (hence my scholarly interest), in the mouth with its stained teeth and fat, rather pink tongue. It is alive still in the man's silence, a whole alternative universe, since the world as we know it is in the last resort the words through which we imagine and name it; and when he narrows his eyes, and grins and says 'Yes, boss, you wanna see me?', it is not breathed out.

I am (you may know my name) a lexicographer. I come to these shores from far off, out of curiosity, a mere tourist, but in my own land I too am the keeper of something: of the great book of words of my tongue. No, not mine, my people's, which they have made over centuries, up there in our part of the world, and in which, if you have an ear for these things and a nose for the particular fragrance of a landscape, you may glimpse forests, lakes, great snow-peaks that hang over our land like the wings of birds. It is all there in our mouths. In the odd names of our villages, in the pet-names we give to pigs or cows, and to our children too when they are young, Little Bean, Pretty Cowslip; in the nonsense rhymes in which so much simple wisdom is contained (not by accident, the language itself discovers these truths), or in the way, when two consonants catch up a repeated sound, a new thought goes flashing from one side to another of your head.

All this is mystery. It is a mystery of the deep past, but also of now. We recapture on our tongue, when we first grasp the sound and make it, the same word in the mouths of our long dead fathers, whose blood we move in and whose blood still moves in us. Language *is* that blood. It is the sun taken up where it shares out heat and light to the surface of each thing and made whole, hot, round again. *Solen*, we say, and the sun stamps once on the plain and pushes up in its great hot body, trailing streams of breath.

O holiest of all holy things!—it is a stooped blond crane that tells you this, with yellow side-whiskers and the grey frockcoat and trousers of his century—since we touch here on beginnings, go deep down under Now to the remotest dark, far back in each ordinary moment of our speaking, even in gossip and the rigmarole of love words and children's games, into the lives of our fathers, to share with them the single instant of all our seeing and making, all our long history of doing and being. When I think of my tongue being no longer alive in the mouths of men a chill goes over me that is deeper than my own death, since it is the gathered death of all my kind. It is black night descending once and forever on all that world of forests, lakes, snow peaks, great birds' wings; on little fishing sloops, on foxes nosing their way into a coop, on the piles of logs that make bonfires, and the heels of the young girls leaping over them, on sewing-needles, milk pails, axes, on gingerbread moulds made out of good birchwood, on fiddles, school slates, spinning-tops—my breath catches, my heart jumps. O the holy dread of it! Of having under your tongue the first and last words of all those generations down there in your blood, down there in the earth, for whom these syllables were the magic once for calling the whole of creation to come striding, swaying, singing towards them. I look at this old fellow and my heart stops, I do not know what to say to him.

I am curious, of course—what else does it mean to be a scholar but to be curious and to have a passion for the preserving of things? I would like to have him speak a word or two in his own tongue. But the desire is frivolous, I am ashamed to ask. And in what language would I do it? This foreign one? Which I speak out of politeness because I am a visitor here, and speak well because I have learned it, and he because it is the only one he can share now with his contemporaries, with those who fill the days with him—the language (he appears to know only a handful of words) of those who feed, clothe, employ him, and whose great energy, and a certain gift for changing and doing things, has set all this land under another tongue. For the land too is in another language now. All its capes and valleys have new names; so do its creatures—even the insects that make their own skirling, racketing sound under stones. The first landscape here is dead. It dies in this man's eyes as his tongue licks the edge of the horizon, before it has quite dried up in his mouth. There is a new one now that others are making.

So. It is because I am a famous visitor, a scholarly freak from another continent, that we have been brought together. We have nothing to say to one another. I come to the fire where he sits with the rest of the men and accept a mug of their sweet scalding tea. I squat with difficulty in my yellow trousers. We nod to one another. He regards me with curiosity, with a kind of shy amusement, and sees what? Not fir forests, surely, for which he can have neither picture nor word, or lakes, snow-peaks, a white bird's wing. The sun perhaps, our northern one, making a long path back into the dark, and the print of our feet, black tracks upon it.

Nothing is said. The men are constrained by the presence of a stranger, but also perhaps by the presence of the boss. They make only the most rudimentary attempts at talk: slow monosyllabic remarks, half-swallowed with the tea. The thread of community here is strung with a few shy words and expletives—grunts, caws, soft bursts of laughter that go back before syntax; the man no more talkative than the rest, but a presence just the same.

I feel his silence. He sits here, solid, black, sipping his tea and flicking away with his left hand at a fly that returns again and again to a spot beside his mouth; looks up so level, so much on the horizontal, under the brim of his hat.

Things centre themselves upon him—that is what I feel, it is eerie— as on the one and only repository of a name they will lose if he is no longer there to keep it in mind. He holds thus, on a loose thread, the whole circle of shabby-looking trees, the bushes with their hidden life, the infinitesimal coming and going among grassroots or on ant-trails between stones, the minds of small native creatures that come creeping to the edge of the scene and look in at us from their other lives. He gives no sign of being special. When their smoking time is up, he rises with the rest, stretches a little, spits in the palm of his hand, and goes silently to his work.

'Yes boss, you wanna see me'—neither a statement nor a question, the only words I have heard him speak . . .

I must confess it. He has given me a fright. Perhaps it is only that I am cut off here from the use of my own tongue (though I have never felt such a thing on previous travels, in France, Greece, Egypt), but I find it necessary, in the privacy of my little room with its marble-topped wash-basin and commodious jug and basin, and the engraving of Naomi bidding farewell to Ruth—I find it necessary, as I pace up and down on the scrubbed boards in the heat of a long December night, to go over certain words as if it were only my voice naming them in the dark that kept the loved objects solid and touchable in the light up there, on the top side of the world. (Goodness knows what sort of spells my hostess thinks I am making, or the children, who see me already as a spook, a half-comic, half-sinister wizard of the north.)

So I say softly as I curl up with the sheet over my head, or walk up and down, or stand at the window a moment before this plain that burns even at midnight: *rogn, valnøtt, spiseskje, hakke, vinglass, lysestake, krabbe, kjegle* . . .

ANTIGONE KEFALA

Sunday Morning

She was at Faliron, on a terrace like Aunt Hariklia's. A bare white terrace from which during the summer they would watch the open air picture theatre next door and see the actors somehow askew, taller and angular, more mysterious because of the distance and slanting angle.

It was a hot afternoon and she stood watching in the sun, the whiteness all around her, the houses silent, the shutters closed, the air clear and still like glass.

Far in the distance between some cypress trees, tall and erect like candles, the voice of a donkey cried out desperate and stubborn. Then she meant to leave but when she reached the door there was no glass any longer, just half a door that came up to her waist and on the other side the head of a leopard appeared and then his body. A mild, friendly leopard with a mellow golden fur and black spots and large doleful eyes, like liquid amber on whose surface trembled delicate lines.

It was obvious then that she would not be able to go through that door, so she tried the next one, and then the next, and every time the leopard was there in the stillness of the afternoon interrupted only by the cries of the watermelon vendors and then she suddenly realised that the walls of the terrace were doors, half doors only through which the huge paws or the sad head of the leopard would appear from time to time to make sure that she was still there, to make her realise that escape was impossible.

The mother was knocking on the door.

'Melina . . . Melina dear . . . a friend to see you in the kitchen.'

She stretched in the double bed. The blinds were drawn and a slim line of cold clear light played on the wall.

She put her housecoat on and came out. The house ticked away in silence. Nothing was heard from the depths of the rooms, only the sun travelling in the stillness.

Richard was near the door, a blue sports pullover on that deepened the colour of his eyes.

He did not speak but waited, his eyes full of light, a warmth flowing out of him, so that she felt elated. She turned her head towards the window to make her hair move, to feel its softness fall across her face. Her body seemed to say—was it still the air at Faliron, the leopard, his eyes? Her body seemed to say, there is more in me that you do not know but which will come alive only if I am moved.

Then he came forward and took her hands, bent down and kissed them. At that moment The Father came in. They both stood still.

'Care for a cup?' The Father said to Richard. 'You are an early bird, you will make her lose her beauty sleep.'

Richard stammered, he turned and blushed slightly.

'We are going to play soccer today,' Richard said, 'I really must go, they are waiting for me in the car. I came to tell you that it will be over at the Medical School if you care to come.'

When he left The Father moved about the kitchen in silence. 'A keen young man, upon my word,' he said and stopped.

Above the sink, in the spotless kitchen the gay flowered boxes stood bright, full of biscuits that both he and The Mother urged her to eat when she came late from the lectures or when she was hungry.

'The youngsters had such appetites, they knew from the boys . . .'

Now he moved slowly preparing breakfast.

'Let me help you,' she said.

D'ONO KIM

Chinaman's Beach According to a Doubtful Lover

Two nymphs lay side by side reaching out for each other with their fingers spread playfully. Before their fingers could meet they decided not to advance any further but to let the water flow between them. This was how I first saw Sydney after the dusty goldfields of Bendigo. I saw the lush green headlands jutting out into the water from the north and from the south, and the two Heads in the distance beckoning me to the open sea.

Here, amid the cradle of coves and spits, between the playful fingers, I had at last found a nook of my own. Do you still remember this small beach almost tucked away under the tall gums where you came to me that night? It was, and still is, the most charming beach of the most beautiful waterways. But that is not why I have now returned once more.

In such bliss I had suddenly fallen asleep, and when I opened my eyes the moon had risen higher and so had the tide with the water lapping at my feet and you were gone. You left me wordless as you had come to me wordless.

On these ripples I have since drawn many pictures of walking you to the end of the sand where the terraced rock rose to the cliff. Though you didn't see it then, a few steps back from the cliff I had a niche shrouded by the leafy trees.

I would have lined it with wild flowers and with crisp sand from the beach in my own wishful hopes, I would have brought to you fresh fish of all colours, and I would have asked you to fish with me.

I must tell you that the day I caught my first fish here I cooked it on the open fire, and it was so good that I believed God was in the water, and I even promised that I would myself return to the water to pay for what I owed by having taken more than my share of the water's offerings. Some anglers who had wandered down to the beach did say, envious of my catch, that I had some oriental magic. But I didn't tell them that fishing was one game that I had not yet been played out of. Fishing had become my life, and fishing was my love. But when the flat calm of the water seemed to deaden all that was alive in it I sat at the water's edge, waiting, and I waited for the love call from the deep, with a line in one hand and with a gaff in the other. Then my eyes fell upon my weapon of love, the crook of the gaff with its sharp point turned to the sun. I had wept before in the middle of the continent sunburnt dry, alone. And here in the middle of the blessed Eden I wept once more because of my love.

You came among those from the clippers in the harbour who would intrude into my cove now and then with women and wine.

The night had just settled in and when the moon lit green the white sand, a group of people came to the beach. From their shouting and laughter I knew there were men as well as women. They were all drunk and still drinking. I could see the unsteady shadows dancing on the beach, waving the bottles and hugging each other, trying not to fall. Like a ritual, they danced and dipped into the water in between their dances, all to pair off eventually in different directions.

In the hush after the last laughter faded away in the trees, I heard not far from me a man being suddenly sick. For a moment I thought he would choke to death with no one coming to his aid.

I made my way down the rock.

By the time I discovered him he had made himself comfortable at the skirt of the beach and was already snoring. The big spider on his arms tattooed black seemed about to flee from his stench.

I got up to leave him in peace.

When I turned round, on the deserted sand was only the moon and you.

You were in a long dress as those women in the public houses wore, but before that I saw your black hair still plaited into a bun and kept in place with a long silver pin. Your face was heavily made-up, coarse enough to lift in scales. Underneath, I could see the wrinkles deepening ahead of your time. The corner of your painted lips was almost twisted, bearing the harsh words you had never uttered for the sake of living on; you had been reared and then taught the virtue of silence and it had bloated your lips now in the world of love. I had seen you before, many times, in the dream houses, in the darker streets of Shanghai.

You had come a long way for your dream.

And you stood there still, but like a ripe open flower that shied away from no eyes.

'Honoured to stand before thee,' I said to you in the only tongue in which I could speak my feelings.

You didn't reply for some time. When you opened your mouth, your voice and tone were all I understood. I had no words to bridge our different dialects.

I merely gazed at you and you gazed at me.

A tear drop appeared on your eyelashes.

Was my look so saddening?

Or did you see me flee in fear from the goldfields, from the gentlest dog in the township baring its teeth at me, did you hear the children's mirth for my alien body humped with a swag, or did I remind you of a love you didn't want to remember?

Your eyes seemed to beam for a moment, and suddenly you burst into laughter and you had already begun to dance. You danced fast. When your dress bloomed you held it with one hand. You held it above your knee and you held my hand with the other, tugging softly but with hidden strength. You danced and I danced with you. With each toss of your head, your shoulder and your whole body, I too tossed and shrugged off all that had burdened me. I groaned, I panted, and I even wailed. Those who had begun to reappear from the trees looked on from the far end of the sand, never coming closer, in dismay.

Maybe it was wise of us to have parted so and not to have stretched our night thin, sparing the barbs of our sad tales—if wisdom was what had been intended between us.

If so, we were destined to sail past each other towards different corners of the water where we must watch the dusk in memory of a lost love.

Have you been faring well?

If you ever pass here again, will you pick up a shell from the sand and write on the beach what we should do with our love?

You know, this beach has since been named after me. The shells washed up on the sand looked like the mandarin's long fingernails, and these reminded people of me. But they were my fingernails groping for you.

MORRIS LURIE

My Greatest Ambition

My greatest ambition was to be a comic-strip artist, but I grew out of it. People were always patting me on the head and saying, 'He'll grow out of it.' They didn't know what they were talking about. Had any of them ever read a comic? Studied one? *Drawn* one? 'Australia is no place for comics,' they said, and I had to lock myself up in the dining room to get some peace. My mother thought I was studying in there.

I was the only person in my class—probably in the whole school— who wanted to be a comic-strip artist. They were all dreamers. There they sat, the astronomer, the nuclear physicist, the business tycoon (on the Stock Exchange), two mathematicians, three farmers, countless chemists, a handful of doctors, all aged thirteen and all with their heads in the clouds. Dreamers! Idle speculators! A generation of hopeless romantics! It was a Friday night, I recall, when I put the finishing touches to my first full-length, inked-in, original, six-page comic-strip.

I didn't have the faintest idea what to do with it. Actually, doing anything *with* it hadn't ever entered my mind. *Doing* it was enough. Over the weekend I read it through sixty or seventy times, analysed it, studied it, stared at it, finally pronounced it 'Not too bad,' and then put it up on the top of my wardrobe where my father kept his hats.

And that would have been the end of it, only the next day I happened to mention to Michael Lazarus, who sat next to me at school, that I had drawn a comic-strip, and he happened to mention to me that there was a magazine in Melbourne I could send it to. We were both thrown out of that class for doing too much mentioning out loud, and kept in after school, to write fifty eight-letter words and their meanings in sentences— a common disciplinary action at that time. I remember writing 'ambulate' and saying it was a special way of walking. Do I digress? Then let me say that the first thing I did when I got home was roll my comic up in brown paper, address it, and put it in my schoolbag where I wouldn't forget it in the morning. Some chance of that. Lazarus had introduced an entirely new idea into my head. Publication. I hardly slept all night.

One of the things that kept me tossing and turning was the magazine I was sending my comic to. *Boy Magazine.* I had never bought one in my life, because it had the sneaky policy of printing stories, with only one illustration at the top of the page to get you interested. *Stories?* The school library was full of them, and what a bore they were. Did I want my comic to appear in a magazine which printed stories, where it would be read by the sort of people who were always taking books out of the library and sitting under trees and wearing glasses and squinting and turning pages with licked fingers? An *awful* prospect! At two o'clock in the morning I decided no, I didn't, and at three I did, and at four it was no again, but the last thing I saw before I finally fell asleep was Lazarus's face and he was saying, 'Publication!' and that decided it. Away it went.

Now let me properly introduce my father, a great scoffer. In those pre-television days, he had absolutely nothing to do in the evening but to walk past my room and look in and say, 'Nu? They sent you the money yet?' Fifty times a night, at least. And when the letter came from *Boy Magazine*, did he change his tune? Not one bit.

'I don't see a cheque,' he said.

'Of *course* there's no cheque,' I said. 'How can there be? We haven't even discussed it yet. Maybe I'll decide not to sell it to them. Which I will, if their price isn't right.'

'Show me again the letter,' my father said, 'Ha, listen, listen. "We are very interested in your comic and would like you to phone Miss Gordon to make an appointment to see the editor." An appointment? That means they don't want it. If they wanted it, believe me, there'd be a cheque.'

It serves no purpose to put down the rest of this pointless conversation, which included such lines as 'How many comics have *you* sold in your life?' and, 'Who paid for the paper? The ink?' other than to say that I made the phone call to Miss Gordon from a public phone and not from home. I wasn't going to have my father listening to every word.

My voice, when I was thirteen, and standing on tiptoe and talking into a public phone, was, I must admit, unnecessarily loud, but Miss Gordon didn't say anything about it. 'And what day will be most convenient for you, Mr Lurie?' she asked. 'Oh, any day at all!' I shouted. 'Any day will suit me fine!' 'A week from Thursday then?' she asked. 'Perfect!' I yelled, trying to get a piece of paper and a pencil out of my trouser pocket to write it down, and at the same time listening like mad in case Miss Gordon said something else. And she did. 'Ten o'clock?' 'I'll be there!' I shouted, and hung up with a crash.

It hadn't occurred to me to mention to Miss Gordon that I was thirteen and at school and would have to take a day off to come and see the editor. I didn't think these things were relevant to our business. But my mother did. A day missed from school could never be caught up, that was her attitude. My father's attitude you know. A cheque or not a cheque. Was I rich or was I a fool? (No, that's wrong. Was I a poor fool or a rich fool? Yes, that's better.) But my problem was something else. What to wear?

My school suit was out of the question because I wore it every day and I was sick of it and it just wasn't right for a business appointment. Anyway, it had ink stains round the pocket where my fountain pen leaked (a real fountain, ha ha), and the seat of the trousers shone like a piece of tin. And my Good Suit was a year old and too short in the leg. I tried it on in front of the mirror, just to make sure, and I was right. It was ludicrous. My father offered to lend me one of his suits. He hadn't bought a new suit since 1934. There was enough material in the lapels alone to make three suits and have enough left over for a couple of caps. Not only that, but my father was shorter than me and twice the weight. So I thanked him and said that I had decided to wear my Good Suit after all. I would wear dark socks and the shortness of trousers would hardly be noticed. Also, I would wear my eye-dazzling pure silk corn yellow tie, which, with the proper Windsor knot, would so ruthlessly rivet attention that no one would even look to see if I was wearing shoes.

'A prince,' my father said.

Now, as the day of my appointment drew nearer and nearer, a great question had to be answered, a momentous decision made. For my father had been right. If all they wanted to do was to buy my comic, they would have sent a cheque. So there was something else. A full-time career as a comic-strip artist on the permanent staff of *Boy Magazine*! It had to be that. But that would mean giving up school and was I prepared to do that?

'Yes,' I said with great calmness and great authority to my face in the bathroom mirror. 'Yes.'

There were three days to go.

Then there occurred one of those things that must happen every day in the world of big business, but when you're thirteen it knocks you for a loop. *Boy Magazine* sent me a telegram. It was the first telegram I had ever received in my life, and about the third that had ever come to our house. My mother opened it straight away. She told everyone in our street about it. She phoned uncles, aunts, sisters, brothers, and finally, when I came home from school, she told me.

I was furious. I shouted, 'I told you never under *any* circumstances to open my mail!'

'But a telegram,' my mother said.

'A telegram is mail,' I said. 'And mail is a personal, private thing. Where is it?'

My mother had folded it four times and put it in her purse and her purse in her bag and her bag in her wardrobe which she had locked. She stood by my side and watched me while I read it.

'Nu?' she said.

'It's nothing,' I said.

And it wasn't. Miss Gordon had suddenly discovered that the editor was going to be out of town on my appointment day, and would I kindly phone and make another appointment?

I did, standing on tiptoe and shouting as before.

The offices of *Boy Magazine* were practically in the country, twelve train stations out of town. Trains, when I was thirteen, terrified me, and still do. Wearing my Good Suit and my corn yellow tie and my father's best black socks and a great scoop of oil in my hair, I kept jumping up from my seat and looking out of the window to see if we were getting near a station and then sitting down again and trying to relax. Twelve stations, eleven stations, ten. Nine to go, eight, seven. Or was it six? What was the name of the last one? What if I went too far? What was the time? By the time I arrived at the right station, I was in a fine state of nerves.

The offices of *Boy Magazine* were easy to find. They were part of an enormous building that looked like a factory, and were not at all imposing or impressive, as I had imagined them to be. No neon, no massive areas of plate glass, no exotic plants growing in white gravel. (I had a picture of myself walking to work every morning through a garden of exotic plants growing in white gravel, cacti, ferns, pushing open a massive glass door under a neon sign and smiling at a receptionist with a pipe in my mouth.) I pushed open an ordinary door and stepped into an ordinary foyer and told an ordinary lady sitting at an ordinary desk who I was.

'And?' she said.

'I have an appointment to see the editor of *Boy Magazine*,' I said.

'Oh,' she said.

'At ten o'clock,' I said. 'I think I'm early.' It was half past nine.

'Just one minute,' she said, and picked up a telephone. While she was talking I looked around the foyer, in which there was nothing to look at, but I don't like eavesdropping on people talking on the phone.

Then she put down the phone and said to me, 'Won't be long. Would you like to take a seat?'

For some reason that caught me unawares and I flashed her a blinding smile and kept standing there, wondering what was going to happen next, and then I realized what she had said and I smiled again and turned around and bumped into a chair and sat down and crossed my legs and looked around and then remembered the shortness of my trousers and quickly uncrossed my legs and sat perfectly straight and still, except for looking at my watch ten times in the next thirty seconds.

I don't know how long I sat there. It was either five minutes or an hour, it's hard to say. The lady at the desk didn't seem to have anything to do, and I didn't like looking at her, but from time to time our eyes met, and I would smile—or was that smile stretched across my face from the second I came in? I used to do things like that when I was thirteen.

Finally a door opened and another lady appeared. She seemed, for some reason, quite surprised when she saw me sitting there, as though I had three eyes or was wearing a red suit, but I must say this for her, she had poise, she pulled herself together very quickly, hardly dropped a stitch, as it were, and holding open the door through which she had come, she said, 'Won't you come this way?' and I did.

I was shown into an office that was filled with men in grey suits. Actually, there were only three of them, but they all stood up when I came in, and the effect was overpowering. I think I might even have taken a half-step back. But my blinding smile stayed firm.

The only name I remember is Randell and maybe I have that wrong. There was a lot of handshaking and smiling and saying of names. And when all that was done, no one seemed to know what to do. We just stood there, all uncomfortably smiling.

Finally, the man whose name might have been Randell said, 'Oh, please, please, sit down,' and everyone did.

'Well,' Mr Randell said. 'You're a young man to be drawing comics, I must say.'

'I've been interested in comics all my life.' I said.

'Well, we like your comic very much,' he said. 'And we'd like to make you an offer for it. Ah, fifteen pounds?'

'I accept,' I said.

I don't think Mr Randell was used to receiving quick decisions, for he then said something that seemed to me enormously ridiculous. 'That's, ah, two pounds ten a page,' he said, and looked at me with his eyes wide open and one eyebrow higher than the other.

'Yes, that's right,' I said. 'Six two-and-a-halfs are fifteen. Exactly.'

That made his eyes open even wider, and suddenly he shut them altogether and looked down at the floor. One of the other men coughed. No one seemed to know what to do. I leaned back in my chair and crossed my legs and just generally smiled at everyone. I knew what was coming. A job. And I knew what I was going to say then, too.

And then Mr Randell collected himself, as though he had just thought of something very important (what an actor, I thought) and he said, 'Oh, there is one other thing, though. Jim, do we have Mr Lurie's comic here?'

'Right here,' said Jim, and whipped it out from under a pile of things on a desk.

'Some of the, ah, spelling,' Mr Randell said.

'Oh?' I said.

'Well, yes, there are, ah, certain things,' he said, turning over the pages of my comic, 'not, ah, *big* mistakes, but, here, see? You've spelt it as "jungel" which is not, ah, common usage.'

'You're absolutely right,' I said, flashing out my fountain pen all ready to make the correction.

'Oh, no no no,' Mr Randell said. 'Don't you worry about it. We'll, ah, make the corrections. If you approve, that is.'

'Of course,' I said.

'We'll, ah, post you our cheque for, ah, fifteen pounds,' he said. 'In the mail,' he added, rather lamely, it seemed to me.

'Oh, there's no great hurry about that,' I said. 'Any old time at all will do.'

'Yes,' he said.

Then we fell into another of these silences with which this appointment seemed to be plagued. Mr Randell scratched his neck. A truck just outside the window started with a roar and then began to whine and grind. It's reversing, I thought. My face felt stiff from smiling, but somehow I couldn't let it go.

Then the man whose name was Jim said, 'This is your first comic strip, Mr Lurie?'

'Yes,' I said. My reply snapped across the room like a bullet. I was a little bit embarrassed at its suddenness, but, after all, wasn't this what I had come to talk about?

'It's very professional,' he said. 'Would you like to see one of our comic-strips?'

'Certainly,' I said.

He reached down behind the desk and brought out one page of a comic they were running at the moment (I had seen it in the shop when I'd gone to check up on *Boy Magazine*'s address), *The Adventures of Ned Kelly*.

Now, Ned Kelly is all right, but what I like about comics is that they create a world of their own, like, say, *Dick Tracy*, a totally fictitious environment, which any clear-thinking person knows doesn't really exist, and Ned Kelly, well, that was real, it really happened. It wasn't a true comic-strip. It was just history in pictures.

But naturally I didn't say any of this to Jim. All I did was lean forward and pretend to study the linework and the inking in and the lettering, which were just so-so, and when I thought I'd done that long enough, I leaned back in my chair and said, 'It's very good.'

'Jim,' said Mr Randell, who hadn't spoken a word during all this, 'maybe you'd like to take Mr Lurie around and show him the presses. We print *Boy Magazine* right here,' he explained to me. 'Would you like to see how a magazine is produced?'

'Yes,' I said, but the word sounded flat and awful to me. I hated, at thirteen, being shown round things. I still do. How A Great Newspaper Is Produced. How Bottles Are Made. Why Cheese Has Holes And How We Put Them In.

And the rest of it, the job, the core of the matter? But everyone was standing up and Mr Randell's hand was stretched out to shake mine and Jim was saying, 'Follow me,' and it was all over.

Now I'm not going to take you through a tour of this factory, the way I was, eating an ice cream which Jim had sent a boy out to buy for me.

It lasted for hours. I climbed up where Jim told me to climb up. I looked where he pointed. I nodded when he explained some involved and highly secret process to me. 'We use glue, not staples,' he explained to me. 'Why? Well, it's an economic consideration. Look here,' and I looked there, and licked my ice cream and wondered how much more there was of it and was it worth going to school in the afternoon or should I take the whole day off?

But like all things it came to an end. We were at a side door, not the one I had come in through. 'Well, nice to meet you,' Jim said, and shook my hand. 'Find your way back to the station okay? You came by train? It's easy, just follow your nose,' and I rode home on the train not caring a damn about how many stations I was going through, not looking out of the window, not even aware of the shortness of the trousers of my ridiculous Good Suit.

Yes, my comic-strip appeared and my friends read it and I was a hero for a day at school. My father held the cheque up to the light and said we'd know in a few days if it was any good. My mother didn't say much to me but I heard her on the phone explaining to all her friends what a clever son she had. Clever? That's one word I've never had any time for.

I didn't tell a soul, not even Michael Lazarus, about that awful tour of the factory. I played it very coolly. And a week after my comic-strip came out in print, I sat down and drew another comic story and wrapped it up and sent it to them, and this time, I determined, I would do all my business over the phone. With that nice Miss Gordon.

Weeks passed, nearly a whole month. No reply. And then, with a sickening crash, the postman dumped my new comic into our letterbox and flew on his merry way down the street, blowing his whistle and riding his bicycle over everyone's lawns.

There was a letter enclosed with my comic. It said that, unfortunately, *Boy Magazine* was discontinuing publication, and although they enjoyed my comic 'enormously', they regretted that they had no option but to return it.

My father had a field day over the whole business but no, no, what's the point of going over all that? Anyhow, I had decided (I told myself) that I didn't want to be a comic-strip artist after all. There was no future in it. It was risky and unsure. It was here today and gone tomorrow. The thing to be was a serious painter, and I set about it at once, spreading new boxes of water colours and tubes of paint all over the dining room table and using every saucer in the house to mix paint. But somehow, right from the start, I knew it was no good. The only thing that was ever real to me I had 'grown out of'. I had become, like everyone else, a dreamer.

FRANK MOORHOUSE

White Knight

He explained to Sandra, a new-wave television producer, that having watched so many *Kojaks*, *Callans* and *Rockford Files* and given his experience with international nuclear intrigue, he was now 'ready to try to write a White Knight formula series for television'.

Yes, it was an old-wave idea, but this would be nuclear White Knight—a Knight who polices the new energy. And a career change.

'My whole life has been a preparation for this,' he said. 'I was not slumped there in front of your television set for those years when we were together, throwing my empty beer cans into your empty fireplace, for nothing. That was preparation for this moment. And so was the time I spent with the IAEA freezing my arse off in Vienna.'

She said, 'As Stephen would say, the White Knight thing all began with the Arthurian legends and Gawain—all these series are about Round Table knights—it can never really be an old-wave idea.' She was referring to Stephen Knight, associate professor, a medievalist.

'*Through the Looking Glass* too,' he said, 'there is a White Knight in *Through the Looking Glass*. I re-read it during my hepatitis. Admittedly, a different sort of White Knight.'

> Alice looked on with great interest as the King took an enormous memorandum-book out of his pocket, and began writing. A sudden thought struck her, and she took hold of the end of the pencil which came some way over his shoulder, and began writing for him.
>
> The poor King looked puzzled and unhappy, and struggled with the pencil for some time without saying anything; but Alice was too strong for him, and at last he panted out, 'My dear! . . . it writes all manner of things that I don't intend—' . . . Alice had put 'The White Knight is sliding down the poker. He balances very badly.' The Queen said, 'That's not a memorandum of *your* feelings!'

Sandra said that she always felt nausea sweep over her when she heard adults quoting Lewis Carroll. People clung to these books to make themselves oh-so-very-childlike and yet, at the same time, suggesting that they could grasp the enigma of existence from reading these books.

He said quickly that he had not touched a Lewis Carroll book for thirty years. 'It was during my hepatitis. I regressed.'

'All right then.'

223

'Hepatitis is a crisis of existential dimension—streets seem threatening and impenetrable. When the liver isn't working some fundamental harmony is shattered. That's what the *Village Voice* says. So you go back to books like Lewis Carroll.'

'You mustn't go on about your hepatitis. People with hepatitis seem to enjoy talking about it.'

'With hepatitis—well, suddenly, you know, that's all that's left.'

But it was agreed that he was to do a treatment for a White Knight series. Sandra suggested he talk with Laura Jones as a possible co-script writer. He made a file and wrote on it in Textacolour 'White Knight', and in brackets, '(ring Laura Jones)'.

Now, turning forty, it was good to know the next life move.

On November 21, he came into his work room with the morning newspapers and a coffee cup, a piece of toast and marmalade held dog-like in his mouth because his hands were full. He dropped the newspapers on the desk where they fell onto the folder saying, 'White Knight (ring Laura Jones)' in green Textacolour. As he watered the plants with a cup of cold undrunk coffee, there on his desk from last week, and wondered again if it did the plants harm, he tilted his head to read the newspaper lying on the desk and read '. . . had been planning a simultaneous suicide ceremony for months to be carried out if the code "White Knight" was broadcast by Leader Jones . . .'

He stopped watering or coffeeing the plants and sat down to read the newspaper with an alertness which became a chill.

> AAP-Reuter—: Georgetown: November 21. People's Temple members in Guyana and the United States had been planning a simultaneous suicide ceremony for months to be carried out if the code 'White Knight' was broadcast by Leader Jones.
>
> The code apparently was not broadcast but Jones summoned his followers to the death meeting by telling them over the loudspeaker, 'The time has come for us to meet in another place.'

Although he had almost recovered from the hepatitis his body was still skewed by it, and it was with a residue of the sickness that he sat there in his swivel chair; even its slight motion gave his body a feeling of precariousness.

Shakily, he finished his toast and marmalade and read the report with a welling anxiety.

He very much doubted that he would begin work that morning on the White Knight series with Laura Jones—aura Jones—as co-script writer. No.

What would have happened to him had Jones broadcast the code White Knight? Should he stay indoors? Would that help? Was it better to move about?

And what sort of questions were these to be asking?

At the New Hellas lunch club that day, having done no work, he said to the political and historical people there at lunch that the Jonestown suicides must be the most bizarre post-Second World War news story 'and my own story is just as bizarre'.

He told them his story.

Donald said, 'So what? There is nothing to be said about it, even if it is the most bizarre news story of the post-Second World War period. And even if your story is equally bizarre, there is nothing to be said about it. It is an historical aberration. It says nothing about the United States that we don't already know—or about the West—it says nothing about the decline or fall of anything. That is often the case with aberrations of history.'

They all turned then to him, as a tennis crowd moves its head, looking to him to prove there was something perhaps to be said about it.

He found, as Donald claimed, that there was nothing really to be said.

'But there must be something to be said,' he came back. 'You people must have something to say. It could not be beyond analysis.'

'What then?'

'I don't know what. All I know is that I was in the fallout zone.'

Donald snorted.

They looked at him—the lunch club—with censure for having introduced a promising subject and for then having nothing to say. They went on to talk about the coming of the republic.

All right, there may be nothing to be said, he thought, nothing to be said there in the New Hellas about the Jonestown suicides, but it asks that something be said. Or was it saying something, not to the lunch club, or to the world, but to him alone.

In bed with Belle, his friend the slut, he said that he thought it was the most bizarre news story of the post-Second World War period. Maybe nothing like it has ever happened in recorded history, he said. And then added his own story.

'Is that not bizarre? Is there not a message in this for me?'

'I'd like to get some sleep now,' Belle said, hitting the pillow in emphatic preparation for sleep. 'Why don't you get decent pillows?'

'I was brought up to be able to sleep on anything,' he told her. He said 'Don Anderson' of the *Australian* bureau in New York says that it was probably the greatest mass suicide in history and I was nearly part of it. But I suspect a Jewish village in Poland might claim the record. There were, I believe, mass protest suicides among the Jews from time to time.'

'Go to sleep now,' she said, 'you mustn't let it preoccupy you. Your libido needs sleep even if you don't.'

'I can't help my libido—hepatitis affects the libido.'

'And turning forty.'

'Turning forty has nothing to do with it. I was actually quoting Knight to Sandra and he's an expert on the Knight's Tale from Chaucer. It all links up.'

'Mmmmm.'

Belle was not the right person for him to be with now he was forty. She claimed to be a representation of his great-grandmother, but that wasn't enough.

That was all right too.

At the Thanksgiving party put on by Sam and Jessie, Jessie being an American, he said to the gathering partygoers that the Jonestown suicides must be the most bizarre news story of the post-Second World War period, 'and I have a pretty bizarre story of my own to tell too— connected with it.'

The guests at the Thanksgiving listened thankfully to his story but he arrived at the end of the story to find that they had nothing to say.

'Imagine the poor stringer in Georgetown,' Jessie said, 'trying to convince the bureau in New York that four hundred Americans got together in the jungle and suicided.'

That was a contribution to the story but it was not the aspect upon which he wanted to focus attention.

Jessie said that the bureau probably told him, 'Go have another drink, Harry.'

'But what about Laura Jones—aura Jones?'

'In New York they probably said "jungle juice",' one of the party said.

'There must be something more to be said about it,' he prompted.

The Thanksgiving conversation could do nothing with it. Everyone became thoughtful.

'Surely things can't be that bad in the United States,' Jessie's father said, at last. He was visiting Australia. 'In our country, can things really be that bad?'

He waited for Jessie's father to say more. But no more was said. The conversation hung there among the thoughtful guests, but nothing more came.

As they all went in for their turkey and pumpkin pie, he said to Jessie's father that he wouldn't take it to mean the decline or fall of the West. Jessie's father said he hoped not.

In the car on the way to the airport to drop Louise, an ex-lover who was passing through on her way back to the United States where she worked in the UK Embassy, he said that he had planned a television series on his IAEA experience with the working title 'White Knight' taken from a lecture by Stephen Knight. He had intended to work on it with Laura Jones—aura Jones—and how on the first day of work the Jonestown suicides occurred according to the plan 'White Knight'. And how he'd been feeling rather suicidal himself.

'Is that a bad omen for the series,' he asked her, 'or is that a bad omen!'

'Or is it a bad omen for you. For you turning forty,' she said. 'Did you read that hepatitis can not only affect your libido but that it can take away your will to live?'

'I have no will to live. Never have had. I could hardly have not read it since you sent it to me marked with a Stabilo pen. And you shouldn't say things like that,' he said, 'to the sick.'

'You told me once that the sick, too, love truth,' she replied. 'And you have to make up your mind whether you take omens or whether you don't take omens. Now that you're forty.'

They kissed at customs control and he felt shielded by the automatic sliding doors of the airport departure tunnel and glad that she was out of the country—her and her Stabilo spells.

In December he turned forty. He spent Christmas and his birthday with Belle, the wrong person. They stayed drunk and debauched in motels around the country and then in the bush, but they knew they were the wrong people to spend birthdays and Christmases with and that they were waiting for someone more suitable to those sorts of occasions to come along in their lives.

'But it feels OK,' she said.

'Oh yes,' he said, with genuine enthusiasm.

In February he met his friend Milton at the international airport on his return from study leave in the US.

Milton said, first thing, 'What about the Jonestown suicides!'

'Why do you mention the Jonestown suicides?'

'I was in this commune in San Francisco when it all happened,' Milton said, who always spent his study leave in a commune. 'We were on the fringe of that scene.'

'Here, let me take your luggage,' he said to Milton, 'but go on, tell me about Jonestown and I'll tell you *my* story.'

'I had this incredible fight with Sheena—really bad in a way neither of us had before with anyone else in our lives or with each other. We generally never fight like that. Pulling hair—smashed mirrors—and she scratched me, flesh under her fingernails . . .'

'A White Knight private investigator would have found the flesh under the fingernails.'

'What?'

'Nothing—go on.'

'It was so bad. We both went off—I went to this bar to drink myself to death. I don't know where she went but we both felt suicidal. She tried to telephone this doctor she knew to get sleeping pills. I kept working out in the bar how to drink enough to kill myself. Next day: Jonestown.'

'Jonestown.'

'Yes, really! A guy at the commune who is into lasers said that the Jonestown thing triggered suicides all over the country. That there was this beaming out from Jonestown and Sheena and I were lucky to have resisted it—just. The signal was too weak.'

'It could have been the hills. The reception is bad in the hills of San Francisco.'

They put the luggage in the car.

'How was Jones going to broadcast the signal?' he asked Milton, who knew these things.

'It was a beam—a head beam.'

'Oh. I thought that it was Alice holding the end of the pen,' he told Milton, jocularly, 'that's our lives.'

'You're right!' Milton said. 'The CIA is in there somewhere.'

'I'll tell *you* my story.'

'Hold on,' said Milton, 'I'll tell you what's really coming down the tube from the Jonestown thing.'

Milton talked dysrhythmically as they drove around the car park looking for an exit. Milton hit his forehead with his hand, 'Of course—I missed at first—the Ballad of the White Knight—White Knight! Jesus the ramifications are fantastic.'

But he thought that Milton seemed to shrink away from him after he had told *his* story of the White Knight.

He did not work in January—the White Knight folder was still lying on his desk from November. When wandering in the city, hours early for an appointment, he bought the seamail *Economist* for November 25.

The *Economist* had 'something to say.'

> The religious sects are the grass forcing itself through the concrete . . . religious innovation is one of the last and best examples of free enterprise . . . half forgotten fragments of animism and the dark other side of the religious coin . . . if things go well the time between now and the 21st century could prove to be as important in the development of human consciousness as, say, the fifth century BC (which saw orderly intellectual thought taking root in Greece); the first century of the Christian era (which saw the offering of a new link between the spiritual and material halves of life); the seventh century (which saw the first real explosion of the idea of man's individual powers and responsibilities) . . . it could lead to a pacification of the long civil war in inner space . . . most appear to have drunk cyanide found mixed with grape drink in a tin tub. Mr Jones had dispensed mock suicide potions before. The spasms of the first children ended any doubt. Many tried to run into the jungle. They were turned back by the camp's armed guards or shot down . . . at one level the story is another example of the special quality of

America; the country where the best is better, but the worst is also worse, than anywhere on the globe.

The pacification of the long civil war in inner space, yet.

Now if the *Economist* leader writer had been at lunch at the New Hellas he would have had something to say. But it was not a Sydney way of talking. We could do with some panoramic thinkers.

AAP-Milton telephone, 'More on Jonestown—I'm over my dysrhythmia now—more stuff is coming down—I'm told there are 913 bodies in a hangar at Dover Air Force base in Delaware. No one will claim them. They will remain there forever. Refrigerated. A complete commune. The dead commune—the title's yours, have it, take it. The ramifications are truly fantastic.'

'It's the grass forcing itself through the concrete,' he told Milton.

'Riiiight!'

Was this the commune which beckoned him? Was this the commune, at last, which wanted him?

He learned from a friend in the US airforce that the bodies were in fact flown from Dover Air Force base to California to be buried. Delaware didn't want them buried there.

Sandra rang about the television treatment on the White Knight series and he told her he had not done any work on it. He told her why.

She said, 'Oh,' and then asked him how he was coping with being forty.

'Fine,' he said.

'Are you sure?'

In April, he read that the code name for the suicide pact was not 'White Knight' but 'White Night'. It had been misreported. There was no explanation of either code name.

He felt something lift from his whimpering psyche but still could not work on the White Knight project.

He rang Milton. 'They had it wrong,' he told him.

'But Jesus,' Milton said, 'you came within one letter of being hit by the laser.'

'I missed by one letter—a kay. I'm A-Okay.'

'Don't joke—that's the way it works. There's a lot of stuff coming out on that sort of thing from Hungary.'

That week while contemplating beginning work 'on the treatment' (and his new life) he fell down writhing with pain on the floor of his office amid the struggling indoor plants.

Gripped with agony, he called a taxi which took him to the doctor and from there he was taken to hospital for emergency surgery.

He came out of the operation with tubes in his mouth, nose, and penis, and with a drip in his arm.

They gave him Pentathol and he saw a sun-filled field of yellow flowers and it beckoned to him. It was, he thought, death beckoning. No doubt. He considered it, saw his great-grandmother and grandfather standing in the field beckoning, but for no obvious reason decided this time to say no he wouldn't go yet into the never-ending warmth of that sun and to death's corny field of swaying yellow flowers. Not yet.

He then fell into a deep sleep and did not die.

He convalesced on his own in a small quiet hotel. He could not go to Belle's house because she was not someone you convalesced with, her life-urge was over-vigorous, and she had once said that she was 'into scars'.

The months of August and September he spent in Canberra, the seat of government, on IAEA business. While in that city a Senator Knight rang and wanted to talk to him about nuclear waste.

Of all the senators why Senator Knight? He told himself that it was White *Night* now that he had to watch—the Knight business was all over. But he went to the appointment cautiously.

Nothing of note occurred.

In August, still in Canberra, he read a poem in the magazine *Quadrant* written by Evan Jones. He did not register the name Jones until he had entered the poem.

Sometimes he read poems because he knew the poet, sometimes because of the title, sometimes he just grabbed a poem and read it as a random sample of 'poetry being written now'. He had read this poem as such a sample.

It was titled *Insomniacs* but he was not an insomniac, that was not the reason he read the poem.

In stanza three he read:

> Insomniacs, bless them, are never afraid of the dark:
> bad nights are called 'white nights' for that dull white
> which lurks behind their eye-lids, dingy, mean.
> Nothing at all like innocence, purity or peace,
> signalling that all the nerves would like to break.
> Something in the whole being is at war.

He put down the magazine. Oh oh, something was still going on. The laser was still searching for him.

That night and for a few nights he sweated after going to bed, fearing that his sleep would now be disrupted—that that had been the message of the poem. Could you die from sleep deprivation?

His two companions in Canberra were named Lewis and after a heavy drinking bout with one of the Lewises, in the week he read the poem, he became ill again with hepatitis.

He could hardly move from his bed, pinned down with an immense lethargy. He found that he could now do nothing else *but sleep*.

It had got him, the laser.

That night while lying in bed with his new sickness in his rooms at University House he heard music from a radio carried on the wind and he heard the announcer say that the piece of music which had reached him on the wind was called *White Night* and that it was played by Kenny White and his orchestra. The wind dropped and he heard no more.

While lying there during the next few days he wondered why his two companions in that city—the seat of government—should both be named Lewis. He asked one and she said that Cottle's Dictionary of Surnames said that Lewis meant 'great battle'.

'Why do you ask?'

He shook his head, the message was there but could not be shared.

This Lewis dropped in the airmail *Guardian* to him to read and he read that the Moscow International Book Fair had refused to allow the book *White Nights* by Israel's Prime Minister Mr Begin to enter the Soviet Union. The book was an account of Begin's persecution and torment in a Soviet labour camp.

In the next airmail *Guardian* he read of a recent screening of Bresson's *Four Nights* which was based on Dostoyevsky's story *White Nights* and he further read that Visconti also had made a film called *White Nights* based on the Dostoyevsky story.

Hepatitis had drained his energy so that clipping even the tissue-thin pages of the airmail Guardian took a long time, but he clipped the two reports and would, from time to time, study them for messages.

The clippings yielded nothing but the word 'guardian' addressed itself to him and he felt comforted by it.

There was, he intuited, an airmail or air-male or heir-male Force of Destruction coming in from around Jonestown and an heir-male Guardian. There was a battle going on for his psyche. He being, of course, the male heir. His suicidal grandfather was mixed up in it somewhere.

As soon as he was well enough he went to the National University library and found all Dostoyevsky's work there except *White Nights*.

He stood there in the gloomy aisles of books sweating from a nervous impotence, having confirmed, once again, that desperate feeling he always had in libraries that what he wanted would not be there, or that he was looking in the wrong place.

'What does it mean that the book *White Nights* by Dostoyevsky is not in the library?' he asked a helpful, new-breed librarian in jeans.

'It could be out on loan.'

He wanted a different category of answer to his questions. But that was asking too much even from a new-breed librarian.

'But all his other books are there in multiple copies.'

'Maybe it is at the binder—that would be another possibility.'

'That all the copies of *White Nights* wore out at the same time? Could you check to see who has all the copies of *White Nights*?'

'That would be confidential. Would you like it to be public knowledge that you, say, borrowed a book on menopause, hypothetically—if you were a woman?'

He did not wish to be drawn into hypothetical discussion—in another gender—on menopause.

'It's odd that's all,' he said, a touch of peevishness in his voice, 'that you have multiple copies of all of Dostoyevsky's work but that all the copies of that title alone are missing.'

She shrugged, and began to fidget nervously with her confidential cards, moving surreptitiously towards the security button.

'Never mind,' he said.

'You're welcome.'

He had never been welcome, not for one day on this planet had he ever felt welcome.

Outside the library, he thought, I am becoming grumpy, I am now forty and I am becoming grumpy.

He recovered and returned to his own city where he told Belle about the *White Nights* and about the books missing from the library and the rest.

'That's odd,' she said, humouring him.

'Don't humour me,' he said, grumpily, 'I think it bears some attention.'

'I cannot explain the *White Nights* thing,' she said, watching him, he thought, closely, 'but I have two copies of Dostoyevsky's *White Nights*, but I don't want you to make anything of it.'

'Why two copies of Dostoyevsky's *White Nights*?'

'I cannot explain why I have two copies and I do not want you to make a thing of it.'

She brought him a copy of the book.

He examined it and read the novella *White Nights*.

He then explained to Belle that white night referred to the mid-summer nights at the sixtieth latitude north.

'So?'

'I am in the midsummer latitude of my life.'

'Oh.'

In November, one year from the Jonestown suicides, an American journalist flew in and telephoned him, Joe Treaster from the *New York Times*.

Joe Treaster wanted to talk to him about the IAEA.

'Who put you on to me?'

'The Department of Information.'

A few days later a friend rang and invited him to a party. 'Joe Treaster from the *New York Times* will be there. You should meet him.'

'Yes, he rang me.'

'Did you know he was the first journalist into Jonestown after the suicides? He's very interesting on it.'

'No!'

He then rang Joe at his hotel but could not reach him and left a message for Joe to ring back.

But he was due in Vienna and could not fit in with Joe's itinerary. They didn't meet, which he thought was probably just as well.

That week Senator Knight from Canberra dropped dead at the age of forty.

He gave up the *White Knight* TV project, not having written a word of it.

He said to Belle that he did not really suffer from the illusion that the universe was rearranging itself to give him a personal message. He knew that was ultimate egoism.

But he could be excused for thinking it was a year of shadows, confusing linguistic signals, ricocheting beams, that maybe a bony hand had been groping for him, inviting him to dance, lanterns had been waved in the dark to guide him towards the cliff. But he was through it now.

'That's a relief,' Belle said, 'I thought for a while there you were loony tunes.'

Later in the next year, having again given up the idea of being a writer, he was working at a university and they had given him a room formerly occupied by a medievalist.

He was seated at the desk for some hours before he realised that a poster of an ivory chess piece on the wall facing him was a white knight— the caption said it was from the Isle of Lewis. The white knight was glum and toy-like and it did not frighten him. He photographed it and during his time at the university became quite fond of it.

GERALD MURNANE

Precious Bane

I first thought of this story on a day of drizzling rain in a second-hand bookshop in Prahran. I was the only customer in the shop. The owner sat near the door and stared out at the rain and the endless traffic. This was all he seemed to do all day. I had passed the shop often and walked through the man's gaze; and during the moment when I intersected that gaze I felt what it might be like to be invisible.

On the day of drizzle I was inside the man's shop for the first time. (I buy many second-hand books, but I buy them from catalogues. Second-hand bookshops make me unhappy. Even reading the catalogues is bad enough. But the second-hand books that I buy do not sadden me. Taking them out of their parcels and putting them on my shelves, I tell them they have found a good home at last. And I warn my children often that they must not sell my books after I have died. My children need not read the books, but they must keep them on shelves in rooms where people might glance at them sometimes or even handle them a little and wonder about them.) The man had glanced at me when I came into his shop, but then he had looked away and gone on gazing. And all the while I poked among his books he never looked back at me.

The books were badly arranged, dusty, neglected. Some were heaped on tables, or even on the floor, when they could easily have been shelved if the man had cared to put his shop in order. I looked over the section marked LITERATURE. I had in my hand one of what I called my book-buying notebooks. It was the notebook labelled: *1900–1940 . . . Unjustly Neglected.* The forty years covered by the notebook were not only the first forty of the century. Written backwards—'1940–1900'—they were the first forty years from the year of my birth to a time that I thought of as the Age of Books. If my life had been pointed in that direction I would have been, just then, not sheltering from rain in a graveyard of books but inspecting wall after wall of leather-bound volumes in my mansion in a city of books. Or I would have been at my desk, a writer in the fullness of his powers, looking through tall windows at a park-like scene in the countryside of books while I waited for my next sentence to come to me.

I put together four or five titles and took them to the gazing man. While he checked the prices pencilled in the front leaves I looked at him from under my eyebrows. He was not so old as I had thought. But his skin had a greyness that made me think of alcohol. The bookseller's liver is almost rotted away, I told myself. The poor bastard is an alcoholic.

I believed, in those days, that I was on the way myself to becoming an alcoholic, and I was always noticing signs of what I might look like in twenty or ten years or even sooner. If the bookseller had pickled his liver, then I understood why he sat and gazed so often. He suffered all day from the mood that came over me every Sunday afternoon when I had been sipping for forty-eight hours and had finally stopped and tried to sober up and to begin the four pages of fiction I was supposed to finish each weekend.

In my Sunday afternoon mood I usually gave up trying to write and looked over my bookshelves. Before nightfall I had usually decided there was no point in writing my sort of fiction in 1980. Even if my work was published at last, and a few people read it for a few years, what would be the end of it all? Where would my book be in, say, forty years' time? Its author by then would no longer be around to investigate the matter. He would have poisoned the last of his brain cells and died long before. Of the few copies that had actually been bought, fewer still would be stacked on shelves. Of these few even fewer would be opened, or even glanced at, as weeks and months passed. And of the few people still alive who had actually read the book, how many would remember any part of it?

At this point in my wondering I used to devise a scene from around the year 2020. It was Sunday afternoon (or, if the working week had shrunk as forecast, a Monday or even a Tuesday afternoon). Someone vaguely like myself, a man who had failed at what he most wanted to do, was standing in gloomy twilight before a wall of bookshelves. The man did not know it, but he happened to be the last person on the planet who still owned a copy of a certain book that had been composed on grey Sunday afternoons forty years before. The same man had once actually read the book, many years before the afternoon when he searched for it on his shelves. And more than this, he still remembered vaguely a certain something about the book.

There is no word for what this man remembers—it is so faint, so hardly perceptible among his other thoughts. But I stop (in my own thinking, on many a Sunday afternoon) to ask myself what it is exactly that the man still possesses of my book. I reassure myself that the something he half remembers must be just a little different from all the other vague somethings in his memory. And then I think about the man's brain.

I know very little about the human brain. In all my three thousand books there is probably no description of a brain. If someone counted in my books the occurrence of nouns referring to parts of the body, 'brain' would probably have a very low score. And yet I have bought all those books and read nearly half of them and defended my reading of them because I believe my books can teach me all I need to know about how people think and feel.

I think freely about the brain of the man standing in front of his bookshelves and trying to remember: trying (although he does not know it) to rescue the last trace of my own writing—to save my thought from extinction. I know that this thinking of mine is, in a way, false. But I trust my thinking just the same, because I am sure my own brain is helping me to think; and I cannot believe that one brain could be quite mistaken about another of its kind.

I think of the man's brain as made up of many cells. Each cell is like a Carthusian monastery, with high walls around it and a little garden between the front wall and the front door. (The Carthusians are almost hermits; each monk belongs to the monastery, but he spends most of his day reading in his cell or tending the vegetables in his walled garden.) And each cell is a storehouse of information; each cell is crammed with books.

A few books are cloth-bound with paper jackets, but most are leather-bound. And far outnumbering the books are the manuscripts. (I have trouble envisaging the manuscripts. One of my own books—in my room, on the grey Sunday afternoon—has photographs of pages from an illuminated manuscript. But I wonder what a collection of such pages would look like and how it would be bound. And I have no idea how a collection of such bound manuscripts would be stored—lying flat, on top of one another? sideways? upright in ranks like cloth-bound books on my own shelves? I wonder too what sort of furniture would store or display the manuscripts. So, although I can see each monk in his cell reaching up to his shelf of books from more recent times, when I want to think of him searching among the bulk of his library I see only a greyness: the grey of the monk's robe, of the stone walls of his cell, of the afternoon sky at his little window, and the greyness of blurred and incomprehensible texts.)

There are very few Carthusian monks in the world—I mean, the world outside my window and under the grey sky on Sunday afternoon. But when I say that, I am only repeating what a priest told me at secondary school nearly thirty years ago, when I was dreaming of becoming a monk and living in a library with a little garden and a wall around me. Apart from the priest's vague answer, the only information I have about the Carthusian Order comes from an article in the English *Geographical Magazine.* But that article was published in the 1930s, at about the time when I was learning to read in my other lifetime that leads back towards the Age of Books. I cannot check the article now because all of my old magazines are wrapped in grey plastic garbage bags and stored above the ceiling of my house. I stored them there three years ago with four hundred books that I will never read again—I needed more space on my shelves for the latest books I was buying.

What I mainly remember about that article was that it was all text with no photographs. Nowadays the *Geographical Magazine* is half filled with coloured photographs. I sometimes skip the brief, jargonized texts of the articles and find all I need to know in the captions under the photographs.

But the 1930s magazines (in the grey plastic bag, in the twilight above the ceiling over my head) included many an article with not one illustration. I imagine the authors of those articles as bookish chaps in tweeds, returning from strolls among hedgerows to sit at desks in their libraries and write (with fountain pens and few crossings-out) splendid essays and admirable articles and pleasant memoirs. I see those writers clearly. I knew them well in the years of my teens, as the 1920s passed and the Great War loomed ahead. When those gentlemen-writers post their *belles-lettres* to editors, they include no illustrations. The gentlemen actually boast of not knowing how to use cameras or gramophones or other modern gadgets, and their readers love the gentlemen for their charming dottiness. (I have never learned to use a camera or a tape recorder, but when I tell this to people they think I am striking a pose to draw attention to myself.)

I do not think the Carthusians would have objected to a gentleman-writer's taking a few photographs of their monastery so I assume that the author of the article trusted his words and sentences to describe clearly what he saw. The monastery was in Surrey, or it might have been Kent. This had disappointed me. When I first read the article I no longer dreamed of becoming a monk, but I liked to dream of monks living like hermits in remote landscapes; and Surrey or Kent was too populous for dreams about peaceful libraries. The only placename I remember from the article is Parkminster. I looked into my *Times Atlas of the World* just now and found no Parkminster in the index. (While I looked I vaguely remembered having looked for the same word more than once in the past with the same result.) Parkminster is therefore a hamlet too small to be marked on maps; or perhaps the monastery itself is called Parkminster, and the monks asked the writer not to mention any placenames in his article because they wanted no curious sightseers trying to peep into their cells.

But, in any case, the article was published in the 1930s, and, for all I know, the Carthusians and their cells and the word 'Parkminster' may have drifted off towards the Age of Monasteries and I may be the only one who remembers them, or at least what was once written about them.

Yet, when I think of the man reaching up to his bookshelves, on a grey afternoon in the year 2020, I see broad gravel paths with trees above them: whole districts of paths with cells beside the paths and in every cell a monk surrounded by books and manuscripts.

The man at his bookshelves—the last rememberer of my book—not only fails to remember what he once read in my book but cannot remember where he last saw my book on his shelves. He stands there and tries to remember.

A lay-brother walks along an avenue of his monastery. Lay-brothers are bound by solemn vows to their monastery, like other monks, but their duties and privileges are somewhat different. A lay-brother is not so much confined to his cell. Each day while the priest-monks are in their cells reading, or reciting the divine office, or tending their gardens, the lay-brothers are working for the monastery as a whole: taking messages and instructions and even dealing, in a limited way, with the world outside the monastery. Each lay-brother knows his way around some suburb of the monastery; he knows which monk lives behind which wall in his particular district. The lay-brother even gets to know, in a general sense, what the hermit-monks keep in their libraries: what books and manuscripts they spend their days reading. A lay-brother, having only a few books himself, thinks of books and libraries in a convenient, summary way. He learns to quote in full the titles of books he has never opened or never seen, whereas a monk in his cell might spend a year reading a certain book or copying and embellishing a certain manuscript and thinking of it for the rest of his life as an enormous pattern of rainbow pages of capital letters spiralling inwards and long laneways of words like the streets of other monasteries inviting him to dream about their cells of books and manuscripts.

A lay-brother walks along an avenue of the monastery. He has an errand to undertake but he is in no hurry. This is not easy to explain to people ignorant of monasteries. Monks behind their walls observe time differently from the people in the world outside. While only a few moments seem to pass on an uneventful, grey afternoon outside the monastery, a monk on the other side of the wall might have turned, at long intervals, page after page of a manuscript. The mystery can never be explained because no one has been able to be at once both outside and inside a monastery.

So, the lay-brother is in no hurry. He stands admiring the vegetables and herbs in each of the gardens of the cells he has been instructed to visit. When each monk has come to the door, the lay-brother asks him a certain question or questions but with no show of urgency. The lay-brother will call again, he says, on the next day or, perhaps, on the day after. In the meanwhile, if the monk could consult his books or his manuscripts for the needed information . . .

There is more than one lay-brother, of course. There may be hundreds, thousands, all striding or ambling through the leafy streets of the monastery while the last of my readers runs a finger along the spines of his books and tries to remember something of my book. And although I think of the lay-brothers as walking mostly through a particular quarter or district of the monastery, I know there are districts and more districts beyond them. In one of those districts, I decide on the grey Sunday afternoon when I have to decide whether to begin my writing or to go on sipping—in one of those districts, in a cell with grey walls no different from all the grey walls in all the streets in all the districts around it, in a collection of manuscripts that has lain undisturbed during many quiet afternoons, is a page where a monk once read or wrote what the man in the year 2020 would like to recall. The monk himself has forgotten most of what he once read or wrote. He could, perhaps, find the passage again—if he were asked to search for it among all the other pages he has read and written in all the years he has been reading and writing in his cell. But no lay-brother comes to ask the monk to look for any such page. Outside the monk's grey walls, no footstep sounds on many a grey afternoon.

The man cannot remember what he once read in my book. He cannot remember where among his shelves he once put away my thin volume. The man fills his glass again and goes on sipping some costly poison of the twenty-first century. He does not understand the importance of his forgetfulness, but I understand it. I know that no one now remembers anything of my writing.

So, on many a Sunday afternoon I leave my writing in its folder. I cannot bring myself to write what will become at last a greyness in a heap of manuscripts I can hardly imagine.

In the bookshop, I paid for my books and pocketed my change. The books were still on the table where the man had stacked them while he checked their prices. The man waited for me to take away the books so he could go on with his gazing, but I wanted to say something to the man. I wanted to reassure him that the books would be safe in their new home. I wanted to tell him that some of them were books I had wanted for a long time—unjustly neglected books that would now be read and remembered.

The topmost book was *Precious Bane* by Mary Webb. I touched the faded yellow cloth cover and I told the man that I had been searching for a long time for *Precious Bane*, that I intended to read it very soon.

The man looked not at the book or at me but out at the rain. With his face towards the greyness at his window, he said that he knew *Precious Bane* well. Or rather, he corrected himself, he had once known the book well. It had been a well-known book in its time. He had read it, but he hardly remembered it, he said, especially since his health was not what it had been. But it didn't matter, he said. It didn't matter if you couldn't remember anything about a book. The important thing was to read a book; to store it up inside you. It was all there inside somewhere, he said. It was all safely preserved. He lifted a hand, as though he might have pointed to some precise point on his skull, but then he let the hand fall again into the position where it normally rested while he gazed.

I took my books home. I entered the titles and the authors' names in my catalogue, and then I put each book in its correct place in my library, which is arranged in alphabetical order according to authors' surnames.

On the following Sunday, when it was time to stop sipping and to begin writing, I thought as usual of the man in the year 2020. He still tried and failed to remember a certain book, the book that I had written forty years before. But after he had walked away from his shelves and had sat down again to sip, I thought of him as knowing that my book was still safely preserved after all.

Then I thought of the monastery, and I saw that the sky above it had been changed. A golden glow was in the air; it was not so much the yellow of sunlight; more the dark gold of the cover of Mary Webb's unjustly neglected book or the amber of beer or the autumn colour of whisky. The light in the sky made the avenues of the monastery seem even more tranquil. The lay-brothers on their way from cell to cell sauntered rather than walked. Each monk in his cell, when he reached for a certain book or manuscript, was utterly calm and deliberate. And when he held up a page to inspect it, the light from his window lay faintly gold on the intricate pen-strokes or the tinted initials, and he found with ease what he had been asked to find.

On that afternoon, and on many Sundays afterwards, I wrote while I sipped. When I next called at the bookshop I had been writing for six months of Sundays.

After I had paid the man for my books, I told him I was a writer. I told him I had been writing on every Sunday since I had last seen him. By the following winter I would have finished what I was writing. And by the winter after that, my writing would have been preserved in a book. I wanted the cover of my book to be a rich, gold colour, I told the man, although he seemed hardly interested. I did not care about the colour of my dust-jacket, but when forty years had passed and the jacket had been torn away or lost and my book had been stored in a far corner of a shop like his, I wanted the gold colour of its spine to stand out among the greys and greens and dark blues of all the almost-forgotten books.

I told all this to the man while he went on gazing out into the sunlight as though it was still the same grey that he had gazed at when he told me about the books he could never forget. But this time the man would not reassure me. He was the last of a dying race, he told me. There would be no more shops like his in forty years. If people in those days wanted to preserve the stuff that had once been in books, they would preserve it in computers: in millions of tiny circuits in silicon chips in computers.

The man lifted his hand. His thumb and his index fingers made the shape of pincers, with a tiny gap between the pads of the two fingers. He held his fingers for a moment against the light from outside and stared at the crack between them. Then he let his hand fall, and he went back to gazing in his usual way.

On the following Sunday I did not go on with the writing that I had wanted to become a book with dark gold covers. I sat and sipped and thought about circuits and silicon chips. I thought of silicon as grey, the grey of granite when it was wet from rain under a grey sky. And I thought of a circuit as a grid of gold tracks in the grey. I saw that the tracks of a circuit would have a pattern hardly different from the paths of a monastery. The circuits I thought of seemed rather more remote from me than any monastery. But the pattern was the same. I could see only thin trails of gold across the grey, but I supposed the gold came from close-set treetops on either side of the long avenues of the circuit. The weather over the circuits would have been an endless calm autumn afternoon, the best weather for remembering.

I still could not imagine what sort of people would walk beneath the overspreading autumn-gold. But a few Sundays after I had first thought about circuits, I began to write about a monastery where a page of writing might have been buried deep beneath a stack of manuscripts in a grey room but that page would never be lost or forgotten. As I wrote, I believed that my writing itself, my account of the monastery, would rest safely forever in some unimaginable room of books under gold foliage in a city of circuits. That monastery, I wrote, was only a monastery in a story, but the story was safe and so, therefore, was the monastery and everything in it. I saw story, monastery, circuit, story, monastery, circuit . . . receding endlessly in the same direction as the lifetime that would have taken me towards the Golden Age of Books.

But as I wrote I came to see that the monastery was not, of course, endless. Somewhere, on the far side of the monastery wall, another greyness began: the greyness of the land of the barbarians, the streetless steppes where people lived without books.

Those people would not always stay on their steppes: the Age of Books would not go on forever. One day the barbarians would mount their horses and ride towards the monastery and turn backwards the history I had so often dreamed of.

I stopped writing. I poured another drink and looked far into the deep colour in my glass. Then I read aloud what I had written of my story, pausing now and then to sip, and after each sip to gaze at the red-gold sunset in the sky over all that I could remember.

GLENDA ADAMS

The Music Masters

Everybody knows that men are the true artists. Where are your great women composers, conductors? Some women think they can sing, but it's more often a screech or a scream. They can also dance a little. But where are your famous women painters, comedians? Women have no sense of humour. But they are educable.

The father sits at the kitchen table with his daughter, listening to the Spike Jones Half Hour on the radio. She isn't allowed to talk or clatter plates, because he doesn't want her to miss a word. Chewing gum on the rail, Cabbage ahead, and Here comes Beezelbom—are among the funniest lines ever written.

This father travels the length and breadth of the city for a Marx Brothers rerun. He takes the daughter to the Prince Edward to see *Night at the Opera* and *Duck Soup*, to supplement her regular education.

When Gummo's sweetheart sings a love song from the deck of the passenger liner taking her to New York, the father groans and holds his ears.

'God love a duck,' he says. 'Screeching women.'

During the intermission, the spotlight falls on one of the balcony boxes, where Noreen and her Hammond organ, a special feature, are waiting. Noreen wears a strapless blue lamé evening dress. Her sparkling silver hair is set in corrugated waves. Her back is as fresh and round and pink as a new velvet pincushion. She sways and bends over the organ, pressing out 'Melody of Love'.

> *Take me in your arms dear*
> *Ten-der-ly*

'Why did they have to bring her on and spoil it all,' the father says.

> *It's a jolly day, today's the wedding*
> *Of the little painted doll.*

'God stiffen the crows,' the father hoots. He hates Noreen and her organ. The daughter thinks she is rather beautiful.

When it is time for *Duck Soup* Noreen turns to the audience and, still sitting on her stool and playing with one hand, she bows. The lights go off and Noreen and the organ disappear.

'There ought to be a law,' the father says.

His favourite scene in *Duck Soup* is at the end, when they all throw edible items at the female singer. He laughs so hard he has to push his dentures back into place.

On the way home, the father tells the daughter that the best movie ever made is *Treasure Island*, because there is only one woman in it, right at the beginning. Once you bring women into it, art is ruined. The Marx Brothers do very well, considering.

The father plays the piano. He specialises in honky tonk and thinks Knuckles O'Toole is the greatest.

The father can play any tune in the world. The daughter can ask for anything at all and he can play it. He always plays in G major, with the left hand very low and the right hand very high, so that it is impossible to sing with him.

When he plays he beats his foot on the floor. He has worn a hole in the carpet. The daughter stands beside him, waiting for a space between the songs to ask him something. He is playing a medley and there is no space. He calls to her to speak up, because he can play and keep time with his foot and listen to her, too.

The mother likes to sing as she hangs out the clothes. Usually she sings

> *I'll be loving you, always.*
> *With a love that's true, always.*

She also likes to sing

> *Now at last the door of my dreams is swinging wide*
> *There upon the threshold stands the blushing bride.*

Often the father requests that she put clothes pegs in her mouth.

The son plays the drums. He has a rubber practice pad that he takes with him everywhere. Whenever he has a spare moment, he takes his sticks out of his back pocket and beats out a two-four, or a four-four, or a six-eight. When anyone speaks to him, he frowns and keeps on playing, his head held critically to one side. People give up trying to talk to him.

The daughter thinks that perhaps she will be a dancer. She has seen every ballet movie.

She has seen *Tales of Hoffmann*. Olympia, the wooden doll, is so lifelike that a young student falls in love with her. But she is only a piece of wood, a puppet.

She has seen *The Red Shoes*. When the girl accepts the red shoes and puts them on, she dances forever. The shoes don't let her rest and they dance her to death.

She has seen *Giselle*, who is loved for a day by the prince. When he forsakes her for a princess, Giselle goes crazy.

She has seen *The Story of Three Loves*. The beautiful young ballerina dances for the artist she loves, even though she knows she has a weak heart and it will kill her. But she does it for him, to help him through an artistic block.

She asks for the *Nutcracker Suite* for Christmas. The father obliges. Six 78 rpms.

She puts on her ballet slippers, puts on side one, and prepares to dance. But instead of flutes and piccolos, there come a banging of tin, a kind of hiccuping, and a bunch of high-pitched voices singing

> *Dja ever see a tin flute dancing?*
> *Nothing is so funny as a hunka tin.*

She bursts into tears. It is Spike Jones's version, and there is hardly any music at all. The father tells her not to be silly. The record is a marriage of two great arts—music and humour.

Bill Haley and his Comets come to town. Also Freddy Bell and the Bellboys. The son gets tickets and buys the record. He wants to know all the words of 'Rock Around the Clock' and perfect his jitterbugging so that he can get up and dance in the aisles at the concert.

He puts the record on repeat and sits beside the record player all morning, writing down the words. He says he doesn't mind practising certain steps with his sister, since she is at least a better partner than his dressing gown cord hooked around the bed post.

The daughter falls in love with a young man who can pom-pom the *Barber of Seville* from start to finish. He can sing the 'Freude, schoener Goetter funken' from Beethoven's Ninth, and he knows all the *Carmina Burana* in Medieval Latin.

He takes her home with him to listen to his record collection.

She chooses *Petrouchka*, planning to tell him about the doll with the heart. He puts on *Turandot*. Then he sits up and sings 'Nessun dorma', pounding on the arm of the couch with his fist.

Next he plays *The Song of the Earth* and sings along with Fischer-Dieskau about the glowing knife in his breast.

The daughter gets home at two o'clock.

The father asks where the hell she's been and what the hell she's been doing. She tells him she has been listening to records.

The daughter falls in love with another man who can read the newspaper, eat a sandwich, talk on the telephone, watch television and memorise songs on the radio, almost simultaneously, or at least in quick succession.

She waits for the TV commercials to tell him something. But he also likes commercials and can sing most of them.

After the 11.30 movie, he turns up the radio and reads a back issue of the *New Yorker*. She curls up beside him. He is reading the history of the orange. She takes the magazine from him and tells him he's the only one. He closes his eyes, smiles and nods his head. He reaches out his arm and turns up the volume on the radio and sings

> *If you can't be with the one you love*
> *Love the one you're with.*

He snaps his fingers to the beat. Next he sings

> *Bye, bye, Miss American Pie*

and falls asleep.

MARION HALLIGAN

The Failure of the Bay Tree

The bay tree grows lusty and evergreen by the terrace steps. It has to be cut back so people can pass by it, with baskets of washing, or lunches on the lawn. Jenny Palmer chops and hacks at it, the secateurs shuddering as they try to bite through the thick stalks. She gives handfuls of bay branches to friends and enemies but still there are too many. Thousands indeed millions of bay leaves will never find their apotheosis in casseroles and terrines and *choucroutes* and pâtés and soups.

But she won't throw them away, she'll put them behind the shed to dry, for *when they are casten into the fyre they cracke wonderfully*; they will snap and spark and scent the air briefly, much to the admiration of guests.

Jenny is good with herbs, she likes to grow them and talk about them.

—Do you know, she will say at a dinner party, rosemary will grow only in the gardens of the righteous? Oh yes. Paul and I had trouble for years, kept planting the jolly stuff and it'd die. Made us very nervous. I mean, it did seem a sign. But we've had one going for a good while now, so we must have mended our ways.

Once somebody said, I always thought it was supposed to grow in the gardens of households where the wife was the boss.

—No no. It's righteousness that does it.

Rosemary, dew of the sea. Christ-scented. Rosemary, protection against evil. Ha ha. And rosemary for remembrance.

Jenny remembers the Anzac Day parades of her youth; even then the old men staggering out this one day, and the spiky sprigs to buy and sniff at on the slopes of the park, singing Lo all our pomp of yesterday Is one with Nineveh and Tyre. Lest we forget. Lest we forget. And with rosemary sharp in the nostrils who could, on that day.

But now Jenny should not remember. She should forget. Have done with grief. Keep busy.

The bay tree now. She sits on the step, the secateurs lax in her fingers. Safe to remember that. Nine years ago, not long, considering how large it is, when Martha Ambrose gave her the tiny twig of a tree with three leaves on it. A house-warming present, when the garden was still a figment of the imagination, and the beginning of her interest in herbs.

Neither witch, nor devil, thunder nor lightning, will hurt a man where a bay tree is; that was Nicholas Culpeper. Martha gave her the quotation as well as the little tree. How it had delighted her. Such a comfort, to know one is safe from these things, she would laugh, as the bay tree put out more and more aromatic and useful leaves.

She sits, amidst the debris of bay branches, and the tears well up and slide down her cheeks, in great oily drops that draw all the marrow out of her, leaving her sunken and salt-encrusted. Mad, mad, to think you are safe, never safe; clever-clever mouthing of fine crisp phrases: dangerous entertainment. The fates grin and click go the scissors; can't believe they are blind, vindictive rather. Punishing for fun.

The bay leaves are green, spicy, peppery. She cracks them and rubs them and sniffs at the shards in her fingers. Perhaps the sharpness will enter the bloodstream along with the oxygen, will purify, clarify, make all fresh. Save us from thunder and lightning, devils and witches.

Sybil is a witch. Why has she never noticed it before? Seen with such clarity, such sharpness? Sybil is a witch, and the theft of the fetish ought to have warned them. Sybil is a witch, so why didn't the bay tree protect against her?

When Jenny realised she was pregnant, she was not pleased. They were intending to have children one day, but not right now. Paul was happy, but pretended to be non-committal. Why not? he said. Might as well be sooner as later. In fact he thought that any later would soon be too late; Jenny was thirty-three, he thirty-five. He blessed the accident which had taken the decision they had been postponing for eight years.

Jenny was thin and liked handsome clothes and to have her hair perfectly cut. She had large dark eyes that looked hard and unfaltering at people, and she never helped out conversations with nods and smiles. Strangers found that disconcerting, but friends had learned to accept it as a mannerism. Even to think of her seriousness as charming. She was amusing and kind, she survived very well in society. Her husband loved her very much, and she him.

She remained cold through the process of the growing child, but efficient. She did it well, as she liked to do everything. She gave up wine, and took iron pills, and watched her diet, and scrubbed her nipples with a nail brush to make them tough for breastfeeding. She went to childbirth classes, and acquired all the necessities of the properly bred middle-class baby: the right number of nappies, an array of suitable and fashionably coloured baby clothes, cot and pram and change-table, all well-designed and healthy.

But she herself didn't change, apart from the unavoidable swelling of belly and breasts. She remained her own person; the baby had to tag along with her job and interests and habits. She was by profession a town planner, she liked orderliness and thought little of the chaos that defined it. Her mind, her thoughts, were as they had always been; having a baby was no more than an extra complication of housekeeping. Properly organised, it would impinge minimally on their lives. She and Paul had good jobs, there was enough money to buy efficiency. She would take the designated maternity leave and breastfeed to begin with to give it a good healthy start in life, both physically and psychologically. After that a nanny.

The pregnancy was relatively easy, given her age, but cumbersome and boring and irritating towards the end as even the best ones are, and the birth long and tiring. She felt exhausted and remote after the final effort that pushed the baby out. So when the nurse placed the little swaddled bundle of child across her chest and she looked at her small round golden face and the tip of her tongue delicately moving about between her lips as though she were tasting the air, Jenny was completely unprepared for the overwhelming, terrifying love that washed through her, breaking down all the firm cool outlines of her self so that it flowed out softly and helplessly to surround the child and keep her safe and was itself so soft and vulnerable she knew at that moment she would never be self-contained again, she was a quivering defenceless surface open to harm.

She forgot the terror of this. Her blood pressure went up rather alarmingly and she was given drugs that made her sleep for a number of hours; when she woke up and the baby was brought to her this intense exciting appalling love was already a part of her, and only a little frightening, and that could be taken for nervousness in the face of this little fragile strange person. And even nervousness didn't last long. The child was a good baby from the beginning, and seemed to like the world. She sucked strongly and gave her mother sweet little orgasms in her belly and Jenny was astonished at the state of sensual delight she found herself so often in.

Paul was tender and amazed at her transformation into a doting mother. He would fetch Caroline for her morning feed, and the three of them would lie in bed together in warm milky contentment, the baby sucking, him snoozing, and afterwards with Caroline tucked up safe in her cot he would put his face against his wife's breasts and the thin sweet milk seemed the taste of perfect happiness.

When it came to the point Jenny couldn't bear to give up the pleasurable leisurely looking after of her baby, and took leave of absence, indefinite, from her excellent job at the National Capital Development Commission. They had much less money, but less expensive habits, so that was all right. And of course there was no question of a nanny; they got the girl next door to babysit when they wanted to go to the cinema or a dinner party.

And so Jenny flourishes in domesticity. Caroline remains such a good baby. Time-consuming, naturally, but not troublesome. Not at all the difficult child that often comes to middle-aged parents. Jenny takes up sewing again, charming little dresses in luxurious Liberty cottons; Caroline is so pretty, these dark old-fashioned flower prints suit her beautifully. She cooks good meals that she and Paul eat together with candles and baroque music after they have put the baby to bed. And she does a lot of gardening; the weather is golden, it's the still painted autumn that occurs in the high country, and Caroline lies on her bouncinette and kicks and gurgles while Jenny weeds and plants and rubs scented geranium leaves between her fingers for her to smell. Whenever his classes at the university allow (he is an anthropologist) Paul comes home for lunch and joins them. They eat bread and cheese in the garden and point out Caroline's charming ways to one another. She is three months old, plump and healthy; her parents think she is remarkably intelligent, very advanced for her age.

Jenny talks to her a lot. It's good for the baby, and fun as well. She's always had a good voice, strong and deep (she was a debater at school), a bit bossy her subordinates at work have said, but Caroline knows only her mellow lilting tones—it's as though her voice like her figure has had its angles rounded and softened and made luscious by motherhood. She tells her stories, little scraps that remain from her own childhood: Snow White and Rose Red, Rapunzel Rapunzel let down your hair, Hansel and Gretel . . .

> . . . And the wicked witch put Hansel in a cage and fed him delicious food in order to make him plump and juicy—just like Caroline, oh what a fat tummy, let's eat her all up. But Hansel was too clever for her, for whenever she said, 'Little boy little boy put out your finger and let me see how fat you are' Hansel would poke a bone out through the bars of the cage and the witch would think, 'Oh no, he's far too skinny'. Witches, you see, have red eyes and can't see very far. But after a while the witch gets tired of waiting and decides to eat him anyway. So she makes poor Gretel, who's been starved on nothing but scraps to eat, light a great big enormous fire in the oven, so she can roast him. And Gretel says, 'I don't know if it's hot enough, will you look in and see?' and when the witch bends down and leans in to the oven Gretel gives her a great big push inside and slams the door on her. So she's all burned up and that's the end of her. And Hansel and Gretel fill their pockets with gold and precious stones and they go back to their little house in the forest and live happily ever after and are never hungry again.

Caroline laughs and chuckles and waves her hands round while Jenny tells her these stories; she is a most satisfactory audience. I know she understands every word I say, says Jenny.

Caroline sleeps so well at night that babysitting her isn't difficult. They usually get Sybil Flanagan from next door, who is in her last year at the Girls' Grammar School. At times she has been a boarder, when her parents were posted overseas, but at the moment they are at home. She

seems a very quiet pleasant girl, clever, and delighted with Caroline; her
rather peaky face, surrounded by the sort of stiff frizzy hair you can't do
a thing with, lights up when she sees her. She sometimes calls in after
school just to have a little play. It's usually at the time Caroline wakes up
from her afternoon sleep. Sybil likes to make tea and talk about life.
She doesn't admire her own parents at all. It's a bit of a bore but Jenny is
good-natured. Once, catching her telling the story of Rumpelstiltskin,
Sybil is enthralled. You should write it down, she says, and Jenny thinks
that it's not a bad idea. She's quite good at drawing, though she's only
done plans for years; she could try writing stories for children, with
pictures. Even she can see that beatific motherhood might not be enough
for ever. Especially looking at Sybil, though of course Caroline will be
nothing like her. The girl leans over the baby and smiles and plays tickling
games, and the gawky, rather grumpy adolescent almost disappears. Little
flashes of happiness touch her face.

So the business with the fetish is rather disturbing. This object is small,
ancient and valuable, an almost spherical terracotta carving of a figure all
breasts and buttocks, the head and limbs vestigial. It fits in the hand and
is beautiful to hold; Jenny has a habit of holding it in her palm and sliding
her fingers over its bulbous surfaces. A fertility object, certainly; Paul
blames their pregnancy, the failure of her until then efficient contraceptive
practice, on this habit. You invoked its powers, they were too strong for
you, he says. That's a joke, of course.

They miss it the day after a dinner party. They'd come home rather late
and quickly paid Sybil and seen her home through the gap in the fence
without going into the sitting-room at all. Jenny can't quite remember
when she last saw it. Surely it was there yesterday afternoon? Would they
have noticed if it weren't? Is anything else missing? So, if it's a burglar,
why just the fetish? They look at one another with sombre eyes, afraid
something nasty is happening. It's precious enough to report to the police,
but they are afraid to do that.

In fact the whole thing is making them feel a bit sick. So when Ted
Flanagan comes in that evening holding the object in his hand and
looking embarrassed and talking volubly about being embarrassed they
are so relieved they simply comfort him.

—Don't worry, they say. It doesn't matter at all. It's not important.

—I don't know what to say, he keeps on saying. It's inexcusable. I don't
know what came over her.

—It's a strange object, says Paul. It's meant to be magic, of course. She
probably couldn't resist having it with her for a while, just, you know,
wanting it near her. Don't give it another thought. Here, let me give you
a scotch.

—It's very good of you to take it like this, says Ted. I was quite
shattered. All I could think of was kleptomania setting in.

—Good heavens, laughs Jenny. What nonsense. We all know Sybil's not that kind of person.

And they continue to have her to babysit good little Caroline, who never wakes. Though Jenny can't help glancing towards the fetish as soon as they come home, and then thinking that of course she's known all the time that it would be there. She often notices that it's been moved; it's in much the same place, but the angle is different, or the shadows. But this isn't surprising, after all she finds it fascinating too. She still sits, on the sofa with her feet curled under her, feeling its ancient powerful curves.

—Still conjuring up the forces? says Paul. Do I see another accident coming up?

—Oh no, says Jenny. They don't need any more children. Caroline is quite enough.

It's winter. It's cold. They've eaten osso bucco for dinner, picking out the marrow with coffee spoons. They've watched television, sitting close on the sofas, enjoying the noise of the wind shut safe away outside. Now the fire is going out, it's time to go to bed. Jenny as always checks that the baby is covered, sleeping soundly. It's just a routine; she enjoys it. Caroline has one arm flung through the bars of the cot, with three fingers folded around the thumb and the index pointed (lovely long fingers, Jenny always thinks, not the usual baby's starfish paws, but then Caroline is an unusually shapely and elegant baby), her favourite way of holding her hands. A comfort, even a ritual. Jenny takes the small fist to tuck it back under the blankets where it belongs on a winter's night. It is cold, cold, cold. And stiff.

She puts her hand to the baby's cheek, in a terrible slow-swift movement of panic that needs to know and doesn't want to find out; it is cold, too, colder than a terracotta idol, colder than clay under snow, cold as only flesh is cold when there is no life in it.

—It's a dreadful thing, says the doctor with tears in his eyes. We don't understand. A perfectly healthy baby, and then suddenly . . . for no apparent reason . . .

In the spring (late, the shops already full of the chirping of Christmas carols) Paul says to Jenny, How about if you were to start trying to get your old job back? I think you might feel better if you could get out of the house, take your mind off things a bit. He hears the triteness of this, but hopelessly. Words cannot help him any more. To name, to describe, to find the right terms, had been to understand; now words are fragile fences round pits of meaninglessness, to be skirted askance.

—I don't mean it'll stop you grieving. But it'll give you something else

to think of as well. I really do think it'd be good for you. Oh love, I think
you should try.

—Soon, she says, smiling vaguely. Not yet. There's a lot to be done
here, I can't really leave it yet.

Now, Martha coming to visit her—coming round to the back of the
house because she sees from her car that she's at home although she hasn't
answered the doorbell, calling in as her friends often do these days because
they worry about her, sad in the gaze of her large dark eyes that still don't
falter because they look in, not out, and see nothing before—now
Martha finds her sitting on the cold back step in the dark of the afternoon
in a debris of bay branches, her face tear-stained, her eyes like stones.

—I see it now, she says, and her words are like stones too. How could
I be so stupid not to understand before? Sybil of course. I should have
seen how wicked. My poor sweet Caroline. Tender little finger poking
through the bars of the cage of the cot. I told her about Hansel and the
bone but she couldn't do it by herself how could a baby manage by herself
and no one to help. Witches have red eyes and can't see very far you know
you'd never guess with Sybil but a finger like that she'd smell it I
know . . .

—But what I don't understand is the bay tree. Martha, the bay tree
failed. Why didn't it work, Martha, it's such a big tree, it could have
worked and I'd still have my . . .

Martha, terror-struck, clutches her as the tears well up and overflow
her eyes again.

MURRAY BAIL

Zoellner's Definition

Definition   The action of determining a question at issue; an ecclesiastical pronouncement. A precise statement on the essential nature of a thing.

Name   The particular combination of vocal sounds employed as the individual designation of a single person or thing. To call a person or thing by the right name.

Zoellner's mother (whose name was also Zoellner) decided to call him Leon. His father preferred 'Max', but today on the birth certificate (and other records stored in cabinets in scattered buildings) he is identified as Leon—Leon Zoellner. In Zoellner's opinion the first name is an accessory only made necessary (perhaps) by the complicated world population. Whenever he thinks of the shape of himself he sees the word *Zoellner*. Like most people Zoellner is intrigued by the name which is used to identify him. In the telephone directory there was only one other Zoellner, an architect with initials R. L. whom he has never met. In Basil Cottle's *Dictionary of Surnames* he found only three names beginning with Z: Zeal, Zeller and Zouch.

Man   An adult male person. The human creature regarded abstractly. The spiritual and material parts of a human person; hence applied to the physical frame of man.

Zoellner has all the appearance of a man.

Face   The front part of the head, from the forehead to the chin; the countenance as expressive of feeling or character; a countenance having a specific expression.

Countenance   Appearance, composure of face; comportment.

He seems to be in mourning, or remembering something; Zoellner has that troubled vagueness. He seems to be listening intently; or he is waiting for something. The face has filled, rounded, folded and settled more or less naturally into the shape of those requirements. There is also the established persistence of his years. This can suddenly fix itself onto another face, or a foot, a metal object, a crowd, or a distant mountain. To be precise, Zoellner glances at these things too rapidly. He is keen. Strange though: looking in mirrors he has trouble describing himself. Perhaps Zoellner is tired of his familiar face, the disappointing lines, inevitable expressions.

Skin   The continuous flexible integument forming the usual covering of an animal body.

This is amazing stuff. The way it stretches and clings to the elaborate shape of Zoellner's ears, and other parts. Hair grows straight through it without a corresponding leakage of blood. Around the lips, however, it sometimes bleeds after Zoellner shaves. His skin is grey like the stone of city buildings. But looking at himself he sees a vertical body capable of locomotion, and none of the fine details of skin.

Eyes   The organ of sight, sometimes including the surrounding parts. The faculty of perception or discrimination of visual objects.

Positioned in fluid his eyes move in his head. Juggled by soft wires apparently, they move freely without pain. His are the colour of wet nuts. Zoellner is positive: he would prefer to be deaf than blind. He has a stubborn wonder of sunrises, pigeons wheeling out from trees, waterfalls (and rain overflowing from blocked gutters), women's teeth, processions, huge wall paintings. Lately he has observed scenes of human misery, perhaps believing that the sight of horror and original emotions will reveal some of the foundations of knowledge. Zoellner has cried, but then most men have—or if they haven't they have felt like it. Zoellner reads. Most of the words produce the same movement: a man chases after God, or a white whale, gold, butterflies, women, evil men, etc. Zoellner wonders why they bother arranging these words. Other books he reads have a man chasing mysterious abstractions such as love, truth, power, respect, revenge and reality. Zoellner stands before a mirror and stares at every section of his face. His eyes are deceived. To touch his left ear in the mirror it is first necessary to find his right ear. It always surprises him. When not reading or looking into mirrors he imagines himself: he sees his shape walking towards him.

Spectacled   Provided with or wearing spectacles. In names of birds and animals having spectacle-shaped markings or appearance of wearing spectacles.

At certain angles the glass reflects light to such a sudden extent that his eyes are invisible. The frames are brown plastic. Apparently they are necessary on his head. He removes them (he has this habit) and rubs his eyes. Zoellner's eyesight is getting worse. When it is tested he is asked to recognize letters from his language printed in rapidly diminishing sizes on a wall-chart. He is not asked to recognize pictures or mountains, or a forest, or a person's face.

Mouth   The external orifice in an animal body which serves for the ingestion of food, together with the cavity to which this leads, containing the apparatus of mastication and the organs for vocal utterance.

Usually this is horizontal and rather wide. Laughing, it twists and floats into a ragged circle; shaving, it is pulled into soft triangles; yawning, the slit becomes a black egg, and his teeth suddenly protrude into it. Zoellner's laugh is sudden and shy; it is both generous and genuine. He is amazed that the skin of his lips is softer and different in colour to the rest of his face. Often he breathes through his mouth. He drops food down the cavity, chews it, rolls it to the back, swallows the ball, repeats.

Actually Zoellner has stopped enjoying the taste of food. With his mouth he touches the lips of others. He has noticed more than once that conversations between people are composed of questions. Thinking about this he compresses lips, making the mouth tiny, the lips themselves are crammed with tiny vertical lines.

Voice   Sound formed in or emitted from the human larynx in speaking, singing or other utterance; vocal sound as the vehicle of human utterance or expression. Sounds regarded as characteristic of the person and as distinguishing him from another or others.

He moves his mouth. It may be said that Zoellner curls his voice around his words; each syllable softly rolls into the next: his words are furry at their extremities: the sentences encircle invisibly from the air. A careful voice, not very loud. Perhaps he is cynical of death? That is what his voice sounds like. Characteristically, after producing a statement he will question it by adding, 'Mmmmm?' Lately he has lowered his voice in mid-sentence; those listening lean forward, rustling slightly. He soon questions others to check their statements—if there is room, if it is possible. His words seem to point. The letter in his language most suited to his voice is the circular *R*. So the words are offered. He hears the noise of his own voice. And then the words are gone. He thinks that spoken words are proof of the present, however temporary. But not the past; for the words, always visible, are departed, untraceable. And not the future; for Zoellner has not yet moved his mouth to re-start his voice.

Cigarette   A small cigar made of a little finely-cut tobacco rolled up in thin paper, etc., for smoking.

Protruding from his face is the white tube made by a machine, its red tip alive with silver smoke. Zoellner sends the smoke down his throat and allows it to fill his body. There it enters the narrowest places and trails throughout. Zoellner half-closes his eyes. He has filled the spaces in his body with a cloud. It pours out from his nose.

Tooth   The hard processes within the mouth, attached in a row to each jaw in most vertebrates except birds, having points, edges, or grinding surfaces, for the biting, tearing, or trituration of solid food. **Teeth**, pl. of TOOTH.

Zoellner does not feel comfortable (is always wondering) when cracking nuts with his teeth. Although, his teeth are described as 'excellent' by several dentists. He has only five repaired areas, or 'fillings' as they are called: steel rods, lights and drills are aimed into the mouth, the holes filled with compositions of mercury and a tenacious cement. These filled-in areas are visible only when Zoellner yawns. Teeth are usually vertical; they have the appearance of polished bones. In the middle stand the largest; but of these, the one on Zoellner's left is leaning across at an angle. The smoke of his cigarettes stains his teeth, the yellow most noticeable in the front. Zoellner has another habit: he closes his mouth and rubs the back of his teeth with the tip of his tongue. This of course cannot be seen by others, when the size, shape, colour and spacing of his teeth are also invisible.

Nose   That part of the head or face in men and animals which lies above the mouth and contains the nostrils.

The entrances to Zoellner's nostrils are partially blocked by hairs: they also protrude outside his nose. His nostrils are dark and rather wide. The nose itself is not noticeably large, but it appears to be soft and porous, caused (perhaps) by the hundreds of tiny black holes. These can be seen when standing very close to his face. There is nothing extraordinary about his nose, and Zoellner himself rarely thinks about it. When blowing through his nostrils into a cloth to remove the mucus he hears the noise (as do others): high, briefly loud, shuffling towards the end. Zoellner wonders why that is necessary. Other animals: do they remove mucus? Lying near a woman his chin is above her head. Looking up she notices (at that rare angle) his nose as an unknown shape related more to the peculiar stub of the chin. From there his face has an over-rounded graven appearance, alien and unattractive. Zoellner touches the nose with his hand.

Ear   The organ for hearing in men and animals. Its parts are the external ear, the middle ear, and the internal ear, or labyrinth.

His father had voiced these words years ago. 'It is better that you have your ears cut off, than never to learn what they are hung on your head for.' They are in fact auxiliary devices jutting from the sides of the head, partially obscured by hair. His ears are a deep red compared to the rest of his face. Zoellner sees that they are growing larger and more bulbous (bloated, bumpier) with his age. Still visible is the mildly circular labyrinth which must channel notes of an orchestra into his brain. These ridges also collect wind and dust. He listens to the actions and voices which surround him. It is necessary sometimes to turn his ear in the noise's direction. Noise, to him, seems true and solid, so true that is it unavoidable; it is, however, his most temporary indicator of time and reality. He touches his ears. Pinching with his fingers the flesh is insensitive.

Hair   The filaments that grow from the skin or integument of animals, esp. of most mammals, of which they form the characteristic coat.

The hair on Zoellner's head is falling out as if he had stood too near to some nuclear blast. In the mornings he wakes up with strands of re-jected hair beside him. The edge of his hair is retreating towards the back of his head. Its colour has changed to muddy grey and gaps reveal raw skin. Worse, he sees that the whiskers around his chin are hardly growing. It is necessary to shave only every three days. He watches his face in the mirror. The hair on top of his head is cut regularly by another man.

Arm   The upper limb of the human body, from the shoulder to the hand; the part from the elbow downwards being the fore-arm.

The length and position of the arms establish his proportions. He thinks of other animals. Standing, his arms hang at his sides and bend out where portions touch his body, the tips of his fingers finish halfway between his groin and knee. His arms swing as he walks and he seems to lean forward for balance. He points, shakes hands; he has many times placed an arm around waists and shoulders of men and women. He leans on his elbow. Out of habit Zoellner uses his right arm more than his left. He writes with that hand.

Leg   One of the organs of support and locomotion in an animal body; in narrowest sense, the part of the limb between the knee and foot.

His legs are now thin and pale, although invisible beneath layers of cloth. They carry him along the street in the evening. There his shape is seen moving between the immovable flat surfaces of buildings. He walks without thinking of his movement; one legs jerks ahead of the other. His mind has migrated his body to some other place, another complicated situation. And he seems oblivious. The street is coated in thick yellow light.

Penis   The intromittent or copulatory organ of any male animal.

This swings in the air between his legs and settles itself horizontally as he sits, legs crossed. It can be seen as he urinates: the wrinkled penis, grey from lack of sunlight, as if a wet forest rock had suddenly been lifted from it. It feels insensitive in his two or three fingers, and during this, the draining of his body, he plays the fluid up and down in circular patterns. Zoellner watches. Inserting himself into the body of a partner, and striving, he is suddenly filled with profound melancholy and pointlessness, or he thinks of other women, fragmented problems, words.

Height   Measurement from the base upwards.

Zoellner without shoes measures 5 feet $6^3/_4$ inches. Metrically this is 1.68 metres. He also weighs 114 lbs. (51.71 kilos). At that height he is considered to have less than the desirable weight. Zoellner is regarded as an under-weight specimen. He thinks more of the space he fills (approx. 7 cu.ft., or 0.1981 cu. metres) and the volumes of air he breathes. Generally he believes that measurements of distance (and time) are nothing more than arbitrary notches. His interest in space is, of course, another question.

Short   Having small longitudinal extent. Of persons: Low in stature.

Zoellner is regarded as a short person. Most other persons would agree.

Clothes   Covering for the person; wearing apparel.

Zoellner covers his body in the same style of clothes worn at this moment in Pakistan, Indonesia, United Kingdom, Argentina, Chile, Germany, Quebec, Japan, Russia, Poland, England, Britain, etc., etc. This consists of shirt, neck-tie, trousers, jacket. Bodies of men are thus covered. There is little decoration in Zoellner's selection. He does feel however the cloth resting on the shape of himself. Beneath the material his body moves. He is walking down the street.

Age   A period of existence. The whole of ordinary duration of life.

He is 52.7 years old. This is a measurement linked to movements of sun and moon; beyond that, when Zoellner tries to feel the bulk of those years, it seems to be a blank period without edges: an imprecise mass. Zoellner tries to pin-point his position in his own curving cycle. Where is he at this moment? He is compelled to judge his age in other ways: is 47 average? At that age he is past the middle, into a minority diminishing group. In his country 68.7 years is the average for death. Both parents have died: he is the member of the Zoellner family left to head towards it.

Reality   The quality of being real or having an actual existence.

Language   The whole body of words and of methods of combining them used by a nation, people, or race. Words and the methods of combining them for the expression of thought.

Words   Verbal expression; used in a language to denote a thing, attribute or relation.

MICHAEL WILDING

Somewhere New

My first encounter with Gavin Mulgrave was by telephone. It was one of those painfully hot mornings, painful not only for the heat itself, which lay still and thick as if you could slice it and take it away as trucks cart snow in New York, but more painful in its potential. It was going to get hotter and heavier. In the afternoon you would sit there trying to take gulps of air and with that harsh, dry dustiness, never properly fill your lungs. You would wait for a southerly to blow up, and electric storms with their huge sheets of lightning purpling the whole city. When the papers were inexplicably short of a pack rape or shark scare or highway pile-up they would sometimes run a front-page photograph of the city taken by lightning the previous night. Sometimes the storms would take place miles out at sea and there would be no thunder, no rain; just the sky illuminated by the huge, silent, spreading flares, like a son et lumière display whose narrative tape has been lost; or been expunged by the static that made radios unusable all afternoon when a storm was building up.

'This is Gavin Mulgrave,' he said.

One of the minor writers of the 20's or 30's had died the week before. I remembered noting it and even looking at the paperback shelves in a bookshop to see if anything of his was still in print. There was nothing.

'We have to get something on him,' Mulgrave said. 'We need a three-minute slot and somebody said you'd be able to knock something out for us. That would be right, wouldn't it?'

'Well—'

'It's not a thesis,' he said. 'It's only three minutes.' He chuckled at that.

'What's it for exactly?' I asked.

' "Today's Writing".' he said. He conveyed an appalled surprise at my not automatically knowing, and simultaneously his dissociative contempt for the programme.

'That's radio?' I queried.

'Yes, it's radio.'

I could see no point at all in doing it. I didn't want to have to think up three minutes of generalities, not in that heat, not for radio which nobody listened to and which was immediately forgotten.

'Do you think you could come down now?' he said. 'We've had a few technical difficulties and we're rather behindhand. I'd like to tape it before lunch.'

'Before lunch?' I repeated. 'I need time to think about it.'

'Read a couple of books in the taxi,' he said. 'You'll probably have to

259

sit around here for ages till there's a studio free, so you might as well bring something to read.'

'You made it then,' he said. 'Let's go into here, this studio's empty. We'll just do a test for the sound and all that. Sometimes it doesn't work and it's an awful bore to have to go all through it again. I like to do it all in one take. I really don't see any point in fiddling around and retaping fragments of an inch and rehearsing every pause. I really don't know what some of the people here manage to do with all the time they spend. If one's efficient one can run it straight off. I hate inefficiency. Besides it's more spontaneous. I like spontaneity.'

He was in his thirties, but whether mid-thirties or late, I could never have guessed. He was medium height, with a slight stoop; he hunched his shoulders up when he leant on the table between us. And then he peered. He had very keen eyes. He was clearly conscious that they were 'piercing' eyes, and he pierced with them as punctuation, as interrogation, as intimidation. His hair was cropped in a short college boy cut; he wore a pastel button-down shirt, pale blue, that emphasized his tan. He hung the jacket of his lightweight suit over the back of his chair. He pushed the mike midway between us and rested his lower lip against his interlocked hands.

'You're much younger than I thought you would be.'

I made some gesture.

'No, I think it's a good thing. I like young people. I think Australia's a young person's country. There's a lot of young talent in Australia. The initiative lies there.'

A signal came from the technician behind a small window.

Gavin said: 'One of the distressing things about modern living is the number of small frogs killed on the roads every day. Now we have in the studio an expert on young frogs whom I'm about to ask a few questions. Mr Desborough—may I call you Paul?—good, well Paul, what are your views on the young frogs?'

I gave him my views on the young frogs. The technician finally indicated that the level and presence were right. Mulgrave seemed happy with the interchange. He said, 'I think perhaps we should do this slot as an interview; it's always more interesting to the listener, as long as the person being interviewed doesn't dry up. It's amazing how many people collapse before an interviewer.'

'I'm happy,' I said.

He reached over and took the book I had brought with me. It was an early Penguin. It had our dead writer's biography on the back and a spate of quotations from his reviews inside the front cover. Mulgrave used this for his questions. As I answered one, he was reading on a few lines further to formulate another.

'Why don't we have some lunch?' he said when it was finished.

'Do you want a playback?' the technician asked.

'I don't think so,' he said, putting on his jacket. 'We can always cut if anything's wrong. Anyway, we'll wait to see how much we've got for the rest of the programme. We don't want to cut and then find we have to tape another item at the last minute. That would be a frightful sweat.'

Lorenzini's bistro was dark and cool.

'I gather in the evenings it's full of all manner of weirdoes,' he said, with one of his piercing looks. He was playing his age, as if he could have no knowledge of the distasteful behaviour of those under thirty.

'I don't know,' I said. 'I hardly ever come here.'

'I should hope not,' he said, pursing his lips; yet his eyes looked round eagerly.

At lunch it was full of broadcasting people in suits.

'Have you done much broadcasting work before?'

'None at all.'

'Really?' he said. 'You surprise me. You took to it like the proverbial duck.'

He ordered cannelloni.

'I suppose it's very hard to get into in England.'

'Yes.'

'I gather you've more or less got to wear your old Harrovian tie and wrap a brigade of guards sash round your waist and drape an Oxbridge scarf over your shoulder before they'll even look at you for an interview.'

'Something like that,' I said.

'It's grotesque.'

He sipped a glass of hock.

'Tell me,' he said, 'what England's like now? Is London still as drab as ever? If you were to believe what they all say, it must be unutterably depressing. I said to Angus Wilson when he was out here, "If it's really as bad as you paint it, what on earth do you stay there for?" It must simply be ghoulishness. A lot of old witches sitting round at a funeral. Everybody says how terrible it is but they all hang on looking for some new colour of decay to appear on the corpse.'

He crumbled a roll.

'I haven't been back for ten years,' he said. 'I've absolutely no impulse to go back. It's enough just to meet the people they send out here. Do you have anything to do with the British Council?'

'No.'

'Well take my advice brother and keep well away.'

He shuddered.

'You wouldn't *believe* it,' he said.

He prodded his cannelloni dubiously. 'Another roll,' he demanded from the waiter. When he addressed the waiter his voice was peremptory, curt.

'It doesn't even have any cultural vitality,' he said. 'What are the magazines? You can list them on one finger. In the States every tin-pot university has its quarterly review.'

'*London Magazine, Stand, Transatlantic,*' I listed.

'Does *Stand* still appear? Does Silkin still sell it round transport cafés? In that same raincoat? Oh, the squalor of it. I feel quite ill. Hawking it round busmen's restaurants and jingling his tin can.'

'I don't remember the tin can.'

'I do. Vividly. I can hear it to this minute.'

He abstracted himself into a reverie, transporting his sun-tan and his slightly plumped cheeks back to the fogs and damps of London. He shuddered on emergence.

'What were we talking about?'

'The shortage of little magazines in England.'

'A positive dearth,' he corrected me. 'I send everything directly to America. I don't even bother sending stories to English publications. The place might as well not exist'.

'Do you publish in Australia?' I asked.

'It would be suicide,' he said. 'Apart from the petty jealousies and the rivalries and ratbaggery here which makes it absolutely essential to keep well clear if one wants to preserve one's skin, who would ever *read* anything one published here? You might as well put it in a bottle and throw it into the harbour. No one in England or America has ever heard of the Australian magazines.'

He signalled to the waiter.

'Besides it would be so humiliating to be rubbing shoulders alongside the minnows passing for writers here. One has to be scrupulously careful where one publishes. Some places are utter graveyards for one's reputation. It takes years to redeem a mistake like that; if you ever can redeem it.'

He ordered a meringue.

'Do you write? I'd like to see something some time. Perhaps we could do a piece on "Today's Writing". I like to feature young writers. I try and keep the fuddy-duddys out as much as possible. But they always seem to wriggle back in. I get a directive from higher-up saying I have to give time to this old goat or interview that old ninny. They really ought to be sent to the knackers yard as a kindness. I can't see myself still writing when I'm ninety. It's like some sort of senile incontinence.'

He wiped his lips with a napkin. The waiter came over.

'Separate bills please,' Gavin instructed him.

'You must keep in touch,' he said. 'I'd like you to do the occasional piece for us. You must come out one weekend.'

'I'd like to,' I said.

'Well we'll see what we can do.'

'I thought we might go to the Ozone,' he said. 'I'm very fond of fish. I don't do much cooking myself. I can't really stand all that fuss. I don't understand what people see in it.'

The lift took us silently to the ground.

'We can get a bus just a few blocks away.'

'I've got my car,' I said.

'Perfect. We'll go in that.'

The sun played over the packed roads. Early model Holdens with inverted surf boards strapped to their roofs looked like marauding sharks, the keels erect fins. At traffic jams the radios from stationary cars broadcast to us the Sydney temperature, the relative humidity, warnings of sharks sighted off northern beaches, and jingles for coca-cola, sunburn oils, and aerosol sand-fly and mosquito sprays. And the station identifying jingles: More music 2SM, the brighter 2UE, 2UW the now sound, and the rest of them. We drove along New South Head Road, past the drive-in car-washes, the lubritoriums, the in-gear boutiques.

'I believe they banned commercial radio in England,' Gavin said. 'It must be unbelievably puritanical there still. Some of the most exciting radio has come from the pop stations,' he said, authoritatively. 'It's free from all the inhibitions. There's none of this cant about improvement. Who wants to be improved? I certainly don't. I'm happy with myself as I am, thank you very much. There's that frightful intrusiveness in England that everyone just accepts. It must be drilled into them at those dreadful boarding schools. The very weather encourages regimentation, marching along in all those damp drizzly days. You couldn't regiment anyone here, the sun prevents it. The sun encourages spontaneity and independence.'

We sat at one of the iron tables at the harbour's edge. Gavin moved his chair beneath the restaurant awning and the bottle of wine to a patch of shade.

'I think the hedonism of the beaches is one of the truly unique qualities of Australia. It's so utterly healthy. There's none of the English neurosis. They don't sit round in damp basements and drafty pubs. Can you imagine a Kingsley Amis in Australia? Or a Brigid Brophy? It just isn't possible. The beaches are the centre of life here instead of those dreadful damp churches. It's an incomparable difference. No one agonizes about culture or class or religion here, they get on with living with their bodies. The body is culture and religion here. They don't have to write or read books and identify with seedy psychopaths. The sun here destroys any of that unhealthy introversion, it drys it out like mould. Everything's vitalist and sinewy here.'

The waves flashed in a complex code to us. A light aircraft droned along the length of the Pacific surf beaches trailing an advertising banner.

'It's an utterly healthy culture. Nobody bothers with theatre or books. That's why radio is making a comeback; you don't have to do anything, you can just switch it on in the sun. It's absurd writing books in Australia. Who would ever want to read them? The glare's too strong on the beaches. You're just pounding your fingers to the bone for a few neurotic housewives and for university intellectuals who've got a vested interest in print culture to keep their jobs. Even cinema's battling. No one wants to be cooped up indoors with this climate. That's why radio is a much more exciting medium to work in than television.'

'There's always winter,' I said.

'But that's *all* there. is. Culture's a seasonal occupation, like cane-cutting or fruit-picking. You can only survive by taking on some other seasonal work—like being a life guard or an opal picker.'

He savoured the bouillabaise.

'You can see the fishing boats they catch the fish in. They go out every night from here. That's why it's so fresh. You can taste the freshness. It's like the whole quality of life here, fresh, young, vital. You could probably go down to the jetty and buy fish off the boats when they come in. Where else could you buy your fish to cook straight off the boat?'

The slow-revving diesels put-putting as they powered the small craft through the Heads, gulls streaming after them, crying out over the fish gut thrown astern.

'You can tell the vitality of a culture by the amount of fresh meat eaten. Everyone I knew in London subsisted on sausages, fishcakes, and faggots. I'm sure most of them never saw a real piece of meat from one year's end to another. They probably wouldn't have known what it was. Something out of *Portnoy*. They all had congenital rickets and scurvy.'

A motor yacht was moored just off the beach and suntanned figures lay on it with wine bottles and raffia hats beside them.

We walked round to Camp Cove and picked our way amongst and over the bronzed figures in trunks and bikinis. They glistened with the sun, the sea, sweat, sunburn oil.

The firmness of the flesh, the taut stomachs, the just covered nipples on the full breasts, the clean undulant lines of throat and breast, belly and crutch, the mascara'd eyes and open mouths, the emanations of warmth and content.

I pulled up at his flat, leaving the motor idling.

'Aren't you going to park?' he asked.

'Well I was going to go straight on home.'

'But you're coming in, aren't you?'

'Well, it's rather late and I have to go out tonight.'

'Oh. Oh, I thought I'd invited you for the evening.'

'I didn't realize,' I said. 'I'm sorry, but I've gone and arranged—'

'When I ask people over at the weekend I always ask them for the evening.'

'I must have misunderstood,' I said.

'You must indeed.'

We sat there, the motor idling.

'Well, I won't hold you up any more,' he said, and fumbled at the door. I had to lean across and open it for him.

'I'm sorry about the misunderstanding, but I can't really change things now.'

'So am I,' he said, 'but it doesn't matter.'

He phoned one midweek and asked me to do a talk on the Prix Formentor, Prix Femina, and Prix Goncourt.

'I don't know anything about them,' I said.

'Don't you follow them?'

'Well no.'

'Really? I'd have thought you would have. Are you positive you couldn't do something? It's rather important. We need something for Friday's programme.'

His voice had a note of reproachfulness.

I suggested someone who might, though I was sure he couldn't do it at the short notice offered. Mulgrave still sounded offended. I wondered if it was that weekend, and he had only proposed this impossible topic as a way of expressing his annoyance. Yet it could have been a way of showing he bore no grudge, offering a prestige item, reasonable money. I decided to ask him to dinner, something I'd thought of but only as a distant possibility.

'When?' he said.

I thought of a time and date.

He cut me short when I began to give him directions for getting there.

'I'll take a cab,' he said.

But he never came. Barbara suggested that he had been offended at my not going back to his flat and had only accepted the invitation to repay in some sort of kind. Which may well have been true. Yet he might simply have forgotten: or had some preferable invitation so that he disregarded ours. We waited. We waited all evening, expecting if not him at least a message. But neither came. I wondered uneasily through the rest of the week if I had remembered the date wrongly, and he might turn up unprepared for. But he never turned up. Or if he did when we were out, said nothing about it. Nothing was ever said. It was as if the invitation and occasion had never existed, or had been an intrusion from some other dimension of space and time.

And then he phoned again to say how grateful he was to me for suggesting the Prix Formentor, Femina, and Goncourt authority, who had a really incisive mind and would be an invaluable addition to his pool of expert commentators for 'Today's Writing'. And what did I think about a late-night poetry programme, new poetry, underground poetry? He'd been investigating radio in the United States, and some of the small culture stations had dynamic ideas.

'I thought I might introduce some of them here. I might get some tapes from the BBC radiophonic workshop and all that gobbledygook. I'd have to do it slowly, of course. You get howled out of town if you so much as mention culture or poetry here. It must be the convict settlement. There's a resistance to anything cultural or new. But there must be lots of young people starved of literary culture here. Where would you ever buy any of the magazines? There's not a decent bookshop in the whole continent. At least in Europe people are aware of literature even if they don't read it. But there must be millions of Australians who go to the grave never knowing any other poetry than I love a sunburnt country. Imagine it.

'Perhaps you'd like to come round and discuss it one evening. I'd like your ideas on it. Why don't you come round to dinner; and bring your friend.'

He tailed away as if he'd lost the name.

'Barbara,' I said.

'Yes, why not?'

'Have you been here before, I can't remember?' he said.

We stood in the middle of his flat. It had a television and a record player and, against a window, a table with a row of books and a typewriter. There was a couch against one wall, and a couple of armchairs. Along the wall leading to the door were bays of steel shelving in which the books were stacked in two rows, utterly functionally. It was not the sort of display shelf you browsed along to get a clue to your host's personality.

'Yes,' I said.

'Did I show you the view? Obviously not, or you would remember. It's breathtaking.'

He opened a french window onto a balcony.

'Step outside,' he said.

It was about ten storeys up. It looked across to the harbour. The warning light on top of the bridge winked. The noise of the traffic and sexual energy of King's Cross rose the ten storeys up to us. I stood well away from the iron railing.

'It's marvellous,' I said, and having given a dutiful surveyal I edged back towards the room.

'Don't you like it?'

'I'm terrified of heights.'

'Are you?' he said. 'Are you really? How fascinating. You really feel vertigo? It's ten storeys, you know. You'd probably pass out before you hit the bottom. Have you read James Dickey's poem about the air hostess?' He chuckled. 'The one who got sucked out of the emergency door of an aeroplane. It goes on for pages, page after page. Falling all the time. It would probably make you nauseous.'

He chuckled.

'I think it's marvellous. I'd ideally like to live on the very top. But you'd have to be a vice king or an abortionist at the least to afford it. And besides the penthouses don't have the sheer sides. They're built in from the edges so you don't get the precipitous effect.'

I was already back inside the room, firmly the other side of the door frame.

'You really are terrified?'

Barbara was leaning over the rails, looking at the minute figures below. To fall on a car from that height would be to crush its roof level with the bonnet and boot. I wished she would come away.

'When there's a gale the whole building sways,' he said. 'You can see the windows swing out of line with the perpendiculars of the next block. Or doesn't that distress you?'

'Yes, it distresses me,' I said.

'Really?'

Ferries wove strings of light across the harbour. The deep hooter of a ship leaving Woolloomooloo or Circular Quay boomed out above the hubbub of the city.

'I love that sound,' he said. 'It's timeless. It's a sound that's been unchanged for seventy years. It reminds me of Crippen. He was the first murderer they ever caught by radio. They radio'd from aboard ship and picked him up when they docked.

'On still nights you can hear the lions,' he said. 'The water carries their roars across from the zoo. I've often thought that if those two Japanese submarines that got in during the war had shelled the zoo they would have been much more effective. Then all the animals would have roamed wild through the streets. Giraffes treading on people. Alligators in the sewers. High buildings would have been the only safe places then. Even they wouldn't have been very safe. Pythons could climb up the drainpipes. And I suppose vultures could have settled on the balcony rail. Imagine waking up one morning and looking into the face of a vulture. If you had any eyes left, that is.'

He finally came inside and locked the window behind him.

'Sit down,' he said.

He sat down himself in one of the armchairs. It faced square on to the television, and the record player was flush to the right of it, the controls within arm's reach.

At first conversation was uneasy. There were recurrent silences, and we didn't fix on any ready topic. Then he went over to the bookshelves and took from the top, where it had been lying flat with a number of volumes of similar size, a large picture book. Barbara always called them picture books whenever she talked about visiting him. The first time it was a book of naval battles, with endless prints of seventeenth, eighteenth, and nineteenth century engagements. And then, satisfied that she was turning the pages and, though she might overhear, was unlikely to talk, he markedly relaxed.

There were no sounds of cooking, nor was there a table laid. At one point Gavin stood up and I thought it might have been to attend to the meal. But he left the room only long enough to collect three glasses and a half-full bottle of white wine.

'How's the poetry programme?' I asked.

'The what?' Sometimes his interrogatives were sharp, curt, as if he had never before heard of the nonsense you were introducing.

'The plan for the late-night underground poetry programme.'

'Whatever made you think of that?'

He sat upright in his chair. His legs crossed, an area of white skin between his sock tops and trouser bottoms was exposed. It contrasted oddly with the tan of his face.

'Firmly underground, I hope,' he added, concessionally explanatory. 'Who reads poetry now anyway?'

I said that I thought the poetry scene in the city was lively, lots of young poets pouring out the stuff.

'Really?' he said. 'Thank my lucky stars I've managed to keep well away.'

Dinner never came.

He began at one stage to describe foods he had eaten, specialties of Mexico City, regional curries, the varieties of Chinese food; even the anonymous bowls of shredded grass in Asian bus terminals began to sound appetizing, would have sufficed. The evening became timeless. My stomach contracted, my head became dizzy, from the wine he occasionally poured. We smoked all our cigarettes. Gavin did not smoke. Perhaps like the chameleon he lived on air. Alone he never feeds, save only when he tryes with gristly tongue to dart the passing flyes. There was no clock in his room. I tried to estimate the time from the traffic sounds outside, but I could not tell whether it had died away to nothing indicating 2 a.m., or was in the temporary lull of about 9 before the cinemas and pubs closed. To stand to leave and have him say, 'Oh, but I invited you to dinner', would be too hideous. It was impossible to ask him. And since he never left his chair, except to hand across a drink, there was no opportunity for us to have a whispered discussion. In the end he made the decision for us, closing the evening.

'I begin work at 5,' he said.

'What, on the programme?'

'Good heavens no. No, on my new book. I get up at 5 and do three hours before breakfast. The light's ideal. It's quiet and cool. So many people never see the morning. It's the best part of the day. It's so easy to work then. I can do a day's work before I have to bury myself in that dreadful building.'

He took us to the lift and smiled as the metal doors slid across in front of us.

It was only eleven o'clock. We went to Henry's hamburger drive-in at Rose Bay and watched the flying boat rock gently on the water as we ate.

When he finally came to dinner he had to be collected. 'I couldn't possibly find my way there. All the streets in Paddington look the same. It's quite impossible to take a cab; the drivers are as lost as you are half the time. No, you'll have to pick me up.'

And picked up and deposited, he sat uneasily. 'I couldn't live here,' he said, 'I don't know how you manage it. It's not because it's a slum, it's the age of it. I could never live in an old house. Think how many people have died here. All those bodies carried out and children born. I have to be somewhere new. This reminds me of England too much. Those dreadful blue plaques throughout London saying Rossetti lived here and George Eliot died there and Uncle Tom Cobley was born somewhere else. Practically every house is covered with them. They're like plague spots. The whole city is positively haunted. It's a wonder they don't bury people behind those little circles. They could mummify them and use transparent plaques. It would at least be more interesting.

'I have to live in new places. A new flat with new furniture. I can't see any point in coming to live in Australia and living in an old building. Old buildings should be left behind in England, with the statues and geriatrics and fungus. There's not one square inch of England that hasn't been trampled over time and again. That's why Australia's so refreshing. It's untouched, it's forward looking, it's alive and vital.'

Caught in that sensual music all neglect monuments of unageing intellect.

'I've been asked to do a piece on Australian intellectual life of all things for some puerile symposium,' he said.

But when I laughed and said at what I thought was his implication, 'You turned it down', he quite ruffled.

'By no means,' he said. 'It needs to be done. And a Texan review has asked me to write a piece on the Sydney scene for them. So I thought if I did those two and a piece for the "Living Abroad" series in *London Magazine* I'd have the basis of a book. I could do it off the top of my head. It would practically write itself. What do you think? It's the sort of book one would probably make one's fortune on; it would get set in schools and universities in current affairs courses; all that sort of thing; Australian Studies. I can get a couple of chapters out of talks for "Today's Writing". I could probably do the whole thing in six weeks. It's the sort of book that needs to be topical. The States would literally lap it up; they're fascinated with Australia.'

He laid down his knife and fork and looked around. 'A glass of water please,' he ordered. Barbara looked startled for a moment, and then went into the kitchen. She put the glass down beside him.

'It's amazing the number of people who think the way to make money out of books is to write a lot of books,' he said. 'They're absurdly wrong, of course. The way to make money is to sell the same item over and over again. You use the work first of all for talks and radio programmes, then you print them as articles, then you put them together as a book, then you sell serial and translation and *Reader's Digest* condensed book rights, and then book clubs and paperbacks, and dramatic and film rights. To say nothing of anthologies and school editions and all that.'

'I can't quite see a book on the intellectual life of Australia selling film rights,' I said.

'But of course it could. They would almost certainly be snapped up. People are always making documentaries for television. The Common-wealth Film Unit makes documentaries. It would be ideal. Think of all the research they would have to do otherwise. Whereas if they just buy the rights of the book they have the structure already established and all the research done.'

He took a second helping of passion fruit meringue.

In the mornings he rose at 5 and wrote a chapter of his book. Then he swam at Redleaf pool, and had a breakfast of tomato juice and fresh fruit, before going to work at 9.

He walked along Camp Cove and swam there just as the dawn came and then took the waiting cab back to the Cross, where after a light breakfast in one of the all-night cafés he began writing by 6.30.

He always went out and read the papers by 5.30 over a breakfast of freshly squeezed orange juice and fresh croissants. Then he would walk round Rushcutters Bay park, breathing in the early morning freshness of the harbour, before beginning his morning's writing.

He got straight out of bed and had his breakfast in a dressing gown on the balcony. He wrote outside there breathing the high clear air bearing the scents of the Botanical Gardens before the traffic had polluted it. At 8.30 he would shower and dress for work.

The weather beacon on the MLC building flashed its predictions at him, the circling beam of the South Head lighthouse lured him to the Pacific, the neon digitted time signs of the Cross kept him to schedule.

Despite my failure over the Prix Formentor, Goncourt, and Femina, he continued to offer me items for his programme. And I began quite regularly to give brief talks and reviews. I enjoyed doing them, and I filed away the carbons of the typescripts, the spellings adjusted to conform to the American norms he demanded: color, honor, odor. There were some very good people who contributed to the programme. Gavin had a knack of finding them and, oddly, of retaining them. And he managed to get hold of people passing through, subsidized by the British Council or the Congress for Cultural Freedom, to give brief interviews or comments. He would sometimes suggest I should meet Iris Murdoch or Anthony Burgess or Kenneth Rexroth or whoever it was he had heard was coming. Though I never did. Nor did I ever meet any of the regular contributors at the studio. The studio sessions were always very brief, crisp, and efficient. He communicated much more on the phone.

His phone calls announcing his new successes became part of the texture of my daily life. If I was not in, he would leave a message to phone him back urgently. There never were any urgencies. Often indeed he would seem put out and interrupted when I did phone back. Though he always had something to say; how the tape of his interview with this person had been sold to a Canadian station; how a meeting with that person had led to a request to write something for some high-paying publication, or an inclusion in a prestigious story anthology. Though more often than not he did not disclose the reason for his successes. He would simply announce that this big magazine or that big radio network had offered him wealth beyond the imagination or honour beyond the aspirations of man. Then by reconstructing his interviews or review programmes of the previous month or so, it was possible to detect the connexion. He once spoke of the assistant editor of an English magazine as accepting contributions only from those writers or critics who edited their own magazines. 'That's why he's so internationally published,' he said, with a serious note that could have been censure, and chuckled. He loved to talk about the scene, the family, the workings of literary establishments. He talked about Podhoretz's *Making It* with delighted frissons of horror, at the blatancy of it, at the naked manipulative ambition, at the insights it provided.

'The big mistake people make is believing you have to be in New York or London to make contacts, but that's absurd. You'd never get in spitting distance there of the important people, it would be like fighting through the dole queues in the North of England. Here I meet everybody. They all come out here to their publishing subsidiaries or to take over other publishers or to promote their books or to go game fishing. It's ideal. And you avoid dying of consumption or pollution or malnutrition.'

And he would relate some other real or potential or hypothetical triumph. I sometimes wondered if he would have been so successful if he had never met me and so had no one to phone up at each chance and hope and success. The competitiveness was as much a stimulus and a reward for him as the far from princely financial returns. But later I encountered, independently, a few other people who were on his phone list, and they too were cast in this competitive, this less successful role. But he kept his friends separate; he could not cope with entertaining more than two people at a time.

The Cross was the beginning and end of most meetings with Gavin. If he came out to dinner, we had to pick him up there and take him back. He sat nervously on the edge of the decaying upholstery of the front seat as we risked our way amongst cabs, buses, and huge semi-trailers with interstate plates and festoons of yellow fairy lights like Christmas trees. Occasionally just the cab would prowl through the narrow streets, the trailer parked somewhere, the driver looking for girls. At various times, related no doubt to the internal dynamic of the vice squad, prostitutes became conspicuous, standing along the main streets. At others, they would operate in pairs from Valiants and Fairlanes coasting beside the footpaths, or move away from the Cross itself to the bottom of William Street, halfway to the city. The small terraces that led off from there to Woolloomooloo and the docks, and to East Sydney and the old prison, were the traditional red light areas. The prison was now a technical college, with the Cell Block Theatre.

'I find it absolutely bizarre,' Gavin would say, and the subject seemed often to recur. 'Imagine listening to music with the ghosts of all those people hanged there. I'd find it quite distracting, the violinist sitting on a trap door with the rope round his neck. I'm sure you'd hear the screams.'

And see the final ejaculation, the posthumous seed shot over the inheriting culture.

'It reminds me of Eichmann writing a thesis on the humanism of Goethe. At least the Nazis were simple barbarians when they built Buchenwald above Weimar. But putting a theatre in the condemned cell, it's the quintessence of Australia.'

He often talked about leaving the Cross. He thought of buying a unit overlooking the Pacific, or a waterfront on the inner harbour with a swimming pool. He said he wanted to have trees around.

'It's absurd not to take advantage of the climate and the natural beauty of the place. It's the Anglo-Saxon heritage, the utter unimaginativeness of the colonists. That's why there are no pavement restaurants or open-air cafés. Do you know, there are only about four restaurants on the harbour.

Imagine what it could be. They still fish in the inner harbour,' he said, a new discovery. 'Every night they trawl for prawns in the mouth of the Parramatta, dozens of little Italian fishing boats. They still fish for the Balmain Bug. It's a delicacy. It's such a marvellous name. But you can't swim there because of the sharks. A lot of the houses on the water have swimming enclosures of wooden palings, but sharks used to get inside at high tide. Then you'd go swimming without realizing. Imagine it. Just you and the frenzied beast in a space the size of a living room.'

But he never left the Cross, not even for the chance of watching a gladiatorial shark contest. It was too convenient for him with its cheap Italian and Austrian, Hungarian and Yugoslav restaurants, its delicatessens staying open into the night. Though he seemed to show little interest in the blue library and the transvestite and female strip clubs. The long grey aluminium coaches brought in their tourists from Queensland and South Australia, the transvestites walked in pairs down Victoria Street, the patrolling cops carried their guns at their hips, and the military police drove round in their trucks. But none of this seemed to impinge on Gavin, high on the tenth floor. Ferry parties were one of the few things that ever reached him. In the evenings ferries hired for celebrations or R & R men from Vietnam ran the entire length of the harbour, booming out amplified rock. This penetrated his flat.

'I thought a poltergeist had turned on my transistor the first time it happened,' he said, happily. He invited me out to the balcony to look across at the ferry with its string of lights and illuminated smoke-stack pass slowly across the water, the rock band resonating between the flat water and the curved night sky. Ferries and ghouls; poltergeists or any other form of horror he entertained happily up there.

'I've discovered why spiders are so disturbing,' he said.

'Are they?'

'Of course they are; inordinately so. It's because they have a ganglion.'

I had to ask what a ganglion was.

'A mind,' he said. 'They have a centre to their nervous system. It's not spread about like strands of nerves in an insect. It's focussed in one centre. When you feel them watching you, they really are watching.'

Peering across with still eyes.

'How's your writing going?' he asked.

His direct questions came without any lead in or warning.

'But what about publishing it? Are you publishing anything? Why don't you write for *Atlantic*? Or *New Yorker*? The big American magazines are the only thing.'

Sometimes I would venture a 'What about yours?' in reply.

'My agent's arranging a couple of projects for me which will keep me very busy.'

'What are they?'

'They're secret at the moment,' he said. He chuckled, his hands clasped.

'What happened to the other book?'

'What book?'

'The book on Australian Culture?'

'Oh that.'

He found another picture book for Barbara.

'Whatever made you think of that?' he said. He switched on the television for a film we positively had to see. He could not understand how we could ever have not heard of it. It was about a pair of hands that, disembodied and of their own volition, strangled people and played the piano. A southerly had blown up and was whining through the aluminium fittings of the high window. He watched television in darkness.

'Do you really recoil from horror films?' he asked. 'How fascinating. Of course, the closed room adds to it. Sometimes I move the set out on to the balcony and watch there. I imagine you'd hate that. But I don't think it would be very comfortable with this wind tonight.'

Which howled around the swaying tower of flats, the strangling hands beamed in to every occupant, terrorizing the entire city.

'You can't go before the final sequence,' he said. 'He transfixes them with a red hot poker and holds them in the fire. It reminds me of making toast on Sunday afternoons in England.'

The horror, the horror.

A number of events occurred in close succession. He phoned one morning to say he was transferring to television. 'It's the only medium today. Radio's dead. No one ever listens to it. Every home has a television and it's playing all the time. It's the medium of the century, there's no doubt about that. I shall have my own programme. It will be a general arts programme. No one wants to know just about books. They want to know about all the arts. The traditional divisions have broken down now. It's only schools and universities and museums that carry on as if they hadn't. But now you get novels that are half fact, half fiction; and all the new underground poets read their work as much as they print it. It's the only way, to see someone actually performing it in front of you. You can't make the old separations any more. Television is the only international medium now. There's no money in steam radio. But with television there's an international exchange of videotapes. I shall use interviews and clips from networks all over the world and the ones I make here will get international release.

And it seemed no time at all later that he phoned to say he was going with a crew to the United States for six weeks. 'We're making a series of documentaries. It's the ideal opportunity. It's the only way to meet people, to travel to where they are. How else can you ever come across them? We shall spend most of our time in New York and San Francisco. I'm terribly excited about it. All the top publishers and editors are in the States. It's an absolutely unique opportunity.'

'That's marvellous,' I said. 'Don't forget to send a postcard.'

'But of course. I'll certainly keep you in touch. I'm going in about three weeks. Do you think you could arrange a meeting with that American friend of yours you mentioned? I need some addresses. Perhaps we could have dinner together. It will have to be quickly. Why don't you invite him to your home? I can't really cope with entertaining large numbers, especially with all this rush.'

'Yes, sure,' I said.

'Good. Do you think you could phone me back and let me know a firm date?'

'Yes,' I said, 'of course.'

He was enthralled by America. It was everything that he had expected. It was greater than he had ever imagined. He had no idea such a place could ever have existed. He even sent back a postcard. He made invaluable contacts, and as soon as he arrived back he began to negotiate his return. It was at this time that I began to make the final arrangements for taking leave.

'Where will you go?' he asked. 'The East coast or the West coast?'

I hesitated, and something in my manner alerted him.

'You're going to America of course?' he said, peremptorily.

'Actually, no, I thought I'd go back to England and—'

'Really,' he said, 'how extraordinary. I can't understand it. I find it quite unaccountable.'

I gestured, conciliatorily.

'How long will you stay for?'

'Well I can get about twelve months,' I began. He picked up my unspecificness.

'You wouldn't stay any longer? You're not planning to go back there for good are you?'

'Well—'

'Oh,' he said.

'I'm not planning anything,' I said. 'The whole point is I haven't made any plans. But if something turned up that appealed to me, then I might stay.'

'I can't imagine what it could be,' he said.

I gestured again, vaguely, conciliatorily, at the open possibilities.

But to him it was now quite clear and closed. 'Well, I hope you enjoy it,' he said; content at least in the certainty that I could not. Yet it was as if I had mortally offended him. He relented enough to have a farewell lunch. But for him it was a farewell lunch. He was convinced that I was returning to the England he had rejected, and that I would never return. His 'Separate checks please', Americanized now, was uttered as almost his final words. He never replied to the three letters I wrote him.

And indeed it was almost the last time we met. For when at the end of the year I returned and re-established contact with him, he was planning to emigrate to Canada. It was near to the States where ultimately he would be able to arrange employment and a visa. He told me this over the phone and then asked, 'Are you still with that—' and he searched for the word—'girl?'

'No, not at the moment, we've sort of —'

He cut across me. 'You must come out to dinner then.' He gave me his address, as if I had never visited him before.

He greeted me at the door but if I had seen him in the street I would never have recognized him. His college boy trimmed hair had blossomed into a wavy Dylanesque mop. He wore tight faded blue jeans and a loose, white sweat shirt hanging out. Throughout the evening I kept looking across to check that it did not blazon out Jesus Lives or Motherfucker. He walked barefooted through the hall and led me to the living room. A young man, also with floppy hair and sweat shirt and jeans, was sitting there listening to the record player.

'My flatmate,' Gavin said.

Conversation was uncertain for a while. I'd no clear idea what Gavin had been doing in the twelve months, what successes were in the bag or what plans were laid. There was an awkward silence when the record player stopped. Then Gavin walked across and took an LP from the top of the bookshelves. 'Why don't you play this?' he suggested to the flatmate. And to a background of a new American group he began to ask me about England.

'It was really terrible? You found it quite unbearable? Is everyone still underfed? I can't imagine what nude theatre must be like there, like the dance of death or something.'

The flatmate giggled, and then settled back to the record.

'There's absolutely no life there at all, is there? The theatre's all from Broadway, isn't it, and the cinema all from Hollywood? The States is the only place. Once you've been there you can't tolerate anything less. You should go there, you know. It makes Australia seem like an underdeveloped country. The wealth is simply incredible. The possibilities are limitless. The whole scene is continually expanding, new forms, new media. It's all excitement. There's always this tension of suppressed violence. It's so explosive. I'm moving heaven and earth to get back. I really don't understand why you don't go there.'

At the end of the record the flatmate went out into the kitchen. I wondered if he was doing the cooking, but there were no sounds to indicate that he was.

After another two sides, Gavin asked, 'Do you smoke?'

'I'm giving up.'

'I didn't mean tobacco,' he said. He chuckled, as ever. He went out to the kitchen and returned with cigarette papers and a salt cruet.

'I never touch alcohol,' he said. 'It destroys the body. It eats into the brain cells and wastes away your liver. I don't know how people ever work who drink. It utterly saps the creative forces.'

The flatmate rolled the joint and we passed it round.

'Marijuana has been the greatest liberator of three centuries,' Gavin said. 'It's revolutionized an entire culture. You can discount ninety per cent of what was thought or written before it was used. The new generation in the States has been utterly transformed.'

The flatmate began to giggle a little, and then withdrew into semi-somnolence.

The conversation became more desultory. My stomach was aching for food.

At eleven Gavin said, 'Time for bed.'

At the door he insisted that we should keep in touch.

But that really was, or has been, the last I saw of him. I was in a coffee shop one afternoon when somebody leaving stopped at my table. I looked up.

'You're Gavin's friend, aren't you?' he said.

'Oh hello, yes, how is he? I've been meaning to get in touch.'

'He's gone,' the flatmate said.

'He's what?'

'He went. Yesterday.' His eyes were bright blue points in his bronzed face and spread of hair. 'He just got up and said, "Really, I can't face any more of it." Then he phoned up Pan-Am and caught a flight out last night.'

I made the usual exclamations that come in surprise. I started to ask him more, but he said, 'I really can't stop, I'm with some people so I must rush. Why don't you give me a ring? I'd love to talk to someone who knew him too. He was such a fascinating man.'

Just before he disappeared into the street I called out, 'Do you have his address? Where did he go?'

'Oh America,' he said, looking back into the doorway.

HELEN GARNER

Did He Pay?

He played guitar. You could see him if you went to dance after midnight at Hides or Bananas, horrible mandrax dives where no-one could steer a straight course, where a line of supplicants for the no-cost miracle, accorded to some, waited outside the door, gazing through the slats of the trellis at his shining head. Closer in, they saw him veiled in an ethereal mist of silvery-blue light and cigarette smoke, dressed in a cast-off woman's shirt and walked-on jeans, his glasses flashing round panes of blankness as they caught the light, his blond hair matted into curls: an angel stretched tight, grimacing with white teeth and anguished smiles. In the magic lights, that's how he looked.

He was a low-lifer who read political papers, and who sometimes went home, or to what had once been home, to his fierce wife who ran their child with the dull cries of her rage and who played bass herself, bluntly thumping the heart rhythm, learning her own music to set herself free of his. They said she was rocking steady.

'To papa from child' wrote the little girl on his birthday card. She was a nuggety kid with cowlicks of blond hair, a stubborn lower lip and a foghorn voice. Her parents, engaged in their respective and mutual struggles, never touched her enough, and imperiously she demanded the bodies and arms of other grown-ups, some of whom recoiled in fear before the urgency of her need. A performers' child, she knew she existed. She knew the words of every song that both her parents' bands played. You'd hear her crooning them in the huge rough back yard where the dope plants grew, chuckling in her husky voice at the variations she invented:

'Don't you know what love is? Don't you love your nose?'

'Call me papa!' he shouted in the kitchen.

'Papa! Papa!' she cried, thumping joyfully round him on her stumpy legs. Having aroused this delight he turned away, forgot her, picked up his guitar and went to work. The child wept loudly with her nose snotting down her face: like her mother, she was accustomed to the rage of rejection and knew no restraint in its expression. In her room she made a dressing table out of an up-turned cardboard carton covered with a cloth. She lined up a brush, a comb and an old tube of lipstick upon it.

The parents had met in a car-park in a satellite town, where kids used to hang out. Everyone wondered how they'd managed to stay together that long, given his lackadaisical ways and her by now chronic anger. The women knew her rage was just, but she frightened even the feminists with her handsome, sad monkey's face and furious straight brows. It was said that once she harangued him from the audience when he was on stage at one of the bigger hotels. Somehow it was clear that they were tied to each other. Both had come from another country, as children. 'When he's not around I just . . . miss him,' she said to her friend. It cost her plenty to say this.

'Old horse-face,' he called himself once, when they ran an unflattering photo of him in the daily paper, bent like licorice to the microphone, weighed down by the heavy white Gibson, spectacles hiding from the viewer all but his watchful corner-smile. He was sickeningly thin; his legs and hips were thin past the point of permission. In spite of guitar muscles, his finger and thumb could meet round his upper arm. One of the women asked him why he was doing this, in bed one morning. 'Finger-lengthening exercises,' he said, and she didn't even laugh.

He was irresistible. His hair was silvery blond, short, not silky but thick, and he had a habit of rubbing the back of his head and grinning like a hick farmer, as if at his own fecklessness. He would hold your gaze a second longer than was socially necessary, as if promising an alliance, an unusual intimacy. When he smiled, he turned his mouth down at the corners, and when he sang, his mouth stretched as if in agony; or was it a smile? It did for women, whatever it was. Some people, if they had got around to talking about it, might have said that there was something in his voice that would explain everything, if you could only listen hard enough: maybe he had a cold; or maybe he did what everyone wants a musician to do—cry for you, because you have lost the knack.

Winter was a bad time in that town. Streets got longer and greyer, and it was simply not possible to manage without some sort of warmth. He was pathetic with money, and unable to organise a house for himself when his wife wouldn't have him any longer. Yes, she broke it. Not only did she give him the push: she installed another man, and told her husband that if he wasn't prepared to be there when he said he would, he could leave the child alone. He ground his teeth that day. He hadn't known he would run out of track, but he knew enough to realise he had no right to be angry. He walked around all afternoon, in and out of kitchens, unable to say what the matter was. He couldn't sit still.

After that he drifted from house to house between gigs, living on his charm: probably out of shame rather than deviousness, he never actually asked for anything. Cynics may say his technique was more refined: pride sometimes begets tenderness, against people's will. He just hung around, anyway, till someone offered, or until it eventuated with the passing of time: a meal, a place to sleep, a person to sleep with. If someone he was not interested in asked him to spend the night with her, he was too embarrassed to say no. Thus, many a woman spent a puzzled night beside him, untouched, unable to touch.

In the households he was never in the way. In fact, he was a treat to have around, with his idle wit and ironic smile, and his bony limbs and sockless ankles, and his way of laughing incredulously, as if surprised that anything could still amuse him. He was dead lazy, he did nothing but accept with grace, a quality rare enough to pave his way for a while at least. If any of the men resented his undisputed sway, his exemption from the domestic criticism to which they themselves were subjected, their carpings were heard impatiently by the women, or dismissed with contempt as if they were motivated only by envy. Certain women, feeling their generosity wearing thin, or reluctantly suspecting that they were being used, suppressed this heresy for fear of losing the odd gift of his company, the illusion of his friendship. Also, it was considered a privilege to have other people see him in your kitchen. He had a big reputation. He was probably the best in town.

After his late gigs he was perfect company for people who watched television all night, warmed by the blue glow and the hours of acquiescence. The machine removed from him the necessity of finding a bed. The other person would keep the fire alight all through the night, going out every few hours to the cold shed where the briquettes were kept, lugging the carton in and piling the dusty black blocks on to the flames. He would flick the channel over.

'That'll do,' she'd say, whoever she was.

'No. That's *War and Peace*. No. Let's watch *Cop Shop*. That's all right, actually. That's funny.'

It wasn't really his fault that people fell in love with him. He was so passive that anyone could project a fantasy on to him, and so constitutionally pleasant that she could well imagine it reciprocated. His passivity engulfed women. They floundered in it helplessly. Surely that downward smile meant something? It wasn't that he didn't *like* them, he merely floated, apparently without will in the matter.

It was around this time that he began to notice an unpleasant phenomenon. When he brought his face close to a woman's, to kiss, he experienced a slow run of giddiness, and her face would dwindle inexorably to the size of a head viewed down the wrong end of a telescope, or from the bottom of a well. It was disagreeable to the point of nausea.

All the while he kept turning out the songs. His bands, which always burnt out quickly on the eve of success, played music that was both violent and reasonable. His guitar flew sometimes, worked by those bony fingers. He did work, then? It could be said that he worked to give something in exchange for what he took, were this not such a hackneyed rationalisation of the vanity and selfishness of musicians; let us divest him of such honourable intent, and say rather that what he played could be accepted in payment by those who felt that something was due. He could play so that the blood moved in your veins. You could accept and move; or jack up on him. It was all the same to him, in the end.

He worked at clearing the knotty channels, at re-aligning his hands and his imagination so harmoniously that no petty surge of wilfulness could obstruct the strong, logical stream. It was hard, and most often he failed, but once in a while he touched something in himself that was pure. He believed that most people neither noticed nor cared, that the music was noise that shook them up and covered them while they did what they had come for. Afterwards he would feel emptied, dizzy with unconsumed excitement, and very lonely.

Sometimes guitar playing became just a job with long blank spaces which he plugged with dope and what he called romance, a combination which blurred his clarity and turned him soggy. In Adelaide he met a girl who came to hear the band and took him home, not before he had kept her waiting an hour and a half in the band room while he exchanged professional wise-cracks with the other musicians. In the light that came in stripes through her venetian blinds she revealed that she loved to kiss. He didn't want to, he couldn't. 'Don't maul me,' he said. She was too young and too nice to be offended. She even thought he liked her. Any woman was better than three-to-a-room motel nights with the band. He was always longing for something.

A woman came to the motel with some sticks for the band. She had red henna'd hair, a silver tooth ear-ring, a leopard skin sash, black vinyl pants. She only stayed a minute, to deliver. When she left, he was filled with loss. He smoked and read all night.

When the winter tour was over, he came south again. He called the girl he thought had been in love with him before he went away.

'I don't want to see you,' she said. 'Have a nice band, or something.'

She hung up. At his next gig he saw this girl in the company of his wife. They stood well back, just in front of the silent, motionless row of men with glasses in their hands. They did not dance, or talk to each other, or make a move to approach him between sets, but it was obvious that they were at ease in each other's company. He couldn't help seeking out their two heads as he played. Late in the night, he turned aside for a second to flick his lead clear of an obstruction, and when he looked back, the women were gone.

When he got to the house the front was dark, but he could see light coming from the kitchen at the back. He knocked. Someone walked quickly up the corridor to the door and opened it. It was not his wife, but the girl. He made as if to enter, but she fronted her body into the doorway and said in a friendly voice.

'Look—why don't you just piss off? You only make people miserable. It's easier if you stay away.'

The kitchen door at the other end of the hall became a yellow oblong standing on end with a cut-out of his wife's head, sideways, pasted on to it halfway down.

'Who is it?' she called out. He heard the faint clip of the old accent.

'No one,' shouted the girl over her shoulder, and shut the door quietly in his face. He heard her run back down the corridor on her spiky heels. He thought she was laughing. Moll.

That night he dreamed: as the train moved off from the siding, he seized the handrail and swung himself up on to the step. Maliciously it gathered speed: the metal thing hated him and was working to shake him off. He hung on to the greasy rail and tried to force the van door open, but the train had plunged into a mine, and was turning on sickening angles so that he could not get his balance. There was roaring and screeching all around, and a dank smell. Desperately he clung, half off the step, his passport pressed between his palm and the handrail.

The train heeled recklessly on to the opposite track and as he fought for balance the passport whisked away and was gone, somewhere out in the darkness. Beneath the step he saw the metal slats of a bridge flash by, and oily water a long way down. He threw back his head and stretched open his mouth, but his very lungs cracked before he could utter a sound.

The band folded. He might get used to it, but he would never learn to like the loosened chest and stomach muscles, the vague desolation, the absence where there ought to have been the nightly chance to match himself against his own disorder and the apathy of white faces. He got a job, on the strength of his name and what he knew about music, doing a breakfast show on FM radio. You could hear him every morning, supposed to start at seven-thirty on the knocker, but often you'd roll over at twenty to and flick on the transistor and hear nothing but the low buzz of no one there. Lie back long enough and you'd hear the click, the hum and at last his voice, breathless but not flustered.

'Morning, listeners. Bit late starting. Sorry. Here's the Flaming Groovies.'

He had nowhere much to sleep, now, so different women knew the stories behind these late starts. Shooting smack, which he had once enjoyed, only made him spew. One night when nothing turned up he slept on the orange vinyl couch at the studio. The traffic noise woke him, and at seven-thirty he put on a record, and chewed up a dried-out chocolate eclair and some Throaties. He thought he was going to vomit on air.

With the radio money, dearly earned by someone with his ingrained habit of daylight sleeping, he took a room in a house beside a suburban railway station. There was nothing in the room. He bought a mattress at the Brotherhood, and borrowed a blanket. He shed his few clothes and lay there with his face over the edge of the mattress, almost touching the lino. In the corner stood his Gibson in its rigid case. He dozed, and dreamed that the drummer from his old band took him aside and played him a record of something he called 'revolutionary music', music the likes of which he had never heard in his life, before the sweetness and ferocity of which his own voice died, his instrument went dumb, his fingers turned stiff and gummy. He woke up weeping, and could not remember why.

The girl who kissed arrived from Adelaide one Saturday morning, unheralded. She invaded the room with her niceness and her cleanliness and the expectation that they would share things. That night he stayed away, lounged in kitchens, drifted till dawn, and finally lent himself to a woman with dyed blond hair and a turn of phrase that made him laugh. When he went back the next night, the kisser had gone.

There were no curtains in the room, and the window was huge. He watched the street and the station platform for hours at a time, leaning lightly against the glass. People never looked up, which was just as well, for he was only perving. At 5.30 every morning a thunderous diesel express went by and woke him. It was already light: summer was coming. He supposed that there were questions which might be considered, and answered. He didn't try to find out. He just hung on.

SILVANA GARDNER

The Assyrian Princess

The Brisbane River is not the Euphrates nor does it resemble a tiger, even in floodtime. The inhabitants are Brisbanites not Ubaidians, but the force which controls human reincarnation is not responsible for relocations, which belong to another department in the Great Cosmos, just as a different section takes care of milleniums. Both of these illustrious organisations are beyond my understanding.

I can't promise familiarity with human reincarnations, either, except my own, and even this is a continuing trial and error which baffles my current existence.

Peculiar associations with objects were the first links to partially jolt my memory to another life, possibly in Assyria. Rather than *partially* I should say *fragmentedly*, for I don't know who my parents were, what I did, where I lived or what my name was, except that I was a princess. What else can one expect after five thousand years of milling through fire, earth, air and water? The elements have a way of pounding brain cells, leaving atoms with weather-beaten corners of strange photos, visual remains haphazardly collaged to what the eye sees and records in its present life.

You don't believe me?

How do you explain, then, the first link was the laboratory?

Squatting at the end of George Street, Gardens on the left, Brisbane River on the right, the Physiology Building was a ziggurat when I started work in the morning.

When I went home in the evening, it became the building it was supposed to be. Each day I went to work, CLICK, ziggurat in the morning, Physiology Building at night.

Forget about my present life as a laboratory assistant. One optical atom records a fortress in Mesopotamia. It's all very well to say *imagination* . . . but the building never became anything else but a ziggurat. It never was a pyramid, a castle or a fifty-storey executive building. This proves a definite link on top of all the others which enriched my life with all kinds of possibilities not to be shared with others. The Law of Karma implies anonymity, otherwise nothing will be gained from the privilege of remembering. Worse still, the flowering of all memories will be blocked, and the mind will play confused tricks, maladjustments, frustrations that, in the midst of a modern young woman's contemporary life crowded with current issues, there will be disconcerting flashbacks to the Tower of Babel, an altar, sacrifices, libations and sanctuaries. The people I work with are Vets. My boss is a Vet who likes Gilbert and Sullivan. Enough said! No link whatsoever between 'The Mikado' and an Assyrian princess. He confided he has an affinity with 'The Pirates of Penzance'. I was tempted to share my affinities but my mind went blank. A warning, for sure.

You may think it grandiose of me to connect an earlier life with royalty, but everyone admits I look incongruous as I scrub the congealed animal blood out of test tubes. They say (sometimes kindly, sometimes not) that my deportment is royal. My secrecy is severely tested . . .

There is another laboratory assistant who stole my white laboratory uniform so that she, too, could look royal. She thought she was Nefertiti, because of her nose. But it's not reincarnation with her, since the current make-up strongly advertises a beauty such as the Egyptian queen's. Possibly all the women in Brisbane think they are Nefertiti when they buy cosmetics with her face on the brand. Reincarnations are never as obvious as this. There's a difference between wishful thinking and a genuine reincarnation, as it happened in my case.

This does not imply I think washing pipettes or cleaning rat cages beneath my station. I'm philosophical about it. It's my karma. I just do everything royally. Especially when the laboratory sink is filled with forty test tubes caked with animal blood, clotted milk and foul-smelling chemicals, especially when some nitwit pulled the plug the day before and there was no overnight soaking. You can't give yourself airs doing a job like mine, handfuls of rat shit will guarantee it!

The window immediately above the repulsive sink faces the river and I can do the wash-up without looking, staring instead at the water till I'm hypnotised by the Tigris tinged with blood, the red flux merging with clear water to ensure animal sacrifices haven't been wasted: the battle *will* be victorious . . .

The blood is the strongest link. As a true Assyrian princess, the sight of blood never offends me. Nineveh flows with blood. We worship its redness. Sometimes we drink it.

The ziggurat houses sheep, specifically kept for the letting of blood. It's true I only watch (you've got to be a graduate to do it) but I know how the syringe can easily be a dagger, skillfully poised to slit the ewe's jugular vein. Not a deep cut. Not deep enough to kill. Just a nick to allow the ruby red fluid to collect in a phial. I love to feel its warmth. The Sedimentation Rate of Platelets is a ruse for a pagan sacrifice. The déjà vu feeling is so strong I once ruined a whole experiment by not hurrying to my boss with the fresh blood. It coagulated before he could add his chemicals to keep it flowing.

He's displeased with me. Says a laboratory assistant can't afford to be a dreamer and even though he understands how a woman could be disturbed by the sight of blood, I should concentrate on my job or else get out. Little does he know . . . AND I'm not dreaming! The fragments of an earlier existence come upon me uninvited, although it's peculiar they are so clear when blood is drawn.

Despite the clarity of the sacrifice, the sequence of events is disjointed. First the sacrifice, then the boss going mad at me, then the cymbals . . . it's impossible to deal with rapid changes with aplomb. I can only apologise and promise to concentrate next time. Royally, of course.

Another link is the pot plants. I have a mania for hanging baskets whose health is fortified with fresh blood. They don't want me to bring them in the laboratory.

They'll make the brick walls look nice, I tell them and withhold the booming voice calling out *hydroponics* the minute I was born. Absolutely not, my boss orders. He worries there won't be enough blood left for his peccadillos. I've seen him throw out one hundred mls the morning after being out late the night before. Another temptation to reveal all. The Laws of Karma are tough.

Since I do not trust reincarnations completely (I'm not a fool) and find it safer to stick with the commonplace of my current life, I go about my business with the mundaneness of any employee, feeling jubilant on pay days.

They talk a lot about sex at morning tea. I don't know what they talk about at night since I do not mix with them. They've tried to involve me with group outings after work but somehow I'm not attracted to the idea. I overheard a girl say: *who does she think she is?*

It must be my royal demeanour which prompted a laboratory attendant (ranks are important in the ziggurat), a youth, to refrain from telling what he did with two girls, locked in a motel bedroom, for three days at Surfers. He'll wait for me to leave before he'll tell the rest of the group. The cheek of him! He obviously doesn't know anything about Babylon. How I would love to tell him of Assyrian sexual practices. *Ménage à trois?* Kindergarten! I could tell him a few things about spring festivals after the lion hunts that would make him blush with embarrassment. Let him see a prudish lab assistant . . . he is too unimportant to break my karma.

There's a new Vet joining the staff next week. Everyone nubile is excited at the prospect. There's much speculation about his appearance. I'm not interested and go about collecting blood, staring through the window to see more of what happened thousands of years ago. I must have been devoted to the priesthood. I smell incense instead of sour milk.

It would be rare for the new Vet to come down to the dungeon where I work. His specialties involve him on the mezzanine floor. But there he is, behind me, as I wash test tubes. How long has he been assessing my arse?

He's dark, like a Bedouin. He's wearing shorts which accentuate his skinny legs covered with lots of black hair. He would be the type whose back is covered with hair like fur. An animal. There's a saying that someone can be so ugly that they're wearing the seven sins. He's wearing the seven sins.

He's using his rank to impress me. I'm not impressed. He leaves. I'm convinced he's come down to see what I look like. He's probably investigated all the female staff to see what's available. What is he expecting? He'll always be a desert merchant, never a priest with seven sins.

There are lions in the hills today. Assurbanipal is going hunting. One minute I'm a princess, the next a lioness. Several sheep are sacrificed for the hunt. Ishtar is a moody goddess. The Bedouin Vet comes down again.

I've been trying to remember who you remind me of, he says as he stands at the door with bleating sheep behind him. Nefertiti? I suggest, privately sneering at his crude attempts at courtship.

No, someone more ancient. The Egyptians came much later than the Assyrians. (He has a genuine copy of an Assyrian frieze where Assurbanipal smites the Elamites.) He talks and talks about Assyrian culture. About Semiramis and her famous hanging gardens. I'm impressed, even though I'm not registering his words.

It's as if I'm being turned into a statue. The final chiselling, the final chip of alabaster falls when the camel driver tells me Stalin was called the Assyrian and I remind him of an Assyrian princess carved in stone.

This is where my reincarnation ends. There will never be any more pictures of the other life. The princess has been terminated. Gone with the elements down the plughole, the water drowning any memory she would've liked to enlarge.

The sheep are poor animals molested every day. One saving grace is that I mustn't have been too wicked a princess, otherwise karma would have seen me an incarcerated sheep. I would have known what it's like to be bled dry, let alone slaughtered.

And who was the Vet who knew me from ancient Assyria?

I never saw him again.

I continue to wash stale blood from test tubes. One day I will wash human blood in a different life. The Laws of Karma are merciless.

JANETTE TURNER HOSPITAL

The Inside Story

Genuflection can be disturbing. I noticed the oddly suppliant man when I signed in, his boot soles gawping at the public while someone attended to his ankles. His knees were crammed together on a stackaway chair, his locked hands rested on its back. God damn you, you sons of bitches, he doubtless prayed.

These things upset me. I was not at all suited to the job, but I got by with endless inner dialogue and a lunatic devotion to curriculum. After the sign-in, the identicheck, and the various double doors, I asked my class: 'Do they always hobble you like that in public?'

What do you mean, in public? they demanded. This is an exclusive place. You've got to belong to be here.

'It seems so . . . so unnecessarily distressing. Surely handcuffs are sufficient?'

It's not so bad, they said. Except for boarding buses. And for dancing. It's a definite handicap at dances.

My class had a very stern rule about cheerfulness. I was often reproached for transgressing it. We can't afford your romantic empathy, they would say. Please check your *angst* in at the cloakroom before you see us.

On the day of the hobbling I had brought the Malamud novel. With *The Fixer* I hoped to broach barricades that had not bent for *Ivan Denisovich*. Curriculum content was a sore point, but nothing could be done about it. The budget would not run to a new set of multiple orders and English 101 was blue chip currency with the parole board, not to be traded in lightly. They were stuck with me and my reading list.

'I thought you would enjoy the prisoner as hero,' I protested.

Hero! they said witheringly. That whining little Denisonovabitch! He's just your regular run-of-the-mill convict. He's a paperback hero here only because he's in Russia. We could tell you a few things that would make us heroes in Russia.

'I detect jealousy,' I said. 'You're jealous of Ivan Denisovich, and of Solzhenitsyn too. You want to be famous prisoners.'

You are a very sassy broad, they said.

'Kierkegaard suggested that we are all equally despairing, but unless we can write and become famous for our despair, it is not worth the trouble to despair and show it.'

You people with a tragic world view, they sighed, you make life so difficult for the rest of us.

George came to the door. He came twice a day in his white coveralls with his pail and putty knife.

'Haven't you got any broken windows?' he would ask wistfully.

He had been doing this for ten years, and is undoubtedly still doing it. A long time ago he killed someone.

Actually, the class did like the Fixer, solitary and unbowed.

'Tell me,' I begged with indecent eagerness—I have a sort of prurient interest in the metaphysical underpinnings of others—'how is it possible to endure such brutality and deprivation? How does anyone survive that? How does he stay human?'

It is comparatively easy, they said, when you are *completely* alone. It is fairly simple when the guards treat you like a dog. The real danger, the greatest threat, is the friendly keeper.

'But the degrading body searches?' I pursued. 'The invasion of the Fixer's physical self? How does anyone survive that?'

The body can adapt to anything, anything at all, they said. Beating, hunger, cold, humiliation. We speak from experience. You would be surprised how simple it is to separate yourself from your body. But head space is another matter. There is no foolproof defence against the invasion of private head space. Ivan Denisovich had it easy. Just plain physical hardship, too exhausting for dreaming or thinking. The Fixer had it much worse, but at least he was alone. We are in graver danger than either of them. We have shrinks and counsellors and classification officers.

'It is not true that the body can adapt to anything at all,' I said. 'I will add Franz Fanon to your reading list. It is ludicrous for you to talk so glibly when you know nothing of torture or concentration camps or Siberian cold.'

It is even more ludicrous, they said quietly (they forgave me many moments of rashness), for you who know nothing of either body invasion or head invasion to presume to judge which is worse. We will not read Fanon—although we've never heard of him but can guess he's another tragic bloody humanist—because that would be the kind of invasion of our head space we can't afford in here.

'But you see—you must see—it is terribly important to answer these questions. How can there be any hope for us if we don't have an ideal of moral survival like the Fixer's? I hear you talking about the "sleaze." I see the gestures you make. I know the men you all consider sleazes. You see, for you too, salvation lies in *not* being a sleaze.'

Oh *salvation*! they said. It is not exactly a major concern here, lady.

'But it is, it is. Or at least damnation is. The sleaze is damned. But he's only someone who has cracked under pressure. And all of us must have a cracking point, given torture. I'm deeply ashamed of it, but I'm sure I'd break at the first instant of physical brutality. Or even before that, at the mere fear of it.'

You are not allowing for the rage, they said. Because you've never experienced it, you can't conceive of the rage you would feel at physical abuse. There's a lot of energy there. It convinces you you're right. The Fixer, for example, could see that he was driving those pigs crazy. He had something they wanted so badly—the sight of him snivelling—that it was pure pleasure not to give it to them.

'I wish I could believe you, but surely fear is greater than rage.'

Not yours, they said. You get so worked up about these things. A good sign, if you're hung up on salvation. You'd get mad as hell and it would jolt you right out of all that garbage of fear you carry around inside your skull. Besides, you can take it from us, and we are experts on this subject, you are not and never could be a sleaze.

No other award, I am embarrassed to confess, has comforted me so much.

'Haven't you got any broken windows in here?' George asked from the door. 'I fix them good.'

He sighed.

'Just ain't nothing for a skilled craftsman to do these days.'

'You know,' Jed said to me privately after class, 'I don't mean to make an issue of it. It's no big thing. But we *do* know what torture is, we just don't give it such a fancy name. See, I was twelve when they had me up for B and E the first time. They were *interrogating* me, you know, licking their dirty lips. Three white cops staring at one naked black kid, scared shitless. Used a fireplace poker to jab me in the balls. You'd be amazed how many cops are perverted queers. But then, you wouldn't believe me. We're the guys your mother told you to stay away from. Nothing but grief, baby.'

One lunch-time, in the staff room, a guard asked me: 'Have those snivelling SOBs told you their cruddy little life stories yet? Every one a bleeding tragedy. They get better and better in the reruns. Mark my word, by the end of the term your whole class will be orphans with unhappy childhoods.'

'Another thing,' Jed said to me. 'Get the hell out of this job. What kind of a nut are you? You think because we like you you're safe. You're too hung up on heroics. That shit just don't mean anything to us. Listen hard now. To me personally, and to a lot of the guys here, you are the sunshine itself. And I would like to pretend that I would lay down my life etcetera for you. Listen, when they throw me in The Hole, I don't give an inch. If I were the Fixer, just me against the screws, I wouldn't crack. But if things were to blow up here—everyone *inside* against everyone *outside*—and you were in the middle of it, I couldn't promise you a thing. I can't tell you what I'd do. I don't even know. I've been through one riot inside and it scared the shit out of me. I saw some ugly things and I did some ugly things. I'll tell you something—people inside dread blow-ups more than the screws do. I'm telling you this so you won't take it personally if anything happens. But I would consider it a favour if you would get your luscious little ass out of here, because you are such a stupid innocent snowflake in this hothouse, you make me weep.'

Protoplasmic, was how I thought of the class. Fluid in shape and structure, observers drifting in and out to watch and listen, credit students being drafted out to yard work or to The Hole or to other penitentiaries, reappearing and disappearing.

I could have looked up records, separated the murderers and thugs from the embezzlers, but I never did. Better not to know. Occasionally fragments of inadvertent information would slip out, but students were generally reticent about their pasts.

One student was a proselytizing TM-er. If you have deep inner tranquillity, he said, you can make disciplined decisions even in times of chaos and crisis. For example, there had been a moment during his last bank robbery when he had a gun pointed at a policeman's head. In the frenzy of that instant he had had to weigh immediate getaway (which would have been possible had he pulled the trigger) against a lifetime of being wanted for a capital offence. If it were not for TM he would have blasted out in the heat of the moment. As it was, he had only a six-year sentence.

'Armed bank robbery!' I was astonished. He was slight and dreaming, with the mystic's eyes of intense vacancy.

'I was charged with six armed robberies.'

'Six!'

'They only have evidence for one,' he said modestly, 'and they wouldn't have got that without plea bargaining. I am a very careful planner. I hate violence.'

Zen and the art of, I thought.

George came to the door again.

'Haven't you . . . ?' he asked sadly.

Oh George, they said, we'd gladly break a window for you. Only it would mean The Hole, you know. Which of course we love—all that privacy and special attention. But we mustn't be selfish. Been there a lot lately. Got to give someone else a turn.

'I fix them good,' said George. 'I'm a real craftsman. Well, let me know . . .'

Christmas was a bad time. During the preceding weeks, a guard came to the classroom door with the day passes, just two or three each day to keep up the air of seasonal expectation. The class was monumentally indifferent. What a bore, they said, when their names were not called. Look at all the snow beyond these cozy walls! Who wants pneumonia for Christmas! No one to cook your meals, no one to see that you're safely tucked in for the night. New Year's re-entry hangover, who wants it?

Joe's eyes always slithered away from official visitors in bored disdain. And just before Christmas, the giver of gifts smiled upon him. Joe stared back.

'None for you, shithead,' said the guard. 'You don't think they'd let an animal like you loose at Christmas, do you?'

Joe's fist hit the desk like a jackhammer on bedrock. Get out of here, you asshole! he blazed, and spent Christmas in The Hole.

'I hate those Steve McQueen movies,' said the bank robber who meditated. 'Very irresponsible. They give young kids the idea that bank robbing is glamorous, just a joy-ride. It is not glamorous, it is hard and bitter work. I may have started young, but I can honestly say'—he said it with moral fervour—'that I never once did it for kicks. I only did it for the money.'

'I have a favour to ask you,' said Jed.

I had been dreading this, being asked to carry out letters or bring something in. But it wasn't that. I must have been lucky. They never inflicted that decision on me.

'It's about Joe,' he said. 'You know how he is. From cold start to karate in one second flat.'

I had noticed this. You should figure out some intermediate steps for anger, I told him. Try grinding your teeth and clenching your fists first. It burns up some of the energy.

That was after the episode of his chivalry. One of the drifters—those people not taking the course for credit but assigned to the school wing for some vague reason or other—had interrupted the class with a lewd joke. Joe had smiled softly and beckoned the drifter out of the room. He returned alone a few minutes later.

'I gave him a little tap on the head,' he told me. 'He'll sleep it off in an hour or so. He shouldn't have been disrespectful to you.'

'Joe's a good man,' said Jed. 'But they have it in for him here because he assaulted a cop. I'm telling you this because he's up for parole again and he has to stay cool. They keep turning him down. He hasn't even been out on a day pass in five years. I'm just asking you as a special favour to avoid any mention of politics, philosophy, civil rights for queers, that kind of stuff, for a couple of weeks. Don't stir up his head space, you know? He has to stay cool.'

I promised. We had a quiet week. No word. No word. Joe skittish as an unbroken colt and still no word from his classification officer. At the end of a week, right in the middle of a discussion of Kafka's *Castle*, he suddenly stood up and bellowed. Like a gored bull.

And then he said in a quite normal voice: 'It's better to blow it and be done with it.'

He blew it with style and with furious fist in the face of the guard who always said, 'Keep your eyes off the lady there, you scum.'

It must have been satisfying.

'At least I was in control,' Joe told me after his spell in The Hole. 'I didn't wait sweating and grovelling for them.'

'Why do you come here, anyway?' my class asked.

'No choice. We tragic bloody humanists have problems with our esoteric educations, you see. At the moment my skills are about as useful in the job market as fluency in Latin.'

'You mean you're just doing it for the money?'

'That's right.'

'Well, thank God. We were always afraid you had some goddamn *humanitarian* reason. Those kind of people make us nervous, you know?'

'Why do you stay?' I asked a guard, one of the few who spoke with the enemy. (Me, that is. And the padres and such.) He had signed up, he said, when they were recruiting for a 'better type' with college degree and idealism and compassion. What a laugh. The institution could only operate in black and white, he said. Grey got it from both sides. Get out, he said, while you're still human. Don't blame the staff for hating your guts though. You're a real threat. You get taken hostage, it's our lives on the line too.

'But why do *you* stay?'

'I stay because ten years in the Penitentiary Service does nothing for a résumé. This isn't exactly a stepping stone to an executive career. I stay because at least it's an income.'

'Why do you do it?' asked another staffer bitterly. 'You think you can reform them with culture? Or you just get your kicks out of making it with a hood?'

'I need the money,' I said. 'Can't get anything else.'

'Yeah?' he said, more kindly. 'It burns me up, those shits getting a college education for free while I bust my guts and risk my life so that *maybe* my son can have one though his pa never did.'

'Why do you do it?' asked my chiropractor.

'I do it so I can pay your bills.'

'If you quit that job,' he said, kneading the snarled nerves and muscles in my back and neck, 'you wouldn't need me.'

Ultimately the decision was taken out of my hands. Couldn't sign in. Emergency conditions, they said at the desk. No one admitted until further notice.

'How much further?'

'Months probably.'

'What happened?'

'A stabbing, followed by the usual pandemonium.'

I read the details in the evening paper. It was Jed, killed by Joe. Nothing but grief, baby.

About six months later, I met a member of my class, out on parole.

'Poor dumb Joe,' he said. 'He never meant to hurt Jed, of all people. You know how he was. They say he's been really weird ever since. Of course he was transferred right out to Maximum, but we get news. They say you wouldn't recognize him. Shuffles around like a sad elephant. Smiles all the time, like old George. You remember old George, the window fixer? They say Joe's like that. Except for when he gets mad again, of course.'

'What happened?'

'Joe got this letter, see, from his old lady. She's going to have a baby and of course Joe hasn't been outside for years. (Stupid dumb broad, why does she have to tell him?) Jed is going around telling everyone to give Joe space, give him time, let him be cool. And we're in the showers, see, and we can actually hear Joe sobbing. At first everyone thinks it's just the sound of the showers, but it has a different sound and it gets louder. Well everyone is minding his own business, and Joe is facing the wall close up to the shower, and Jed is giving everyone the hard look just in case, but then gradually the showers are turning off and Joe is consequently sounding louder. So I think Jed is planning to turn more showers back on, because he steps across near Joe and Joe just turns and bellows and stabs. Christ it was a mess with the showers and steam and fountains of blood and all.

'You know,' he said. 'The guys would like it if you'd write once in a while. Especially Joe probably. He always liked you, Joe did.'

I would like to stop feeling guilty about never having written to Joe, or anyone inside. I should never have taken that job. At least, thank God, as Jed sometimes used to remind the class, I was only doing it for the money.

PETER CAREY

Room No. 5 (Escribo)

I scratch my armpit and listen to the sound, like breakfast cereal. The hotel room has a title, *Escribo*. It was an office. Occasionally there is a rumbling upstairs, a vibration, and water cascades through the ceiling and splashes into the bidet beneath.

Trucks rumble through the town. They are filled with soldiers. It is likely that Timoshenko is finally dying, in which case there may be a coup, or possibly none, possibly a dusty road stretching across the plain and a wrapper from one of those bright green confections lost somewhere among the grasses.

The restaurant smells of piss and is humid. Condensation covers the tiled floor which is streaked with a fine grime. A large footprint with a rubberised pattern repeats itself. Jorge was here yesterday. Jorge may not be important to anything. He is a captain in Timoshenko's army but his ability to affect things is probably small.

Jorge's customs post is six kilometres along the road over the bridge. It will probably rain. If Timoshenko dies things may alter. The wind may blow from a different direction. It may continue hot. The sound of gunfire could be mistaken for thunder, or vice versa. In the urinal humidity of the restaurant possibilities smear into one another. Some young boys drink Coca-Cola and lean against the coffee machine. Outside there are more, revving Zundapps.

You lie on the bed and smile at the ceiling. I wonder what you think. Your smile is permanent and I have given up asking you about it. I have decided that you are smiling about a day five years ago. I have not yet decided what happened on that day. And, as you won't tell me, it is I who must decide, but later. I can think of nothing that might make you smile.

I asked you if you were frightened to die, now. You smiled and said nothing.

I asked the question to stop you smiling.

I don't know who you are. You have not stopped smiling since I found you at Villa Franca. You have not stopped smiling except to make love, and then you frown, as if you had forgotten what you were going to say. Your smile is full and gentle. It is a smile of softness and of complete understanding but you refuse to explain it and I do not know what you understand and you continue to refuse me this.

You wish for more yoghurt. Again, for the eighth time today, we leave this room and go to the cafe opposite the Restaurant Centrale. You eat yoghurt. I watch. The soldiers who sit at the other tables watch loudly. They watch us both. You frown, as if making love, eating yoghurt. I cannot bear the sight of it, the yoghurt, the texture of it is repulsive to me, like junket, liver, kidney, brains, Farax, and Heinz baby foods.

Your yoghurt finished, you look at me and smile. Your eyes crease around the edges. The strange thing about your smile is that it has never once become less real or less intense. It is a smile caught from a moment in a still photograph, now extended into an indefinitely long moving film. You look around the cafe. I tell you not to. The soldiers are not schooled in the strange ways of your smile and may misinterpret it. They have already misinterpreted it and sit at tables surrounding us.

If Timoshenko dies they will rape you and shoot me. That is one possibility, have you considered it?

I watch the spider as it crawls up your arm and say nothing. You know about it as you know about many things. You insisted on going through the border post ten minutes after me. Is it for that reason, because of your inexplicable behaviour, that they held you there so long. I saw, through the window of the verandah, the officials going through your baggage. They held up your underwear to the light but did not smile. Things are not happening as you might expect.

I wish you to frown at me. What would happen if I asked you, gruffly, to frown at me here, in public? You would smile, suspecting a joke.

When the soldiers see us walking towards the cafe they call to us. I ask you to translate but you say it is nothing, just a cry. They wait for us to come and eat yoghurt. It is a diversion. While they remain at the cafe there cannot be a general alert. For that reason it is good to see them. They, for their part, are happy to see us. They called out 'Yoguee' as we walk up the hill towards them. When we arrive at the table there are two bowls of yoghurt waiting. For the third time I send one bowl back. The waiter refuses to understand and jokes with the soldiers. You say that his dialect is difficult to catch. It is a diversion.

The heat hangs over the town like a swarm of flies. Trucks rumble over the old stone bridge. It stinks beneath the bridge. If you couldn't smell the stink by the bridge the scene would be picturesque. I have taken photographs there, eliminating the stink. Also a number of candid shots of you. I wish you to appear pensive but you seem unable to portray yourself.

There are some good dirty jokes concerning the Mona Lisa's smile and the reasons behind it. Your smile is not so enigmatic. It is supremely obvious. It is merely its duration that is puzzling.

I do not know you. Your accent is strange and contains Manchester and Knightsbridge, but also something of Texas. You have been to many places but are vague as to why. You have no more money but expect some to arrive at the Banco Nationale any day. We wait for your money, for Timoshenko, for night, for morning, for the ceiling to rumble and the water to pour down. I have put newspaper in the bidet to stop the water from the ceiling splashing. I have begun a letter to my employers in London explaining my absence and there is nothing to stop my finishing it. I have hinted at a crisis but am unable to be more explicit. They, for their part, will interpret it as shyness, discretion, or the result of censorship.

At this moment the letter lies conveniently at the top of my suitcase. If the suitcase is searched the letter will be found easily. It is possibly incriminating, although it is constructed so as to reveal nothing. Knowing nothing, it is possible to reveal everything. That is the danger.

NIGHT

It is night. You lie in the dark with your face hidden in the pillow. You lie naked on top of the blanket; you like the texture of the blanket. It is hot and the blanket is grey and I lie beside you on the sheet, peering at the light entering the room through closed shutters. I have considered it advisable to keep the shutters pulled tight—the room is at street level and has a small balcony that juts out a foot or two above the cobbled roadway.

I touch your thigh with my toe and you make a noise. The noise is muffled by the pillow and I do not understand it.

I sleep.

When I wake you are no longer there. My body is electrified by short pulses of panic. The shutters are open and a truck drives by, beside the balcony and above it. I hear the driver cough. Men in the back of the truck are singing sadly and softly. I listen to them hit the bump at the beginning of the bridge and hear the hard thump and clatter. The sad singing continues uninterrupted, as if suspended smoothly above the road.

You are no longer there. I dare not look for your bag, but you have left a handkerchief behind. I could rely on you for that, to leave small pieces of things behind you.

It is not the money. I am not concerned with the money. The Banco Nationale has not impressed me with its efficiency and I have no faith in its promises and assurances. They cashed your last traveller's cheque and gave a hundred US dollars instead of ten. You laughed and took the money back, but not from a sense of caution.

In the bank there was an old woman in black who had her money in a partially unravelled sock. You stood behind her and smiled at her when she turned to stare at your dress. If the money were to arrive in an old sock I would have more confidence, but you say it is coming from Zurich and I have little hope. No, it is not the money, which we both undeniably need. The panic is not caused by the thought of you disappearing with or without the money, nor is it caused by the thought of the secret police, although I am not unconcerned by them.

But the panic is there. I fight it consciously. In my mind I rearrange the filing system in my London office. There are some red tabs I have been anxious to order. I busy myself writing classifications on these red tabs. I write the names of my districts: Manchester, Stockport, Hazel Grove. At Hazel Grove I lose my place. I lie on the sheet covered by small pinpricks of energy and hear a man shout something that sounds like '*Escribo*'. I am sure he could not know the sign on the door of our room. Unless you have told them, and they have shouted it deliberately, to frighten me. For you say nothing of the police or the political situation when I attempt to discuss it. As for the newspapers, you say they are boring, not worth translating, and that, in any case, they are unlikely to report Timoshenko's death immediately. You say you have no idea why they would not let us back across the border last Sunday and claim that you accept their story as reasonable and correct. You have also suggested that it was because 'the border closes on Sunday' but that was not a very good joke. And, by now, it is essential that we wait 'until my cheque comes from Zurich'. You seem bemused, as patient as a sunbather.

Is it because you want to see the ending, how the story works out? Because I remember the way you were in Riano when we went to the cinema to see that American film, something about the FBI. You laughed continually and the audience made small hissing noises at you. But you waited, because you wanted to see the end. Then we went to a cafe for a drink and you sipped your sweet vermouth and said, 'Wasn't it awful?'

There is a scratching at the door. You enter quietly, wearing my shirt over your dress. I can hear that your feet are bare. And I can smell you, the smell of your pulse. It is as if you opened a window on the inner regions of your soul. The smell is of rain on the wheat plains. Water and sand, seeds, cow dung, spit, wildflowers, and dry summer grass.

You enter the room softly on your bare feet and I lie on the cool sheet watching you watching me.

I say, where were you.

You say, I went for a walk . . . by the river.

I say, it stinks by the river.

You say, I know.

You have nothing but your skirt and my shirt on. You shed them limply and come to my bed, frowning gently.

DAY

The shutters are still open and a small boy watches us. He has climbed up from the roadway onto our small raised balcony. I place a sheet over you and stand up, gesturing to the child that he must go. He refuses to budge, staring fixedly at my cock. He has a large square head and small stupid eyes. Go, I say. But I do not move out onto the balcony where I could be viewed from the street. I could possibly be misinterpreted and that would be unfortunate.

Instead, I close the shutters and wait for him to go. I wait five minutes by the watch on your sleep-limp wrist. He is still there. I make myself comfortable and wait.

He is probably from the police. That amuses me, but not sufficiently, because it is not totally impossible. Things are becoming less and less impossible.

I do not care about the police but would like to know why they refused to let us back across the border last Sunday.

Jorge is a captain in Timoshenko's army at the border post. I am informed of his name because he has been called that, Jorge, by people in the restaurant. Jorge has told you that there is a war across the border. Either that or that the people across the border are anxious to attack this country when Timoshenko dies. Or possibly both things. You say there was a difficulty with the grammar, a doubt about the meaning of a certain verb and one or two words that are phonetically confusing. But you have accepted all three possibilities as being true and reasonable. He bought you a drink and insisted that you sit at his table to drink it. I was more confused than hurt, more anxious than angry. It seemed possible that he was teasing, that he had fabricated or arranged a war to have you sit at his table.

That is why we now eat at the Restaurant Centrale. But sooner or later he will come to buy you a second drink and to announce that the war is continuing indefinitely. I have no plan for dealing with him. He appears to be well covered and practically invulnerable.

In all likelihood I shall watch you both from my table.

Jorge's small spy is still there on the balcony and is peering through the shutters. I turn my back on him and go back to the filing system which is now devoted to the streets of London. I begin to arrange them in alphabetical order but can get no closer to A than Albermarle Street.

Outside the boys are revving up their Zundapps. Trucks continue to pass over the bridge but there seem to be more of them. It is as if they have been brought out by the heat. Today will be most unpleasant. It is hotter now than it was at noon yesterday.

The ceiling rumbles and the water begins to pour through, slowly at first and then in a torrent. I place fresh newspaper inside the bidet and watch Timoshenko's face absorb the water, becoming soggy and grey.

AFTERNOON

I watch you eat your yoghurt. You appraise each spoonful carefully, watching the white sop slide and drip from your spoon. There are beads of perspiration on your lip and you ask me to ask for the water. I have forgotten the word and remember it incorrectly. The waiter appears to understand but brings coffee and you say that coffee will do. Later, when I pay, I notice that he does not include the price of the coffee. Has he forgotten it? Or is it an elaborate joke, to bring coffee, pretending all the time that it is water. After eight days in this town it is not impossible.

We leave the cafe and walk up towards the museum. You shade your eyes and say, perhaps it will open today, although you know it will be closed.

After the museum we walk through the same cobbled streets we have walked for eight days, attempting to find new ones. There are no new streets, they are the same. They contain the same grey houses faced with the same ornate ceramic tiles. I photograph the same tiles I photographed yesterday. You take my arm as we enter the square for the last time and say, the money has come, I can feel it.

We walk slowly to the Banco Nationale. It is still early. After we have checked there we will return to our room, there is nothing else.

The money has arrived. You discuss it with the teller. You appear uncertain, moving from one foot to the other as you lean against the counter watching him calculating the exchange on the back of a cigarette packet. The two of you consult frequently. You look at me uncertainly and produce some dark glasses from your handbag. Among your numerous small possessions these are a surprise to me. I thought I could number your possessions and had, one night, compiled a mental list of them. It is called Kim's game, I believe, although I have no idea why.

It is cool and quiet in the bank. You whisper to the teller in his language. The rest of the bank staff sit in shirt sleeves at their desks and watch. Occasionally they say something. A thin-faced clerk addresses a question to me. I shrug and point to you. Everybody laughs and I light a cigarette.

I have no confidence in the money or its ability to get us back across the border. There is a bus later this afternoon.

I ask you to ask the teller about the war across the border. You lean towards him, kicking up your legs behind the counter as you lean. He replies earnestly, removing his heavy glasses and wiping perspiration from his badly shaven face. I notice that he has a small tick in his cheek. He has the appearance of an academic discussing a perplexing problem. When he has finished he replaces his glasses and resumes his calculations.

You say nothing.

I ask you. The anxiety is returning—I cannot connect your behaviour to anything. I am not anxious for the course of the war itself, nor for the sake of the money. I touch your flesh where it is very soft, above the elbow and you jump slightly. I ask you what he has said.

You say, he says everything is OK . . . he heard on the radio that it is OK.

And Timoshenko? I ask you. The clerk looks up when he hears the words but resumes his work immediately. My finger plays with the fabric of your blouse where it clings to your arm. And Timoshenko?

You say, Timoshenko is OK . . . the operation was a success . . .

Did he say?

No, I read it this morning . . . in the newspaper . . . I meant to say. You look at your dusty sandaled foot and scratch the bare calf of your leg. I notice now how you scratch the bare calf of your leg like that. I wonder how such a habit starts. There are many small red scratch marks on your leg. You say, Timoshenko is OK.

I go to stand at the window and look across to our hotel. A number of small boys are fighting on the balcony of our room.

I return to the counter and lean against it as if it were a bar and I were in a western. I lean backwards with my elbows on the bar and watch you sideways. I say, ask him about the border, will they let us across.

He wouldn't know.

I know, I say, it doesn't matter.

BEFORE

In Villa Franca you were in the Banco Nationale when I met you. You wore the same blouse and asked if I would mind you travelling with me. I said, I would be happy for you to. Your eyes were soft and grey, seeming wise and gentle. You had, so it seemed, lived less than a block from me in London. It was difficult to work out the chronology, you appeared to shift around so often.

You said, you don't look as if you work in insurance. And I wasn't sure what you meant.

BORDER

I prepare for Jorge as the bus groans around the mountain road towards the border. It is full of old women and stops constantly to let them off. There are also a few men who wear squat hats, heavy farmer's boots, and black umbrellas. The heat is intense. You gaze out the window and say nothing. We have not discussed the border or any of its implications. I do not believe in the war or Timoshenko.

The border post is at a break in the mountains. There is a small wooden bridge and two buildings that look like filling stations. Soldiers stand around the bridge with machine guns hung casually from their limp shoulders. One kicks a stone. There is a woman and a child sitting in the dust by the customs house steps. The woman waves flies away from her face with a newspaper. The child sits stock still and stares at the bus with dull interest.

There are now only six of us in the bus. Three men with squat hats and black umbrellas and an old woman who carries two chickens by the legs, one in each hand. The chickens appear to be asleep.

We have been here before. Last Sunday. We wait for Jorge and the continuation of his little joke. You sit beside me in the bus and huddle into the window, alone with your reflection in the dusty fly-marked glass. I say, it is OK. You say, yes it is OK. Your eyes hide behind dark glasses and I see only my own face staring at me questioningly.

In the customs shed we form a line. There is an argument about the chickens and one is confiscated. A soldier tethers its feet to the bottom of an old hat stand from which a machine gun hangs heavily.

Jorge stands at the head of the line looking along it like a sergeant major. He waves to us and waddles down, a riding crop tucked under his fat folded arm. The riding crop betrays his heroes but looks ludicrous and somehow obscene. He has two broken teeth which appear to be in an advanced state of decay.

You talk to him and he continues to look across at me. Finally you turn to me and say, he says it is OK . . . the war was nothing . . . an incident . . . they often have them.

You do not appear happy. Your forehead is wrinkled with a frown that I yearn to smooth with my palm.

I shake Jorge's hand. I am immediately sorry. The chicken is in danger of upsetting the hatstand. The soldier removes the machine gun and places it on the counter.

AFTER

The bus travels through the flat grey granite as dusk settles. Large rocks pierce the gloomy surface of the earth. There are no trees but a few sheep who prefer the road to the country on either side, possibly because it is softer. It is cooler here on the other side of the border, on this side of the mountains.

Rain begins to fall lightly on the windows, making soft patterns in the dust. I open the window to smell the rain. You are frowning again. I hold my hand out the window until it is wet and then place my palm on your forehead.

I say, why do you frown?
You say, because I love you.
I say, why do you smile?
Because I love you.

POSTSCRIPT

In Candalido I ask you about the first time we crossed the border and why you crossed separately.

You say, it is because of the underwear, because they always do that . . .
at the small border posts . . . take out the underwear.

I say, why should I mind?

You say, it was dirty.

KRIS HEMENSLEY

A Portrait

I was beside myself.

Q   You were afraid?

A   I was quite beside myself.

Q   Was someone following you?

A   I quickened my pace, but just as quickly slowed down. The echo of my increased tread more audible than my usual walk, the resounding of which had pulled me out of my stroll in calmer mind not long before. I had often walked off an evening of wine & heavy talk in the past. I spent many summer hours in this way—the hours after midnight—sometimes earlier. Not every night was spoken for—many were free. I am not a man given to feeling lonely. No-one has ever told me they thought of me as a lonely man.

Q   Are you a lonely man?

A   I have been lonely—in fact, very lonely in the past.

Q   Were your friends ever aware of your loneliness?

A   It's not my usual demeanour i hasten to say.

Q   But on those occasions . . .

A   Once a friend of mine noticed. He startled me. I thought i had carried it off well—my front of being tired of talking thus content to skirt the table & conversation—& to leave well before midnight. I said to my friend not to walk with me. I fancied a stroll by myself. I wanted to walk thru the town. Echoes or no echoes. But he insisted. He said he had things on *his* mind. I let him talk. Just before he left, he put his hand on my shoulder & said that he was leaving us soon. That he didnt really want to go but he couldnt stop himself or the arrangements which had been made. He asked me not to fail in my correspondence. It's what we depend on after all, isnt it? he said. It's what stalls the ultimate departures. I wanted to ask him what he meant by that but he was gone too fast. He waved to me, shouted something, goodnight, & my name, or something. I wanted to run after him. I said, goodnight baby, in a little voice hardly louder than a whisper. And then i felt a terrible panic come over me. I wanted to run after him & away from myself.

Q   You werent feeling well?

A   I had the usual anxiety symptoms. But the thing that really set me back was the suddenness of my shadow—the way that it shot upon me & then away from me. *I found myself beside myself.* I wanted then to entirely fade away. To leave my shadow against an old wall standing on the edge of a plot recently bulldozed of condemned tenements. I wanted to join the chipped orange bricks of the old wall . . .

Self Portrait

Q Would you say that you are talking to yourself?

A 'Now'?

Q I mean, in your writing?

A My current writing?

Q You *are* writing currently?

A No—i'm not as it happens—i'm not at all.

Q When you were writing, would you say you were talking to yourself—or, to put it another way, were you writing for yourself?

A I dont know. That's a hard question. I mean, i dont know.

Q Then—you *might* be writing for yourself?

A I wouldnt have said so myself. If i had been asked to describe what it
is that i do, i doubt if i would have said that i wrote for myself, or talk
to myself, which was how you described it in the first place. No, i'm
not sure. I wouldnt know.

Q For whom then do you write?

A I really dont know!

Q These questions might of course be quite irrelevant—i merely ask out
of interest!

A Yes of course. I sometimes wonder myself about these things. I know
that i write. I can see that i do. You ask me 'for whom' which at least
confirms that i do.

Q Do you write for me?

A For you?

Q Yes—would you write for me?

A I dont know! Obviously i've never written before for you—you
mean, in the sense of a commission? That sounds so medieval! No—
i couldnt write for you! I dont know you for a start! And anyway,
i'm not a representational artist! What i mean is, i take it you would
want something to see for your money—not that you've mentioned
money!—something recognizable?

Q If you write neither for yourself nor for anyone else, then you must
write for no-one. Are you conscious of writing for no-one?

A The way you propose that almost gives it a personality!

Q Gives No-one a personality?

A Yes. No-one. Nemo. Or—cut away his dash—plain Mr Noone. Of
Noone's Balloons, or Noone's Lucky Arcades. Purely fictitious of
course!

Q Do you know *anyone*?

A That's as abstract as 'no-one', surely?

Q   You think so?

A   Yes i do.

Q   Do you mean you dont know anyone?

A   I really dont know what you mean by 'know'.

Q   Well—on an informal level—you know, a nod & a smile—to know someone.

A   I dont know anyone on those terms.

Q   Does anyone know you?

A   Oh yes. Lots of people know me. They know me to look at, to say hello to, to nod & smile at. But that's hardly knowledge is it?

Q   I would have thought it was. On a very simple level.

A   No. I dont accept that for a minute. I dont call that knowing at all. That's not-knowing! I mean to say—on those terms i not-know everyone!

Q   Perhaps you write for them?

A   You're joking?

Q   Maybe i am! But, you *might* be writing for them. Or let us say—they might be reading you?

A   Oh no! Never! Not that anybody reads me at all—that would be wishful thinking! But—writing for people i not-knew—that's crazy!

Q   Do you know me?

A   Not really! You've asked me questions & i've answered them . . .

Q   We've talked in other words?

A   No—not at all. We havent talked. You've asked questions, i've answered them.

Q   Would you say that you not-knew me then?

A   Well—at least you have questions to ask of me. The people one not-knows never ask questions!

Q   Well—what's the next stage?

A   Ah. The next stage. The next stage is—it's hard to say what the next stage is. I havent the words!

Q   Can you write it?

A   I dont know—maybe i could.

Q   Would it be worth writing?

A   I think so.

Q   Would you try & write it?

A   I might.

Q   Now?

A   OK.

Q   Right now?

A   Alright. But, by myself! I'll have to work it out by myself.

Q   Yes. Certainly. I'll go. I'll leave you to it. I imagine this is the first time you will have written something for someone else?

A   Is it? Am i doing that? I wasnt aware i was writing for someone else?

Q Oh, but i think you are. I asked you if you could write it & you are now going to see if you can. The motivation came from me . . .

A Well—i am, or i think i am, writing it for myself because it's something i would like to find out for myself. It's incidental that you were the motivation.

Q Without sounding what might be called personal, i think that the original motivation is not at all incidental. It's the all-important factor surely?

A Well—without being personal—i would say that everyone is incidental to the writing—nothing else counts.

Q In effect then—i am incidental? The world is incidental?

A Not that you are the world—but, yes. Incidental. And so am i. I am also incidental.

Q Incidental to your own writing?

A Yes. And to the world. The world around me & the world of writing which includes the world of my writing. I am not what is primary. I am an instrument.

Q A writing instrument?

A Yes. You could say that.

Q Will you say it?

A *I AM A WRITING INSTRUMENT!*

Q There was something irrevocable about the way you said that—as if daring the gods!

A Was there?

Q Yes . . .

A Not that i believe in the gods—whoever & wherever they might be!

Q Maybe they dont believe in you either?

A Ha! Ah well! I'll just have to keep on writing—maybe they'll notice one day!

Q So you *are* writing for the gods?

A Haha! You're too clever for me!

Q I've caught you out?

A Yes. I'm writing for the gods! The truth's out!

Q No-one will believe you.

A No-one believes the truth anyway, so that doesnt bother me!

Q *I* believe you!

A Hahaha!!!!

VICKI VIIDIKAS

End of the Moon

And she says, standing in a narrow room overlooking a dark street, I just presumed Sam and you turned on . . . And turns to you with her pale moon face and you stammer, well I have, I do, I mean . . . Sam doesn't, he doesn't need to . . . And she laughs a little awkwardly murmuring doesn't need to, and her face takes on veils and her features seem to dissolve.

She walks through the lounge room into the kitchen to make coffee, and you don't follow her but stop by a wooden cabinet with latticed glass doors, and start opening drawers with little knobs on them like Chinese jewellery boxes, and there are lots of slender necked pipes, different sizes laid out inside the drawers, and down the bottom a glass hookah . . . And you sigh and think not again, you've been here before, but then you stop something in your mind and think maybe it'll be different this time, maybe . . .

You are sitting in the lounge room with the blinds drawn looking at a bookcase that has about half a dozen books in it, then *Nova* magazines and *Vogue* and *Bazaar* and occasionally a *People* . . . And she's sitting on a brown vinyl settee with her moon face staring into space or sometimes her white hands picking bits of wool off her jumper, and you don't feel like talking because the room seems asleep and the atmosphere lethargic, and you sort of feel it'd be an effort to be enthusiastic . . . Her moon face is sleeping, her pale face is waiting in a tomb, a mummy . . .

Then he walks in thinly with a plastic pouch in his hand, and she makes a vague gesture towards you and he turns and looks at your face and you know he hasn't seen you and somehow you feel cheated . . . Then he sits down and there's a dull silence, a lack of energy, not that you don't like silence, you do, but some kinds . . . depending on the people who share it . . . And he says do you want to turn on? and moon face nods tiredly, it's nothing new and you feel slightly uneasy and vulnerable of course. Then he looks at you with a question or an answer on his face, and goes to the wooden cabinet and selects one of the pipes and undoes the pouch . . . You're thinking how does he know which one to choose? and packs the bowl in dead silence, and you wonder at how expertly he does it, you never did learn to do it well yourself . . . And lights up and passes the pipe around and when it's your turn you shake a little, it's been long and when you were there before lots of bad things were happening . . . And you draw in and suck your cheeks and swallow and hope it's not the beginning of bad things, no, you think they couldn't possibly be repeated, but then you're not so sure and shake every time the pipe comes round, and try to hide your nerves and hope they haven't noticed.

Sam is somewhere up the road giving painting lessons to doctors' wives, and you know it's less than five minutes away to get to him but you feel cut off as if you'd have to swim dark oceans and climb savage mountains, and maybe when you got there he'd be dead anyway or not want you anymore . . .

Moon face is rocking on the lounge and the guy is just staring mutely into space and then there's a strange feeling between you three, the silence fills with currents, somebody laughs and the three of you are laughing and it's all so secret you've really got some joke on the world, and you can see the laughter rising in small coloured bubbles to the ceiling that looks as if it's made of cake . . . And you become one of them, you're a laugh bubble locked inside with your knees drawn up and an invisible circle around and protecting you . . . And you're floating and you've definitely got something on the world and you no longer care about moon face or the guy or running into . . . And you can't think of repetition, whether you've been through all this before . . .

There are remembrances of black velvet collars with silver leashes in the night leading . . . Or velvet hooks which catch your skin and slippery nails that tear at your thighs, and the black is breathing and expanding, your mind filling with the dark that is oh so soft yet frightening to lie back in, your body filling with the long silver needle and the doctor's face becoming a dummy that's trying to pretend it is real, but you lying back and knowing there's nothing behind it, nothing . . .

Your lips are blue, the face twitching with colour, the room is filled with flying ants with sharp teeth, grow bigger and sting, and you don't want to be hurt, not after the laughing, no, you don't want to feel pain, that blood rip black . . . anymore . . .

Where are you Sam, oh there, and you smile at him and try to ask him how his painting students went, and he looks at you kind of queer and says, what's the matter with you? You laugh and say, I'm just in a fine mood, a fine fine mood, and you laugh again and it arches out in a long wobbly taper from your throat, your throat of blood . . . And somehow it seems sort of hysterical so you lie on the floor staring at the ceiling and wondering what happened to moon face and the other . . . Maybe they're down the street less than five minutes away, and you feel you'd have to climb savage mountains and swim dark oceans to get to them if you wanted to, and somehow they're so vague now except there was a tomb, a mummy, many bandages, and somehow you don't want to . . .

KATE GRENVILLE

No Such Thing as a Free Lunch

It's a fancy place in the way places are fancy here. Dim yellowish walls which anywhere else you might take the liberty of calling shabby. Ah— but the paintings! One doesn't like to look naive and peer too closely, but clearly they're originals, little gems dashed off by the masters, signed with a flourish. My compliments to the chef and to Claude for his wonderful restaurant. The lights are dim but of course no mere vulgar pink. This, my dear, is the dimness of quality. Among the sparkling white linen and the shadowy old chairs—old but good—large elegant men sit back at ease with a bottle of de Rothschild still half full in front of them. Poised women sparkle discreetly, leaning languorously, laughing in streams of silver bells.

Oliver does not, of course, expect me to exclaim aloud my awe or to shame him by clumsy colonial enthusiasm. Super cool now behind the black cummerbund of the maitre de. Skirt round this chair, don't brush the tablecloth as you pass and for heaven's sake try not to knock those flowers over. Chin up, back straight, now. No scurrying. Well done.

The chair is being pulled out for me and the oily face inclining with bogus respect. Madame? Slide in slowly now. Weight on the balls of the feet so that he can slide the chair in under me. Well done. What a team.

Oliver is of course totally au fait and absolutely au courant with this place. Evening Luigi, how are you this evening glad to hear it. Where's Claude tonight I don't see him. A few new faces I see. Well now what do you recommend tonight Luigi? The plovers' eggs in sauce de la maison? Plovers' eggs it shall be. That is, unless, of course . . . he inclines his smooth polished Public School face towards me . . . no that will be fine Luigi, two plovers' eggs. And I think a bottle of the '68 don't you? Yes. Fine.

Of course I come here pretty often you know. The odd business lunch and pleasurable um dinner. Nice quiet place. Bit pricey of course but utterly worth every penny.

At the next table a young man with pale eyes like a blind fish in a dead-white hairless face is talking steadily, calmly, without the slightest shadow of a doubt, to his companion who is elegant in black silk and blond coiffure. Her perfect face framed in the bell of her hair stares at him. She nods, murmurs. Absolutely oh yes. Quite. How amusing. Quite. Her dark eyes never leave his decomposing-flesh face. Oh how splendid. How absolutely. She leans forward to him, one hand supporting an elegant cheekbone, the other resting, forefinger pointing, on the table.

Oliver unfolds his napkin and arranges it in his lap.

Now we were talking were we not about *Lear*, without a doubt the greatest play ever written. Genius with a capital G. That strange quality not so very far from madness which we like to call Genius.

His voice is properly reverent in the face of Genius with a capital G. I venture to differ. *Hamlet*, perhaps?

Oh no dear. You're quite wrong about that. Without any argument his masterwork, his chef d'oeuvre as it were. Definitely his greatest. No. I was just talking to Hail about this very subject last week and he was telling me. No, I'd say you'll have to look at it again. Ah the wine thanks Luigi.

The correct half-inch in the glass. Lift it to the light and peer at it with one eye. Swill it round in the glass. Sniff. Close eyes the better to appreciate this really remarkably fine aroma. Tilt the head back, toss it in and swill it around the back teeth before finally swallowing. Purse the lips. Yes lovely. Not quite up to the '65 naturally but what would you?

At the next table the food has arrived. The long slender fingers delicately grasp the knife and fork and convey dainty morsels to the perfect mouth. Chewing discreetly, she nods and leans forward, swan-like, between mouthfuls, all intelligent interest. Her companion picks petulantly at his food and lifts a disdainful forkful to the blank hole of his mouth.

Well now what were we saying yes the Theatre. Of course the Theatre is without a doubt the highest form of art. No doubt that a fine piece of theatre played by truly professional actors well there's nothing can touch it in terms of sheer artistry. Now the films. I know you work in the films. Well I'm sure there's a lot of merit in certain films but you won't convince me that it's a medium in which art can flourish. Fine for a night's simple entertainment of course absolutely. Quite hits the spot at certain times. And of course for the mass of people, the bulk of the population, well I don't of course want to sound snobbish or in the slightest degree elitist but I'm sure you'll understand when I say that some pleasures require an educated palate.

Another swig of wine hits his educated palate and he closes his eyes and leans back.

Now what would you call a really good film, I mean a film that's not simply a piece of entertainment now I did see a good film a while ago, what was the name of it now. Remarkably fine film within the limitations of the medium. Now a film like that takes the medium to its highest point and there's no doubt there's a lot of merit in it, without a doubt that film is one of the masterworks of that particular medium. But compare it with a piece of true theatre and you'll just have to agree with me.

The plovers' eggs arrive and look distinctly nasty.

I think you'll find that these are really remarkably fine. You'll enjoy these, no question of it.

Now you're obviously an intelligent girl I'd be interested to hear your views on this. Clearly you're not just a run of the mill type of person. Obviously you're more intelligent than most and I'll be interested in your opinion. Now the way I see it is this, you've got two distinct and separate things going on and only one of them can rightly be called Art. And of course there's not a shadow of a doubt in my mind that.

The plovers' eggs are like the insides of golf balls.

Yes the chef here really is remarkably fine no-one to touch him in the whole of London. Now I was talking to Claude last week and I said Claude your chef is a treasure. I think you'll agree that this is the finest food of its kind you've ever tasted.

Absolutely tip top Luigi up to the usual high standard do convey my felicitations to Pierre. I think you'll have to agree that burp. Pardon me.

Now if you'll just excuse me a moment. Bows slightly the embodiment of breeding.

The dead fish at the next table is also making his way to the door at the back. When he's out of sight the immaculate blond slumps forward at the table and covers her face with her hands. Under the table I see her kick off a shoe and scratch the back of her leg with her toes. She sits for a few moments with her face in her hands hidden by the bell of her hair. She looks up at last, straightens her back, resumes the graceful listening attitude, takes a sip of wine. She catches my eye. Without cracking the perfect symmetry and beauty of her heart-shaped face, she gives me a slow patient wink from one brown eye. Then with a wide pink cat's mouth she yawns—tremendously, tonsil-exposingly, eloquently.

ANGELO LOUKAKIS

Being Here Now

I sit outside the theatre and can do nothing but exercise my memory. As I wait to see if he will live (they tell me this open-heart stuff has a ninety-five per cent success rate), I make him young again. I find him in another life. The late fifties, early sixties, they were his salad days.

Say Christmas around 1960.

My memory lets me down on this, but, on the theory that there were always heatwaves in our little Arncliffe, I would say this was a week of heat. Why not? I can remember nearly everything else.

He comes up from the yard behind the shop, in his singlet. It's soaked in sweat.

'We can do nothing about this heat. We have to live with it. Open the doors, close the doors, what's the difference? We are baking in hell.'

'Doesn't matter,' I say. 'Christmas is soon. Aren't we gonna put up decorations? All the big shops have decorations, why can't we have some?'

'*Kala. Pare* six bob from the till. Six bob only. Go up the paper shop. But listen, don't bring me back rubbish.'

I take at least eight bob and go via Frank's Milk Bar so I can play the pinball first. The Hawaii machine, two games for one shilling, replay for lucky number. And only then do I go, two doors up, to the paper shop and buy glass baubles and tinsel and a cardboard Santa. Mrs Mack wraps it up in brown paper, and after that, I start back to our Mixed Business.

I always hate the bits of footpath with no awnings in the summer because it's always so stinking hot. And so I run the last little bit to our place, and finish up red and panting anyway. But I have to get inside quick, don't I?

He doesn't look in the parcel straight away. He always thinks I never do as I'm told. So he just asks, and I tell him what I got. He doesn't say anything else, so I must have done right, probably . . .

'But still we have to get the trees don't forget,' I say.

'Tomorrow.'

The sister comes and calls me, because they are wheeling him out of the operating theatre and into intensive care. How is he? Reasonable. It was a bit complicated. A couple of things the surgeon wasn't expecting. He is stable, however.

When I see him, he doesn't recognize me. He is doped up and will remain that way for a couple more days, they tell me.

The next day when I come to visit he is asleep, and I wait in a chair by his bed. Where was I? I was going to go to the markets today, to buy the trees.

I had this pet thermometer which I bought at the chemist and carried around with me everywhere. No doubt I had it in my pocket that December morning.

⎯⎯⎯⎯➤●◄⎯⎯⎯⎯

I do up the button on my shirt pocket so it doesn't fall out when we push the Renno around the corner. I help him do this every day so it can roll down the hill and get started. There's something wrong with the battery. There's always something wrong with the battery.

And it's hot again today. In the car, I look at the temperature on my thermometer. Eighty degrees at nine a.m.

I love it at the markets, the Haymarket, the way he knows everybody, their names, and everybody knows him.

'We go to the Chinese man for Christmas trees, but first we got to get fruit and vegetables,' he says. He sends me to get a trolley. Then he lets me wheel it to the first stand, and then it starts to get full, and then he takes over.

A box of lettuce, a box of tomatoes, a half-case of cucumbers, a sack of onions . . .

'Enough until after Christmas,' he says. I know we don't sell much. He pushes all the stuff back to the car and I help him put it in. I watch the muscles move on his arms. He's got big hands too. (I look at mine and compare them to his as he lies there, still groggy, twenty-four hours after they slit his chest open. His hands are still large. Mine are still small. Except for them, every part of him seems wired to something, and there are drips in his forearms.)

Then he says—

'Go to the Chinese man, you know the one, and wait. I'll be there in a minute for the trees.'

I know what he does. When he sends me to wait somewhere at the markets, it's so he can go to one of the pubs and have a couple of quick ones. I don't care. Only I'm not supposed to tell my mother what he does, he told me once.

When he comes back, he's smiling at me, looking like it's *him* that's done something wrong for a change. But not really wrong, and we're both in it together, aren't we? He kisses me, even though he knows I don't like him doing it when anybody is around.

And now, twenty years later, he's lying in this hospital bed. He's been coming round for the last hour or two. Finally, he moves his arm, meaning that I should come closer.

'What time it is?'

'Two in the afternoon.'

'I woke up so quick,' he says slowly.

He is thinking it is the afternoon of the day of his operation.

'It's not the same day. It's two o'clock the next day. It's Wednesday today,' I tell him. He nods and then closes his eyes again. He seems so incredibly tired. I stay a little longer, then leave to go back to the office.

Today, three days after his operation, they tell me he is going to be alright. I settle back to pass the time while he sleeps, playing my game, putting it all back together again. There was a time when he wasn't such a mess. I wish it were still here, that time.

Mr Chin starts up like he always does—

'Is he a good boy?'

'Yes, he's a good boy,' my father answers.

'Help his father?'

'Yes, he help his father.'

Mr Chin smiles at me.

'Help your father, son. Jackie here works hard. I work bloody hard myself.'

Mr Chin calls everyone Jackie. My father's name is Pavlos. 'Help your father son,' I keep thinking as he picks out three small trees. I take out my thermometer as we head back to the car. Ninety today. How are we gonna get the trees in the car? The ends will have to stick out the window, he says.

We pull them out of the car first when we get back. One is for us, one is for Mrs Riley, and one is to put in the shop for sale—only one because our customers usually get their trees from the big fruit and veg. up the road.

Christmas Eve? I would have delivered the tree that was ordered, like I always did. My father puts our own tree in an old five-gallon ice-cream tin with some water, and carries it into our living room behind the shop. He puts some Christmas paper around the tin to hide it. Then I'm allowed to put the decorations up.

Christmas morning 1960? Presents. Some clothes, a model airplane kit from Phil, son of the lady who cleans the shop once a week. And I get a Meccano set from my parents. This part I like. But then my father says Kosta and Maria and Dimitri and some other friends of my mother's are going to come around in the afternoon—same as every Christmas. They'll make Greek food, which I like, but they'll play records on the radiogram too, which I don't. Her records are always whining ones, and everyone is always singing high notes. And that's how it was.

And I'm thinking maybe after lunch I'll remind him of those times. He likes to hear stories about the past, not much less than he likes telling them.

I watch him eat, slowly cutting up his cottage pie and piling small amounts of potato onto his fork. I know he doesn't like this sort of food. He likes plenty of *salsa*, lamb and beans done Greek style, everything juicy. He pushes the bowl of custard with half an apricot on top to one side. He does like tea, however, which he eventually drinks leaning back against the pillows.

'Almost Christmas . . . Are you feeling sentimental?' I ask him.

An ironic smile, and he points to the dressing on his chest.

'Here is my present,' he shakes his head, and then tears well in his eyes.

'I've been thinking of Christmas when I was a kid . . . Do you remember when I was always at you to buy the decorations? And I came to the markets to buy trees? Remember? Every year I used to . . .'

'Not *every* year,' he says. 'You come a couple of times.'

'I used to deliver them to your customers.'

'Sometimes . . .' He smiles again. 'You didn't like to make the deliveries. You complained. I want to go out! I want to ride my bike! . . . You forget.'

'Remember the trouble we used to have with those old Rennos? Trying to get them started to go to the markets?'

He grins again. 'The Renno was a good car.'

'That's not what I thought,' I say, knowing that when he interrupts me like this, I may as well give up. He's not in his listening mood. Anything you say he just takes as a cue for himself.

'The doctors say everything is OK, you are going to be alright.'

I hold his hand but he doesn't seem to notice. He seems to drift off for a few moments, then he says—

'Yes. The surgeon come to see me before. Same thing, he said.'

'It's a pity you won't be out for Christmas.'

'Pah. I don't care about Christmas. You know that.'

'Not even if you were in Greece?' I say, trying to get him onto his favourite subject.

My old man lives in his mind, and always, for as long as I've been aware of these things, has done. It's the only way he can cope with his life, which he hasn't liked for years, but hasn't been able or willing to fix either. In recent years I've spent plenty of energy trying to find things we could talk to each other about—although he himself has never bothered to do the same. I haven't been able to find too many. My father is a very selfish man.

'If I had stayed in Greece, I never would be sick. In Australia everybody gets sick, doctors, hospital all the time.'

'It's the change of diet. Too much animal fat. No exercise. Too much stress. All those things have . . .'

'No, it's the water,' he says. 'And the climate. All my life here, forty years, I never had a drink of water taste good. Clean water. From the mountains, and cold. I remember still the taste . . . You telling me before about Christmas when you was a kid. When I was young, not just twenty, but *fifty* years before, I can remember, and I can tell you.'

'So tell me.'

'We had plenty holidays. St Nicholas Day and Christmas and New Year and *Ta Fota*. We play cards, everybody get together and we play cards on the eve of New Year—*ti Kali Hera*, we call it. In winter don't forget, I'm talking about. In the village we kill one or two pigs and make sausages. Only one time a year we had sausages. That was Christmas time. And the smell, and the taste, mmm . . .'

'Did it snow where you were?'

'Yes, sometimes it snow too.'

The nurse comes to take pulse and blood pressure readings, and while she's doing that I go for a walk down the corridor.

I am so tired of humouring him, even as sick as he has been. I've humoured him for years, and I'm doing it now. I wonder when it's going to end. Probably never.

I've been looking after him for years, although he doesn't seem to realize, or want to acknowledge the fact. I've arranged for this operation. I'm paying his bills. And what's my return? Nil. He doesn't really care about me.

He switched off years ago. When he decided that fate had dealt him blows he just hadn't deserved, he cut everyone out. My mother, myself, everyone. He couldn't cope, so he made life a misery for everyone else.

As I walk back towards his part of the ward, I see the nurse exit.

'How are they, Mr Krinos's readings?'

'They're fine. He's doing well.'

When I get to his bed he says—

'You didn't go. I thought maybe you go back to work.'

'No I'm still here.'

'I remember some more. You talk before about Christmas, what you did. And I tell you about snow in the old country?'

'Yes.'

'I remember something more . . . One time, near Christmas, or end of the year—I'm talking maybe 1927, '28—my father tell me he have a job for me—to take some potatoes, a sack of potatoes he grow himself, to my uncle up in Varvisa. Varvisa is the village high up from us in the mountains. I was twelve, thirteen *chronos*. I never been to that place by myself before—but I know where it is. That's what I say to myself.

The donkey I been riding everywhere else, so my father say, take the donkey, put the potatoes in the pack, and take him up to Varvisa.

'It was afternoon when he tell me to do this job. Really, it takes one day to go up to Varvisa and come back down. He gives me only half-day. But I love my father and I do what he say. I take the donkey and start to go to my uncle in Varvisa.

'The road is very long. Ten kilometres. Twelve kilometres, maybe more. And . . .'

He can't find the word, and tilts his hand upwards instead.

'Steep,' I say.

'Steep. Yes. Steep . . . Only times before I went to this village I went with my father. And this time I think to myself, I know how to go there. So, I'm going. One hour. Two hour. Should be about three hour. But three hour pass and no *horio*, no Varvisa. Then four hour. It's after four o'clock. It's late. Then I see I am lost. I am lost. I have to think what to do. What can I do? I turn around and come back down.

'And I am very upset. All the way I come back down I think how stupid I am, how every time I do wrong thing. My father send me to do the job, like man, and I can't do it.

'Anyway, I am back in Ritopolis, oh, after dark, and I put the donkey in the shed, and quietly I take potatoes and pack off him. I am doing this and my father hear the noise and he come to the shed. He has the lamp with him, because it is dark in there, and he see me. Me and the potatoes.'

'What did you say?'

'I say nothing. I am very upset. I remember even now. I start to cry. He say to me "I send you to do job, to your uncle, and you come back like this. What's the matter with you? Where you been?" He ask me questions and questions, and me, I am crying.'

And my old man's eyes, which had been welling up as he was speaking, finally spill over.

'It's alright,' I say to him, 'It's alright. That was a long time ago. It's all over now. All over. Come on. You're alright.'

I take his hand, and the tears start to subside.

'You've been through a lot,' I say. 'The operation was hard, I know. But you're going to be better now.'

He nods hopefully. He just nods. Looking like the kid he really is. And immediately succeeds in turning me off again. He is so self-indulgent it is unbelievable. How I am going to put up with his old age is beyond me. There's no-one else to look after him. He's only in his sixties and already he's a fond old fool. I don't know what the answer is. I know I can't go on resenting him like this, I'll finish up with some disease myself.

I think there's nothing I can do but just put up with it. Depressing as that prospect is. I decide I should leave him for today.

'I'm going now,' I try to tell him, but he's so tired, he's already falling asleep. A meal and fifteen minutes talk is enough to wipe him out at this stage of his recovery.

I walk away from the ward. The answer is to try not to think what things might be like tomorrow. Being here now is what I should be aiming at. Great.

ANIA WALWICZ

red sails

she was told in my red sails book in sweden a long time ago that red sails
will come into my harbour they told my little girl that red sails will come
with true love mister true love to me i am told now that red sails are about
to enter when i am all ready for when she is grown up red sails will appear
for sure it will happen exactly like that i tell now in my book that red sails
are about to come very soon and very soon any day now and any day then
i will be mister true then i will be mister true to me i will be mister true
love i will become true true to me mister truelove to me i will be mister
true love my only only and no other to me told her that red sails will
appear come over horizon line i know that red boat is on its way it won't
be long it gets closer and closer closer than ever i'm very near nearly ready
but not quite yet not just i'm not quite you know but very soon any day
and any very nearly nearly my true love mister i'll come over i'll be true
i'll get over i'll come to me i'll come to i'll be my true love red boat love
i just have to wait and i wait my red boat is on on its way i trust i hope
she was told in sweden a long time ago they told my little girl that when
i'm all grown up and ready for when it's all over a red sail boat will come
into my harbour and i'll become mister true to me i'll be mister true true
mister love to me i'll be my one and only only red sails will sail around
the world to come to me why don't you come to me come to me i'm
ready for nearly nearly but you know i'm not quite yet i'm not quite
steady i'm harbour and i wait for me to come true to me to be my true
love and no other and i wait she was told in sweden in my book that when
she is all grown up and ready for when i'm all right and fully fully red sails
will appear i know that it will exactly like that it gets near and near nearly
there when i'm ready ready and fully i'll be true to me i'll be mister true
love and i wait come to me why don't you come to me and i wait i'll be
true love to me i'll be true love mister love me i will be my true and only
one i'll be mister true love to me i just wait red sails come i'm nearly
nearly almost there almost but not quite and i wait when will i come i just
have to wait believe me it will any day very soon red sails are gets closer
to me nearer and nearer closer than ever just a touch but not yet red sails
will come when i'm ready for when i'm fully fully when i'm all right and
i'm not quite quite i just wait and see red sails will appear then i'll be
mister true love to me i'll be true to me then i'll meet me i'll be my one
and only one to me i'll be true red sails about to enter and about to i am
harbour and i wait i have to trust my story book told my little girl to wait
till i'm all grown up and ready for when i'm fully fully when it's all over

this boat will come with red sails on then i'll turn true love to me then i'll be my true mister true love and i wait red sails just around the corner in sweden a long time ago they told my little girl to see when i'm all grown up and ready for red sails will arrive my i'll be true to my only only love me please come to me i'll come true to me only then very soon just about to and about to gets near when feels right to me i'm ready for but not yet completely i have to wait when i'm steady level head when will you come over red sails coming true to me i will be a meant for longtimes i'm closer than ever i'll be true love mister red sails will appear when i'm fully fully sure now i'll i can feel i'll be mister true love i'll come home to me in full focus i know by ten i'm going to sail in red sails it gets near closer and closer i'm sailor and i sail back to me i was away i was sailing in my head i was out of me then i'll come back to me be true sailor mister love me do i'm nearly ready for but i'm not quite there just wait till level head then i'll be real for steady i'm about to and about to and not yet i'm nearly there but not yet not quite i'm almost almost and i wait

DAVID BROOKS

The Line

Late, on the hottest night of the year, he sits by the window. For a long time he searches for a line and at last he finds it, beginning at the tip of his pen and continuing across the page beneath the words *continuing across the page beneath* until it reaches the edge and, independent of ink and human motion, and pausing only briefly as if about to dive, moving thence on to the desk and past the candle and the glass towards the sill.

From there, against the first faint stirrings of a cool breeze from the river, it slips through the wire screen and out across the fuchsias and the lawn. Traversing the pavement, rising above the trees, and following no streets or feasible cross-country route, it passes westward over Roe Street and the Beggar's Lane to the playing-fields and the old stone buildings of the university. Not stopping at these, nor in the café quarter, and following roughly the course of the river, it passes through the wide updraught of denser oxygen above the park, directly above the last bedless lovers in an F. J. Holden and the pointing arm of the statue of Sir John F., the founding father of the city, and thence across the long, perfect reflection of the Great Port Bridge and into the sleeping suburbs. After almost one mile of these, just grazing the upper branches of an avenue of flowering gums, it slows and descends, approaching cautiously the third front window of a darkened house four miles or three pages of the city directory from where first it left the orderly confines of the introductory paragraph of a tale for which it may, in truth, have never been intended.

To follow it by car (public transport, needless to say, is unthinkable), one would have—to employ again the city directory—to begin on page 48, in the square designated by the fine blue lines that descend from either side of the letter *B*, and those which stretch towards the left from the number 53 at the far right-hand margin. Bearing in mind that one's general direction must always be westward, one would then move at first in a southerly direction along Alton Road until Balcott and, turning right at the church with the great rose window, move diagonally across two map squares to where the page joins 47 and, crossing at first Charles Road, Balcott leads into Dean Parade. Now moving directly westward, one traces Dean through four squares of the light blue grid—past the city pool, the council offices and the Ladies' College—and passes beneath the freeway into Estuary Road, where the Floral Beach Parade and map 46 begin. Following the Floral Beach Parade diagonally across the upper right, beside Dog Swamp and the Herdsman Cemetery, one finds oneself, having strayed north-westerly, referred to map 36, where the Floral intersects Green Street and turns towards the sea. At Herbert Street one takes a left-hand turn. Moving again southward, one drives beneath flowering gums to a lane beginning, of course, with the letter *I*, and halts at the darkened frontage of number 38, at a considerable disadvantage and at least half an hour behind the line which, unshackled by a pedestrian imagination, has already entered the third window from the left—left open to catch the cool sea breeze—and passed between billowing curtains towards a bed upon which sleeps a woman with soft white skin and auburn hair, her face partly hidden by her furled right arm and a fold of the single sheet. Uninhibited by this last barrier, the line has long since found her, and, not without an initial parabolic digression, proceeded along her left calf and thigh and come to rest, peacefully and without thought of return.

She, of course, knows nothing of this. She has, in fact, been borrowed from Alain Dufort, and was last seen on a balcony above a courtyard lined with palms. All she could tell is that, when she awoke, she had been dreaming of an old man on an esplanade, feeding seagulls that, for their own mysterious reasons, suddenly rose, and, banking westward, traced with their soft grey wings an ambiguous message, free of grid or narrative, on a dark sky promising rain.

KERRYN GOLDSWORTHY

Roses and My Brother

The geography was all wrong for them, but my mother grew roses. It took dedication, which she had. Inside the gate there were roses and grapevines, violets and geraniums, snapdragons, nasturtiums, Iceland poppies. Outside the gate there was the horizon.

My father's father owned the horizon, at least by the law of the land. 'The law of the land' was a phrase he liked. We called him Papa, which had Victorian overtones that suited him. He had a large old-fashioned desk with a maze of drawers and pigeonholes and a key on a narrow loop of green ribbon; every year he sat down at it and filled in pages of perfect tax returns. Referred to, with capitals, as Papa's Desk, it was a numinous object with a force-field of mystery and power that had something to do with money, and it was, of course, kept locked. My grandfather habitually wore a hat. He was the sort of man-in-a-hat you see driving firmly along in the right-hand lane, well below the speed limit.

He was a good man, whatever that means. It was one of the few things he had in common with my father. In their turn, in the tiny town, they both always ended up being asked to be a pallbearer whenever there was a funeral. They could both be trusted to carry the dead, steadily and with ceremony, and not to slip.

Inside the gate there was shade and green and the vines grew over our heads, dangling down bunches of grapes like purple earrings for lady giants. We snapped the red dragons on the ends of our fingers; we pressed the poppy petals in the dictionary, between pontoon and popular. My mother made us rosebud sprays to pin to our dresses for good luck in exams. She showed us what happened to the dew in the saucers of nasturtium leaves: it gathered into a globe like a clear marble, a little pure world. My mother taught me the word *world*, and the word *word*. She made a merry-go-round birthday cake with a striped canopy and silver-paper horses that went round and round. She made us smocked dresses and draw-string blouses and did amazing things with lace and ribbon and rick-rack braid. She went to country dances with huge boxes for the supper-room, full of silver trays and paper-lace doileys and cream puffs made into little swans with proper beaks and wings. She was firm with large animals, she read us 'The Forsaken Merman' while we practised hemstitch and herringbone, and when my father got sick she went out and drove the tractor, before dawn, in the rain.

Outside the gate, we went to school, and on weekends and holidays my father took us with him in the truck, round the lambing ewes and out on fox-extermination expeditions: three small girls in knitted cardigans and matching pixie hoods, learning to gaze collectedly on birth and death. If somebody walked into this room with a sharp knife and a sheep and said to me 'Here, stop writing and kill this sheep,' I could probably do it properly without being sick; I remember, from watching, how it's done. Outside the gate my father showed us things being killed and born and my grandfather did not approve; my mother was friends with everybody and my grandmother did not approve. Then my grandparents retired and moved away to the city, and my parents let out the breath they had been holding for ten years.

My grandfather planted nine fruit trees in his back yard in the city. They revealed in him a capacity for recklessness and opulence saved up and hidden all his life. It had been a life of neat lines, straight fences and tidy columns of arithmetic, but in his old age in his back yard he grew peaches and nectarines and apricots in ridiculous profusion and excess. In his tiny orchard the trees were planted in straight lines and there was never any mess on the ground, but every summer the branches hung so heavy with perfect golden globes that he had to prop them up to stop them dragging on the ground, or breaking under the weight of his harvest. They sang in the sun. If you stepped out through the back door on a clear day you were dazzled. The neighbours were kept in summer fruit by the boxful and bucketful for streets around. He made huge pans of jam.

In the front yard, he grew roses. He left the labels on the bushes.

They came back often to the farm to visit. One year my grandfather said to my mother that her roses needed pruning properly. What he meant was that he would do it. My mother ground her teeth and handed him the secateurs as if they were a pair of duelling pistols. My grandmother said to my mother that her daughters needed disciplining properly. What she meant was that she would do it. My mother ground her teeth and changed the subject. My grandfather went outside with the secateurs and cut my mother's hard-won roses back almost level with the ground, to sad little black twigs.

In that tense quartet of adults my mother and my grandfather were the true adversaries, for they were at once the most different and the most alike. It was usually my grandmother who precipitated open quarrels, but between my mother and my grandfather was the subtle hidden struggle of two strong-willed people who know that deep harmony is possible, if only they could get it right. In their opposite ways they loved the same things: order, beauty, gardening, and my father. The invasion of the garden was not malicious butchery; he was simply doing what he considered right. My mother did not cry readily or often, but when she saw what my grandfather had done, she wept.

My father's dislike of small boys probably had its roots in the way he felt about his own childhood. Wherever it came from, it was genuine and intense, and if he'd ever had a son, each would have made the other's life a misery. He was well pleased with daughters, and he wanted to get us out of there and away to the city before we married farmers' sons and disappeared forever. The irony of this was not lost on my mother, who had married a farmer's son.

But my grandfather never really forgave my mother for failing to provide him with an heir. He foresaw the disappearance of the farm and the family name, and it hurt him; unlike my father he had failed to learn a farm's best lesson, which is that immortality is the prerogative of gods. My grandfather would have taken it for granted that a grandson would carry it all on—even a grandson who might have preferred to be a singer or a sailor, and to float away forever on tides of music. My grandfather would have tried to stop him; and in doing everything in his power to make sure, he would simply have been doing what he considered right.

I have always wanted a brother, but if I'd had one I can't see how he could ever have been a happy man. What with my father and my grandfather, any brother of mine would have been born into a trap; no matter whether he had escaped or not, no matter what or whom he had been like, there would have been struggle and bitterness in store for somebody.

My mother thought her roses had been killed, though if she had been entirely convinced she would not have nursed their delicate, dead-looking little skeletons so assiduously for so long. And a few seasons later, there they were, climbing and spilling up and down the fence and along the path, reaching new heights of golden abundance in the sun. When my grandfather pointed out how well they had responded to his treatment, my mother might have been forgiven for taking the secateurs and stabbing him in the back. But my mother is a generous woman and held her peace, though to say that she was grateful would be going too far. Sometimes I think about my mother's son, my brother. I wonder what he would have been like, and if he would have needed saving, and whether she could have saved him, if he had.

TIM WINTON

My Father's Axe

Just now I discover the axe gone. I look everywhere inside and outside the house, front and back, but it is gone. It has been on my front verandah since the new truckload of wood arrived and was dumped so intelligently over my front lawn. Jamie says he doesn't know where the axe is and I believe him; he won't chop wood any more. Elaine hasn't seen it; it's men's business, she says. No, it's not anywhere. But who would steal an axe in this neighbourhood, this street where I grew up and have lived much of my life? No one steals on this street. Not an axe.

It is my father's axe.

I used to watch him chop with it when we drove the old Morris and the trailer outside the town limits to gather wood. He would tie a thick, short bar of wood to the end of forty feet of rope and swing it about his head like a lasso and the sound it made was the whoop! of the headmaster's cane you heard when you walked past his office. My father sent the piece of wood high into the crown of a dead she-oak and when it snarled in the stark, grey limbs he would wrap the rope around his waist and then around his big freckled arms, and he would pass me his grey hat with bound hands and tell me to stand right back near the Morris with my mother who poured tea from a Thermos flask. And he pulled. I heard his body grunt and saw his red arms whiten, and the tree's crown quivered and rocked and he added to the motion, tugging, jerking, gasping until the whole bush cracked open and birds burst from all the trees around and the dead, grey crown of the she-oak teetered and toppled to the earth, chased by a shower of twigs and bark. My mother and I cheered and my father ambled over, arms glistening, to drink the tea that tasted faintly of coffee and the rubber seal of the Thermos. Rested, he would then dismember the brittle tree with graceful swings of his axe and later I would saw with him on the bowman saw and have my knees showered with white, pulpy dust.

He could swing an axe, my father.

And that axe is gone.

He taught me how to split wood though I could never do it like him, those long, rhythmic, semi-circular movements like a ballet dancer's warm-up; I'm a left-hander, a mollydooker he called me, and I chop in short, jabby strokes which do the job but are somehow less graceful.

When my father began to leave us for long periods for his work—he sold things—he left me with the responsibility of fuelling the home. It gave me pride to know that our hot water, my mother's cooking, the livingroom fire depended upon me, and my mother called me the man of the house, which frightened me a little. Short, winter afternoons I spent up the back splitting pine for kindling, long, fragrant spines with neat grain, and I opened up the heads of mill-ends and sawn blocks of she-oak my father brought home. Sometimes in the trance of movement and exertion I imagined the blocks of wood as teachers' heads. It was pleasurable work when the wood was dry and the grain good and when I kept the old Kelly axe sharp. I learnt to swing single-handed, to fit wedges into stubborn grain, to negotiate knots with resolve, and the chopping warmed me as I stripped to my singlet and worked until I was ankle-deep in split, open wood and my breath steamed out in front of me with each righteous grunt.

Once, a mouse half caught itself in a trap in the laundry beneath the big stone trough and my mother asked me to kill it, to put it out of its misery, she said. Obediently, I carried the threshing mouse in the trap at arm's length right up to the back of the yard. How to kill a mouse? Wring its neck? Too small. Drown it? In what? I put it on the burred block and hit it with the flat of the axe. It made no noise but it left a speck of red on my knee.

Another time my father, leaving again for a long trip, began softly to weep on our front step. My mother did not see because she was inside finding him some fruit. I saw my father ball his handkerchief up and bite on it to muffle his sobs and I left him there and ran through the house and up to the woodpile where I shattered great blocks of she-oak until it was dark and my arms gave out. In the dark I stacked wood into the buckled shed and listened to my mother calling.

I broke the handle of that axe once, on a camping trip; it was good hickory and I was afraid to tell him. I always broke my father's tools, blunted his chisels, bent his nails. I have never been a handyman like my father. He made things and repaired things and I watched but did not see the need to learn because I knew my father would always be. If I needed something built, something done, there was my father and he protected me.

When I was eight or nine he took my mother and me to a beach shack at a rivermouth up north. The shack was infested with rats and I lay awake nights listening to them until dawn when my father came and roused me and we went down to haul the craypots. The onshore reefs at low tide were bare, clicking and bubbling in the early sun, and octopuses gangled across exposed rocks, lolloping from hole to hole. We caught them for bait; my father caught them and I carried them in the bucket with the tight lid and looked at my face in the still tidal pools that bristled with kelp. But it was not so peaceful at high tide when the swells burst on the upper lip of the reef and cascaded walls of foam that rushed in upon us and rocked us with their force. The water reached my waist though it was only knee-deep for my father. He taught me to brace myself side-on to the waves and find footholds in the reef and I hugged his leg and felt his immovable stance and moulded myself to him. At the edge of the reef I coiled the rope that he hauled up and held the hessian bag as he opened the heavy, timber-slatted pots; he dropped the crays in and I heard their tweaking cries and felt them grovelling against my legs.

During the day my mother read *They're a Weird Mob* and ate raisins and cold crayfish dipped in red vinegar. We played Scrabble and it did not bother me that my father lost.

Lost his axe. Who could have stolen such a worthless thing? The handle is split and taped and the head bears the scars of years; why even look at it?

One night on that holiday a rat set off a trap on the rafter above my bed. My father used to tie the traps to the rafters to prevent the rats from carrying them off. It went off in the middle of the night with a snap like a small fire cracker and in the dark I sensed something moving above me and something warm touched my forehead. I lay still and did not scream because I knew my father would come. Perhaps I did scream in the end, I don't know. But he came, and he lit the Tilley lamp and chuckled and, yes, that was when I screamed. The rat, suspended by six feet of cord, swung in an arc across my bed with the long, hairy whip of tail trailing a foot above my nose. The body still flexed and struggled. My father took it down and went outside with its silhouette in the lamplight in front of him. My mother screamed; there was a drop of blood on my forehead. It was just like *The Pit and the Pendulum*, I said. We had recently seen the film and she had found the book in the library and read it to me for a week at bedtime. Yes, she said with a grim smile, wiping my forehead, and I had nightmares about that long, hairy blade above my throat and saw it snatched away by my father's red arms. In the morning I saw outside that the axe head was dull with blood. After that I often had dreams in which my father rescued me. One was a dream about a burning house—our house, the one I still live in with Elaine and Jamie—and I was trapped inside, hair and bedclothes afire and my father splintered the door with an axe blow and fought his way in and carried me out in those red arms.

My father. He said little. He never won at Scrabble, so it seems he never even stored words up for himself. We never spoke much. It was my mother and I who carried on the long conversations; she knew odd facts, quiz shows on television were her texts. I told her my problems. But with my father I just stood, and we watched each other. Sometimes he looked at me with disappointment, and other times I looked at him the same way. He hammered big nails in straight and kissed me goodnight and goodbye and hello until I was fourteen and learnt to be ashamed of it and evade it.

When his back stiffened with age he chopped wood less and I wielded the axe more. He sat by the woodpile and sometimes stacked, though mostly he just sat with a thoughtful look on his face. As I grew older my time contracted around me like a shrinking shirt and I chopped wood hurriedly, often finishing before the old man had a chance to come out and sit down.

Then I met Elaine and we married and I left home. For years I went back once a week to chop wood for the old man while Elaine and my mother sat at the Laminex table in the kitchen listening to the tick of the stove. I tried to get my parents interested in electric heating and cooking like most people in the city, but my father did not care for it. He was stubborn and so I continued to split wood for him once a week while he became a frail, old man and his arms lost their ruddiness and went pasty and the flesh lost its grip upon the bones of his forearms. He looked at me in disappointment every week like an old man will, but I came over on Sundays, even when we had Jamie to look after, so he didn't have cause to be that way.

Jamie got old enough to use an axe and I taught him how. He was keen at first, though careless, and he blunted the edge quite often which angered me. I got him to chop wood for his grandfather and dropped him there on Sunday afternoons. I had a telephone installed in their house, though they complained about the colour, and I spoke to my mother sometimes on the phone, just to please her. My father never spoke on the phone. Still doesn't.

Then my mother had her stroke and Jamie began demanding to be paid for woodchopping and Elaine went twice a week to cook and clean for them and I decided on the Home. My mother and father moved out and we moved in and sold our own house. I thought about getting the place converted to electricity but the Home was expensive and Elaine came to enjoy cooking on the old combustion stove and it was worth paying Jamie a little to chop wood. Until recently. Now he won't even do it for money. He is lazier than me.

Still, it was only an old axe.

II

Elaine sleeps softly beside me, her big wide buttocks warm against my legs. The house is quiet; it was always quiet, even when my parents and I lived here. No one ever raised their voice at me in this house, except now my wife and son.

It is hard to sleep, hard, so difficult. Black moves about me and in me and is on me, so black. Fresh, bittersweet, the smell of split wood: hard, splintery jarrah, clean, moist she-oak, hard, fibrous white gum, the shick! of sundering pine. All my muscles sing, a chorus of effort, as I chop quickly, throwing chunks aside, wiping flecks and chips from my chin. Sweat sheets across my eyes and I chop harder, opening big round sawn blocks of she-oak like pies in neat wedged sections. Harder. And my feet begin to lift as I swing the axe high over my shoulder. I strike it home and regain equilibrium. As I swing again my feet lift further and I feel as though I might float up, borne away by the axe above my head, as though it is a helium balloon. No, I don't want to lift up! I drag on the hickory handle, downwards, and I win and drag harder and it gains momentum and begins a slow-motion arc of descent towards the porous surface of the wood and then, halfway down, the axe-head shears off the end of the handle so slowly, so painfully slow that I could take a hold of it four or five times to stop it. In a slow, tumbling trajectory it sails across the woodheap and unseats my father's head from his shoulders and travels on out of sight as my father's head rolls onto the heap, eyes towards me, transfixed at the moment of scission in a squint of disappointment.

I feel a warm dob on my forehead; I do not scream, have never needed to.

The sheets are wet and the light is on and Elaine has me by the shoulder and her left breast points down at my glistening chest.

'What's the matter?' she says, wiping my brow with the back of her hand. 'You were yelling.'

'A dream,' I croak.

III

Morning sun slants across the pickets at me as I fossick about in the long grass beside the shed finding the skeleton of a wren but nothing else. I shuffle around the shed, picking through the chips and splinters and slivers of wood around the chopping block, see the deep welts in the block where the axe has been, but no axe. In the front yard, as neighbours pass, I scrabble in the pile of new wood, digging into its heart, tossing pieces aside until there is nothing but yellowing grass and a few impassive slaters. Out in the backyard again I amble about shaking my head and putting my hands in my pockets and taking them out again. Elaine is at work. Jamie at school. I have rung the office and told them I won't be in. All morning I mope in the yard, waiting for something to happen, absurdly, expecting the axe to show like a prodigal son. Nothing.

Going inside at noon I notice a deep trench in the verandah post by the back door; it is deep and wide as a heavy axe-blow and I feel the inside of it with my fingers—only for a moment—before I hurry inside trying to recall its being there before. Surely.

I sit by the cold stove in the kitchen in the afternoon, quaking. Is someone trying to kill me? My God.

IV

Again Elaine has turned her sumptuous buttocks against me and gone to sleep dissatisfied and I lie awake with my shame and the dark around me.

Some nights as a child I crept into my parents' room and wormed my way into the bed between them and slept soundly, protected from the dark by their warm contact.

Now, I press myself against Elaine's sleeping form and cannot sleep with the knowledge that my back is exposed.

After an hour I get up and prowl about the house, investigating each room with quick flicks of light switches and satisfied grunts when everything seems to be in order. Here, the room where my mother read, here, Jamie's room where I slept as a boy, here, where my father drank his hot, milkless tea in the mornings.

I can think of nothing I've done to offend the neighbours—I'm not a dog baiter or anything—though some of them grumbled about my putting my parents into the Home, as though it was any of their business.

I keep thinking of axe murders, things I've read in the papers, horrible things.

In the livingroom I take out the old Scrabble box and sit with it on my knee for a while. Perhaps I'll play a game with myself . . .

V

This morning when I woke in the big chair in the livingroom I saw the floor littered with Scrabble tiles like broken, yellowing teeth. Straightening my stiff back I recalled the dream. I dreamt that I saw my body dissected, raggedly sectioned up and battered and crusted black with blood. The axe, the old axe with the taped hickory handle, was embedded in the trunk where once my legs had joined, right through the pelvis. My severed limbs lay about, pink, black, distorted, like stockings full of sand. My head, to one side, faced the black ceiling, teeth bared, eyes firmly shut. Horrible, but even so, peaceful enough, like a photograph. And then a boy came out of the black—it was Jamie—and picked up my head and held it like a bowling ball. Then there was light and my son opened the door and went outside into the searing suddenness of light. He walked out into the backyard and up to the chopping block in which an axe—*the* axe—was poised. I felt nothing when he split my head in two. It was a poor stroke, but effective enough. Then with half in either hand—by the hair—he slowly walked around the front of the house and then out to the road verge and began skidding the half-orbs into the paths of oncoming cars. I used to do that as a boy; skidding half pig-melons under car wheels until nothing was left but a greenish, wet pulp. Pieces of my head ricocheted from chassis to bitumen, tyre to tyre, until there was only pulp and an angry sounding of car horns.

That does it; I'm going down to the local hardware store to buy another axe. It's high time. I have thought of going to the police but it's too ludicrous; I have nothing to tell: someone has stolen my axe that used to be my father's. A new axe is what I need.

It takes a long time in the Saturday morning rush at the hardware and the axes are so expensive and many are shoddy and the sales boy who pretends to be a professional axeman tires me with his patter. Eventually I buy a Kelly; it costs me forty dollars and it bears a resemblance to my father's. Carrying it home I have the feeling that I'm holding a stage property, not a tool; there are no signs of work on it and the head is so clean and smooth and shiny it doesn't seem intended for chopping.

As I open the front gate, axe over my shoulder, my wife is waiting on the verandah with tears on her face.

'The Home called,' she says. 'It's your father . . .'

VI

The day after the funeral I am sitting out on the front verandah in the faint yellow sun. My mother will die soon; her life's work is over and she has no reason to continue in her sluggish, crippled frame. It will not be long before her funeral, I think to myself, not long. A tall sunflower sheds its hard, black seeds near me, shaken by the weight of a bird I can't see but sense. The gate squeals on its hinges and at the end of the path stand a man and a boy.

'Yes?' I ask.

The man prompts the boy forward and I see the lad has something in a hessian bag in his arms that he is offering me. Stepping off the verandah I take it, not heeding the man's apologies and the stutterings of his son. I open the bag and see the hickory handle with its gummy black tape and nicks and burrs and I groan aloud.

'He's sorry he took it,' the man says, 'aren't you, Alan? He—'

'Wait,' I say, turning, bounding back up the verandah, through the house, out onto the back verandah where Elaine and Jamie sit talking. They look startled but I have no time to explain. I grab the shiny, new axe which is yet to be used, and race back through the house with it. Elaine calls out to me, fright in her voice.

In the front yard, the father and son still wait uneasily and they look at me with apprehension as I run towards them with the axe.

'What—' The man tries to shield his son whose mouth begins to open as I come closer.

I hold the axe out before me, my body tingling, and I hold it horizontal with the handle against the boy's heaving chest.

'Here,' I say. 'This is yours.'

NOTES ON CONTRIBUTORS

MENA ABDULLAH (1930–) was born in Bundarra, northern New South Wales, to parents of Indian origin. She worked as an administrator for the Commonwealth Scientific and Industrial Research Organisation. Her volume of stories, *The Time of the Peacock* (1965), was written in collaboration with Ray Mathew (q.v.). The 'rusilla' of her story is the rosella, an Australian native bird of the parrot family.

GLENDA ADAMS (1940–) was born in Sydney and lived for many years in New York. She teaches creative writing at the University of Technology, Sydney. Her fiction includes the short story collections *Lies and Stories* (1976) and *The Hottest Night of the Century* (1979) and the novels *Games of the Strong* (1982), *Dancing on Coral* (1987) and *Longleg* (1990).

ETHEL ANDERSON (1883–1958) was born in Leamington Spa, UK, to Australian parents. Educated in Sydney, she lived for several years in India (*Indian Tales*, 1948) and England (*Adventures in Appleshire*, 1944). *At Parramatta* (1956) is a collection of interlinked stories set in Australia at the time of the Crimean War. Her work includes poetry: *Squatter's Luck* (1942), *Sunday at Yarralumla* (1947); essays: *Timeless Garden* (1945); and fiction: *The Little Ghosts* (1959). *The Best of Ethel Anderson* was edited by J. D. Pringle in 1973.

MURRAY BAIL (1941–) was born in Adelaide and worked in advertising for several years in India and England. He has written stories: *Contemporary Portraits and Other Stories* (1975), reissued as *The Drover's Wife and Other Stories*; novels: *Homesickness* (1980), *Holden's Performance* (1987); a monograph on the painter Ian Fairweather (1981); and *Longhand: A Writer's Notebook* (1989).

MARJORIE BARNARD (1897–1987) was born in Sydney. She took a first in history at the University of Sydney and worked as a librarian for several years. Her fiction includes a book of children's stories, *The Ivory*

Gate (1920), and *The Persimmon Tree and Other Stories* (1943); her non-fiction includes *Macquarie's World* (1941), *A History of Australia* (1962) and a study of Miles Franklin (1967). Under the name M. Barnard Eldershaw she collaborated with Flora Eldershaw (1897–1956) on the novels *A House is Built* (1929), *Green Memory* (1931), *The Glasshouse* (1936), *Plaque with Laurel* (1937) and *Tomorrow and Tomorrow* (1947), on a number of historical works, and on *Essays in Australian Fiction* (1938). *But Not for Love: Stories of Marjorie Barnard and M. Barnard Eldershaw* was published in 1988.

BARBARA BAYNTON (1857–1929) was born in Scone, New South Wales. She wrote a volume of stories, *Bush Studies* (1902), and a novel, *Human Toll* (1907). Her life, from outback governess to marriage into the English aristocracy is told by Penne Hackforth Jones in *Barbara Baynton: Between Two Worlds* (1989). *Barbara Baynton*, a selection of her work, edited by Sally Krimmer and Alan Lawson, was published in 1980.

LOUIS BECKE (1855–1913) was born in Port Macquarie, New South Wales. He spent some twenty years adventuring in the Pacific islands, the subject of his early books *By Reef and Palm* (1894), *His Native Wife* (1895) and *The Ebbing of the Tide* (1896). His account of Bully Hayes is the basis of Rolf Boldrewood's *A Modern Buccaneer* (1893). He wrote a number of novels in collaboration with Walter Jeffery, including *A First Fleet Family* (1896) and *The Mutineer* (1898). The *Adventures of Louis Blake* (1909) is substantially autobiographical.

DAVID BROOKS (1953–) was born in Canberra. He is a senior lecturer in Australian literature at the University of Sydney. He has written poetry: *Five Poems* (1981), *The Cold Front* (1983); stories: *The Book of Sei and Other Stories* (1985), *Sheep and the Diva* (1990); and essays: *The Necessary Jungle* (1990); and edited *Security of Allusion: Essays in Honour of A. D. Hope* (1992).

PETER CAREY (1943–) was born in Bacchus Marsh, Victoria, and worked in advertising for many years. He has lived in England and currently lives in New York. He has written stories: *The Fat Man in History* (1974), *War Crimes* (1979); and novels: *Bliss* (1981), *Illywhacker* (1985), *Oscar and Lucinda* (1988), *The Tax Inspector* (1991) and *The Unusual Life of Tristan Smith* (1994). Carey has also written screenplays.

MARCUS CLARKE (1846–81) was born in Kensington, London. He came to Australia at the age of sixteen and established himself as a journalist and dramatist. His writings include stories: *Holiday Peak and Other Tales* (1873), *Four Stories High* (1877), *Stories* (1983); novels: *Long Odds* (1869), *His Natural Life* (1874), '*Twixt Shadow and Shine* (1875), *Chidiock Tichbourne* (1893); and historical studies: *Old Tales of a Young Country* (1871). *A Colonial City*, a collection of his journalism edited by

L. T. Hergenhan, was published in 1972; and in 1976 *Marcus Clarke*, a selection edited by Michael Wilding, was published. Brian Elliott's biography appeared in 1958.

CHARMIAN CLIFT (1923–69) was born in Kiama, New South Wales. She joined the Australian Women's Army Service during the Second World War, and then became a journalist. Clift was married to George Johnston (1912–70) with whom she wrote the novels *High Valley* (1949), *The Big Chariot* (1953) and *The Sponge Divers* (1955).They lived for many years in Greece, and she recorded their experiences in *Mermaid Singing* (1956) and *Peel Me a Lotus* (1959). Her other writings include novels: *Walk to the Paradise Gardens* (1960), *Honour's Mimic* (1964); and essay collections: *Images in Aspic* (1965), *The World of Charmian Clift* (1970). Her stories are collected in the joint Clift–Johnston volume *Strong Man from Piraeus* (1984).

PETER COWAN (1914–) was born in Perth. He has worked as an itinerant labourer, served in the RAAF during the Second World War, and taught at the University of Western Australia. He has written stories: *Drift* (1944), *The Unploughed Land* (1958) *The Empty Street* (1965), *The Tins* (1973), *New Country* (1976), *Mobiles* (1979) *Voices* (1988), and a selection edited by Bruce Bennett, *A Window in Mrs X's Place* (1986); novels: *Summer* (1964), *Seed* (1966), *The Color of the Sky* (1986), and *The Hills of Apollo Bay* (1989); and biography: *A Unique Position—A Biography of Edith Dircksey Cowan 1861–1932* (1978) and *Maitland Brown* (1988). He is an editor of *Westerly*.

ELEANOR DARK (1901–85) was born in Sydney, the only daughter of the writer Dowell O'Reilly (1865–1923). She wrote novels: *Slow Dawning* (1932), *Prelude to Christopher* (1934), *Return to Coolami* (1936), *Sun across the Sky* (1937), *Waterway* (1938), *The Little Company* (1945) and the historical trilogy *The Timeless Land* (1941), *Storm of Time* (1948) and *No Barrier* (1953). *Lantana Lane* (1959) is a collection of interlinked episodes based on experiences of farming in Queensland with her husband Dr Eric Dark. The house in which they lived in the Blue Mountains of New South Wales, Varuna, is now a writers' retreat.

THELMA FORSHAW (1923–) was born in Sydney. She served in the WAAAF during the Second World War, and has been a secretary, advertising writer, and book reviewer. A collection of her short stories, *An Affair of Clowns*, was published in 1967.

SILVANA GARDNER (1942–) was born in Zadar, Dalmatia. She came to Brisbane as a child and is a writer and artist. Her poetry includes *When Sunday Comes* (1982), *Hacedor* (1982), *With Open Eyes* (1983), *Children of the Dragon* (1985), and *The Devil in Nature* (1987).

HELEN GARNER (1942–) was born in Geelong, Victoria. For some years she was a schoolteacher. Her fiction includes *Monkey Grip* (1977), *Honour and Other People's Children* (1980), *The Children's Bach* (1984), *Postcards from Surfers* (1985), *Cosmo Cosmolina* (1992).

KERRYN GOLDSWORTHY (1953–) was born in South Australia. She has written the short story collection *North of the Moonlight Sonata* (1989); and edited the anthologies *Australian Short Stories* (1983) and *Coast to Coast* (1986).

KATE GRENVILLE (1950–) was born in Sydney. She has written stories: *Bearded Ladies* (1984); novels: *Lilian's Story* (1985), *Dreamhouse* (1986), *Joan Makes History* (1988); and non-fiction: *The Writing Book: A Workbook for Fiction Writers* (1990), *Making Stories: How Ten Australian Novels Were Written* (with Sue Woolfe, 1993).

MARION HALLIGAN (1940–) was born in Newcastle, New South Wales, and lives in Canberra. In 1992 she was appointed chairperson of the Literature Board of the Australia Council. She has written stories: *The Living Hothouse* (1988), *The Hanged Man in the Garden* (1989), *The Worry Box* (1993); novels: *Self-Possession* (1987), *Spidercup* (1990), *Lover's Knots* (1992); and *Eat My Words* (1990), a book about food.

ELIZABETH HARROWER (1928–) was born in Sydney and grew up in Newcastle. She lived for several years in London and has worked in publishing and journalism. She has written the novels: *Down in the City* (1957), *The Long Prospect* (1958), *The Catherine Wheel* (1960) and *The Watch Tower* (1966).

KRIS HEMENSLEY (1946–) was born on the Isle of Wight, UK, and came to Australia in 1966. He has been an active editor of little magazines, including *Earth Ship*, *The Ear in a Wheatfield* and *The Merri Creek or Nero*. His many volumes of poetry and prose include *Domestications* (1974), *Here We Are* (1975), *The Poem of the Clear Eye* (1975), *The Rooms and Other Prose Pieces* (1975), *Sulking in the Seventies* (1975), *Down Under* (1978), *Games: An Exhibition 1970–72* (1978), *A Mile from Poetry* (1979), and *Christopher* (1987).

JANETTE TURNER HOSPITAL (1942–) was born in Melbourne, grew up in Brisbane, and lives in Canada. She has taught in schools and universities. She has written stories: *Dislocations* (1986), *Isobars* (1990); novels: *The Ivory Swing* (1982), *The Tiger in the Tiger Pit* (1983), *Borderline* (1985), *Charades* (1988), and *The Last Magician* (1992).

ELIZABETH JOLLEY (1923–) was born in Birmingham, UK, and came to Western Australia in 1959. She has worked as a nurse and a teacher. She has written stories: *Five Acre Virgin* (1976), *The Travelling Entertainer* (1979), *Woman in a Lampshade* (1983), *Stories* (1984); novels: *Palomino*

(1980), *The Newspaper of Claremont Street* (1981), *Mr Scobie's Riddle* (1983), *Miss Peabody's Inheritance* (1983), *Milk and Honey* (1984), *Foxybaby* (1985), *The Well* (1986), *The Sugar Mother* (1988), *My Father's Moon* (1989), *Cabin Fever* (1990), *The Georges' Wife* (1993); non-fiction: *Central Mischief* (1992); and radio drama: *Off the Air: Nine Plays for Radio* (1994). *Elizabeth Jolley: New Critical Essays*, edited by Delys Bird and Brenda Walker, was published in 1991.

ANTIGONE KEFALA (1935–   ) was born in Braila, Romania, to Greek parents, and educated in New Zealand. She has worked as a teacher, librarian and arts administrator. She has written poetry: *The Alien* (1973), *Thirsty Weather* (1978), *European Notebook* (1988), *Absence* (1992); and fiction: *The First Journey* (1975), *The Island* (1984), *Alexia* (1984).

D'ONO KIM (1936–   ) was born in Pyongyang, Korea, and educated in Seoul, Tokyo and Sydney. He has worked as a librarian. He has written novels: *My Name is Tian* (1968), *Password* (1974), *The Chinaman* (1984); and a play: *The Bell* (1990). He has also written libretti for the composer Anne Boyd.

RUDI KRAUSMANN (1933–   ) was born in Austria to Austrian and German parents. He came to Australia in 1958 and worked as a language teacher, journalist and broadcaster. He edited the magazine *Aspect: Art and Literature* and has written prose: *From Another Shore* (1975); poetry: *The Water Lily and Other Poems* (1977), *Paradox* (1980), *Flowers of Emptiness* (1982), *Poems* (with drawings by Garry Shead, 1990); and drama: *Three Plays* (1989).

HENRY LAWSON (1867–1922) was born on the goldfields of Grenfell, New South Wales, to a Norwegian father and Australian mother. He worked as a labourer and journalist. His writings include stories: *Short Stories in Prose and Verse* (1894), *While the Billy Boils* (1896), *On the Track* (1900), *Over the Sliprails* (1900), *Joe Wilson and His Mates* (1901), *Children of the Bush* (1902), *The Rising of the Court* (1910), *Triangles of Life* (1913); and verse: *In the Days When the World Was Wide* (1896), *Verses Popular and Humorous* (1900), *When I Was King* (1905), *For Australia* (1913), *My Army, O, My Army* (1915), *Song of the Dardanelles* (1916). The standard edition of his work is edited by Colin Roderick, who has also written *Henry Lawson: A Life* (1991). Selections of Lawson's work are edited by Brian Kiernan, John Barnes, and Geoffrey Dutton.

ANGELO LOUKAKIS (1951–   ) was born in Sydney to Cretan parents. He works in publishing. He has written stories: *For the Patriarch* (1981), and *Vernacular Dreams* (1986); a novel: *Messenger* (1992); and non-fiction: *The Greeks* (1981) and *Norfolk Island* (1984). He has also written television drama.

MORRIS LURIE (1938–) was born in Melbourne to Jewish parents from Poland. He studied architecture and spent some time working in advertising. Lurie has lived in England, Greece, Denmark and Morocco. He has written novels: *Rappaport* (1966), *The London Jungle Adventures of Charlie Hope* (1968), *Rappaport's Revenge* (1973), *Flying Home* (1978), *Seven Books for Grossman* (1983), *Madness* (1991); stories: *Happy Times* (1969), *Inside the Wardrobe* (1975), *Running Nicely* (1979), *Dirty Friends* (1981), *Outrageous Behaviour* (1984), *The Night We Ate the Sparrow* (1985), *Two Brothers Running* (1990); prose pieces: *The English in Heat* (1972), *Hackwork* (1977), *Public Secrets* (1981), *Snow Jobs* (1985), *My Life as a Movie* (1988); plays: *Waterman* (1979); and an autobiography, *Whole Life* (1987). He has also written children's books.

DAVID MALOUF (1934–) was born in Brisbane to parents of Lebanese and Jewish descent. He taught in schools in the UK and at the University of Sydney. He now divides his time between Australia and Italy. His writings include fiction: *Johnno* (1975), *An Imaginary Life* (1978), *Child's Play* (1981), *Antipodes* (1985), *Harland's Half Acre* (1984), *The Great World* (1990), *Remembering Babylon* (1993); poetry: *Bicyle and Other Poems* (1970), *Neighbours in a Thicket* (1974), *First Things Last* (1980), *Wild Lemons* (1980), *Selected Poems* (1981); a memoir: *12 Edmondstone Street* (1985); and drama: *Blood Relations* (1988). A selection of his work, edited by James Tulip, was published in 1990. He wrote the libretto for *Voss*, for composer Richard Meale, from Patrick White's novel.

ALAN MARSHALL (1902–84) was born in Noorat in western Victoria. Crippled by infantile paralysis in childhood, he spent the rest of his life on crutches. He worked as an accountant in a shoe company, a lonely hearts columnist for *Woman*, and a journalist. His writings include a novel: *How Beautiful Are Thy Feet* (1949); stories: *Tell Us About the Turkey, Jo* (1946), *How's Andy Going?* (1956), *Short Stories* (1973), *Hammers over the Anvil* (1975), *The Complete Stories of Alan Marshall* (1977); accounts of his travels: *These Are My People* (1944), *Ourselves Writ Strange* (1948); and an autobiographical trilogy: *I Can Jump Puddles* (1955), *This Is the Grass* (1962), *In Mine Own Heart* (1963). Other books include an interpretation of Aboriginal myths, *People of the Dreamtime* (1952), and the collections *Alan Marshall Talking* (1978), *Alan Marshall's Australia* (1981) and *Alan Marshall's Battlers* (1983). There is a biography by Harry Marks, *I Can Jump Oceans* (1976).

RAY MATHEW (1929–) was born in Sydney. He left Australia in 1961, and has since lived in London, New York and Italy. He has written plays: 'Sing for St Ned' (1960), 'The Life of the Party' (1961), *A Spring Song* (1961), *We Find the Bunyip* (1968); poetry: *With Cypress Pine* (1951), *Song and Dance* (1956), *South of the Equator* (1961); a novel: *The*

Joys of Possession (1967); and stories: *A Bohemian Affair* (1961), and *The Time of the Peacock*, with Mena Abdullah (1965).

FRANK MOORHOUSE (1938–) was born in Nowra, New South Wales. He worked for a while as a journalist and as an organiser with the Workers' Educational Association. His writings include stories: *Futility and Other Animals* (1969), *The Americans, Baby* (1972), *The Electrical Experience* (1974), *Tales of Mystery and Romance* (1977), *The Everlasting Secret Family and Other Secrets* (1980), *Forty-Seventeen* (1988); novels: *Conference-ville* (1976), *Grand Days* (1993); and collections of journalism: *Days of Wine and Rage* (1980), *Room Service* (1985), *Late-shows* (1990). He was a co-editor of *Tabloid Story*, and edited the story anthologies *Coast to Coast* (1973), *The State of the Art* (1983) and *Fictions 88* (1988). His screenplays include *Between Wars* and *The Coca-Cola Kid*.

GERALD MURNANE (1939–) was born in Melbourne. He lectures in creative writing at Victoria College and is fiction editor of *Meanjin Quarterly*. His fiction includes *Tamarisk Row* (1974), *A Lifetime on Clouds* (1976), *The Plains* (1982), *Landscape with Landscape* (1985), and *Inland* (1988).

OODGEROO NOONUCCAL (formerly Kath Walker) (1920–93) was born on Stradbroke Island, off the Queensland coast, into the Noonuccal tribe. She was State secretary of the Federal Council for the Advancement of Aboriginals and Torres Strait Islanders, and director of the Noonuccal–Nughie Education and Cultural Centre on North Stradbroke Island. Her books include the volumes of poetry *We Are Going* (1964), *The Dawn is at Hand* (1966), and *Father Sky and Mother Earth* (1981), the stories *Stradbroke Dreamtime* (1972), and *My People: A Kath Walker Collection* (1970).

BARRY OAKLEY (1931–) was born in Melbourne. He has been a schoolteacher, advertising copywriter, journalist, and is now literary editor of *The Australian*. He has written novels: *A Wild Ass of a Man* (1967), *A Salute to the Great McCarthy* (1970), *Let's Hear It for Prendergast* (1970), *The Craziplane* (1989); stories: *Walking Through Tigerland* (1977); plays: *The Feet of Daniel Mannix* (1975), *Bedfellows* (1975), *A Lesson in English* (1968, 1976), *The Ship's Whistle* (1979), *The Great God Mogadon and Other Plays* (1980), *Marsupials and Politics* (1981), *Beware of Imitations* (1985); and non-fiction: *Scribbling In the Dark* (1985).

HAL PORTER (1911–84) was born in Melbourne and grew up in Bairnsdale, Gippsland. He worked as a cub reporter, schoolteacher, hotel manager, hospital orderly, actor, theatrical producer and librarian. His writings include stories: *Short Stories* (1942), *A Bachelor's Children* (1962), *The Cats of Venice* (1965), *Mr Butterfry and Other Tales of New Japan* (1970), *Fredo Fuss Love Life* (1974), *The Clairvoyant Goat* (1981),

Selected Stories, edited by Leonie Kramer (1971); novels: *A Handful of Pennies* (1958), *The Tilted Cross* (1961), *The Right Thing* (1971); autobiographies: *The Watcher on the Cast Iron Balcony* (1963), *The Paper Chase* (1966), *The Extra* (1975); plays: *The Professor* (1966), *Eden House* (1969); poetry: *Elijah's Ravens* (1968), *In an Australian Country Graveyard* (1974); and non-fiction: *Stars of Australian Stage and Screen* (1965), *The Actors: An Image of New Japan* (1968), *Bairnsdale: Portrait of an Australian Country Town* (1977). There is a biography by Mary Lord (1993) who has edited a Hal Porter selection (1980).

KATHARINE SUSANNAH PRICHARD (1883–1969) was born in Levuka, Fiji, where her father was a newspaper editor. She worked as a governess and a journalist and spent some years in England. In 1920 she was a founding member of the Communist Party of Australia. Her writings include novels: *The Pioneers* (1915), *Windlestraws* (1916), *Black Opal* (1921), *Working Bullocks* (1926), *The Wild Oats of Han* (1928), *Coonardoo* (1928), *Haxby's Circus* (1930), *Intimate Strangers* (1937), *Moon of Desire* (1941), *Subtle Flame* (1967) and the goldfields trilogy *The Roaring Nineties* (1946), *Golden Miles* (1948) and *Winged Seeds* (1950); stories: *Kiss on the Lips* (1932), *Potch and Colour* (1944), *N'Goola* (1959), *On Strenuous Wings* (1965), *Happiness* (1967); poetry: *Clovelly Verses* (1913), *The Earth Lover* (1932); an autobiography: *Child of the Hurricane* (1963); and non-fiction: *The New Order* (1919), *The Real Russia* (1934), *Straight Left* (1982). There is a biography, *Wild Weeds and Wind Flowers* (1975), by her son, Ric Throssell, who has also edited a volume of selected stories, *Tribute* (1988).

HENRY HANDEL RICHARDSON (1870–1946) was born Ethel Florence Lindesay Richardson in Melbourne. She was educated in Melbourne and at the Leipzig Conservatorium. After living in Strasbourg, Richardson spent most of her life in England. Her writings include novels: *Maurice Guest* (1908), *The Getting of Wisdom* (1910), *The Young Cosima* (1939), and the trilogy *The Fortunes of Richard Mahony—Australia Felix* (1917), *The Way Home* (1925), *Ultima Thule* (1929); stories: *Two Studies* (1931), *The End of a Childhood* (1934), *The Adventures of Cuffy Mahony* (1979); and an autobiography: *Myself When Young* (1948). There is a biographical and critical study by Dorothy Green, *Ulysses Bound* (1973), and a biography by Axel Clarke, *Henry Handel Richardson: Fiction in the Making* (1990).

PADDY ROE (1912?–   ) was born near Broome into the Nyigina tribe. He has worked as a drover and windmill repairer. His stories have been recorded by Stephen Muecke (1951–   ) who wrote a doctorate on narrative analysis of contemporary Aboriginal narratives in the Kimberleys, and directs the creative writing programme at the University of Technology, Sydney. Paddy Roe's stories are collected in *gularabulu* (with Stephen Muecke, 1983), and *Reading The Country* (with Stephen Muecke and Krim Benterrak, 1984).

CHRISTINA STEAD (1902–83) was born in Sydney. She worked as a teacher and secretary. She left Australia in 1928, living in England, Europe and the USA until returning in 1974. Her writings include novels: *Seven Poor Men of Sydney* (1934), *The Beauties and Furies* (1936), *House of All Nations* (1938), *The Man Who Loved Children* (1940), *For Love Alone* (1944), *Letty Fox: Her Luck* (1946), *A Little Tea, A Little Chat* (1948), *The People with the Dogs* (1952), *Cotters' England* (1966/67), *The Little Hotel* (1973), *Miss Herbert (The Suburban Wife)* (1976), *I'm Dying Laughing* (1986); and stories: *The Salzburg Tales* (1934), *The Puzzleheaded Girl* (1967), *Ocean of Story* (1986). Selected letters were edited by R. G. Geering in two volumes, *A Web of Friendship (1928–1973)*, and *Talking into the Typewriter (1973–1983)* (1992). There are biographies by Chris Williams (1989) and Hazel Rowley (1993).

DAL STIVENS (1911–) was born in Blayney, New South Wales. He has been a bank officer, public servant, journalist and press officer; and was foundation president of the Australian Society of Authors in 1963. His writings include stories: *The Tramp and Other Stories* (1936), *The Courtship of Uncle Henry* (1946), *The Gambling Ghost and Other Tales* (1953), *Ironbark Bill* (1955), *The Scholarly Mouse* (1957), *The Unicorn and Other Tales* (1976), *The Demon Bowler and Other Cricket Stories* (1979); novels: *Jimmy Brockett* (1951), *The Wide Arch* (1958), *Three Persons Make a Tiger* (1968), *A Horse of Air* (1970); and non-fiction: *The Incredible Egg* (1974). A volume of *Selected Stories* has been edited by H. P. Heseltine (1969).

ETHEL TURNER (1870–1958) was born in Yorkshire, UK, and came to Australia at the age of ten. She is best known for her children's books *Seven Little Australians* (1894) and its sequel, *The Family at Misrule* (1895), *Miss Bobbie* (1897) and *Flower o' the Pine* (1914), but she also wrote adult novels such as *The Story of a Baby* (1895). Other titles include *The Little Larrikin* (1896), *Three Little Maids* (1900), *Gum Leaves* (1900), *In the Mist of the Mountains* (1906), *The Stolen Voyage* (1907), *That Girl* (1908), *Fugitives from Fortune* (1909), *The Raft in the Bush* (1910), *Fifteen and Fair* (1911), *The Cub* (1915), *Captain Cub* (1917), *Brigid and the Cub* (1919), and *Judy and Punch* (1928). Selections from her diaries 1889–1930 have been edited by Philippa Poole (1979).

VICKI VIIDIKAS (1948–) was born in Sydney to an Estonian father and an Australian mother descended from Ned Kelly's family. She lived for a number of years in India. She has written stories: *Wrappings* (1974); and poetry: *Condition Red* (1973), *Knäbel* (1978), and *India Ink* (1984).

ANIA WALWICZ (1951–) was born in Swidnica, Poland. She attended art school in Melbourne and is a painter and performance artist. Her books include *Writing* (1982), and *Boat* (1989).

JUDAH WATEN (1911–85) was born in Odessa into a Jewish family that settled in Western Australia in 1914, and moved to Melbourne in 1926. He lived for some years in England. His writings include novels: *The Unbending* (1954), *Shares in Murder* (1957), *Time of Conflict* (1961), *Distant Land* (1964), *Season of Youth* (1966), *So Far No Further* (1971), *Scenes of Revolutionary Life* (1982); stories: *Alien Son* (1952), *Love and Rebellion* (1978); travel writing: *From Odessa to Odessa* (1969); and a book for children: *Bottle-O!* (1973).

PATRICK WHITE (1912–90) was born in London to Australian parents. Educated in Australia and the UK, he was an intelligence officer in the Middle East during the Second World War. He lived in England, Europe and the USA, returning to Australia in 1948. White received the Nobel Prize for literature in 1973. His writings include novels: *Happy Valley* (1939), *The Living and the Dead* (1941), *The Aunt's Story* (1948), *The Tree of Man* (1955), *Voss* (1957), *Riders in the Chariot* (1961), *The Solid Mandala* (1966), *The Vivisector* (1970), *The Eye of the Storm* (1973), *A Fringe of Leaves* (1976), *The Twyborn Affair* (1979), *Memoirs of Many in One* (1986); stories: *The Burnt Ones* (1964), *The Cockatoos* (1974), *Three Uneasy Pieces* (1987); plays: *The Season at Sarsaparilla, A Cheery Soul, The Ham Funeral* and *Night on Bald Mountain* in *Four Plays* (1965), *Big Toys* (1978), *The Night the Prowler* (1978), *Netherwood* (1983), *Signal Driver* (1983); an autobiography: *Flaws in the Glass* (1981); and non-fiction: *Patrick White Speaks* (1989). A biography by David Marr was published in 1991.

MICHAEL WILDING (1942–) was born in Worcester, UK and came to Australia in 1963. His writings include stories: *Aspects of the Dying Process* (1972), *The West Midland Underground* (1975), *Scenic Drive* (1976), *The Phallic Forest* (1978), *Reading the Signs* (1984), *The Man of Slow Feeling* (1985), *Under Saturn* (1988), *Great Climate* (1990), *This is for You* (1994); novels: *Living Together* (1974), *The Short Story Embassy* (1975), *Pacific Highway* (1982), *The Paraguayan Experiment* (1985); and non-fiction: *Marcus Clarke* (1977), *Political Fictions* (1980), *Dragons Teeth* (1987), *Social Visions* (1993), *The Radical Tradition: Lawson, Furphy, Stead* (1993). He was a co-editor of *Tabloid Story*.

TIM WINTON (1960–) was born in Perth. He has written stories: *Scission* (1985); novels: *An Open Swimmer* (1982), *Shallows* (1984), *That Eye, the Sky* (1986), *Minimum of Two* (1987), *In the Winter Dark* (1988), *Cloudstreet* (1991). A critical study, *Reading Tim Winton*, by Richard Rossiter and Lyn Jacobs was published in 1993.

JUDITH WRIGHT (1915–) was born in Armidale, New South Wales. She is a distinguished poet and writer on conservation. Her books include poetry: *The Moving Image* (1946), *Woman to Man* (1949), *The Gateway* (1953), *The Two Fires* (1955), *Birds* (1962), *Five Senses* (1963),

City Sunrise (1964), *The Other Half* (1966), *Alive* (1973), *Fourth Quarter and Other Poems* (1976), *The Double Tree* (1978), *Phantom Dwellings* (1985); stories: *The Nature of Love* (1966); non-fiction: *The Generations of Men* (1959), *Preoccupations in Australian Poetry* (1965), *Because I Was Invited* (1975), *The Coral Battleground* (1977), *The Cry for the Dead* (1981), *We Call for a Treaty* (1985); and children's fiction: *Kings of the Dingoes* (1958), *The Day the Mountains Played* (1960), *Range the Mountains High* (1962).

SOURCES AND ACKNOWLEDGMENTS

The editor ànd publisher thank copyright holders for granting permission to reproduce copyright material.

Abdullah, Mena and Mathew, Ray. 'Because of the Rusilla' from *The Time of the Peacock*, Angus & Robertson, Sydney, 1965.

Adams, Glenda. 'The Music Masters' from *The Hottest Night of the Century*, Angus & Robertson, Sydney, 1979.

Anderson, Ethel. 'Juliet McCree is Accused of Gluttony' from *At Parramatta*, Angus & Robertson, Sydney, 1956.

Bail, Murray. 'Zoellner's Definition' from *Contemporary Portraits*, University of Queensland Press, St Lucia, 1975.

Barnard, Marjorie. 'Dry Spell' from *The Persimmon Tree*, Currawong, Sydney, 1943; reproduced with the permission of Alan Alford, c/o Curtis Brown (Aust.) Pty Ltd, Sydney.

Baynton, Barbara. 'Squeaker's Mate' from *Bush Studies*, Duckworth, London, 1902.

Becke, Louis. 'Challis the Doubter' from *By Reef and Palm*, George Allen & Unwin, London, 1894.

Brooks, David. 'The Line' from *The Book of Sei and Other Stories*, Hale & Iremonger, Sydney, 1985; reproduced by permission of the author.

Carey, Peter. 'Room No. 5 (Escribo)' from *The Fat Man in History*, University of Queensland Press, St Lucia, 1975; also reproduced by permission of the author, c/o Rogers Coleridge & White Ltd, 20 Powis Mews, London W11 1JN.

Clarke, Marcus. 'Human Repetends' from *Australasian*, 14 September 1872.

Clift, Charmian. 'Three Old Men of Lerici' from *Strong Man from Piraeus*, Nelson, Melbourne, 1984; © Charmian Clift Estate, c/o Barbara Mobbs, Sydney.

Cowan, Peter. 'Requiem' from *Drift*, Reed & Harris, Melbourne, 1944; reproduced by permission of the author.

Dark, Eleanor. 'Hear My Prayer' from *Tales by Australians*, edited by Edith Fry, British Authors Press, 1939; reproduced with the permission of Michael Dark, c/o Curtis Brown (Aust.) Pty Ltd, Sydney.

Forshaw, Thelma. 'The Widow-maker' from *An Affair of Clowns*, Angus & Robertson, Sydney, 1967; reproduced by permission of the author.

Gardner, Silvana. 'The Assyrian Princess' from *Westerly*, June 1985; reprinted in *Beyond the Echo*, edited by S. Gunew and J. Mahayuddin, University of Queensland Press, St Lucia, 1988; reproduced by permission of the author.

Garner, Helen. 'Did He Pay?' from *Postcards from Surfers*, McPhee Gribble, Melbourne, 1985.

Goldsworthy, Kerryn. 'Roses and My Brother' from *North of the Moonlight Sonata*, McPhee Gribble, Melbourne, 1989.

Grenville, Kate. 'No Such Thing as a Free Lunch' from *Bearded Ladies*, University of Queensland Press, St Lucia, 1985.

Halligan, Marion. 'The Failure of the Bay Tree' from *The Hanged Man in the Garden*, Penguin Books Australia Ltd, Melbourne, 1989.

Harrower, Elizabeth. 'The Beautiful Climate' from *Modern Australian Writing*, edited by Geoffrey Dutton, Fontana/Collins, London, 1967.

Hemensley, Kris. 'A Portrait' and 'Self Portrait' from *Games: An Exhibition 1970–72*, Rigmarole of the Hours, Melbourne, 1978; © Kris Hemensley, reproduced by permission of the author.

Hospital, Janette Turner. 'The Inside Story' from *Dislocations*, University of Queensland Press, St Lucia, 1987; Virago, London, 1994; first published in the United States by Louisiana State University Press.

Jolley, Elizabeth. 'Poppy Seed and Sesame Rings' from *Frictions*, edited by Anna Gibbs and Alison Tilson, Sybylla Feminist Press, Melbourne, 1982.

Kefala, Antigone. 'Sunday Morning' from *Tabloid Story Pocket Book*, Wild & Woolley, Sydney, 1978.

Kim, D'ono. 'Chinaman's Beach According to a Doubtful Lover' from *The Chinaman*, Hale & Iremonger, Sydney, 1985.

Krausmann, Rudi. 'The Street of the Painters' from *Tabloid Story Pocket Book*, Wild & Woolley, Sydney, 1978.

Lawson, Henry. 'The Union Buries Its Dead' from *Short Stories in Prose and Verse*, Louisa Lawson, Sydney, 1894.

Loukakis, Angelo. 'Being Here Now' from *For the Patriarch*, University of Queensland Press, St Lucia, 1981.

Lurie, Morris. 'My Greatest Ambition' from *Outrageous Behaviour: Selected Short Stories*, Penguin Books Australia Ltd, Melbourne, 1984.

Malouf, David. 'The Only Speaker of His Tongue' from *Antipodes*, Chatto & Windus, London, 1985.

Marshall, Alan. 'Trees Can Speak' from *How's Andy Going?* Cheshire, Melbourne, 1956; reproduced by permission of Longman Australia Pty Ltd.

Moorhouse, Frank. 'White Knight' from *Forty Seventeen*, Penguin Books Australia Ltd, Melbourne, 1988.

Murnane, Gerald. 'Precious Bane' from *Strange Attractions*, Hale & Iremonger, Sydney, 1985; reproduced by permission of the author.

Noonuccal, Oodgeroo. 'Carpet Snake' from *Stradbroke Dreamtime*, Angus & Robertson, Sydney, 1972.

Oakley, Barry. 'Father Carroll' from *Walking in Tigerland*, University of Queensland Press, St Lucia, 1977.

Porter, Hal. 'First Love' from *The Cats of Venice*, Angus & Robertson, Sydney, 1965.

Prichard, Katharine Susannah. 'N'Goola' from *N'Goola*, Australasian Book Society, 1959; permission courtesy of the copyright owner R. D. Throssell, c/o Curtis Brown (Aust.) Pty Ltd, Sydney.

Richardson, Henry Handel. 'Conversation in a Pantry' from *The End of a Childhood*, Heinemann, Melbourne, 1934.

Roe, Paddy. 'Lardi' from *gularabulu*, edited by Stephen Muecke, Fremantle Arts Centre Press, Fremantle, 1983.

Stead, Christina. 'A Harmless Affair' from *Ocean of Story*, Penguin Books Australia Ltd, Melbourne, 1986.

Stivens, Dal. 'The Man who Bowled Victor Trumper' (also known as 'Indians have Special Eyesight') from *The Courtship of Uncle Henry*, Reed & Harris, 1946; reproduced with the permission of Dal Stivens, c/o Curtis Brown (Aust.) Pty Ltd, Sydney.

Turner, Ethel. 'The Child of the Children' from *The Child of the Children*, Ward Lock, London, 1959.

Viidikas, Vicki. 'End of the Moon' from *Wrappings*, Wild & Woolley, Sydney, 1974.

Walwicz, Ania. 'red sails' from *Boat*, Angus & Robertson, Sydney, 1989.

Waten, Judah. 'Mother' from *Alien Son*, Angus & Robertson, Sydney, 1952.

White, Patrick. 'Clay' from *The Burnt Ones*, Eyre & Spottiswoode, London, 1964; © Patrick White, 1964.

Wilding, Michael. 'Somewhere New' from *Aspects of the Dying Process*, University of Queensland Press, St Lucia, 1972; reproduced by permission of the author.

Winton, Tim. 'My Father's Axe' from *Scission*, McPhee Gribble, Melbourne, 1985.

Wright, Judith. 'The Weeping Fig' from *The Nature of Love*, Sun Books, Melbourne, 1966; reproduced by permission of the author.

Every effort has been made to trace the original source of all copyright material contained in this book. Where the attempt has been unsuccessful, the publisher would be pleased to hear from copyright holders to rectify any errors or omissions.

AUTHOR INDEX